CONTINENT OF
HUNTER-GATHERERS

Frontispiece Garnawala 1, Wardaman country, northern Australia, 1990 (Photo: Bruno David. David et al. 1994. Courtesy of the Binjari Association, Wardaman community).

CONTINENT OF HUNTER-GATHERERS

New perspectives in Australian prehistory

HARRY LOURANDOS

Department of Anthropology and Sociology
University of Queensland

PUBLISHED BY THE PRESS SYNDICATE OF THE UNIVERSITY OF CAMBRIDGE
The Pitt Building, Trumpington Street, Cambridge CB2 1RP, United Kingdom

CAMBRIDGE UNIVERSITY PRESS
The Edinburgh Building, Cambridge CB2 2RU, United Kingdom
40 West 20th Street, New York, NY 10011–4211, USA
10 Stamford Road, Oakleigh, Melbourne 3166, Australia

First published 1997

Printed in Hong Kong by Colorcraft

Typeset in Times Roman 11/13 pt

National Library of Australia Cataloguing in Publication data

Lourandos, Harry, 1945– .
Continent of hunter-gatherers : new perspectives in
Australian prehistory.
Bibliography.
Includes index.
ISBN 0 521 35106 5.
ISBN 0 521 35946 5 (pbk.).
1. Hunting and gathering societies – Australia.
2. Aborigines, Australian – Antiquities. 4. Man, Prehistoric –
Australia. 5. Australia – Antiquities. I. Title.
994.01

Library of Congress Cataloguing in Publication data

Lourandos, Harry, 1945–
Continent of hunter-gatherers: new perspectives in Australian
prehistory/Harry Lourandos.
    p.   cm.
Includes bibliographical references and index.
ISBN 0-521-35106-5 (hc: alk. paper). – ISBN 0-521-35946-5 (alk.
paper)
1. Man, Prehistoric–Australia. 2. Hunting, Prehistoric–
Australia. 3. Economics, Prehistoric–Australia. 4. Australian
aborigines–Antiquities. 5. Australia–Antiquities. I. Title.
GN871.L68 1997
994'.01–dc20   96–28528

A catalogue record for this book is available from the British Library

ISBN 0 521 35106 5 hardback
ISBN 0 521 35946 5 paperback

To the memory of my mother and her sisters

and

To all Aboriginal Australians

CONTENTS

FIGURES

TABLES

PREFACE

Australian Aboriginal prehistory or long-term history

In this book I have tried to take a fresh look at the prehistory or long-term history of Australia and its Aboriginal people by moving away from more traditional approaches which viewed people as part of the natural landscape, largely controlled by long-term environmental changes and trends. Hunter-gatherers, and Australian and Tasmanian Aborigines in particular, have been seen in this light; as representatives of the 'original human society', where change was minimal, and where biological and socio-cultural factors, even the number of people on the ground, were largely determined by the natural environment. In contrast, here, hunter-gatherers are seen not as passive peoples, but as people interacting dynamically with both the natural and socio-cultural world over which they had a considerable measure of control. In this way, hunter-gatherer peoples, or those whose lifestyle is predominantly aimed in this direction, no longer need stand apart from others, such as horticulturalists and agriculturalists, and people of so-called more complex societies, with whom they are so often contrasted.

I have therefore compared traditional approaches to Australian Aboriginal hunter-gatherers and their prehistory with more recent viewpoints which look to the more dynamic elements of these people's society and history. I have set the Australian information also within a world context of hunter-gatherers of both past and present. Not that there is general consensus among these recent perspectives; nor should we expect it. The interpretations, indeed the collecting of the data themselves, have taken place within a lively, competitive set of debates and discourses both within Australia and internationally. While attempting to include as much of this information as possible, and to make reference to the growing number of participants in this young and expanding discipline, I have also tried to steer my own course, presenting my own point of view. I have attempted also to trace the development of ideas and interpretations. By presenting the information as clearly and in as much detail as possible (with referencing), I hope I have also made it accessible to readers, so that they can make up their own minds.

The evidence itself is, however, constantly changing or being modified. As we go to press new claims are being made of a radically early chronology for the prehistory of Australia. From the site of Jinmium in the Kimberley of northwestern Australia have been reported fallen panels of rock art engravings dated at between 58,000 and 75,000 years ago, and stone artefacts at between 116,000 and 176,000 years ago. The site lies below an outcrop of sandstone, on which there are circular engravings, and is composed of deep sandy layers, which have been dated by thermoluminescence techniques (*Sydney Morning Herald* 21.9.96; forthcoming in *Antiquity*). This evidence has, however, already been subjected to close scrutiny and is viewed as controversial, largely due to problems associated with the dating methods (see also Chapter Three).

Another people's prehistory, or history

Traditionally, prehistory, like its data, was considered as yet another resource for scientific investigation; as there for the taking. With some notable exceptions, little consideration was given to the descendants of that past – the Australian and Tasmanian Aboriginal people – let alone their viewpoints. This attitude has now changed considerably. Australian prehistoric archaeology is now a highly politicised, complex arena of negotiation. Increasingly it has become mandatory in most states for archaeologists to negotiate with local Aboriginal communities before seeking permits to excavate, and to present them with written reports on the project when completed. Aboriginal participants are generally welcomed in fieldwork projects, and in some states this is compulsory. Today, it is becoming increasingly common for anthropologists and also archaeologists to work on behalf of particular Aboriginal communities who employ them as specialists and direct their research. Archaeology and its findings on the prehistoric past are part of the consciousness of Aboriginal communities, to use in whatever way suits them (see Pardoe 1992; Webb 1995).

The recent renaissance in Aboriginal society and culture throughout Australia and Tasmania has drawn upon, and been empowered by, knowledge of the distant and more recent past; and is embedded in a reassertion of Aboriginal identity and its association with the land. Land rights claims are central to the social and economic betterment of many Aboriginal communities, and the tie to land is often validated through traditional, including archaeological, information. Aboriginal views of the past often complement, and sometimes also conflict with, those of the professional archaeologist and anthropologist.

In these ways, the situation in Australia parallels that of other countries where the recent history of indigenous people has been interwoven with that of the past; and where indigenous people have been, and are, striving to shake off the colonial past. The inheritance of colonialism includes the ways indigenous people's history and 'prehistory' was presented and interpreted, often to the disadvantage of the people themselves; often as a means of social control. The story of Aboriginal Australia and Tasmania is much the same. Unilinear evolutionary models of the nineteenth and early twentieth century, for example, presented by anthropologists and archaeologists, which placed these peoples on the lowest rungs of the socio-cultural evolutionary 'ladder', have largely served to preserve the status quo; to keep Aboriginal Australians and Tasmanians in their place – as dependent, 'conquered' peoples, largely divorced from land, society, economy and their past. The traditional models of Australian prehistory, discussed above, with their emphasis upon the dominance of the natural environment over Aboriginal society – assigning to the latter a passive role – producing long-term stability and lack of change, have, in their own way, also reinforced these conditions.

Studies of hunter-gatherer peoples worldwide, many of whom have been subjected to similar recent historical processes, have been coloured in similar ways. These attitudes often have been projected also upon hunter-gatherer societies of the past, including those of the Pleistocene. The more recent research of Aboriginal Australians and Tasmanians has emerged from these historical and social contexts, and much, including this book, is largely reaction to what has gone before. This book, therefore, attempts in some ways to redress these unequal relations between the people whose history is being studied – the Australian and Tasmanian Aboriginal people – and the rest of us who wish to be enlightened by it.

ACKNOWLEDGEMENTS

I would like to thank first John Mulvaney for offering me the opportunity to write this book, and for his continuing help and encouragement throughout the years. I also thank Robin Derricourt for his encouragement and patience through the most difficult of times.

I thank all my colleagues and fellow students with whom I have worked over the years, and who have contributed to my appreciation and understanding of archaeology, anthropology and Australian prehistory; at the University of Sydney, the Australian National University, the University of New England, the University of Queensland and the Tasmanian Museum and Art Gallery. I would like to thank especially the many students who have always been the most important to me and whose enthusiasm and insight drove me on.

I would like also to single out a few people who along the way contributed greatly to my understanding of Australian prehistory; in Australia, Jim Allen, John Clegg, Roland Fletcher, Josephine Flood, Jack Golson, Jenny Hope, Phil Hughes, Rhys Jones, Isabel McBryde, Betty Meehan, Wilfred Shawcross, Marjorie Sullivan, Alan Thorne, Peter White and Richard Wright; and overseas, Barbara Bender, Clive Gamble, David Harris, Brian Hayden, Paul Mellars, Jim O'Connell, Doug Price and Olga Soffer. During the writing of this book I was especially encouraged and helped by Sandra Bowdler, Judy Bieg, Julia Clark, Jenny Figueiredo, Sue O'Connor, Colin Pardoe, Annie Ross, Bruno David, Bryce Barker, Monica Minnegal, Irene Saunderson, Su Solomon, Paul McInness, Brigid Cassidy, Lara Lamb and Sue Davies. Jacques Bierling and also Ian McNiven produced the illustrations. I also thank John Mulvaney, Robin Derricourt and Clive Gamble for commenting on an earlier draft. Thanks go also to Phillipa McGuinness, Jane Farago and Jean Cooney for their helpful editorial assistance and support.

INTRODUCTION:
CHANGING PERSPECTIVES

Australian Aborigines are held by anthropologists as classic examples of hunter-gatherer societies, and are often used as 'models' of past so-called non-agricultural peoples, including those of the Pleistocene period. Recent studies, however, including those in anthropology, ethnohistory and archaeology, are revising more traditional opinions concerning Australian Aborigines and, more generally, hunter-gatherers of both past and present. It is now acknowledged that a much broader range of hunter-gatherer societies existed throughout the world and in all periods of time than was previously considered to be the case. Similarly, perceptions of Australian Aborigines and their history have also changed, for many reasons, and this history has been seen afresh as significantly more varied as regards socio-cultural factors, demography and economy, to name but a few aspects. The effects of colonialism, introduced diseases, population decimation and social dislocation left their mark on the continent long before anthropologists arrived. In this book I have tied together information from disparate sources – social anthropology, ethnohistory and archaeology – so as to discuss the varied Australian Aboriginal socio-cultural patterns in both time and space. This material is set within archaeological and anthropological debates concerning the history and development of hunter-gatherer societies in both the long and short term.

In some ways it forms part of a revisionist anthropology and archaeology of Australian Aborigines, and hunter-gatherers in general. It explores new directions and new interpretations and, hopefully, offers new insights on and models of Australian hunters of the near and distant past. In my examination of the ethnohistorical and ethnographic information I have focused upon regional variation and on aspects at variance with more traditional models of Australian Aborigines. With the archaeological evidence, which encompasses such

1

enormous stretches of time, I have highlighted socio-demographic processes within a broad ecological setting.

The Australian past

The traditional model viewed Australian prehistory with an emphasis on long-term equilibrium between numbers of Aboriginal people and natural resources. That is, Aboriginal demography was seen as largely under the control of long-term environmental forces, and socio-cultural changes (where they could be identified) were largely negligible. This viewpoint is clearly expressed by Joseph Birdsell in the following two quotations.

> It is now realised that these economically simple peoples, and all of the Pleistocene occupants of Greater Australia, live in fact in a skilfully regulated state of homeostasis. Such people were in equilibrium with their environment and this balanced condition was maintained, despite some fluctuations, by a rather complex series of actions, beliefs and traditions. (Birdsell 1977: 149)

Birdsell viewed Aboriginal economy (and extractive efficiency, or production, in particular) as being relatively homogeneous and unchanging.

> A hunting and collecting economy of the most generalised sort was present throughout the entire continent and the material culture upon which extractive efficiency was based showed only minor regional variations. (Birdsell 1957: 53)

Today, as we have seen, much greater socio-cultural variation is acknowledged throughout Australia, in both space and time, than traditional models allow. Undoubtedly the more recently obtained wealth of archaeological and palaeontological data, and revision of ethnohistorical and ethnographic information, have helped form these new impressions. While present interpretations generally acknowledge the more *dynamic* nature of past socio-cultural, demographic and environmental processes, they also appear divided on two fronts: they either emphasise natural environmental forces, or view socio-cultural (including demographic) factors as less *directly* tied to environment.

Hunters and gatherers

Since the first international conference on hunter-gatherers in 1966 – the *Man the Hunter* conference (Lee and DeVore 1968) – there has been a considerable widening of the approaches to the study of hunter-gatherers and their past. Emphasis has been placed upon a wider range of social, political, economic and demographic themes concerning these societies. It has also been appreciated that a considerable overlap exists between hunter-gatherer and other societies: agriculturalists, for example. As well, the evolution of hunter-gatherer societies towards varying levels of cultural complexity is being considered.

Hunter-gatherer societies, such as those of the north-west coast of North

America, which were populous, socially stratified, sedentary, with developed procurement and storage technologies, were once considered to be anomalous. That this level of cultural complexity could have developed without an agricultural component is now being given greater credence in the case of both recent and past non-agricultural peoples. Social structure, demography, aspects of economy, technology and sedentism among hunter-gatherer-fisher peoples are now recognised as being influenced by a range of key factors, including both the natural and cultural environments, together with the individual histories of particular societies. For example, many hunter-gatherer societies have had a long history of contact with a variety of neighbouring peoples, including agriculturalists, and, more recently, with quite complex societies, including states and empires. These external contacts may have produced a variety of changes in the original hunter-gatherer society (Denbrow 1984; Gordon 1984; Schrire 1984; Bird-David 1988; Woodburn 1988). In the course of time, individual societies also have fluctuated between varying degrees of hunting-gathering-fishing and horticulture. Many Southeast Asian and Amazonian horticultural groups, for example, have reverted to hunting and gathering (Lathrap 1968; Keesing 1981; Griffin 1984), while other hunter-gatherers have become specialised economic mediators providing produce to agriculturalists and others (Hoffman 1984).

In this way, the broad models used in the main studies of hunter-gatherer societies traditionally, those focusing upon ahistorical and static factors, have been replaced in recent years by more dynamic approaches. These consider long- and short-term historical processes within and between hunter-gatherer and other societies, together with the question of change (Bender and Morris 1988; Myers 1988). Socially and politically, the traditional emphasis upon the hunter-gatherer 'band' as the unit of study has also been superseded by highlighting the wider system of alliances of which individual 'bands' were a part.

The new focus, therefore, falls upon the complexity of political relations of individual hunter-gatherer societies and their neighbours, and the history of these events. Leadership and territorial disputes concerning land and other resources thus become central themes of discussion (Leacock and Lee 1982; Ingold et al. 1988a, 1988b). Indeed, the very category *hunter-gatherer* has been questioned recently, being seen as yet another narrow classification. This category is viewed as the product of broader world social formations (colonial, capitalist) of which historically these peoples were part, and by which they have been subjugated (Wilmsen and Denbrow 1990; also Lee 1992). In an attempt to surmount this so-called growing crisis, Lee advocates that anthropology and hunter-gatherer studies need to become 'a working discipline that sees science, humanism and critical reflection as three components of a single field' (Lee 1992: 41). While these final issues may at first sight appear only remotely linked to our topic, as I indicated in my Preface, they are of direct concern to indigenous peoples and their history.

What I have here termed the traditional approach places an environmentally deterministic emphasis in interpreting the hunter-gatherer present and past; it has in the past decade or two been replaced by the acknowledgement of more complex relationships between society, demography and environment. It is now recognised that the traditional dichotomy which divorced hunter-gatherer and agricultural societies is by no means clear. Many now prefer to see a continuum of societies bridging the earlier two economic classifications (Bray 1976; Harris 1977a, 1977b; Lourandos 1980a, 1980b). For example, many hunter-gatherers practise varying levels of land and resource management, which significantly overlap with horticultural-agricultural practices. When viewed through time the continuum becomes, in part, an evolutionary cline along which differential development may have occurred; for example in society, economy, demography and technology among other areas. The cline, however, should not be seen as either unilinear or deterministic, but instead as incorporating a large number of *possibilities* and *relationships*, which may have appeared in different ways at different times in the past.

Australian prehistory – its background and data

Not all readers of this book will be familiar with prehistoric archaeological data, the way they are excavated, analysed and dated, nor with the enormous stretches of time involved (in this case 40,000 years or more), nor with the frameworks in which all this evidence is gathered, ordered and interpreted. These issues are therefore briefly introduced here.

Australian archaeological data incorporate a wide range of site types, among which the most investigated include rock-shelters and caves with their deeply stratified sedimentary sequences. More subject to the vagaries of preservation are open sites which, in coastal and aquatic regions, include shell middens, which are accumulations of shell and other organic remains and sediments. A third important group of sites includes sand dunes, which often incorporate archaeological material within their matrix. These sites are generally excavated stratigraphically by stripping off the 'natural' layers of material which have been accumulated through time, one atop the other. An artificial grid of squares is superimposed upon the surface of the site and individual squares (often one metre square or 50-centimetres square) are excavated in turn. The material from each level is then recorded, and processed either in the field or laboratory, generally both (Connah 1982). Examples of all these can be found in Chapters Four to Seven: these sites include rock-shelters and caves, shell middens and dunes.

Sites are dated most often by radiocarbon (C-14) dating, with samples taken from organic material (such as charcoal, bone and shell). Such techniques often produce generalised dates which can be equated with conventional chronology. In this book I either give the radiocarbon date itself, together with the laboratory number for identification; for example, 3,250 ± 25 years BP (Beta-1234), or a

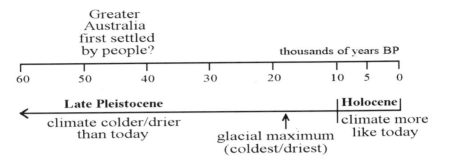

a Time chart of the late Pleistocene and Holocene periods in Greater Australia. A general climatic description is also provided.

generalised date, which in this case would be c. 3,250 years BP (that is, about 3,250 years before the present). Otherwise I present an even more general date, in this example, c. 3,000 BP, as the case may warrant. Other dating methods, based upon various techniques, are also employed.

Given the huge units of time involved in Australian prehistory, geological time periods are generally used as the basic chronological framework. In this case, the two major epochs involve the late Pleistocene (from before 40,000 until about 10,000 years ago), when the climate was generally colder and drier than today, and many parts of the earth were glaciated; and the Holocene period (from about 10,000 years ago until today), when climates more similar to today's predominated (Figure a). Each of these major climatic phases is composed of sub-phases during which changes in climate occurred, which are identified as colder and drier, warmer and wetter periods, with corresponding changes to vegetation types and rises and falls in sea levels. In general, during the period of time covered by this book, the climate became colder and drier after about 30,000 years ago, reaching its coldest, driest phase during the glacial maximum, around 18,000 years ago. Since then, conditions have generally become warmer and more humid, particularly so during the Holocene period, that is to say, the last 10,000 years. During the early Holocene, however, climate was generally warmer and wetter than today. Sea levels also fell to their lowest around the time of the glacial maximum, and have slowly risen since then, stabilising at the present level between 6,000 and 5,000 BP. In general, the archaeological prehistoric data are viewed against this environmental backdrop (Figure b).

Concentrated archaeological research in Australia is less than two generations old (Mulvaney 1975, 1979; White 1981; Horton 1991; Golson 1993), and thus only a minute sample of the potential evidence has been unearthed and analysed. As well, sites are often fortuitously discovered. The interpretations of this material, covering as they do such vast time periods and a continent the size of Europe or the United States of America, which was larger still during the Pleistocene period, can only serve as *general* models. In time, no doubt, they

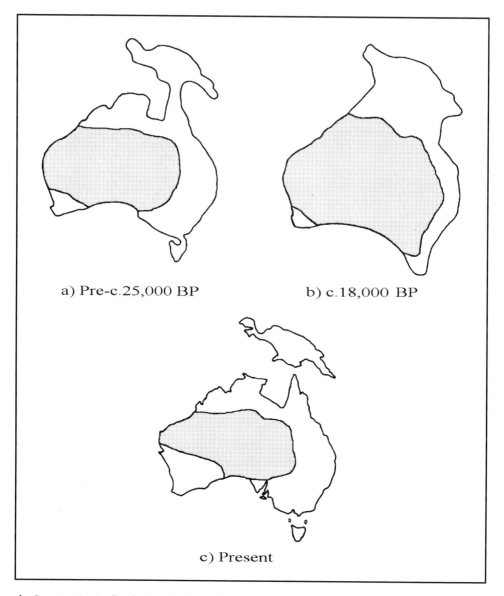

a) Pre-c.25,000 BP   b) c.18,000 BP

c) Present

b Greater Australia during the late Pleistocene and Holocene periods. Changing sea levels and the general extent of the arid zone are indicated during three time periods (based on Ross et al. 1992: 99, Figure 5.17).

will be modified with the availability of new information and new perspectives, as indeed they have consistently been updated throughout the last forty years or so of research. Nevertheless, the interpretations and models presented in this book represent a sample of competing explanations, and the ways these have been derived especially over the last twenty years of research. The slant or perspective I have taken is of course my own, but I have attempted to focus upon the main debates and to place these within both a national and international context of hunter-gatherer studies, past and present. I have also attempted to include as much of the relevant data and interpretations as possible, so as to let the reader make up his or her own mind.

This book

This book considers the prehistory of Greater Australia (which includes mainland Australia and the islands of New Guinea and Tasmania), together with aspects of the ethnography and ethnohistory of Australia and Tasmania, in light of the debate on hunter-gatherer cultural dynamics in both the long and short term. Chapter One discusses the above debate itself, focusing upon the issue of hunter-gatherer cultural variation in time and space. Special attention is paid to key factors, including environment, demography, economy and society, which are discussed in regard to both ethnographic and archaeological information and ways that these can be applied to studies of Australian Aborigines. Chapter Two considers Australian Aboriginal ethnography and ethnohistory in light of the preceding chapter, with emphasis upon changing perceptions, and draws comparisons between mainland Australian and Tasmanian hunter-gatherers and New Guinean hunter-horticulturalists.

Chapter Three discusses the Southeast Asian background to the colonisation of Greater Australia, and the earliest archaeological sites. The skeletal information and its varied interpretations are also considered and finally an assessment is made of environmental impact as regards use of fire and extinction of Pleistocene fauna. The next four chapters ·(Four to Seven) consider in detail the archaeological sequences of both Pleistocene and Holocene periods across Greater Australia, including tropical northern Australia, and its offshore islands, arid and semi-arid Australia, the temperate southern parts of the continent, and Tasmania which has been separated from the mainland for perhaps 12,000 years.

In Chapter Eight I discuss continental changes, in particular stone artefacts and their temporal and spatial patterns, and therefore their role in interpreting the archaeological record. Chapter Nine assesses the interpretations, old and new, of the ethnographic and archaeological data, and provides some new explanatory models for the prehistory of Greater Australia. Finally, Chapter Ten concludes with some general models and by placing Australian prehistory within a regional and world context.

In most chapters, in particular those covering the data, there is a section called Overview which provides a summary at the end of relevant parts; the Overview sections can be either consulted separately or skipped over, as the reader chooses. There is also a glossary of terms and some brief notes on dating methods (and their limitations) at the end of the book.

CHAPTER 1

HUNTER-GATHERER VARIATION IN TIME AND SPACE

If indeed hunter-gatherer societies of past and present did cover a very broad range in socio-cultural variation, and overlapped with other societies such as agriculturalists, how then can this be characterised? And how can we investigate changing patterns in socio-cultural variation on both long- and short-term time scales, sometimes involving thousands of years and even longer? These are the questions guiding the discussion presented in this chapter. They are directed at both ethnographic and archaeological evidence and at hunter-gatherer societies in general, with the aim of evaluating the evidence from Aboriginal Australia in later chapters.

The question of complexity

Recent discussions concerning socio-cultural variation within hunter-gatherer societies have focused upon the question of 'complexity', and in particular how more 'complex' hunter-gatherer behaviour emerged (Price and Brown 1985b; Cohen 1985). Although no consensus exists regarding definitions, the term 'complexity' generally concerns all aspects of hunter-gatherer society, and can be viewed as an elaboration of parts, including economy, demography and society, among others. Some have gone so far as to distinguish between so-called 'simple' and 'complex' categories of hunter-gatherer society and, further, to explain shifts from one group to the other (Cohen 1985; Henry 1985). One problem, however, with the latter approach is that it polarises hunter-gatherers, and thus avoids the general question of explaining the development of socio-cultural variation itself. For variation can occur within as well as between both of the latter categories. Also, by distinguishing so called 'simple' hunter-gatherers from others, it merely relocates the traditional 'towards agriculture' debate in time – in this case, phrased in terms of 'towards complexity'. The problem, in this way, remains roughly the same – how to explain shifts from one less 'complex' system to another more 'complex' one (see also Soffer 1985).

While in some cases a dichotomous approach might be justifiable, I suggest that in order to avoid classifying hunter-gatherer societies as one category or another we view the general range in socio-cultural variation as a continuum. In this way, particular characteristics or traits can be isolated independently of general categories such as 'simple' or 'complex'. These two classes can then form the two ends of a continuum, with individual societies or traits located along it. Note that the continuum should not necessarily be seen as unilinear or directional in time or space, as no one trajectory is suggested. A varied patchwork of societies may have appeared in both time and space. The viewpoint adopted here, therefore, is that all human societies are in some ways complex, that considerable variation exists within and between societies, and that this can be evaluated best by adopting a clinal model. Individual societies may have moved back and forth along such a continuum in both the long and short term, as well as spatially. This point is well illustrated by ethnographic case studies which indicate short-term changes (for example, annual or seasonal) as well as long-term ones. Changes can be expected, therefore, in all variables, including economic, demographic and social aspects, and the cline can overlap with different societies, including agriculturalists among others. Also, we should not assume static conditions, but that these are potentially always dynamic, with general limits set by both socio-cultural and natural environments.

Long- and short-term trends

The uniqueness of the hunter-gatherer past, as compared with other human societies, is the extraordinary length of time involved. Time is often scaled in thousands of years. In order, therefore, to understand and analyse these vast periods varying temporal scales need to be employed, and on both long- and short-term time axes. Similarly, varying spatial or geographical scales also need to be considered: for example, local, regional and even more general (including continental). Questions directed at one temporal or spatial level may take on quite a different meaning in another context or at another level. For example, it would not be accurate to directly compare a short-term with a long-term observation (or interpretation), nor a local with a regional or continental one. Likewise, general questions aimed at long-term, regional or continental scales, would be inappropriate if directed at a short-term, local case study. In other words, all analyses and their frames of reference need to be clearly defined from the outset. This applies equally to the application of different bodies of theory (Marquardt 1985).

There are also obvious problems in interpreting historical processes taking place within these long time-frames. For example, general ecological and socio-cultural theory was not developed with these problems in mind, but usually operated on smaller time scales. Geological time-frames, on the other hand, while in nature long-term and thus able to be employed here, are generalised and therefore also limited. These general issues have been discussed in relation to large slices of hunter-gatherer time including the Eurasian Palaeolithic (Bailey 1983a) as well as Australian prehistory (Frankel 1988; Lourandos 1993), although no clear resolution is apparent. Therefore, in order to confront some of these issues, I have attempted in this book to distinguish, where possible, between different temporal and spatial scales, so as to allow for more accurate comparison between epochs, regions and their varied and sometimes competing interpretations.

Theoretical approaches

We must also consider more general theoretical approaches to issues of hunter-gatherer socio-cultural variation in time and space. The traditional approach has been to emphasise both cultural and biological adaptations (in a neo-Darwinian sense) by hunter-gatherer societies to particular natural environments. This perspective is essentially ecological (Bettinger 1991), and has a strong emphasis upon general systems theory (Flannery 1968). In North America, for example, this perspective can be traced to the school of 'cultural ecology', which has been associated closely with Julian Steward (1955), and was adopted by the so-called 'processual' archaeologists (Binford and Binford 1968; Binford 1983; Wenke 1981). The most recent developments of this approach lie in what are called 'optimal foraging' studies, which consider the underlying ecological structure and evolutionary significance of hunter-gatherer subsistence practices (O'Connell and Hawkes 1981; Winterhalder 1981; Hawkes et al. 1982; Hawkes et al. 1985).

The importance of socio-cultural factors in the process of adaptation also has begun to be more fully appreciated and, therefore, their role in long-term cultural change in the archaeological record (Flannery 1968, 1972, 1976; Struever 1968). In this way people were viewed as adapting to both a natural and a socio-cultural environment. When considering questions of adaptation, therefore, the parameters of both these environments need to be defined for particular points in time.

The debate concerning the relative importance of natural or cultural influences is complex, but generally it can be characterised by approaches either emphasising the dominance of *external* influences like environment and demography (Binford 1983: 221), or of *internal* dynamics, including socio-cultural factors (Bender 1978, 1981, 1985; Lourandos 1983a, 1985a, 1988a; Ingold et al. 1988). Often the former approach takes on a techno-environmental hue, with social factors being relegated to secondary status. At best, this theoretical divide between ecological and social or structural approaches has produced lively debate (Gould 1985: 427–434; Price and Brown 1985a: 435–442; Bettinger 1991: 144–149); but at worst, it has clouded the basic issue of seeking to integrate the major theories.

Recent ecological approaches, however, successfully accommodate social factors (Ellen 1982); and in discussions regarding both ecological and social realms, social influences have been assigned a primary role (Ingold 1980, 1988). The latter is also the approach I have adopted in this book. Natural and biological constraints are viewed here as limiting factors, with all *decision-making* passing through a cultural filter. In this sense, society plays a dominant role (also Friedman and Rowlands 1978; Marquardt 1985; Shanks and Tilley 1987; see also Gamble 1986a: 59). In some ways, environmental and biological constraints also are influenced by cultural practices, as may be seen for example in cultural manipulation of both the natural environment and human demography (see below, this chapter).

Demography, therefore, although viewed by some as a primary force in human history (Cohen 1977), is also seen to be influenced in many ways by society (Hassan 1975; Bender 1978, 1981). For example, George Cowgill (1975) has argued that because of this complex relationship, demography must not be considered as a 'prime mover' in human history, but as both 'cause and consequence' of other factors.

Traditional approaches to Australian prehistory also have been largely from a cultural ecological perspective, with an emphasis upon natural environmental and biological influences. Cultures are seen as adapting functionally to particular environments through time and space. Some of the most influential theories forming the basis of Australian prehistory have also adopted an essentially static viewpoint, where socio-cultural and demographic changes are of little significance, and long-term equilibrium predominates (see Introduction and Chapter Nine). However, use of the concept of 'static equilibrium' in systemic studies has drawn considerable criticism in anthropology in general, with recent weight being given to more dynamic processes and, hence, upon 'dynamic equilibrium' (Ellen 1982: 186–191, 273). A similar shift in emphasis also can be detected in more recent approaches to Australian prehistory, with increasing attempts also to integrate social factors within more traditional ecological frameworks.

Investigating socio-cultural variation

How can we investigate socio-cultural variation among hunter-gatherer societies of the past and present? I now pursue this question particularly in regard to environment, demography, economy and society. The aim here is to highlight some of the main issues regarding hunter-gatherer socio-cultural variation in time and space, and ways that these can be recognised in both ethnographic and archaeological records. Where possible, I also have considered models of spatio-temporal trends and processes. It should be pointed out, however, that the degree of archaeological resolution of many of the issues discussed here depends upon the use of varying spatio-temporal scales of analysis; including, long- and short-term observations, and local, regional and continental perspectives. The results that can be obtained, therefore, depend largely upon the type of questions asked.

Environment

Environmental factors, as discussed above, set the limits or constraints within which cultural choices, by hunter-gatherers and others, are made. Indeed, people's perception of the natural environment in which they dwell is essentially a cultural phenomenon, one based upon interpretation and, therefore, choice (Bender 1978; Ingold 1980). For many years, however, as I have already stressed, environmental factors were seen as largely determining hunter-gatherer cultural choices and patterns in both long and short term. The Australian archaeological literature, and to some extent the ethnographic, has been strongly influenced by approaches such as these. Aspects of this form of environmental determinism can still be found directly or indirectly influencing even recent interpretations (see Chapters Four to Seven). Today, however, environmental (and more sophisticated ecological) approaches generally allow for more complex relations between environment, the socio-cultural domain and demography (Ellen 1982, 1988). Although the question still remains of clearly distinguishing between social and ecological relationships (Ingold 1988).

Some of the more general relationships between environment, society and demography can be viewed in the following way. The distribution of natural resources in time and space can influence the pattern of hunter-gatherer subsistence and settlement. For example, spatio-temporal concentrations of resources can allow for more concentrated hunter-gatherer settlement patterns, perhaps expressed as increased levels of sedentism (that is, duration of stay), and more intensive exploitation practices, or both (Lourandos 1968, 1980a, 1980b; Jochim 1976; Winterhalder and Smith 1981; Binford 1980). Habitats such as these include mosaic ecosystems of diverse, patchy distribution of resources, for example, wetlands, riparian (river bank) communities and the littoral (coastal). In contrast, resources which are widely separated in time and space allow for more dispersed settlement patterns (see below, this chapter). In each environment, however, a range of possible hunter-gatherer exploitation patterns may exist.

In large regions, these relationships between people and environment may be expressed clinally. In Australia, for example, clines such as these were detected stretching from the arid zones of central Australia (a region of sparse resources) to the humid northern coastal strip with its more dependable, concentrated resources. Socio-cultural factors, however, also may have influenced these clines (see below, this chapter).

In time, and given changes in climate, whole ecosystems may have altered and with them their patterns of resource distribution or structure. Thus, marked increases or decreases in the biomass of large areas may have taken place and have influenced changes to hunter-gatherer patterns of settlement and resource use. Changes similar to these have been suggested for temperate regions during the shift from Pleistocene to Holocene climatic regimes. For example, in north and central Europe the distribution of resources during the colder, drier Upper Palaeolithic was markedly different to that of the succeeding, more humid, warmer Mesolithic. Hunter-gatherer subsistence, settlement and demographic patterns, therefore, in these parts of Europe are viewed as having been significantly influenced by these major alterations in climate and related resource availability (Price 1985, 1987; Zvelebil 1986; Rowley-Conwy 1986).

Similarly, regional shifts in distribution of natural resources during the Holocene are viewed as having influenced significant transformations in hunter-gatherer responses in the Mississippi riverine region of northeastern North America (Brown 1985). Terminal Pleistocene–early Holocene climatic alterations, and their changing patterns of resource distribution, have also been associated with economic shifts by hunter-gatherers to more intensive harvesting of local resources (such as cereals, legumes and nuts) and further still to their domestication, as in the case of the Levant (Henry 1985; Bar-Yosef 1987). Broadly comparable discussion on the effects of changing climate and environment upon Australian Aboriginal patterns of land and resource use is found below, in Chapters Four to Seven.

The temporal and spatial distribution of natural resources, therefore, can influence hunter-gatherer economy, society and demography, and general patterns may be discernible; however, the broad range in cultural responses, as indicated by the archaeological record worldwide, suggests significant local variation, the result of both environmental and socio-cultural factors.

Demography

The traditional viewpoint of hunter-gatherer demography was of thinly scattered, dispersed populations with rather mobile patterns of settlement. Variations to these general patterns, such as dense, settled communities, were often explained as due to extraordinary local factors such as high seasonal or annual bioproductivity. Today, it is recognised that demography among hunter-gatherers varied greatly seasonally, annually and in the long term; and that demographic patterns overlapped significantly with those of other societies including horticulturalists, agriculturalists, and pastoralists among others.

Along the northwest coast of North America, from northern present-day California to southern Alaska, complex demographic patterns were observed among the hunter-gatherer-fisher populations. The range in variation extended from permanent, settled villages of over a thousand people to more mobile and dispersed communities. Ecological factors influenced this pattern to some extent so that, for example, societies tended to be densest, most settled and ranked socially in the northernmost latitudes where bioproduction was most concentrated seasonally and most unstable. But other factors, including historical, socio-cultural and technological (for example, storage, labour organisation and the like), were also important and influential (Suttles 1968; Schalk 1982; Ames 1985). Comparable, complex socio-economic patterns also existed in northwestern Alaska (Sheehan 1985). We might expect, therefore, a similarly complex regional demographic pattern among other hunter-gatherer societies divorced in both time and space from the above, including those of Australia (see Chapter Two).

Demographic patterns in both time and space lie at the crux of many questions concerning the history and operation of hunter-gatherer societies, both long- and short-term, and therefore key aspects of these are discussed here in some detail. More traditional viewpoints have focused upon ecological factors underlying hunter-gatherer demography. For example, under the influence of the ecological studies of Wynne-Edwards (1962), the demography of hunter-gatherer populations was seen as largely controlled by ecological-environmental factors. Like other animal populations observed, hunter-gatherer societies were seen as controlled by 'optimum numbers', those most attuned to particular environments (Carr-Saunders 1922). Population sizes of hunter-gatherers were seen as regulated well below the 'carrying capacity' of the environment (Binford 1968). Hunter-gatherer societies were viewed, therefore, as being in long-term equilibrium with their environment, their numbers regulated homeostatically by a range of environmental and socio-cultural factors. Joseph Birdsell thus wrote of the Australian Aborigines:

> It is now realised that these economically simple peoples, and all of the Pleistocene occupants of Greater Australia, live in fact in a skilfully regulated state of homeostasis. Such people were in equilibrium with their environment and this balanced condition was maintained, despite some fluctuations, by a rather complex series of actions, beliefs and traditions. (1977: 149)

Using ethnographic information of Australian territorial sizes, obtained from the work of Kryzwicki (1934) and Tindale (1940), Birdsell (1953, 1957), an American geneticist, hypothesised that traditional Aboriginal population sizes and densities were closely attuned to environmental factors – measurable by rainfall. He attempted to demonstrate, by using a large statistical sample, that Australian population and territorial size was directly proportional to rainfall, with the lowest populations (and largest territories) in harsh, arid zones such as central Australia, and the densest populations (and smallest territories) in biologically rich coastal strips, such as those of the tropical northern coast of Arnhem Land (see Chapter Nine). He obtained high statistical correlations in his sample between sizes of tribal areas and environmental productivity as measured by rainfall. However, the important variable of population density was assumed rather than demonstrated. These results were presented as a universal model for all 'generalised' hunter-gatherers, both past and present, and has been widely influential (for example, Stanner 1965; Yengoyan 1968; Godelier 1975).

More recent studies, however, have tended to question the assumed close connection between environmental fertility and high population sizes. As discussed above in relation to the northwest coast of North America, a range of socio-cultural factors also affect demographic patterns, and, therefore, we might expect these to occur differentially in both time and space. Strong cultural factors thus may underlie Birdsell's demographic cline which stretched from the central Australian desert to the northern coast, as Cohen suggested (1975). As well, in other parts of Australia, such as the fertile mouth of the Murray River in the southeast of the continent, Birdsell's figures did not fit the expected pattern, suggesting that a wide range of factors, other than rainfall, were in operation (Hallam 1977a). Methodological problems concerning Birdsell's analysis have also been discussed. For example, the concept of 'carrying capacity' has been questioned as being, among other things, difficult to measure (Hayden 1975] and largely a social construct (Cowgill 1975).

Birdsell considered that the size of Australian Aboriginal groups also was controlled by density-dependent factors. For example, according to his calculations local groups (which can be equated with 'bands') tended to average around fifty people, and 'tribes' around five hundred (1953, 1957). While some have questioned these estimates (Hiatt 1968), these figures also might represent the influence of cultural controls upon Aboriginal demography and its spatial distribution.

Ethnographic observations of hunter-gatherers, including those of Birdsell on the Australians I have discussed above, indicated that cultural factors helped to keep populations in check. Such factors included territoriality, infanticide, senilicide and post-partum sexual taboos among others (Hayden 1972; Hassan 1975). More recent information, however, would suggest that although cultural practices such as these might serve well in the short term, they would be less effective as long-term population controls. Over longer periods of time, hunter-gatherer populations could expand almost unnoticed, at very low levels. For example, it has been hypothesised that growth rates during the Palaeolithic were very low, in the order of 0.001 to 0.002 percent (Hassan 1975: 42). Such very low growth rates would not be noticeable in the short term and thus hunter-gatherer populations could expand in a relatively stable fashion over long periods of time. Population sizes and densities, therefore, might have changed through time. Gray (1985), for example, has argued similarly for Australian prehistory; that whatever growth rates might have taken place, overall rates appear to have been quite low (see Chapter Two).

Cowgill (1975), basing his arguments upon both historical and recent ethnographic evidence from a range of societies, has argued convincingly that human demography, including that of hunter-gatherers, is clearly so interwoven with socio-cultural factors that it is not possible to consider it an independent variable. For human societies, therefore, demographic factors, in both long and short term, need to be considered as much a part of the socio-cultural as the biological realm (Hassan 1975; Polgar 1975). This line of reasoning also is followed in this book (see also Chapters Nine and Ten).

Because of its interrelationship with other factors, therefore, demography cannot be considered an independent or primary force in long-term historical events affecting hunter-gatherer societies, among others, although it has often been attributed this status. Demography, for example, has been viewed as the main thrust behind the shift to the domestication of animals and plants and agriculture (Boserup 1965; Cohen 1977; for opposing views see Hassan 1975; Polgar 1975; Bender 1978). However, where long-term archaeological sequences of hunter-gatherer societies exist, major cultural changes (including shifts towards agriculture) are not necessarily accompanied by, nor the products of, changing demographic patterns (such as population increase, sedentism and the like). Regions where this evidence can be found include Peru (Cohen 1977; Polgar 1975) and Tehuacan and Oaxaca in Mesoamerica (Flannery 1968). In general, the archaeological data from these areas indicate more complex socio-cultural, demographic and environmental patterns through time. The archaeological trends also appear to have been long-term, measurable in thousands of years.

But demography refers to more than just rises and falls in population; it also relates to the geographical spread or dispersal of population and the ways this may alter in the short term (for example, seasonally or annually), as well as long term. Once again, traditionally it has been assumed that hunter-gatherer societies dispersed and aggregated into larger units throughout the year and through time according to the distribution of natural resources. When and where resources were either in abundance or thinly dispersed, so too were hunter-gatherer populations (Flannery 1968). This general correlation between availability of natural resources and the dispersal patterns of hunter-gatherers is not disputed here. For example, more settled or sedentary hunter-gatherer societies are closely related to regions where seasonality (and thus clumping of resources in time and space) is more marked. However, it needs to be pointed out that other factors (for example, socio-cultural) also affect the size and density of hunter-gatherer groups as well as the patterns of mobility and duration of settlement (that is, sedentism). For example, in Aboriginal Australia while large and lengthy intergroup gatherings were often associated with local resource gluts it is clear in many cases that resource availability was not the main reason for these events and that resource productivity was manipulated in a variety of ways (see further in Chapters Four to Six).

In an ethnographic analysis of societies from the eastern Highlands of New Guinea, Tia Negerevich (1992) has recently shown that patterns of sedentism and mobility were not directly linked to either environmental or social factors.

For instance, residential patterns cross-cut societies oriented more towards either hunter-gatherer or horticultural strategies. Traditional distinctions, therefore, between hunter-gatherer and horticultural settlement patterns did not apply in this example. Once again, this serves to illustrate that the spatial (dispersal) patterns of hunter-gatherers, through time, are not solely subject to biological, ecological-environmental or social factors.

In summary, therefore, there appears to have been a much greater variation in the demography of hunter-gatherer societies that have existed throughout the world than has previously been acknowledged. Hunter-gatherers stretched from populous, dense and sedentary societies to dispersed, mobile, small populations, and overlapped with horticultural and agricultural societies. The demography of hunter-gatherers was dynamic and influenced not merely by environmental–ecological factors but also by socio-cultural forces among others. Because of this interdependence with the natural and cultural world, therefore, demography should not be considered a lone card when evaluating explanations of causality and change in the history of hunter-gatherer societies.

Archaeological evidence of past demography is especially problematical being based, apart from skeletal evidence, upon settlement and land-use patterns. Skeletal material also can provide evidence on diet (Hobson and Collier 1984; Hayden et al. 1987) as well as, for example, on stress factors associated with overcrowding of populations (Cohen and Armelagos 1984; see also below Chapter Six). Changes in population sizes and densities have been recognised by alterations in the numbers of archaeological sites occupied through time, the nature of sites and their rate of usage (as in rock-shelters, caves and open sites) (Hassan 1981; Ross 1985; Bailey 1983b). Quite apart from estimating relative changes in population are the difficulties of disentangling demographic data from the effects of environment and cultural changes. This is especially relevant to the Australian material (discussed in Chapters Four to Seven) and other contexts such as the Mesolithic of northwestern Europe (Rowley-Conwy 1986; Price 1987; Zvelebil 1986). Other regions where similar issues involving demography within hunter-gatherer contexts have been discussed include: the Upper Palaeolithic in southwestern France (Jochim 1983; Gilman 1984; Mellars 1985) and in eastern Europe (Soffer 1985); the Archaic period of northeastern North America (Brown 1985); the Natufian of the Near East (Henry 1985; Bar Yosef 1987); and Peru (Cohen 1977).

Economy

Hunter-gatherer economy, composed of land and resource management strategies, has been viewed traditionally as relatively elementary and subsistence-based, guided in many ways by environmental-ecological factors. Australian Aboriginal economies, for example, were considered to be 'parasitic' (Meggitt 1964), and much like those of other hunters living off the land as ordinary 'carnivores and herbivores' (Polgar 1975: 3). Higher levels of production and the accumulation of surplus, for reasons of storage and redistribution, were considered as atypical, or as aspects of more complex, perhaps agricultural, societies (Polgar 1975: 11). It is becoming increasingly apparent, however, that a very wide range of economies existed among hunter-gatherer populations, and that these overlapped and were interrelated with agricultural and other economies, such as those of pastoralists, as well as with more complex socio-economic systems, including 'states' and more recent capitalistic formations (Ingold, Riches and Woodburn 1988a, 1988b).

The prior distinction between 'food producers', or agriculturalists, and 'food collectors', or hunter-gatherers, also has been revised. All human societies can be considered as 'producers' in the sense that food, and other commodities, are appropriated by a division of labour (Sahlins 1974; Ingold 1980). The hunter-gatherer economy itself can be seen to operate at two main levels: (a) the domestic or local group level; and (b) the wider intergroup level (Sahlins 1974). At the first, the domestic, level a very wide range of possible hunter-gatherer-fisher patterns can be found. Many more incentives existed, however, for accumulating surplus (and storage) and its redistribution at the second, the intergroup, level, where patterns of communal feasting and exchange existed in complex secular and ritualistic contexts. This intergroup feasting, ceremony, communal production and exchange, operated also as mechanisms of mediation amongst largely autonomous societies lacking as they do in many ways centralised political controls. Complex intergroup ceremonial and secular behaviour, therefore, can be viewed as the political arena of hunter-gatherer societies and was underwritten by the economy, by production (see below, this chapter).

These socio-economic, intergroup patterns can be found, to varying degrees, among hunter-gatherer and other societies (including agriculturalists). In this way, hunter-gatherers are little different to other societies. Once again, the traditional distinction which divides hunter-gatherers from others becomes unnecessary.

It is now generally recognised that a wide range in variation exists in hunter-gatherer economic patterns, and some of the main forms are discussed here. I focus particularly upon issues concerning, first, surplus and storage; second, settlement patterns; and, third, intensification and technology.

SURPLUS AND STORAGE

The accumulation of surplus, in the form of food, goods and other material commodities, occurred to varying degrees in all hunter-gatherer societies. In some societies, such as the African !Kung San (Lee 1979), this occurred in a relatively limited fashion, whereas in others, including those of the northwest coast of North America (Suttles 1968), and Inuit coastal communities of northwest Alaska (Sheehan 1985), accumulation of stored surpluses of food and other goods took place seasonally. In the latter two regions, surplus was used in elaborate systems of intergroup feasting, ceremony and exchange. Storage also took place of intangibles, such as relationships between individuals and groups via exchange, ceremony, marriage and the like. Relationships of this kind can be viewed as long-term social storage or investment, which could at times be converted back into hard and fast commodities through access to land and resources of others, wives, trading connections, knowledge and further influential social relationships (Testart 1982). All hunter-gatherer societies stored in this way, but where seasonality was more marked, as in the higher, more temperate (and sub-Arctic) latitudes of the world, there was more opportunity to store in bulk during seasons of plenty, when resources were more concentrated in time and space. Storage of surpluses was employed here also to overcome the harsher seasons of scarcity such as winter. Opportunities for storage of economic surpluses, however, existed in many environments around the world where seasonal concentration of resources took place. But whether or not such opportunities were seized upon by particular hunter-gatherer societies depended on a wide range of socio-cultural, historical and demographic factors, among others. Accumulation of surplus, therefore, was not only stimulated by subsistence needs, but also for political and wider socio-economic reasons, as I have shown above in relation to intergroup socio-political mediation (also see below, this chapter).

Storage also occurs in contexts where a return on labour is either immediate or delayed. For example, James Woodburn (1980, 1982) has argued that hunter-gatherers can largely be placed into categories lying at two ends of a spectrum. Those that practised (i) more 'immediate-return' strategies, where goods and services were obtained within a short duration (often a day or so), and those where (ii) 'delayed-return' strategies operated. Among the latter, lengthy delays from several weeks, months to years were involved. He argued that 'immediate-return' systems are fairly typical of hunter-gatherers such as the Hadza, !Kung, Mbuti, and Malapantaram and Pandaram of southern India, while the second class ('delayed-return' systems) compares more closely in organisation with agricultural societies. He also placed Australian Aborigines in the second class, along with the North American Haida, Kwakiutl, Ainu and some Inuit (Eskimo) societies, that is, more socially complex hunter-gatherer-fishers (see also Testart 1982). While acknowledging that all human societies have elements of 'immediate' and 'delayed' practices, often in complex, subtle combinations, placing socio-economic practices along a spectrum or continuum (which overlaps with agricultural societies) allows us to compare, in a relative way, their similarities and differences. As I have mentioned already, such continua or clines need not be viewed in a simplistic unilinear fashion.

SETTLEMENT PATTERNS

Variation also exists in hunter-gatherer settlement patterns, which are influenced by a wide range of factors – including environmental, socio-cultural, and demographic among others. Lewis Binford (1980) for example distinguished between two types of settlement patterns: the first with more mobile, 'residential' or 'mapping on' strategies, where hunter-gatherers moved themselves to spatially dispersed resources in relatively homogeneous environments; and the second more sedentary, 'logistical' strategies, where resources were obtained and brought back to a central base camp in more heterogeneous (perhaps seasonal) environments. He hypothesised that different archaeological patterns would result from the two practices. Binford observed these two patterns to operate within different natural environments: the first among the African Bushmen and the second among North American Nunamiut. That is, that they may have largely reflected the ecological structure of the particular environments in which the latter two groups resided.

However, we can also reformulate Binford's observations so as to use them in a more general way. We could hypothesise instead, therefore, that the two strategies may have operated also in comparable natural environments but in *different ways* in the past. That is, that they represent two different socio-cultural strategies for using *similar* environments. In other words, 'residential' and 'logistical' strategies can be hypothesised also as ends of a spectrum of possible economic-settlement patterns operating *within any environment at any time* (Lourandos 1987a; see also Ames 1985; Cohen 1985). While all hunter-gatherer settlement patterns may be seen as a combination of the above two strategies, these categories allow us to distinguish two ends of a spectrum of behavioural patterns which are discernible archaeologically. Henceforth, the terms 'residential' and 'logistical' will be used in modified form, as above, throughout this book.

Further, the reformulated observations of both Binford and Woodburn (above) can be combined to form a composite archaeological model of possible socio-economic behaviour (Figure 1.1). Once again, the terms are used here in a modified form and not as originally employed by the two authors. At the two ends of this hypothetical behavioural spectrum, therefore, I have grouped (i) 'immediate-return' strategies with 'mapping on' (or 'residential') behaviour, and (ii) 'delayed-return' strategies with 'logistical' behaviour. If we were to state this in another way, here we have (a) more dispersed (more mobile) economic-settlement patterns, as distinct from (b) more concentrated (more sedentary) patterns. Archaeological settlement patterns, therefore, might be expected to lie somewhere along this continuum (Lourandos 1988a). The model also allows us to investigate differences in degrees of mobility and sedentism and to link these to economic practices (Figure 1.1). Archaeological evidence of more sedentary behaviour has often been expressed as more concentrated use of archaeological sites, for example linear settlement (Struever 1968; Hayden 1981), repeatedly used base camps (Binford 1980) and more intensive use of rock-shelters and caves (Gilman 1984; Mellars 1985; Gamble 1986a; also Soffer 1989). Although this evidence and its interpretation are by no means unproblematical.

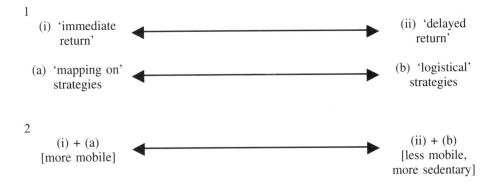

Figure 1.1 Two hypothetical models, or continua, of hunter-gatherer socio-economic and settlement patterns.

We might expect also that hunter-gatherer societies in the past may have moved back and forth along this spectrum. That is – and no unilinear trajectory need be suggested – with societies choosing from various alternative strategies as the circumstances arose. These decisions, therefore, need not only reflect past environmental-ecological patterns, but socio-economic and demographic ones as well (see below this chapter). The archaeological model presented here (Figure 1.1) is also employed throughout this book in analysing the Australian data.

'Logistical' organisation, 'delayed-returns' and storage carry implications regarding organisational and social complexity. Ideological changes in relation to material goods and their control (whether communal, individual and the like) are also involved (Testart 1982). A wider range, therefore, of socio-cultural patterns is possibly involved here. I now turn to discuss some of these issues.

INTENSIFICATION AND TECHNOLOGY

Hunter-gatherers were not passive victims of environmental forces and circumstances as traditional viewpoints supposed. To some extent they had the ability to control environmental productivity and economic levels of production, and to intensify production for a variety of reasons. They attuned their wide array of economic strategies, techniques and technology to perceived variations in availability of resources, changes in demography and social circumstances, among others (for example, Thomson 1939; Suttles 1968; Damas 1968; Winterhalder and Smith 1981). Environmental productivity was to some extent brought under control by techniques such as fire management of ecosystems and their plant and animal communities, water management of swamps and their resources, as well as management via a variety of procurement strategies. (Australian Aboriginal examples of similar behaviour can be found in Chapters Two, and Four to Seven). Indeed, in many cases the primary aim may have been to maintain general levels of bioproductivity, that is by regulation or regularisation, rather than to increase them (Hayden 1981; Lourandos 1980a, 1980b).

As well, economic levels of production could be intensified (or extensified) according to circumstances. While such practices could take place within the domestic (local group) level of economy as noted earlier, economic intensification was clearly magnified at the intergroup level (Sahlins 1974). This was also the case in Aboriginal Australia where accumulations of surplus and storage were increased for intergroup purposes, such as communal gatherings, feasts, ceremonies and exchanges. Examples of this can be found in most major environments of the mainland (Lourandos 1988b). The size of the surplus, in many ways, may have depended upon the duration and scale (for example, number of participants) of these festivities.

A wide range of techniques was employed to expand production for these purposes, many of which also were employed (often seasonally) at the domestic economic level. These techniques may have been used for a variety of reasons, such as to maximise, regulate or regularise time, labour, or efficiency, in economic productivity or production. The reasons may not have been directly economic, but concerned a variety of factors. Techniques included: labour-intensive collecting, processing and storage of plant foods; communal hunting (for example, net hunting) and fishing. Fishing techniques included the use of nets, traps, weirs, artificial drainage systems, and more complex equipment allowing the resources of a wider range of environments to be tapped. In this way, from an ecological perspective, lower (trophic) levels of the food chain could be exploited and generally with these devices, also a wider range of smaller-bodied animals with high annual rates of regeneration (referred to by ecologists as the 'r' selected variety) (Pianka 1978). Although the nature of the resources themselves (for example, the latter), and their ecological relationships, have often been used to explain their introduction and its effect (Hayden 1981), the point that needs to be stressed here is that it is the social context in which they are used – how they are used – that may be the more important factor (Soffer 1989). As well, devices such as traps and nets captured prey en masse thus saving time, energy (Torrence 1983) and people-power.

Redeployment of labour (along age, sex and group lines) was a further tactic (and is discussed in Chapters Four to Seven). While many practices can be viewed as aimed at immediate or short-term returns, as discussed, others can also be seen as producing a 'delay' on return. Of the latter, we can include fixed facilities such as fish traps, weirs and drainage systems (used, for example, in fishing), fixed hunting nets and traps, and more 'logistically' organised hunting base camps. These facilities were likely to involve more concentrated or permanent residence in particular locales (seasonally or annually). Practices such as these aimed at, or resulted in, expanding and extending the hunter-gatherer-fisher repertoire of techniques, and expanding the hunter-gatherer ecological niche, and have been well recognised worldwide in both ethnographic and archaeological contexts (Bender 1978; Hayden 1980, 1990; Lourandos 1983a, 1985a; Price and Brown 1985; Zvelebil 1986). The potential exists for observing these also in the Australian archaeological record (see Chapters Four to Seven).

Other means by which the hunter-gatherer econiche could be expanded include more intensive use of particular environments, some of which may have been considered more 'marginal' by past societies. In this case 'marginality' is seen as a socially perceived construct. Environments such as these might include wetlands, closed forests (including rainforest), and offshore islands. In this way, a wider range of environments could be exploited or more intensively utilised. Where a mosaic complex of microenvironments pertained, as in more favoured, richer areas, ecological management of resources, together with more finely tuned synchronisation in the use of resources, may have helped to regulate and/ or increase natural productivity and economic production. Intensification of production, however, need not have been primarily economically driven but was embedded in the broader socio-economic context (Bender 1978; and as regards Aboriginal Australia: Lourandos 1983a, 1985a, 1988b; Hynes and Chase 1982; Chase 1989).

In time, therefore, considerable variation in hunter-gatherer settlement and economic patterns may have taken place. I have already suggested some ways this may be investigated archaeologically, but there are still more. David Harris, for example, has outlined in detail possible economic 'pathways' along which hunter-gatherers may have travelled in time (1977b; see also 1989). In some cases historically these have led to the domestication of plants and animals, and in others not. Of the five main routes that he considered, three have led to domestication. These include the following key resources: (a) grasses and forbs; (b) roots and tubers; and (c) exploitation of social ungulates. He argued that the final two examples – (d) harvesting of tree nuts, and (e) fishing and hunting of aquatic animals – led instead to complex patterns of resource management, being limited as potential items of domestication and 'farming' by their respective biology. Harris' model can be extended to other classes of resources also, to illustrate their potential use and manipulation by hunter-gatherers and others. Archaeological examples of management and manipulation of wild resources by past hunter-gatherer societies are now increasingly being investigated, with prime examples including: Mesolithic Europe (Price 1985, 1987; Zvelebil 1986); the Mesolithic Near East (Henry 1985; Bar Yosef 1987); and the Jomon of Japan (Akazawa 1986). Further examples are provided from Aboriginal Australia and its past (see below Chapters Four to Seven). While emphasis has been placed on the biological and ecological constraints of these resources and their natural environments, the socio-demographic contexts in which these processes occurred also now need to be discussed in some detail.

Hunter-gatherer society

Here we consider the very wide range of social variation among contemporary hunter-gatherers and the implication this has for the interpretation of the archaeological record. Firstly, ethnographic hunter-gatherer societies range from relatively open, more egalitarian societies, for example African Bushman, to highly territorial, socially stratified societies, including those along the northwest coast of North America, western Alaska, and the Calusa of Florida. Many of the latter societies operated like chiefdoms (for example, the Kwakiutl and Calusa) with hereditary access to rank, control of distribution of resources, and acquisition of slaves. Warfare was also prevalent, and often the source of slaves and annexation of territory (Suttles 1968; Sheehan 1985; Marquardt 1988).

Indeed, these societies reflect a degree of social complexity beyond that of many subsistence agricultural societies. The Calusa, for example, displayed a state formation, including a paramount chief and standing army. For many other hunter-gatherer societies, including those of Australia, the society retained its basic egalitarian fabric with elements of social stratification. Examples of the latter in Aboriginal Australia include hierarchically organised religious cults, the existence of prominent leaders and 'big men', and competition between groups for resources and territory, among other things (see more on this in Chapter Two).

Relationships, therefore, between basically more open, more egalitarian and more 'complex' (more territorial) hunter-gatherer societies can be seen as clinal, presenting a mosaic of patterns, even within specific geographical regions, such as the northwest coast of North America. So-called egalitarian hunter-gatherer societies have been characterised by Woodburn as essentially having a fluid group structure, with an emphasis upon mobility, and relatively 'immediate-return' economic strategies (Woodburn 1982). He argued also that, in contrast, more 'complex' hunter-gatherers are characterised by bounded, discrete groups, more formal leadership, and 'delayed-return' economic strategies. We might add that the latter also are often associated with aspects of higher population density, increased levels of sedentism (decreased mobility) and 'logistical' economic patterns (including storage). More egalitarian societies, as defined here can, therefore, be seen as relatively 'open' social systems in contrast to the relatively more 'closed' systems of more 'complex' societies (see below this Chapter).

Social complexity also has been viewed by some (Johnson 1982; Ames 1985; Cohen 1985) as density-dependent; that is to say that stress factors caused by levels of population density stimulate the development of particular social strategies, including the forming of hierarchies. Greater social complexity, they argue, would exist where levels of population density were greatest in both time and space, and that these patterns are supported to some extent by ethnographic and archaeological data. While not denying the importance of such physical constraints upon social formation, it should also be pointed out that social structure too has its own particular dynamic, including the influence of historical and cultural factors. Social structures, including hierarchies, may become formalised and institutionalised thereby exerting a strong influence upon future events. Johnson (1982), for example, distinguished between vertical and horizontal social hierarchies, among others. Both these forms can be found in Aboriginal Australia; vertical formations may appear in the competition between groups, and horizontal structure can be seen in the stratified initiation systems into politically powerful religious cults, in which there were positions of social authority. Social differentiation has been investigated archaeologically through burial practices of past hunter-gatherer populations and has revealed aspects of differential status, as in the Natufian graves of the Levant (Henry 1985) and Archaic societies of northeastern America (Brown 1985), and more subtle distinctions as in the Mesolithic burials of Scandinavia (Price 1985; for Australian examples see Chapter Six; also Meehan 1971).

Alliances between groups also served to bind together local and regional hunter-gatherer populations. Systems of alliance included both relatively 'open' and 'closed' formations, as well as very extensive systems, often referred to as 'tribal' formations (Bender 1978; Cohen 1985; Lourandos 1983a, 1985a).

SOCIAL NETWORKS

The complex of alliance systems, of which individual bands are a part, have been viewed from a number of perspectives. For example, Joseph Birdsell (1953, 1957, 1968) followed by Martin Wobst (1974, 1976), discussed these social formations in terms of 'mating networks', in relation to their adaptive value in biological reproduction. Birdsell's data, as we have seen, were based upon Australian Aboriginal ethnographic information. But alliance formation concerns a broader range of relationships than 'mating' or marriage, as studies of Australian Aboriginal kinship have indicated (Maddock 1972). For example, alliance provided individuals and groups with more widespread opportunities, including not only partners in biological and social reproduction, but reciprocal rights to the land and resources of others (which may have operated also as a kind of insurance in times of need); also opportunities related to social contacts, information, ceremonies, exchange and the like.

The ecological significance of these elaborate, relatively open, 'support' systems was outlined by Aram Yengoyan (1968, 1972, 1976), and also by Maurice Godelier (1975) from a Marxist perspective.

> This network of related individuals and groups permits local groups to move into different areas of exploitation, especially during severe droughts and periods of economic hardship. The extension of kin relations via section groupings thus 'insures' for each local group the ability of movement into adjacent areas. (Yengoyan 1968: 199)

Yengoyan's basically ecological interpretation of the insulating effect of relatively open alliance systems is generally supported by other anthropologists of the Australian arid zone (Meggitt 1962; Gould 1980; Tonkinson 1978; Myers

1986). Yengoyan argued that the most complex social systems operated in the harshest Australian environments – the arid zones, where natural resources were scarcest and thus the need for social support greatest. Yengoyan's interpretations of the degree of social complexity of the central Australian networks has, however, been challenged. Sub-section systems, for example, appear to have arrived only recently in the region (Hamilton 1982a, 1982b). The force of Yengoyan's model is diminished further by the fact that complex social networks existed also outside of harsh, arid areas, for example in well-watered, fertile coastal regions, like southeastern Australia. Very extensive alliance systems had developed in central and southern present-day Victoria; and in many ways these networks were even more complex than those of the arid zone.

Both 'open' and 'closed' aspects of alliance operated in Victoria. For instance, at the 'tribal' level relatively closed networks may have reflected, in some way, the high biogeographical diversity of the region and thus denser Aboriginal populations and tighter overall territorial packing. Population density was, therefore, related in some ways to the distribution of natural resources (as already discussed above). In Victoria, however, extensive, more 'open', pan-tribal social networks overlaid and united these smaller, more 'closed' territorial units (see Chapter Two). In the same way, huge socio-political networks also existed further north, in present-day New South Wales (the Wiradjuri and Kamilaroi) (Howitt 1904: 303; Howitt and Fison 1880). These super networks cannot, therefore, be explained as direct expressions of environment productivity. Australian super networks were often associated also with extensive exchange systems, and this is so also in other, relatively complex hunter-gatherer societies (for example those of Archaic mid-continental North America).

The conclusions that may be drawn from these comparisons between Australian arid zone and humid coastal environments, is that complex alliance systems do *not only* act as cultural shields against constraints set by particular natural environments, as previously thought. In more fertile environments, like southeastern Australia, they must have served other purposes as well. I suggest that these complex networks also operated to offset constraints set by particular social or socio-demographic environments. In more fertile regions, alliance systems may have shielded people against greater levels of competition between groups, brought about by overall denser concentrations of population (see below, this chapter). That is, larger networks, among other alliance formations, may have developed to offset the constraints imposed by social 'closure'.

Birdsell (1953, 1957) argued that territorial packing of Aboriginal populations in richer Australian environments indicated greater economic autonomy of social groups; with less necessity for reliance upon neighbours and far-flung allies. I would argue, however, that the formation of extensive networks in Victoria and elsewhere suggests the reverse; that autonomy was at a premium. The complexity of Victorian networks, to me, indicates their relatively interdependent and dynamic nature. Forming alliances in these ways gave people the option of overcoming the limitations imposed by population density and heightened territoriality. Complex social networks, therefore, may have functioned, in part, to regulate or manage the relations between people and environment, between people and people, in a demographically and socially complex and problematical region. Demographic packing of Aboriginal population in the region of Victoria had resulted in a complex, dynamic and competitive interrelationship of relatively more 'open' and 'closed' social formations.

In ethnographic accounts of hunter-gatherer and horticultural societies, alliance has been viewed as regulated or managed by a complex of mechanisms. These include communal intergroup feasting, resource procurement, ceremonies, rituals and exchange (Sahlins 1974: 123–130; Bender 1978, 1981). A classic ecological study of a Highland New Guinea horticultural society, the Tsembaga-Maring, indicated that intergroup behaviour similar to that outlined above served to manage the demography (including population size) of the region (Rappaport 1967). Further research, from a social perspective, has suggested that these intergroup events in Highland New Guinea acted as more than population controls; serving also as socio-political devices and to manage relations between societies largely lacking other forms of centralised political controls (Modjeska 1982). Broadly similar interpretations have been offered of the evidence from Aboriginal Australia where, in some ways, comparable intergroup behaviour took place (Lourandos 1983a, 1985a, 1988b). Essentially, therefore, similar intergroup practices can be seen as reinforcing alliance and as regulating socio-political relations between Australian populations, and thus directly and indirectly affecting their demography in both short and long term. To view this behaviour, however, as primarily aimed at demographic control would be to underestimate the socio-cultural factors that largely guide it. After all, would we assess our own socio-political relations solely as agents of demographic control?

Alliance networks also make demands upon economy (that is, upon productivity and production) as Bender (1978, 1981) has demonstrated. This is particularly evident at the intergroup level, where ceremonial activity, feasting, exchange and social interaction are intensified. Sahlins (1974) has argued that amongst small-scale societies, including hunter-gatherers, horticulturalists and the like, economic intensification is more likely to be associated with intergroup relationships, rather than at the domestic or local group level of economic organisation. Internal relations within and between groups can, therefore, be seen as producing a dynamic which bears upon a group's economy and its level of production.

The Tsembaga-Maring, for example, invested up to thirty percent of their garden produce to support pig herds that were mainly slaughtered for communal feasting associated with intergroup ceremonies at intervals of around ten years. Domestic pigs, therefore, were not raised to supplement the diet; everyday pork was obtained by hunting wild animals (Rappaport 1967). In other Highland societies, investment in pig herds for similar reasons was up to fifty percent of garden produce (Modjeska 1982). The production of communal foods in Aboriginal Australia to uphold intergroup occasions can be viewed in a similar light. These resources were the equivalent, in some ways, of the pig and other items in Highland New Guinea and other regions, and were employed for broadly similar purposes – largely serving to manage intergroup relations (Lourandos 1988b). Although these changes in resource use have been viewed traditionally within agricultural contexts – in regard to questions concerning the origins and intensification of agriculture – the main point here is that they apply equally to hunter-gatherers.

MORE 'OPEN' SYSTEMS

More 'open' social formations, as already observed, are charactised by less formality and greater flexibility and fluidity of relationships between individuals and groups. Rules of exclusion ('closure') are overcome by a variety of means; in these ways large numbers of people can be integrated in loosely formed alliances, which can be 'reassembled' as need be. Communication within and between such networks often was facilitated by more 'homogeneous' cultural traits, including aspects of ritual as well as items of material culture. These more homogeneous patterns, whether expressed in symbolic form (for example, rock art) or portable items (in exchange, for example) have their archaeological equivalents in widespread distribution of homogeneous artefact sets. Clive Gamble (1986a), for instance, argued along these lines to explain geographically dispersed artefact distributions in Palaeolithic central Europe prior to the glacial maximum, when the region resembled an arctic desert. He argued that these 'open' alliance formations served to unite widely dispersed populations under these harsh conditions, which in some ways resembled those of recent arid Australia (see above; also Soffer 1987b).

EFFECTS OF 'CLOSURE'

It may be hypothesised also that changes in demographic structure (that is, changes to population density, dispersal and size) would provide a context for changes to socio-economic relations. It may be suggested that as demographic relations become more complex or dynamic (competitive), therefore, these circumstances can be expected to, first, affect the nature of 'open' and 'closed' intergroup relationships and, second, make increasing demands upon economy. *The socio-demographic dynamic, I suggest, is the result of increasing levels of 'closure' in association with heightened competition between and within groups of people.* Competition in more 'open' systems, it can be argued, would be more readily alleviated by generally greater flexibility of relationships. Processes such as these should also be viewed in their historical context, for patterns of behaviour can become more formalised and thus exert strong influence on future decision-making. Historical trajectories could in this way be forged. A model to help explain these events would be of a trend from a more 'open' social system to one with greater levels of 'closure' (see also: David and Lourandos in press; Lourandos and David in prep. a). Relatively more 'closed' social or alliance systems would produce demographic conditions involving increasing social constraints, for example upon access to partners, land and resources, and further social connections (see also Gilman 1984). As we have seen, however, demographic shifts need not be related directly to environmental changes or to population increases or decreases; socio-cultural factors, among others, also might be involved.

Behaviour associated with territorial constraints such as these would include: marking of territorial boundaries through mechanisms such as art, ritual precincts, cemeteries and the like; increased ritual and exchange associated with intergroup occasions, feasting, and so on; and increased aggression (overt or ritualised). These features of (overt) territorial behaviour (including social 'closure') can be found in many ethnographies of hunter-gatherers, including those of the Australian Aborigines, and have been discussed in detail in recent archaeological literature (see below, this chapter and Chapter Two). Territorial constraints (including more sedentary patterns) may also lead to alterations in social organisation (including the development of hierarchies), which may have been overcome in other contexts by factors such as increased mobility (Johnson 1982; Ames 1985; Cohen 1985). Another related feature is the expansion of alliance systems, which at the one time unite larger populations (thus surmounting territorial constraints) and produce more complex social patterns (including hierarchies and centralising tendencies) (Bender 1978, 1981, 1985). These features are found also in Australian Aboriginal ethnographies, for example those of southeastern Australia (Lourandos 1983a, 1985a) (see also above, this chapter).

The implications of the above for archaeology are that indicators of these socio-economic processes may by revealed in the following ways: by increased cultural regionalisation (denoting territoriality), increased ritual and territorial markers (denoting more 'closed' social structures), and complex, widespread exchange patterns (denoting expansion of alliance systems). Territorial indicators would include ceremonial sites and cemeteries (Bender 1985; Brown 1985) and stylistic markers (for example, artefacts, art, and the like), which also denote regional style-zones (Wobst 1976; Conkey 1985; Gamble 1986a). Exchange items may have wider and more complex patterns of geographical distribution. Regionalisation, or increased territoriality in relation to subsistence and settlement patterns, would include the following: (a) increasing trends towards use of smaller-sized territories and locales (for example, fishing spots); (b) 'logistical' strategies, and possibly increased sedentism (indicating longer-term base camps); and (c) the presence of fixed facilities (indicative of 'delayed-return' systems, like weirs, fish traps and so on). Associated also may be evidence for economic shifts, such as resource intensification or specialisation as examples of changing patterns of production. Changes in social organisation (including forms of hierarchisation) can be found in the range in variation of burial practices, and palaeopathological signs of stress on populations (for example, due to overcrowding) are sometimes observable in skeletal evidence (Cohen and Armelagos 1984; Cohen 1985).

All the above general indicators are subject to their own limitations. In order to avoid generalisations, therefore, in this book I make reference to specific examples, both archaeological and ethnographic. The archaeological indicators (direct or indirect) of increased territoriality, demographic packing, 'logistical' strategies and the like among hunter-gatherers, have been discussed for various regions, including southwestern France during the late Upper Palaeolithic. For example, Michael Jochim (1983) considered that the classic cave art of the region served as territorial markers, and thus to regulate rising hunter-gatherer population densities. The latter were indicated by increases in numbers of sites and their usage (see also Gilman 1984; Mellars 1985). A further archaeological example comes from the Woodland period of Archaic northeastern America, where elaborate ritual and mortuary precincts may have served as territorial markers and were associated with widespread exchange and, in some cases, more sedentary settlement (Struever 1968; Bender 1985; Brown 1985). As many of these examples illustrate, *long-term trends* in particular variables (for example, 'sedentism', mortuary precincts and the like) were established over thousands of years, in a rather slow, conservative fashion (for instance, Brown 1985; Mellars 1985). Reversals and oscillations were also observed in both long and short term (for instance, Soffer 1985). It is argued here that broadly similar long-term trends can be observed in the Australian prehistoric evidence which is covered in Chapters Four to Seven below.

I am not, however, arguing here that changing patterns of socio-cultural variation and 'complexity' are only associated with aspects of 'closure'. Variation and complexity, no matter how defined, can occur at any level or in any context. For example, the relatively 'open', extensive social networks of arid Australia also included more varied, 'complex' aspects. What I have outlined here are the conditions especially associated with 'closure'.

Overview

The main issues regarding hunter-gatherer socio-cultural variation, in long- and short-term contexts, that have been discussed here are, first, that environmental factors influence the temporal and spatial distribution of natural resources and therefore the range of cultural, economic and demographic choices available to hunter-gatherer societies. Changes to the natural environment, its ecological structure and its resources, therefore, exert influence upon the alteration, or arrangement, of hunter-gatherer strategies.

Second, the demography of human populations is interwoven with socio-cultural factors. For example, fertility levels, population size and density, and social patterns of aggregation and dispersal (including mobility and sedentism), are to a large extent influenced and controlled by socio-cultural, as well as environmental, forces.

Third, hunter-gatherer economies operate at two main levels: the domestic, and the wider intergroup. At both levels a wide range of possible economic patterns applies including both extensive and intensive strategies, which can be altered through time. Economic intensification, however, appears to have been more prevalent at the intergroup level.

Finally, hunter-gatherer society also may be structured at varying levels of complexity. Here a distinction was made between what are termed relatively more 'open' and 'closed' social systems. Aspects of complexity are associated with both, and these formations are influenced also in various ways by demography and environment.

Many of these features of socio-cultural variation can be analysed by using both ethnographic and archaeological data, some of which were discussed above. It has been argued here that – depending on the questions asked of the archaeological data – the resolution often largely rests upon varying spatio-temporal scales of analysis. For example, possible long- and short-term spatio-temporal trends can be perceived in the archaeological record. Indirect as well as direct data, however, often also need to be employed. In the following chapters, the Australian ethnographic and archaeological information will be viewed in light of the issues and models explored here. The general nature of the book allows for a broad range of topics to be discussed also at a general level, and more specific issues in regional case studies.

CHAPTER 2

AUSTRALIAN ABORIGINAL
HUNTER-GATHERERS

In this chapter we discuss the ethnographic and ethnohistorical information on Australian Aboriginal hunter-gatherers and place emphasis upon changing perspectives, population sizes and densities, territory, trade and exchange and, in some detail, Australian and Tasmanian ethnographic case studies. As well, Australian and Tasmanian hunter-gatherers are compared generally to New Guinean hunter-horticulturalists.

Changing perspectives

Recent changes in perceptions of Australian Aboriginal society can be attributed to a number of factors. Early colonialism of the late eighteenth century brought about a severe reduction of Aboriginal populations due to introduced disease and European aggression (see below, this chapter), which resulted in a significant loss of evidence on traditional Aboriginal society. Anthropological studies came more than a century later, and were based largely upon observations of people of arid and tropical regions of the continent. Little was known, for example, of Aboriginal society in the fertile, southern temperate zone of the continent. The particular emphases of anthropological theoretical perspectives also left their mark. For example, 'structural functionalism' – one of the main anthropological approaches employed in Australian Aboriginal studies this century – was largely ahistorical in approach and generally avoided economic enquiry (Hamilton 1982b). The recent surge of interest in Aboriginal culture has also stimulated anthropological attitudes. To some extent also, ethnohistorical studies have thrown light on little-known sectors of the continent, such as the southeast. The overall impression, therefore, that has been obtained from this more recent information is of a broader and more complex range in traditional Australian Aboriginal societies.

Here we consider several issues: population, territory, economy and their relationship to Aboriginal society. Apart from emphasising a relatively low Aboriginal population size and density, earlier traditional attitudes to Aboriginal economy viewed it as 'generalised' (Birdsell 1957), and because of its reliance upon natural resources such as wild foods, as passive or 'parasitic' (Meggitt 1964). In contrast, recent ethnographic and ethnohistorical studies have considerably revised this viewpoint by pointing to complex Aboriginal land and resource management (see below, this chapter). In the earlier perspective, Aboriginal economies, for example, were not considered as generating significant surpluses, and storage was also underestimated. In contradiction to this view, more recent ethnohistorical studies, among others, indicate that sizeable surpluses of stored (and often laboriously processed) foods, including a range of plants, fish and the like, were accumulated, especially in connection with intergroup occasions such as ceremonies, feasting and exchange (Lourandos 1988b; see also below, Figure 2.1). Elements of a 'market' economy as regards the trading of both the narcotic *pitchuri*, and also of fashioned axe blanks, operated in northwestern Queensland. Both examples may have been dismissed previously as due to European contact.

Perspectives on the organisation of Aboriginal society, and in particular the role of leaders, women, and rights to land and natural resources, have also been considerably revised. Traditional approaches, which emphasised the egalitarian and so-called anarchic side of Aboriginal social organisation (Meggitt 1966; Maddock 1972) may now be contrasted with recent studies discussing the ethnopolitics of acquisition, control and inheritance of land and resources (Sutton and Rigsby 1982). Prominent leaders also played a decisive role in the latter events and, for example, controlled important fertile sectors of territory in Cape York Peninsula (Von Sturmer 1978; also Keen 1989).

Recent Aboriginal land rights disputes have clearly highlighted competitive and complex Aboriginal attitudes to land and its control. Similar attitudes are also reflected in past accounts. Clan elders, for example, were acknowledged as powerful and prestigious individuals in southwestern Victoria (southeastern Australia). In this region, further status and prestige was obtained through ceremonial rank, polygyny, shamanism, organisation of spectacular mass hunts and participation in extensive exchange networks. In southwestern Victoria, competition between groups involved a wide range of natural resources, including territory, and is recorded by many early European observers throughout Victoria (Lourandos 1977a, 1980a, 1985a). Further aspects of competition between groups is expressed in the elaborate material culture of weaponry (shields, clubs and the like) used for display and combat. Elaborate examples of this equipment exist from Victoria (Smyth 1876) and also northeastern Queensland (Reynolds 1987).

The position of women, their separate political, economic and ceremonial domains, and their relationship with male affairs and power structures, is discussed in detail by Annette Hamilton (1980, 1982a) and Diane Bell (1983) (see also Meehan 1982; Gale 1970; Balme and Beck 1993). These observations have, for many reasons, not been recorded in traditional male-oriented anthropological studies.

The complexity of kinship and ceremonial practices of Australian Aboriginal society have long been appreciated (for example, Maddock 1972), but less so their connection with economy and the material realm of Aboriginal culture. The traditional impression was one of an 'imbalance' between complex structural-ceremonial relations and rather elementary economy and equipment. I would suggest that these misconceptions were produced by early colonial historical processes leading to population decimation and societal dislocation. Traditional Aboriginal economy, I would argue, which was embedded in a complex socio-demographic structure, would have decayed long before most recorded anthropological observations. More recent neo-Marxist analyses, however, draw a close connection between Aboriginal religious and ceremonial practices and the operation of the economy. Bern (1979), for example, has argued that the ideology of economic relations lies in the rich Australian religious life (cults, ceremonies and the like). Hamilton expressed a similar viewpoint:

> For, although men act in the ritual sphere using means reminiscent of action in the economic world under capitalism, and attempt to find more and more secure ways of ensuring the transmission of rights to *ritual* property from fathers to sons, the material basis on which the male religious life rests is gained through the labour of the women. This 'real' base, however, does not appear anywhere at the ideological level; men continue to act as if ritual manipulations are the sole determinant of human production, and concern themselves exclusively with defining access to the rituals which constitute their 'business world' in which women feature mainly by their absence. (1982a: 106)

Manipulation of religious affairs, therefore, may be viewed in terms of the political economy.

Earlier ethnographic accounts also have hinted at a close association between the level of production and the demands of social relations. For example, the classic studies of the Tiwi people of Bathurst and Melville Islands of northern Australia by Hart and Pilling, indicate that production of resources was increased and surpluses provided by the development of relatively efficient domestic labour units in the form of large polygynous households (1960). Due to their larger retinue, such households were also relatively sedentary. Thus increased female labour was employed to host lengthy feasts associated with status funerals. In this way, a polygynous, gerontocratic system, with one individual male recorded as having twenty-nine wives, for example, controlled both production and reproduction. The distribution of wives, goods, services, feasts and rituals and the like, was governed, and competed for, by a minority of 'big men' (the ethnographers' term).

While the Tiwi are not necessarily a typical Australian Aboriginal society, they display many similarities with other Australian societies. For example, Thomson (1949) detailed the elaborate exchange systems of Arnhem Land and their close association with ritual leaders and the production of items of exchange (see below). Keen (1982) has recently pointed to the ways in which varying kinship systems allow for differential levels of polygyny. Both examples are indications of ways in which social relations may affect the level of production. In the first case, specialist craftsmen emerged, together with production being stimulated for purposes of exchange. In the second, the potential size of the domestic labour force (polygyny) was to a large degree controlled by the form of the particular kinship system. Thus the Murngin system allowed certain individuals to acquire up to ten wives. Polygyny, and the related existence of prominent leaders, has also been recorded for other Australian regions, as noted above.

These arguments may also be extended to the material aspects of the economy, that is, to technology and equipment. Leonn Satterthwait (1980) considered that the wide range of specialised procurement equipment, as measured by the number of 'techno-units' in his analysis, firmly placed Australian Aboriginal society within the class of 'complex' hunter-gatherers, an observation also made by others (see Chapter One). It may be argued that population decimation and societal dislocation following European settlement of the continent severely disrupted Aboriginal patterns of use of this varied equipment. The apparent 'under-utilisation' of efficient techniques, such as processing and storage of plant foods, observed by Richard Gould (1980) might be explained best in this way. Further examples of economic material culture are discussed below.

Population size and density

Traditionally it has been thought that Australian Aboriginal people were thinly spread around the continent, with the highest densities in fertile tropical coastal regions. But many of the early estimates of the late eighteenth and early nineteenth centuries are contradictory and biased. This is especially so of the southern reaches of the continent where European settlement had its most immediate impact. For example, for the rich area of southwestern Victoria, Fyans (Bride 1898: 191) estimated between three and four thousand people, while for the entire region of Victoria, Smyth (1876, 1: 32, 35) deduced a population of merely three thousand. Apart from the difficulty of assessing the densities of mobile populations in the bush, there appears to have been a genuine ignorance of the facts, as well as a desire to underplay true sizes. With a rapidly declining Aboriginal population due to both introduced diseases and European eradication, it served the interests of many (including officials and landholders), to follow the latter course. In general, the Aborigines were viewed as a conquered people whose culture and numbers were rapidly on the wane. Inferences of a small original population further strengthened this viewpoint.

By 1912, the anthropologist Baldwin Spencer roughly estimated the Aboriginal population of the Northern Territory at 50,000 people (White and Mulvaney 1987: 116). It was not, however, until 1930, that the federal government assigned Radcliffe-Brown to assess the Australian Aboriginal population sizes at the time of the 1788 settlement. Radcliffe-Brown's estimates were based largely upon historical sources which varied in reliability (1930). He also assumed that tropical areas were more fertile and that their Aboriginal populations were more numerous.

> ... the available evidence points to the original population of Australia having been certainly over 250,000, and quite possibly, or even probably, over 300,000. (Radcliffe-Brown 1930: 696)

The figures quoted, therefore, were minimum estimates, but through usage these estimates have come to be quoted as the average (for example, Maddock 1972: 22). A recent re-examination, however, of the ethnohistorical literature has unearthed new information which has resulted in this estimate being revised upwards. Tasmanian population sizes were re-evaluated by Rhys Jones (1974) who largely employed newly available evidence – the Tasmanian journals of George Augustus Robinson (Plomley 1966). Jones was able to estimate the number, size and location of Tasmanian local groups, or 'bands', and in so doing revised the overall Tasmanian population at the time of contact from around 2,500 up to between 3,000 and 5,000 people.

A detailed reassessment of the population sizes of southwestern Victoria has produced even higher estimates than those for Tasmania (Lourandos 1976, 1977a, 1980a, 1980b: 77–100). I based my analysis also on new information derived from George Augustus Robinson's (Victorian) journals of 1840–41, which at the time existed only as manuscripts and were unpublished. Population densities were likewise deduced from the number, size and location of recorded clans or 'bands' of the region. The conservative nature of the material was also acknowledged, having been obtained following a period of population decline brought about by introduced diseases such as smallpox (Lourandos 1980b: 77). This evidence, therefore, contradicted the assumption that the highest Australian population densities had been in tropical coastal areas, and that coastal population density was closely tied to latitude (Jones 1971a: 371) (see Table 2.1). The southwestern Victorian population estimates also correlated closely with those derived from neighbouring coastal and inland regions, such as the Coorong Estuary, South Australia, and the Goulburn River area from central Victoria. Finally, I concluded that:

> The evidence suggests that areas such as southeastern Australia which were quickly occupied by Europeans, had larger Aboriginal populations than was generally admitted

Table 2.1 A comparison of population densities of some Australian and Tasmanian hunter-gatherer and New Guinea shifting agricultural societies, showing an unbroken continuum (based on Lourandos 1980a: 248). Data: Tasmania (after Jones 1974: 326; Victoria (after Lourandos 1977a); Arnhem Land (after Hiatt 1965: 17); central New Guinea (after Modjeska 1977: 37) ; Trans-Fly (after Ohtsuka 1977).

Population	Population density (sq. kms. per person)	Economy
Tasmania		
Southeast Tasmania (Oyster Bay) (coastal)	11–14	hunting-gathering
Northwest Tasmania (coastal)	5–10	hunting-gathering
Australia		
Southwest Victoria (Northern Tjapwurong) (inland)	2.5–3.3	hunting-gathering-fishing
Southwest Victoria (Peek Whuurong) (coastal)	1.4–2.5	hunting-gathering-fishing
Northeast Arnhem Land (Gidjingali) (coastal)	1.29	hunting-gathering-fishing
New Guinea		
Baktaman (central PNG)	1.3	shifting cultivation (taro), h-gathering
Saiyolof (central PNG)	1.1	shifting cultivation (taro)/h-gathering
Wonio (Trans-Fly)	1.0	shifting cultivation (taro), h-gathering
Southern Hewa (central PNG)	1.6	shifting cultivation (sweet potato), hunting
Oksapmin (central PNG)	0.13–0.1	shifting cultivation (taro, sweet potato)
Duna (central PNG)	0.1–0.25	intensive shifting cultivation, mounded sweet potato

or perceived by early chroniclers. This argument further suggests that the total Australian Aboriginal population which Radcliffe-Brown [1930] estimated at 300,000 should be revised upwards, perhaps by a factor of two or three, if the Victorian examples are an indication. (Lourandos 1980b: 100)

These investigations were taken further by the economic historian Noel Butlin (1983, 1993), who argued that diseases introduced in 1788 in southeastern Australia exacted a heavier toll on Aboriginal lives than had been appreciated. He employed the above southwestern Victorian population estimates to bolster his arguments. Smallpox epidemics, he argued, were severe, requiring relatively dense populations to spread the disease. The effects of smallpox had effectively raced ahead of European settlement across southeastern Australia. Other infections included respiratory and venereal diseases, as well as measles. The implications of this evidence are that early European observers outside the Sydney area were not viewing the traditional Aboriginal society but one decimated by widespread diseases. Through a process of model-building, Butlin estimated the population of southeastern Australia (that is, present-day Victoria and New South Wales) at 250,000, which is four times the figure calculated by Radcliffe-Brown. A revision of the Australian figures at the same order of magnitude would arrive at a total population closer to one million, or at least around 900,000 (see also White and Mulvaney 1987). This accords generally with my own assessment, above.

Although Butlin's arguments related to southeastern Australia, broadly similar evaluations are now being directed at northern Australia (from the Kimberley region to Cape York), where contact with Indonesian fishing fleets had persisted for several hundred years. MacKnight (1986) argued that diseases, including smallpox, also may have spread from this northern region of external contact prior to the establishment of European colonies in southern Australia.

The available Australian estimates of population density (see Table 2.1; also below, this chapter) have probably not taken into account the extent of demographic decline at the time of European contact, and therefore under-represent the true densities. Nevertheless, the picture obtained indicates relatively high densities around the humid seaboard of Australia, in particular the southeastern, eastern and northern coastlines. As we have seen, densities from southeastern Australia (for example southwestern Victoria), approximate the highest densities, such as those from tropical regions, for example Arnhem Land. Further inland population densities are lower than those of the more fertile coastal regions, although estimates from productive inland regions, such as the Murray Valley region of southeastern Australia, are relatively high. The lowest densities are from the most arid inland regions. Of particular interest is the observation that the highest Australian densities overlap with the lower end of the range of population densities from New Guinea. On the other hand, Tasmanian population densities are three to four times lower than those of environmentally comparable areas such as southwestern Victoria. These issues are discussed further below.

Territory

Over two hundred distinctive languages were spoken in Aboriginal Australia (Dixon 1980: 1), and although 'tribal' or dialectal languages existed (see below), most people were bilingual or multilingual. Aboriginal society was clan-based and groups of related clans, speaking similar languages, coalesced socially and politically into larger named units, often referred to as 'tribes'. Groups of 'tribes' or dialectal languages, also formed socio-political alliances. In reality however, individuals and groups were aligned linguistically, socially and politically to each other in varying ways. Because of these overlapping ties, definitions of 'tribe' have always been somewhat problematical. For convenience, however, linguistic units and territorial boundaries generally have been used to locate geographically 'tribal' groups (Tindale 1974).

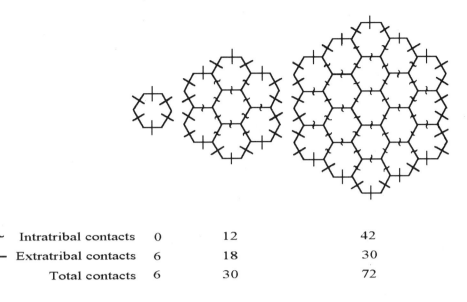

	Intratribal contacts	0	12	42
~				
—	Extratribal contacts	6	18	30
	Total contacts	6	30	72

Figure 2.1 A model of the interaction between local groups of hunter-gatherers (based on Birdsell 1958: 197).

Aboriginal social formations have also been considered from biological and ecological perspectives. Birdsell (1958) modelled Australian Aboriginal alliance formations by focusing upon groups of clans bound into biologically viable 'mating networks' (see Figure 2.1). W. E. Stanner (1965) considered the ecological basis of Aboriginal territorial organisation in terms of cultural adaptation to varying natural environments. This approach had similarities to the North American research of Kroeber (1939) and Steward (1936), and was developed further by Nicholas Peterson (1976), who reasoned that the main ecological unit in Aboriginal society was based upon the major drainage basins of the continent (see Figure 2.2). Drainage basin populations, therefore, were seen as the principal biological and cultural unit.

While these models explain the Australian material to a large extent, the situation is, in effect, more complex due to the dynamic social and political nature of group alliance and territoriality. This can be illustrated quite well for southwestern Victoria (see Figure 2.3; see also below, and Chapter Six). Here major drainage basins were cross-cut by important networks of 'inter-tribal' boundaries. Had only the drainage basin population for the region been considered this would not fully explain the socio-political complexity that occurred in the centre of the basin (Lourandos 1977a). When considering Australian Aboriginal territoriality, therefore, we need to carefully examine the dynamics of the socio-political realm as well as those of the ecological and biological.

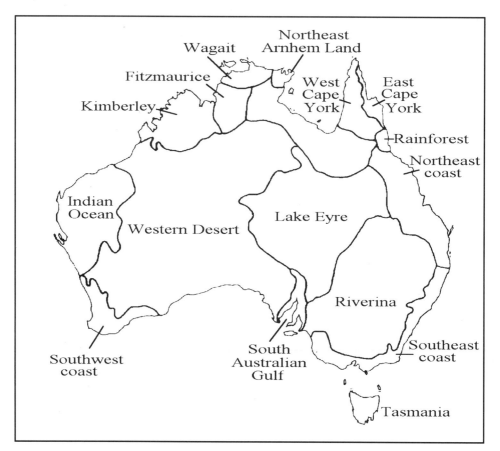

Figure 2.2 Culture areas of Aboriginal Australia based upon drainage basin divisions (based on Peterson 1976: 66, Figure 8).

Exchange and trade

Traditional Aboriginal exchange and trade, often encompassing extensive sectors of the continent, has been discussed in detail by McCarthy (1939, 1940), Mulvaney (1976) and McBryde (1984) among others. This account, to a large extent, follows John Mulvaney's general assessment. Reciprocal exchange was documented for most Australian areas studied, with an emphasis upon alliance formation between individuals and groups. These transformations appear to have been predominantly social and ritualised in form, although economic motivation was also involved. Ceremonial exchange systems were also extensive in all major environmental zones; ethnographic accounts such as those of Arnhem Land are complimented by ethnohistorical information from all other parts of the continent (see Figure 2.4). Gifts, including tokens and symbols, as well as ceremonies and other religious information travelled between exchange partners or via a chain

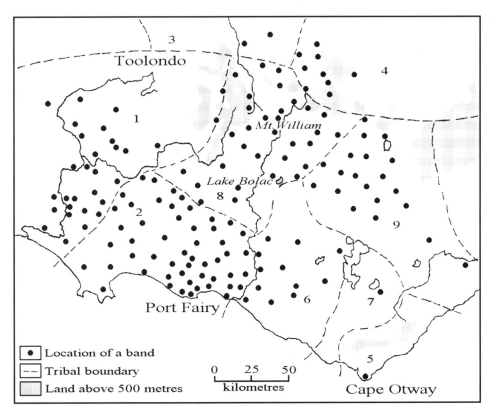

Figure 2.3 Social networks of southwestern Victoria, including socio-linguistic divisions (numbers) and locations of bands or clans (based on Lourandos 1980a).

of contacts along traditional routes. Long distances were covered by individuals and groups; up to 200 kilometres in coastal areas, and up to around 500 kilometres in arid zones. 'In theory, some individuals could have traversed 800–960 km (250 to 300 miles) in completing two journeys within a limited time period for ochre and pituri' (Mulvaney 1976: 79; see also below).

A very broad range of commodities, including goods and foodstuffs, was exchanged (for example, Roth 1897: 100–151; Spencer and Gillen 1899: 586–587; Howitt 1904: 712–719; Horne and Aiston 1924: 21, 34, 47, 80, 104). Specialisation in crafts and goods was also widespread (Roth 1897; Spencer and Gillen 1899: 586; Horne and Aiston 1924). Long-distance journeys took place for items such as ochre, *pituri* (*pitchuri*, a narcotic) and sandstone grinding slabs, which were also obtained by women (Hamilton 1980; also Watson 1983). Individuals controlled important greenstone axe quarries in Victoria, which served as centres for extensive exchange systems in southeastern Australia (Howitt 1904: 311–340; see also Chapter Six).

Some items travelled great distances across Australia.

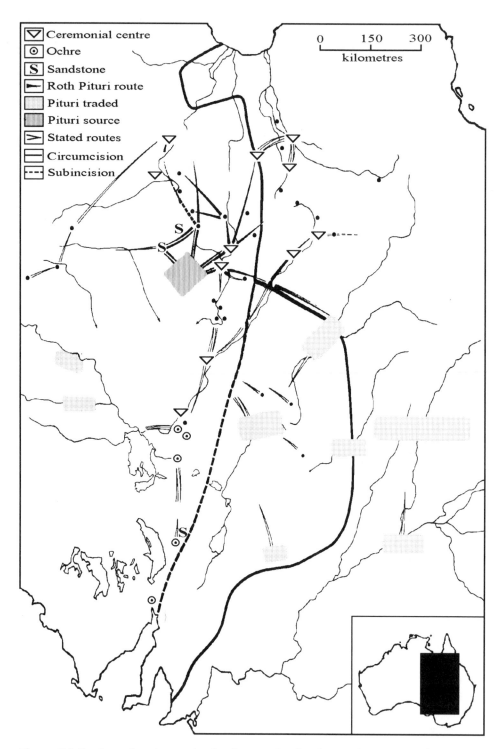

Figure 2.4 Trade and exchange in the Cooper Creek–Diamantina region of pituri, ochre and grindstones (sandstone), also showing the continental divisions of groups practising circumcision and subincision rites (based on Mulvaney 1976: 87, Map 6).

Legend:
- ▽ Ceremonial centre
- ⊙ Ochre
- S Sandstone
- ➤ Roth Pituri route
- Pituri traded
- Pituri source
- ➤ Stated routes
- Circumcision
- --- Subincision

0   150   300
kilometres

Shell, stone, ochre, pituri and wooden tools and weapons all circulated over hundreds of kilometres ... Shell pendants crossed the continent. Even a wooden hooked boomerang was seen by Carnegie (1898: 343, 392) at least 1200 km (800 miles) west of its area of manufacture ... Pituri was a valued item over 800 km (500 miles) from its source (cf Dunbar 1944: 177). (Mulvaney 1976: 80)

Shells, including baler shells, from the Gulf of Carpentaria (northeastern Australia), found their way to South Australia (Mulvaney 1969: 96). Mulvaney considered that food was only rarely exchanged, although it also provided the resource base for hosting lengthy intergroup ceremonial and exchange gatherings which took place in all environments across the continent (1976: 80). Food, however, including 'cooked' or 'smoked' eels were exchanged in southwestern Victoria (Dawson 1881; Lourandos 1980a).

Some objects travelled rapidly across vast distances: *pituri* is recorded as having moved 480 kilometres in just a few weeks and Flinders Range ochre was transported 30 kilometres a day for distances in excess of 320 kilometres (Mulvaney 1976: 90). Ceremonies also were exchanged rapidly; for example, the Molonga ceremony appears to have been exchanged in just 25 years (1893–1918) across a distance of over 1,600 kilometres. The ceremony spread from western Queensland (North Georgia River) to the Nullarbor Plain in South Australia (Mulvaney 1976: 91, 92), and the rapid dissemination of ceremonies has also been reported by others (for example, Backhouse 1843: 435; Petrie 1904: 19).

AUSTRALIAN AND TASMANIAN ETHNOGRAPHIC CASE STUDIES

We now consider case studies from a range of mainland Australian and Tasmanian environments which have been drawn from both ethnographic and ethnohistorical information. The studies have been selected to provide, in some ways, a sample of these environments; they also form a backdrop to many of the archaeological study areas that follow in Chapters Four to Seven. Emphasis has been placed, where possible, upon settlement and subsistence patterns, social relations and demographic structure, and upon the use and manipulation of land and plant resources in particular. Information varies, however, between studies as it was collected originally for a variety of purposes and in different ways. Comparisons are also drawn between the mainland and Tasmanian evidence and hunter-horticultural societies of Papua New Guinea. Finally, this information is assessed in the light of the arguments presented in Chapter One.

The tropical north

Today, the climate of tropical northern Australia is highly seasonal with high summer rainfall and dry winters. Northwesterly monsoons generate summer rainfall in the north, and the east coast is influenced by southeasterly trade winds.

Rainfall is highest in elevated areas including the Kimberley of the northwest, Arnhem Land in the central north and the Great Dividing Range in the east. The highest rainfall of all occurs in the Cairns–Innisfail area of the northeast. There are also marked similarities between the climates of northern Australia and those of southern, coastal Papua New Guinea.

In general, open sclerophyll forests and savanna, dominated by *Eucalyptus* among other genera, are the predominant vegetation forms, with open tussock grasslands much further inland in more arid regions. In the high-rainfall coastal area of the northeast, the dominant vegetation gives way to a complex mosaic of rainforest and other closed-canopied sclerophyll communities.

Arnhem Land

Detailed recent ethnographic studies have been carried out by Betty Meehan (1982), who focused particularly on the activities of the Anbara women, and Rhys Jones (1981) and John Altman (1987), which complement the earlier accounts of Donald Thomson (1949). Aboriginal communities living in or near coastal wetlands were seasonally semi-sedentary, and more mobile at other times of year. A strong emphasis was placed upon plants and their management (discussed further later in this chapter) and production was increased to meet the demands of lengthy ceremonial events (Altman 1987: 191–223). In general, there are strong similarities between parts of Arnhem Land and western Cape York. The Tiwi of Bathurst and Melville Islands were island-based fisher-hunter-gatherers and had little contact with the mainland, and their polygynous socio-economic system was described above.

Western Cape York

Thomson's early study of the Wik Monkan of western Cape York (1939) clearly focused on the ecological complexity of the lives of tropical coastal peoples. So diverse were their seasonal subsistence and settlement patterns, with such a range in resources and equipment, that Thomson thought a casual observer seeing them at different times of year might mistake them for different peoples. The climate of the region is markedly seasonal, the wet season extends from late November to March, the dry season from April to November. Towards the end of the Dry (as it is called here), vegetation is desiccated and the country was burnt off by the Aboriginal people. In contrast, during the Wet, vegetation grows prolifically and extensive areas of lowland are inundated. Much of the Cape York Peninsula is savanna forest, with large salt pans around the coast which are flooded in the wet.

The Wik Monkan recognised four or five main seasons of the year. Of these, three are described here, together with a simplified account of Wik Monkan settlement and subsistence patterns.

The Dry – May to November: during this season, people generally were nomadic, but as the vegetation dried up, movement became restricted to areas of permanent water. The seeds and tubers of water lilies, together with fruit (Nonda plum) were now eaten. On the coast people resided near the forest edge, digging wells for water, the food staples being the tubers of swamp plants which were eaten raw or processed into cakes. Stored vegetable food, including tubers from the prior season, were also utilised. Storage in the main, however, was associated with ceremonial occasions. Shelters were ephemeral, and more substantial cold season huts were constructed between May and June; fish were caught with poison in waterholes. Wallaby hunting drives took place along bushy coastal corridors where the animals sought refuge during this season.

The Wet – first half of October to December: Temporary shelters were soon replaced by well-constructed permanent huts, and bark canoes were now used in hunting and travel. The height of the Wet occurs between January and March, and can last from four to four-and-a-half months, and camps at this time were permanently established on higher ground. People fished, caught crabs, and gathered shellfish and a wide range of birds' eggs, as well as plant foods. Hunting methods now changed completely, with the larger kangaroos stalked individually under the cover of heavy windstorms.

The *Ontjin* (end of Wet, start of Dry) – mid-March to late July: The time of the great vegetable harvest immediately followed the wet season. Bark food troughs were made and the staple foods were plants including yams, lily tubers, and seeds. Fish were caught in weirs and traps as floodwaters retreated, and fish nets were also used (Beaton 1982). The wet season camps broke up slowly at first, and people finally dispersed by canoe along the waterways. Finally, the lengthy nomadic phase of the annual cycle began.

Eastern Cape York

Specialised marine-oriented societies were described for eastern Cape York, in areas such as Princess Charlotte Bay and the Flinders group of islands. These Aboriginal people established relatively narrow coastal territories and saw themselves as 'beach people' (Hynes and Chase 1982), in contrast to groups from the hinterland whom they referred to as 'inland people'. They possessed specialised, elaborate marine technology, with dugong hunting and fishing as predominant economic activities. A variety of plant and land use strategies were also employed (see also later in this chapter). A separate social unit occupied the nearby offshore islands of the Flinders group. In the rich rainforested region, from north of Cairns to Ingham in the south, a complex group of territorially-based communities with high population densities were relatively sedentary, processed a range of plant species and interacted through ritual, exchange and intergroup combat (Figure 2.5) (Dixon 1976).

Coastal islands

Individual Aboriginal social groups appear to have occupied many of the offshore islands of the tropical eastern, northern and northwestern coastline of Australia. These peoples relied heavily on marine resources and to varying degrees on terrestrial foods. In many cases they possessed specialised technology, in particular maritime equipment, including efficient canoes and a variety of fishing

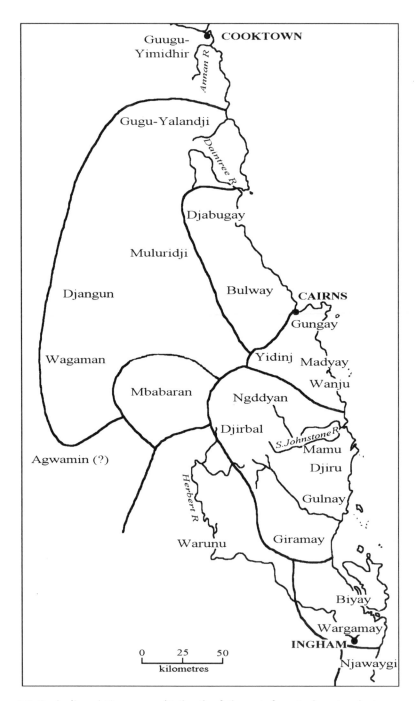

Figure 2.5 Socio-linguistic groups ('tribes') of the rainforested region between Cairns and Ingham, north Queensland (based on Dixon 1876: 209, Map 1).

gear. Their relationships with peoples of the mainland and other islands were also complex.

BENTINCK ISLAND (GULF OF CARPENTARIA)

Bentinck Island was described by Tindale (1977) as being one of the most densely populated regions of Australia. It is positioned at southern latitude 17 degrees, and has an estimated area of 140 square kilometres, together with lesser used outlying islets and sandbanks of 180 square kilometres. Population size was about 123 people divided into eight 'hordes'. As the interior of the island sustained few people, the Kaiadilt people had a marine-oriented economy, with an emphasis on fishing. Still surrounding the island are scores of extensive stone-walled fish traps.

WHITSUNDAY ISLANDS (CENTRAL GREAT BARRIER REEF)

The Whitsunday Islands (situated between southern latitudes 20 and 21 degrees) form the largest offshore island group on the east coast of Australia, close to present-day Proserpine. The product of vulcanism, these islands are steeply elevated, with a climate of hot, wet summers and dry winters, with rainfall averages of around 1,826 mm in summer. Vegetation varies markedly between islands, and many of those in the north are clothed in rainforest. While ethnohistorical information is sparse (Rowland 1986; Barker 1989, 1991), it is known that the islands were inhabited by a separate socio-linguistic group, the Ngaro (Tindale 1974: 182). These people utilised the resources of islands and reefs over a distance of more than 100 kilometres, with the aid of sewn ironbark canoes, but to what extent they were associated also with part of the nearby mainland is unclear. The size of the population was reputedly around 100 people; however, decimation by European diseases and conflict with Europeans may also have been responsible for reduced numbers. Population density for the islands based upon these figures is around 1 person per 98 hectare, which is comparatively high (Rowland 1986: 82; see also Table 2.1).

Whitsunday Island, the largest of the group, was the only island permanently occupied, with the main base camp located on a rare area of level ground where fresh water, shelter and abundant marine and terrestrial resources were also available. 'The diet of these people included turtle, flying foxes, birds, yams, wild cherries, Burdekin plum, damson trees, trochus shell, baler shell, green ant and cockatoo apples' (Rowland 1986: 77). Raw materials for manufacturing stone artefacts were obtained from quarries on South Molle Island. More sophisticated outrigger canoes were observed also near the Whitsunday Islands and the Melanesian origins of this form of watercraft seem clear, and point to the southerly extension of external social contacts from this northerly region (Rowland 1986: 82–83).

KEPPEL ISLANDS (SOUTHERN GREAT BARRIER REEF)

A group of small islands, the Keppels, lies some 13 kilometres off the coast of Queensland, near Rockhampton, at southern latitude 23 degrees. The total area of all the islands is only 22.5 square kilometres (Rowland 1982b: 114), and a separate socio-linguistic community of under 100 people appears to have resided permanently on this island group. Population densities are difficult to gauge, largely because of the small land-to-size-of-coastline ratio. A conservative estimate, therefore, of one person per 26 hectare has been proposed by Rowland (1982b: 10–11), which is comparable to densities from other smaller tropical islands of Queensland, such as Dunk and Sunday.

Rowland considered these people to have been 'specialised marine exploiters. In fact, if they had not been, the islands would have been too small to exploit' (1982b: 118). Cultural differences between the Keppel Islands and the mainland were noted by Roth (Roth 1898; Rowland 1980: 3–4), and items employed on the Keppel Islands, as distinct from the mainland, included: (a) a one-piece bark canoe; (b) fish hooks of coconut or turtle shell; (c) stone drills used in fish-hook manufacture; and (d) harpoons with detachable heads. The last three items all have Melanesian parallels. Hut forms also differed from those of the mainland, and missing from the Keppel group were items such as boomerangs, and varieties of shields and nullas, all of which are found on the nearby mainland.

Land and resource management

TROPICAL PLANTS

Strong similarities exist between the suite of tropical plants employed by Australian Aborigines and plant species of regions along Australia's northern frontier. Golson, for example, has pointed out the affinities between northern Australian plants and those of the Indo-Malaysian region:

> It is that the level of correspondence between food uses of the same genera in Malaysia on the one hand and Arnhem Land (43 per cent) and Cape York (49 per cent) on the other ... may well be due as much to ancient patterns of exploitation brought to Australia from the Malaysian region by its early inhabitants as to the property of the flora itself. (Golson 1971: 207)

CYCADS (*CYCAS MEDIA, MACROZAMIA*)

Aboriginal management by fire of stands of cycads has been reported for both northern Cape York (Harris 1977a: 429), and the central Queensland highlands (Beaton 1982). Both examples illustrate that by firing natural groves of cycads their overall productivity can be increased. This can be achieved by synchronising seed production within stands of cycad (Beaton 1982: 52). 'Burning also makes seed harvesting easier, and stimulates asexual reproduction' (Harris 1977a: 429). The cycad seeds appear to have been a staple food in open canopy woodlands, and they still are in Arnhem Land. 'Their attraction as a food source lay in their abundant yield of large seeds, in the ease of harvest, in the possibility of storage, and in their occurrence in concentrated stands' (Harris 1977a: 428). David Harris' calculations indicate that cycad seeds have a relatively high nutrient status, and their yield compares favourably with that of some cultivated plants. He also considered that the large stands of cycad of today may be the product of Aboriginal burning.

Cycad seeds are toxic (carcinogenic), but a number of laborious leaching techniques were available. Leaching involved soaking seeds in water and then drying them. Fermentation necessitated placing the seeds in water for several months. Roasting of seeds was a further possibility. As well, old seeds would be leached through natural weathering processes. The availability of sufficient quantities of water may have dictated the methods used (Beaton 1982). The abundance of seeds thus produced may have necessitated the involvement of an increased task force:

> If such husbandry of a wild plant food was important in the Aboriginal exploitation of the resource then the possible yield suggests a co-operative effort, involving perhaps many more people than a small residential and economic unit like the Australian 'band'. (Beaton 1982: 54)

Beaton considered that the management of cycad stands, together with the costs (in terms of energy expended) of processing the seeds, may have involved large groups of people, perhaps congregating together for joint ceremonial and trading purposes (see also Chapter Four).

TROPICAL YAMS

Tropical yams, for example varieties of *Dioscorea* sp., are also toxic and require lengthy leaching time in water. Quantities of yams were also stored in eastern Cape York, for example, in pits, following the height of the harvest season (see above) and storage was increased in preparation for the assembly of large numbers of people in connection with ceremonies (Thomson 1939). Yams were also important staple plants across humid northern Australia, for example in Arnhem Land (Thomson 1949; Jones 1981; Meehan 1982) and on Bathurst and Melville Islands (Hart and Pilling 1960; Goodale 1971; Levitt 1981).

MANAGEMENT

Aboriginal management and manipulation of plants and the connection of these practices with those of 'cultivation' was the subject of two important ethnobotanical studies by Harris (1977a) and Hynes and Chase (1982). Harris compared the plant-using economies of Cape York with those of the nearby Torres Strait Islands, which are tied culturally also to Melanesia. He concluded that a *continuum* of broad-spectrum economic strategies existed across the region, rather than a dichotomy between hunting-gathering and horticultural practices. Limited horticulture and gathering of wild and managed plants was practised along the southern Papuan coast and nearby islands of the northern Torres Strait. In the islands of the Torres Strait horticultural practices are few, while on the Australian eastern Cape York Peninsula management of some plants took place, together with exploitation of a wide range of plant and animal species. The orientation of subsistence, therefore, was more horticultural the closer one approached the Papuan mainland, and closer to foraging in the environs of the Australian mainland. The use of horticultural crops was only one of a range of forms of resource specialisation employed in the region. Whereas some plants, for example yams, were *managed* and occasionally planted in Cape York, they were *cultivated* on the northern Torres Strait Islands (Harris 1977a: 452–453).

Of Harris' two Cape York study areas, the east coastal Lockhart region provided the greatest ecological diversity. Information also was obtained from Aboriginal informants. Rainfall is high and habitats vary from coastal wetlands to strips of rainforest and open-canopy woodlands. Yams (ten varieties, including *Dioscorea*) were the food staples and required considerable processing (leaching and roasting). Yams were mainly obtained from sandy soils near beaches and mangrove swamps. Other plants also required processing, for example the staple mangrove fruit (*Bruguiera gymnorhiza*).

Propagation of yams also took place: '... it used to be common practice at the time of harvest for the top of the tuber from which regeneration takes place to be either left in the hole or broken off and replanted in the same or nearby hole' (Harris 1977a: 437). This is a widespread northern Australian practice, for example in Arnhem Land, where a range of roots and tubers are treated in this way (Specht 1958: 481; Jones 1975; Peterson 1976; Hynes and Chase 1982: 40). Yams were also planted on offshore islands, to extend their range and as a 'stored' supply. Hynes and Chase add that such 'stores' also assisted visitors who at times may have become stranded on the islands (1982: 40). In general the combination of regulated harvesting and frequent replanting reported from the Lockhart region suggests that yams were a managed rather than just a gathered resource there. Indeed it may be said that their exploitation approximated horticultural in several ways, without the labour involved in tillage and the higher yields per plant that cultivation affords (Harris 1977a: 437).

Hynes and Chase (1982) examined the broad coastal strip of eastern Cape York, from Temple Bay south to the Stewart River, which also incorporated the Lockhart area examined by Harris. There is strong agreement between Hynes and Chase's interpretation of Aboriginal land and plant use and that offered by Harris. Hynes and Chase focused upon the concept of 'domiculture', or the ecological relationship between people and plants within 'hearth-based' habitats, which composed the core parts of the domain of the local group. They argued that these habitats were managed in a variety of ways. Controlled burning increased productivity and yams and coconuts were planted. Coconut trees were also owned, and shade trees were planted around base camps and a range of other plants were seeded about these camping places. Artificial, managed habitats were thus created and maintained around both permanently and less frequently occupied locales. Distribution and productivity of plants was, therefore, largely under control. Also, territorial rights were demarcated by planting and, 'Infringements upon the rules of harvesting were said to be dealt with severely and were considered to be of the grossest form of greed' (Hynes and Chase 1982: 40).

For the Torres Strait–Cape York region as a whole, Harris concluded:

Although all the subsistence systems examined were broad-spectrum in character . . . there is nevertheless considerable evidence of intensive or specialised use of particular resources within the broad-spectrum patterns. In the coastal ecosystems of the Lockhart area and the insular ecosystems of the western Torres Strait specialised exploitation of marine animal resources developed, complemented by some parallel specialisation in the use of terrestrial plant foods. The procurement of fish, shellfish, turtles and dugong was a major subsistence activity in both areas. It played a central role in social life and was supported by elaborate techniques of fishing and canoe building, especially in the Torres Strait islands (Haddon 1912: 154–171, 205–217). (Harris 1977a: 454)

Summary: the tropical north

Specialised marine-oriented societies inhabited the tropical coast of northeastern Australia and its offshore islands. The emphasis here was upon fishing, hunting of dugong and turtle using specialised technology including complexes of stone fish traps, a range of canoe types and fishing gear (harpoons, fish hooks). Aspects of the latter technology also had Melanesian parallels. Similarities were also found with coastal and island dwellers of northwestern Australia. Variation also was evident as in eastern Cape York, and parts of east Arnhem Land, where peoples were seasonally sedentary, practiced storage and were terrestrially oriented. In the north Queensland rainforests relatively dense populations practised specialised use and management of plants, and were markedly territorial with intergroup combat and ceremonial events.

The arid zone

This enormous region presently encompasses over one-third of the Australian continent, and was much more extensive during part of the Pleistocene (Figure 2.6). Environmentally the region is varied; today in the north climate is seasonal, aligned to the tropical monsoon with its heavy summer rainfall and dry winters, while in the south the climate is less seasonal and thus more unpredictable. Together with the adjoining semi-arid belt these dry environments make up two-thirds of present-day Australia.

The Western Desert

Gould carried out ethnographical and archaeological studies in the western desert in the region of the Warburton Ranges between 1966 and 1967 (1968, 1969). The region has an annual rainfall of less than 200 mm, which varies considerably from year to year. Heavy rains can fall between January and February, but otherwise water is confined to rocky outcrops, soaks and wells dug by the local people. The landscape is of parallel sand dunes, flat sand dunes, and rocky ridges with better supplies of water, and the vegetation is predominantly spinifex grass, with mulga scrub in better watered areas. The Ngatatjara, dialect speakers of Pitjantjatjara, are the traditional owners of this land, and lived in aggregations

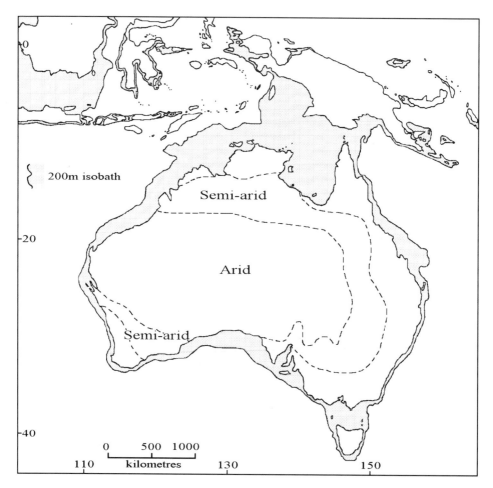

Figure 2.6 The Australian arid and semi-arid zones of the present day. A humid belt lies beyond the semi-arid region. Also indicated (shaded area) is the Pleistocene coastline at the 200-metre submarine contour (climatic information adapted from Bowler 1971: 50, Figure 5:1).

of extended families of between ten and thirty people. Larger groups of around 150 people have been reported, and as many as 270 people in slightly more humid areas to the east, in 1935.

As rainfall is erratic, no strict seasonal round was observed and instead people occupied areas of permanent water first, and groups broke up and moved away as the meat intake declined. In contrast, permanent waterholes were reserved until last, generally during extended periods of drought, and people were described as 'eating their way into' a permanent waterhole (Gould 1969: 267). They then consumed food within a 10–20-kilometre radius of the waterhole, before moving on to the next source of water. Gould considered that the Ngatatjara settlement pattern was the mirror image of that reported by Lee for the !Kung Bushmen of the Kalahari Desert (1968). The two families reported by Gould had moved camp nine times in over four months, over an area of around 2,000 square kilometres.

Eight main vegetable staples, available at different seasons throughout the year, were recorded for the Ngatatjara, and these plant foods were transported by women daily back to camp. Some fruit were sun-dried or fire-dried and then stored, and seeds were processed into bread, which was also stored indefinitely in caches up in trees. Communal hunting took place using fire, brush pounds, and natural game traps, and women spent one-third more in time collecting and preparing food than did men. Knowledge of chains of waterholes was governed by the group's religion or law, and mostly held by men; but women also had access to some of this information.

The Alyawarra practised a seasonal pattern broadly similar to that of the Ngatatjara. Jim O'Connell's ethnographic study of these people showed that following rain, which generally fell in summer, people fanned out to ephemeral water sources and their natural resources, which included roots, tubers and, later, fruits and grass seeds (1977: 269). In contrast, during the dry season of winter, people resided near permanent water, such as around the larger streams, where roots and seeds were gathered. At this season group sizes were small.

Little Sandy and Great Sandy Deserts

Contrasting information to the above has been provided by Peter Veth's research in the Little Sandy and Great Sandy Deserts of northwestern Australia, which have a climate less markedly seasonal than the Sandy Desert but more predictable than that of the Gibson Desert (1987, 1989a). Summer rains fall between December and February, with ephemeral water sources becoming increasingly dry after April. From September temperatures increase, and only permanent soaks and rockholes remain. Veth's information was based on ethnographic and archaeological research. This region traditionally belongs to the Martujarra (Mardudjara), which is a collective term for four western desert dialect groups (Tonkinson 1978). Some of these people had resided in their area up until the 1960s.

Settlement patterns and group sizes were closely associated with the seasonal availability of water, and people were mostly mobile during the summer wet season, utilising widespread ephemeral sources of water. After April, residential moves became increasingly less frequent, and targeted existing water sources. The cooler months following the summer rains provided abundant resources. For example, grass seeds ripen from April to July, herbaceous species are available between July and September, and acacia seeds from September to February. By the end of the dry season, people from neighbouring dialect groups had congregated at the remaining permanent springs and soaks, and meetings were held. Veth characterised this predictable settlement pattern of increasing sedentism around sources of permanent water as based upon reliable rainfall and abundant mid-year resources. He contrasted this system with the less predictable pattern outlined by Gould, where sources of permanent water were reserved until last.

Cooper Creek

The broad riverine region of Cooper Creek is fed by rainfall in the northeastern ranges of Queensland, and passes through an arid landscape. Up to three 'pulses' or bursts of bioproduction per annum occurred in this area (Smith 1986: 30). Following the seasonal summer rains, people dispersed into the dune fields which flank the broad rivererine corridor, and as standing water dried up they retreated back towards permanent water in the river basin (W. Jones 1979; Kimber 1984). Late summer floods rejuvenated the extensive stands of grasses and their seeds, and further forays into the sand dune country followed winter rains. When settlement was restricted to the riverine corridor, however, emphasis was placed on grass seeds, in particular *Panicum decompositum* and *Portulaca oleracea*.

Substantial population sizes (numbers of several hundred people) were noted in the Cooper Creek region (W. Jones 1979) and a series of intensive management strategies were employed to extend the availability of seed foods (see below). Other measures also were taken to expand the econiche of the riverine corridor, including the sinking of deep wells to tap ground water and therefore extend people's access to the more marginal dune fields (W. Jones 1979: 140–143; Kimber 1984).

The semi-arid zone

The Darling Basin of New South Wales

The Darling River rises in the eastern highlands and flows for 1,600 kilometres, before entering the Murray River. For half this distance the river crosses the semi-arid plains of the Darling Basin. While climate is seasonal, with hot summers and cool winters, rainfall is variable (although evenly distributed annually) and ranges from 150 mm. to 300 mm. per annum. Drought, however, is also common. Discharges occur most often in the river, and are lowest in early spring and summer, and substantial flooding takes place every five to eight years, inundating areas up to 30 kilometres from the river. Open acacia-savanna and shrub-steppe grasslands predominate, with eucalypt-savanna along the river.

This region was inhabited by linguistically related social groups, collectively known as Bagundji, or 'river people'. Harry Allen, who compiled the ethnohistorical information, calculated that the Bagundji clustered along the river during spring and summer and whenever the river was high (1972, 1974). At these times groups were semi-sedentary and at their largest (averaging around 45 people) spaced at 45-kilometre intervals along the river. Population densities averaged around one person per kilometre of river frontage. Allen estimated that these densities were around one-third of those from the more productive Murray

River region (1974: 313). If we allow for decimation by diseases and European intervention, I suggest that these population estimates may be too low.

Specialised techniques were used for fishing, birding, hunting and the collection and processing of plants. Fishing nets up to 90 metres in length were employed, together with stone traps and wickerwork weirs. Similarly, large nets were strung across water courses to snare ducks, which was a collective pursuit. Communal activities also included net fishing and the collection of bullrush roots and grass seeds (see below). As rainfall and river discharges are sometimes unpredictable, an opportunistic economic pattern was envisaged by Allen. During winter, groups of people were smaller and while some groups remained near the river, others apparently were more nomadic, also moving further away to more ephemeral sources of water. Hunting appears largely to have replaced fishing during this season, and specialised hunting techniques were employed as men seldom carried spears. Animals as well as emus were driven into large nets, similar in size to those used in fishing. Plant foods that were utilised included seeds of acacia, saltbush (*Chenopodium* sp.) and flax (*Linum* sp.), as well as fruits and tubers.

Extensive stone-walled complexes of fish traps and weirs were constructed on a large stretch of the Darling River, near present-day Brewarrina, in northwestern New South Wales. Some of these structures are still extant, and are comparable, both physically and in their use, with those of southwestern Victoria which are described later in this chapter. These fishing stations of the Darling were centres for intergroup feasting, ceremony and exchange, enacted by a broad-based local network of social groups (Mathews 1903).

Land and resource management

In both the arid and semi-arid areas of Australia, the collection of seeds, including those of grasses, was a principal economic strategy (Meggitt 1964: 30; Allen 1972, 1974: 313–315; Smith 1985, 1986). Of 140 plant food species in central Australia, more than 70 were exploited for their seeds (Latz 1982), including five considered to be staple foods – *Acacia aneura, Eragrostis eriopodra, Panicum decompositum, Portulaca oleraca* and *Tecticornia verrucosa*. Edible plants were harvested from a large number of plant species including trees, shrubs, grasses and forbs (Smith 1986: 29).

In semi arid New South Wales, large riverine groups of people (such as those along the Darling River) may have lived principally on seeds of acacia and grass during the summer (Allen 1974: 314). Seeds were also employed to extend periods of sedentism at particular camping sites (Tindale 1964: 402). Within the Cooper Creek riverine corridor, people resorted to *ngardu* (*Marsilea quadrifolia*) (Horne and Aiston 1924: 52–57), which was avoided in central Australia, where it was regarded as unpalatable. The use of *ngardu* at Cooper Creek may have been related to seasonal increases in Aboriginal numbers, group sizes and sedentism in the region (Smith 1986: 30). Seeds like *pitaru* were generally employed by the Diyari during lean times such as drought, and likewise, *ngardu* appears only to have been used in the Darling Basin area during dry seasons, when Aboriginal groups were concentrated along the river (Newland 1920–21: 12; Dunbar 1943–1944; 175; Allen 1972; Smith 1986: 31).

This pattern of seed use can also be related to harvesting and processing procedures. In these terms, seeds were costly foods requiring labour-intensive methods of harvesting and processing. Studies indicate that one kilogram of flour (from various seeds) involved between two and five hours of labour; and when harvesting time was added, this rose to between five and eight hours (Brokensha 1975: 25; O'Connell and Hawkes 1981: 124–5; O'Connell et al. 1983: 90–92; Cane 1984: 79; Smith 1986: 31).

> Labour costs included collecting seeds before they were ripe, as well as sun-drying or roasting of the seeds. Other methods were to stack the grass before burning it. Threshing and husking of seeds was also involved. (Allen 1974: 313)
>
> . . . the ricks or haycocks, extended for miles . . . and not a spike of it was left in the soil, over the whole of the ground . . . The grass was beautifully green beneath the heaps and full of seeds. (Mitchell 1839, I: 238–239, 290–291; cited in Allen 1974: 313)

Seed-grinding equipment in many areas also had to be imported over long distances, which necessitated increased labour and social costs. For example, in the western desert and Lake Eyre basin, stone was traded and exchanged by way of complex kinship networks. In the western desert men obtained stone by travelling to the source, using kinship ties along the way. Used equipment was also traded, and these valuable stones were bequeathed by female siblings to their daughters (Hamilton 1980: 8–9).

Management of seeds helped to stabilise and increase seed productivity. For example, in the Cooper Creek riverine plain measures were taken to manage plant yields (W. Jones 1979; Kimber 1984). Dams constructed of earth were strategically placed so as to irrigate large areas of grassland. Seed was sown by hand and released in areas where it did not grow naturally, and the wide range of infield harvesting and storage methods helped to extend the season of availability of seeds by several months (W. Jones 1979: 140–143). The methods involved harvesting seeds at various stages of their growth and maturity.

Storage of seeds was extensively practised in arid and semi-arid regions (Allen 1974: 314–315). For example, pits were employed as seed storage depots (Allen 1974: 314); and northwest of the Darling River, seeds were wrapped in grass and coated in mud. Large quantities of seed also were stored in whole-skin bags of wallaby or small kangaroo. One tonne (1,000 kilograms) of stored seed was observed in central Australia, placed in 175 wooden dishes, each one five feet long and one foot deep.

Quantities of seeds were also employed to support large groups of people during ceremonial occasions (Spencer and Gillen 1912: 259; Hamilton 1980:

14–15). These gatherings often followed the end of the wet season when resources were in abundance, and stores of seeds were put aside to help extend the duration of these events (Smith 1986: 30). Tindale noted both the importance of seed foods and the difficulties in managing labour during intergroup occasions:

> ... even the duration and scale of the most important of the men's initiation ceremonies are likely to be determined by the revolt of the women following the exhaustion of ready supplies of women's gathered foods within a radius of three or four miles. (Tindale 1972: 245)

Sub-tropical Australia

Coastal southeastern Queensland

Southeastern Queensland (between latitudes 25 and 30 degrees) is flanked by the Great Dividing Range in the west, the Macpherson Range in the south, and the Pacific Ocean in the east. It also includes a number of large offshore islands. The protected estuary of Moreton Bay is a rich coastal environment including plentiful sea mammals, such as dugong (Hall 1982). In contrast, the narrow coastal hinterland (the Wallum ecosystem) is comparatively poor in resources (Walters 1989: 218), with comparatively well-endowed river valleys further inland (Hall 1986: 99). Climate is transitional between tropical and temperate, with wet summers (October to March) and drier winters. Maximum rainfall of 1150 mm. per annum has been recorded in the eastern ranges.

Around 5,000 Aboriginal people were estimated to have resided in the Moreton Bay district (including 3,000 on the coast) by Simpson, the Crown Lands Commissioner and Protector of Aborigines from 1842 to 1853. From these figures Jay Hall (1982: 83–84) has calculated a population density of around 1.25 square kilometres per person and higher, which is comparable to high coastal densities such as we have already noted for Arnhem Land and southwestern Victoria (Table 2.1, p.37). As these figures are from historical contexts following known diseases such as smallpox, they should be considered underestimates. Individual socio-linguistic groups inhabited the main islands of Moreton and North Stradbroke, the narrow Wallum coastal strip each side of the Brisbane river, and the more extensive riverine hinterland between the mountains and the coast. Local groups numbered around 60 people on average (Hall 1982: 84), and defence of territorial boundaries is recorded, with specific resource zones controlled by individuals within the group (Winterbotham 1959: 39).

Populations of the coast and islands appear to have been relatively sedentary (Hall 1982: 84–87), and local communities had constructed groups of huts strategically at intervals of between five to six kilometres along the coast. Groups of substantial, well-built huts may have been wet-season dwellings, with around six huts being the average number. More ephemeral huts were also built. Coastal subsistence centred upon swamps, estuaries, beaches and lowland forest, and the predominant procurement strategies included fishing by men, and the gathering and processing of fern-root by women. A wide range of fishing techniques was used, the most common of which was the scoop net. Set nets, brush weirs across creeks, and spears were also employed. Large hauls of fish were obtained during the winter mullet runs, and surplus fish were wrapped in grass, hung in dilly bags and thus stored for a number of weeks. Dugong were herded by men into large nets, which were sometimes staked across channels leading to beds of sea-grass, and dolphins were trained to herd schools of fish into shallow waters where they were netted and speared (Hall 1982: 86). Women processed large quantities of fern-root or *bungwall* (*Blechnum indicum*), which was a daily staple, and these plants were collected from coastal swamps, then roasted, scraped, cut up with stone knives and pounded into cakes.

Large intergroup social gatherings were associated with the coastal sea-mullet (*Mugil cephalus*) runs in winter (Hardley 1975; Nolan 1986), and especially with the triennial summer bunya nut (*Araucaria bidwillii*) feasts held in the Bunya Mountains and Blackall Ranges, as well as other resources. A rotation of communal events, therefore, took place throughout the year (Lilley 1984: 20–22; Satterthwait 1986: 30; Morwood 1987: 339). People came from over 200 kilometres away to attend the bunya gatherings and visitors 'near at hand would all turn up, old and young, but the tribes from afar would leave the aged and sick behind' (Petrie 1975, cited in Walters 1987: 221). While feasting, such as the Bunya, has been viewed by some as supplementing dispersed food resources (Draper 1978; Morwood 1987), others have argued that rather than a dietary or directly economic motivation, the purpose of these gatherings was essentially social (Sullivan 1977: 60; Hall 1982: 85).

NORTH COASTAL NEW SOUTH WALES

The north coast of New South Wales (between latitudes 28 degrees and 34 degrees) is well endowed with large rivers and estuaries, complex wetlands and a lush sub-tropical hinterland of rainforest, more open forest and steep, rugged ranges. It lacks, however, the productive rock platform ecological zone of the south coast. Population density has been estimated in this region at between 1.5 and 3 people per square kilometre, compared with one person per 12 square kilometres further inland on the western slopes of the Great Dividing Range (Belshaw 1978: 73).

Isabel McBryde viewed the populations of the Clarence River valley as moving inland during winter (1974: 17, 266). Conversely, for the Ballina group, Julia Coleman (1982: 2) drew on a number of references and argued that prior to European settlement, large Aboriginal populations resided in small coastal territories around 12 kilometres across (Ainsworth 1922: 17–18; Dawson 1935: 25; Pierce 1971: 4). Subsistence was based upon the resources of the sea, estuary and coastal plain. 'Villages', including sizeable and well-constructed huts, were located at strategic points (such as good fishing grounds) along the coast and estuaries, such as the Clarence. Coleman suggested that these semi-sedentary populations resided close to stone fish traps which are still in evidence along the coast (1982: 5–7).

Around 1,000 people gathered for weeks during the seasonal migrations of fish in winter (July–September) (Coleman 1982: 4,7). People moved beyond their local territory to attend fights, corroborees, initiations and marriages, and one battle between men of the Macleay and Bellingen rivers against men of the Clarence involved around 700 participants. 'Women, children and old people frequently accompanied the warriors, the fights then being followed by up to a month of feastings, wedding, corroborees' (Coleman 1982: 4). Coleman concluded that the prior model of mobile and sparsely populated Aboriginal society for the region may have been the product of European disruption of traditional demographic patterns.

Temperate southern Australia

Coastal New South Wales

The south coast of New South Wales (between latitudes 34 and 36 degrees) has a narrow coastal plain, flanked by the wooded mountains of the Great Dividing Range. This well-watered region is composed also of numerous rocky bays, inlets, estuaries, sandy beaches, and productive wetlands. Ethnohistorical and environmental studies of the region suggested that the Aboriginal population was semi-sedentary in coastal areas, where resources were most plentiful, dependable and accessible. In contrast, during the leaner season of winter, the people may have been more nomadic, dispersing inland in smaller groups (Poiner 1976). A comparable study of the Bateman's Bay area of the far south coast indicated that populations within the estuary may have been semi-sedentary year-round (Attenbrow 1978).

New England Tablelands

This elevated region of the Great Dividing Range, 900–1,500 metres above sea level (between latitudes 29 and 31 degrees), shares some similarities with the southeastern highlands. Deep gorges divide the plateau from the coast, while the western gradient is comparatively gradual. Although opinions vary (for example, see McBryde 1974: 338), the tablelands appear to have been occupied by one socio-linguistic group, the Aneiwan, and to have been what is termed a 'marchland' area (an area to which a number of groups had access) between strong tribal groups in the east and west and occupied on a permanent basis by perhaps one tribe, with the balance of the population occupying the area only for periods of the year (Belshaw 1978: 76; see also Bowdler 1981: 107; also Chapter Six). The social groups referred to are those of the coast and of the inland western plains.

Plentiful aquatic resources were available in swamplands before these were drained by European pastoralists (Godwin 1983), and large standing nets were constructed for hunting purposes (McBryde 1978b: 239). These large and productive nets also may have been employed in collective hunting drives, associated with large-scale, populous intergroup activities (Godwin 1983; also Satterthwait 1987). Sandra Bowdler suggested that plant foods may have included or been dominated by the yam-daisy (*Microseris scapigera*) (1981: 106).

Southeastern highlands

This most elevated region of mainland Australia (between 35 and 38 degrees southern latitude) is composed of desiccated plateaux at varying levels between 600 metres and 1,500 metres above sea level. The highest peak is Kosciusko at 2,228 metres, and rainfall varies from 3,000 mm. in the highest parts, a portion of which falls as snow, to 400 mm. in areas of rain shadow. The region can be categorised as wet coastal and inland mountains, with drier tablelands in between.

Detailed ethnohistorical and archaeological studies of this region have been conducted from the Monaro area around Canberra, to the Victorian Alps (Flood 1976, 1980). The socio-linguistic groups residing in the uplands can generally be distinguished from those of the east coast and inland western plains. They appear to have had a shared social system based upon two 'classes' of female descent. They also appear to have been generally more mobile, with ephemeral bark huts and a more limited range of material equipment than their eastern and western neighbours. These characteristics have been attributed to the harshness of the highland environment (Flood 1976: 37), and a form of highland confederacy may have existed also (Flood 1980: 72). Population densities, although tentatively reconstructed, may have been around one person per 26 square kilometres for the Monaro region, to one person per 36 square kilometres for the southern tablelands (Flood 1980: 43). Josephine Flood also cautions that these estimates do not allow for the decimation of populations caused by smallpox; traditional population sizes, therefore, would presumably have been higher.

Patterns of settlement and subsistence were derived from a combination of ethnohistorical and archaeological evidence (Flood 1976: 40–42, 1980: 176–195). Aboriginal people appear to have more intensively inhabited the lower valleys, that is below 300 metres, such as the valley of the lower Snowy River, which are forested (dry and wet sclerophyll), contain plentiful resources (eels, possums, plants) and have a mild winter climate. Fish was a chief resource. Beyond 300 metres extends a region of treeless plains, and from the evidence Aboriginal settlement of this zone appears to have been relatively slight. Higher still, at 900 to 1,830 metres, the presence of increased numbers of camp sites and ritual sites have been interpreted as evidence of large-scale seasonal (summer) intergroup gatherings (see below).

In summary, below the treeline, all ecological zones appear to have been inhabited, in contrast to the more sparse signs of occupation of the alpine zone.

A generally nomadic pattern of seasonal transhumance is indicated; with semi-nomadism in winter and a concentration of people in the lower valleys.

Annual intergroup festivities were held on the higher slopes during summer, with people coming from as far as 160 kilometres away. These occasions were well organised, with messengers despatched well in advance. Something like 500–700 people gathered for ceremonies, initiations and feasting, which centred upon the Bogong moths (*Agrotis infusa*) (Flood 1980: 61–82). These moths migrate annually in their millions in summer to aestivate on the high peaks of the eastern highlands. They cluster in quantity in rock crevices and were captured in nets, roasted and winnowed. The moths have a high fat content and were pounded into 'cakes', which, when smoked, lasted for perhaps several weeks. The eating of moths, however, appears to have been largely an exclusively male prerogative, and moths were also found on the home territories of all of the participating highland social groups. The motivation, therefore, for these highland gatherings cannot be viewed primarily as a food-getting exercise, but as socially promoted (Flood 1980).

Complex socio-political behaviour was associated. Pre-arranged ceremonies were often performed by visiting groups on the lower slopes, before they ascended to the higher ceremonial grounds. Some groups seized the opportunity to settle disputes. 'Sometimes this place and season is chosen to decide animosities by actual battles, and the conquered party lose their supply of Bogong for the season' (Bennett 1834, I: 273; Flood 1980: 75). Payten also mentions that on the corroboree grounds of the lower slopes 'pitched battles' were fought between the Victorian and New South Wales social groups (in Flood 1980: 74). As well, stricter territorial rights over moths pertained, with individual groups appearing to have owned particular highland peaks where moths clustered (Flood 1976: 44). As an indication of the close connection between moths and ceremonial occasions, ceremonial bora-grounds were often located close to where the moths clustered (Figure 2.7).

In conclusion, I would suggest that the Bogong highland feasts and ceremonies helped to cement alliances between highland groups and their neighbours. These activities constituted the political relations of the 'confederacy' of highland groups, referred to above. This interpretation is reinforced by further ethnohistorical evidence of strong alliances between highland groups, which were strengthened by shared enmities with neighbouring inland and coastal peoples. Regarding the Omeo, Ovens, Monaro and Queanbeyan peoples of the highlands, Von Lendenfeld wrote in 1895:

> Probably the customs of these four tribes were identical, because they lived in frequent intercourse and combined against their common enemies. (1895: 388; in Flood 1980: 72)

The enemies referred to were the adjacent inland and coastal peoples; the same conclusion was also drawn by George Augustus Robinson concerning the same

Figure 2.7 Socio-linguistic networks of the southern highlands of Australia, indicating 'tribal' movements in the exploitation of Bogong moths (based on Flood 1980: 71, Figure 8: also Tindale 1974).

region. For example, the coastal Kurnai of present-day Gippsland, Victoria, were also regarded as traditional enemies of these mountain peoples (Flood 1980: 72–73), as I discuss further on in this chapter.

Southwestern Victoria

The temperate, fertile plain of southwestern Victoria (between 37 and 39 degrees in southern latitude) is some 80 kilometres in width, bounded by the Great Dividing Range to the north and the Indian Ocean to the south. Rainfall averages about 1400 mm. per annum in the uplands, and 760 mm. per annum on the plain, and the climate is 'mediterranean', with autumn–winter rainfall, and dry

Figure 2.8 A group of Aboriginal men of the Upper Yarra region, Victoria, photographed in 1853. Those standing wear traditional cloaks made from a number of skins (of either possum or young kangaroo) sewn together. Those seated wear European blankets. The men display a variety of traditional weapons including shields, clubs, spears and boomerangs. La Trobe Library.

summers. A network of small perennial creeks, marshes and wetlands covered the plain, much of which was water-logged during winter. Sclerophyll forest (and rainforest) grew in areas of higher rainfall, with savanna and grasslands in higher areas. The climate is drier beyond the ranges, averaging 500 mm. per annum.

The ethnohistorical account of the Aboriginal inhabitants of the region has been largely obtained from the manuscripts of George Augustus Robinson (1839–1849) protector of Aborigines, and writings of Dawson (1881) (Lourandos 1977a, 1980a, 1980b, 1983a, 1985a, 1987b) (see also Chapter Six). A number of social networks occupied the plain, the major division being between the densely populated, coastal Gunditjmara or Mara, and inland groups such as the Tjapwurong, who were affiliated with the broader Kulin network. Population density ranged from a maximum of 0.7–0.4 people per square kilometre among the Gunditjmara, to 0.4–0.3 among the northern Tjapwurong. 'Bands' generally numbered between 16–20 to 100 people or more (Table 2.1, p.37).

Although resources were more abundant in spring and early summer, there seems to have been no marked scarcity recorded. Variation in resource availability however, may have occurred during times of summer drought or

Figure 2.9 Earth mounds of southwestern Victoria. This is part of a group of thirteen mounds, the largest observed by George Augustus Robinson (1841); they were the camping places of individual Aboriginal groups who utilised the extensive earthworks and eeling facilities at Mount William (based on Robinson 1841).

winter low periods. Populations were densest and sedentism most pronounced where resources were abundant, reliable and accessible (see also Poiner 1976), for example, in wetlands, riverine areas and the coastal hinterland. In these favourable locations the population appears to have been semi-sedentary year round. Permanent base camps or 'villages', as they were called by early observers, were located only in these optimal locations, and comprised some ten to thirteen large, well-constructed, domed wooden huts plastered in clay. Some of these dwellings had stone sub-structures, or were built into circular pits. The most prominent settlement form, particularly in seasonally water-logged parts of the interior, were earth mounds. These artificial, and frequently sizeable constructions, often occurred in groups and served as permanent camping locations, especially during the wet season (Figure 2.9). Domed huts were often observed constructed atop earth mounds. Wetlands had a high level of annual regeneration of local and migratory species (migratory fish such as eels, birds, and plants). These locations also adjoined fertile microenvironments such as the forest and open plains. A range of plants was harvested, of which the favoured – and perhaps most important – was the tuber, yam-daisy (*Microseris scapigera*), which was collected in large quantities daily by women on the open plain. (See further this chapter for other plant collecting and management practices.)

Populations were more mobile and less dense in the open plains and wooded ranges, where resources were more dispersed and less dependable. A broad range of seasonal fishing, hunting and food procuring equipment was employed. Stored foods included eels and animal meat, and large quantities of acacia gum; eels and meat were cooked or smoked, eels and whale meat buried, and acacia gum cached as winter food.

Large intergroup gatherings, of between 400 and 1,000 people and more, were held at various locations and seasons within the district and involved ceremonies, trade, exchange and competitive games. For example, the most prominent centre of exchange was Lake Keilambete. At these occasions communal food-procuring activities included large-scale hunting drives in both summer and winter, led by prominent men. These hunts sometimes involved a human circle 20 to 30 kilometres in diameter. People also took advantage of seasonal resource abundance to congregate in large numbers, for example during the seasons of eeling, whaling and collecting of native fruit.

During the eeling season in autumn elaborate fish traps or weirs were constructed of stone, clay and brushwork. Near Lake Bolac, a semi-permanent village extending for a distance of some 35 kilometres along the river bank was established for the fishing season for a duration of two months. Individual social groups controlled or owned specific fish weirs (Dawson 1881: 94). Ceremonies were also held here, and these could involve up to a thousand people or more.

Some 40 kilometres further north, near Mount William, elaborate artificial drainage systems were constructed for eeling purposes. Nearby were 13 extra large earth mounds, where individual social groups camped while fishing. Robinson described these labour-intensive earthworks in the following way:

> At the confluence of this creek with the marsh observed an immense piece of ground – trenches and banks resembling the work of civilised man but which on inspection were found to be the work of the Aboriginal natives – purpose consisted of catching eels – a specimen of art of the same extent I had not before seen . . . these trenches are hundreds of yards in length – I measured in one place in one continuous triple line for the distance of 500 yards. The triple water course led to other ramified and extensive trenches of a more tortuous form – an area of at least 15 acres was thus traced out . . . These works must have been executed at great cost of labour . . . There must have been some thousands of yards of this trenching and banking. The whole of the water from the mountain rivulets is made to pass through this trenching ere it reaches the marsh . . . (Robinson 1841, 7 July) (see Figure 2.10)

Marked territorial behaviour was associated with access to land and to all key seasonal resources, such as eels. Disputes concerned the transgression of land and resource use, and in some cases led to bloodshed. Intergroup meetings included communal food procurement, as well as the feasting, ceremonies and exchange already referred to, and these meetings were most often held close to territorial boundaries so as to avoid trespass and therefore further conflict (Lourandos 1977a).

Aspects of this general settlement and subsistence pattern have also been found in other parts of southeastern Australia, for example southeastern South Australia towards the Coorong estuary and mouth of the Murray River, and the wider Murray River region (for example, Pardoe 1988). In the latter area, relatively high population densities, marked territoriality and semi-sedentism were common, together with the use of earth mound habitation sites. Further east, in coastal Gippsland, Aboriginal populations were characterised in similar ways and as relying heavily upon fishing (Robinson in Kenyon 1928).

Complex alliance networks operated also in the wider region of central and

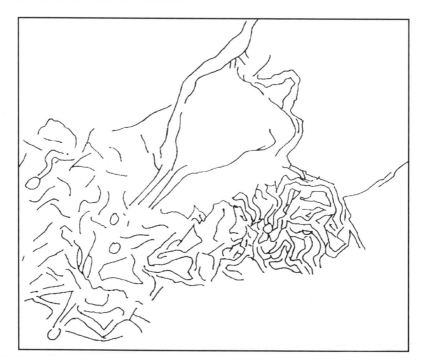

Figure 2.10 A small section of the large-scale drainage systems at Mount William, southwestern Victoria, ground plan as drawn by George Augustus Robinson in 1841. This complex consisted of some fifteen acres of excavated drains, which Robinson compared to agricultural systems he had observed in England (based on Robinson 1841).

southern Victoria, and these ranged from the local or clan level to kinship networks that transcended tribal language groupings (Figure 2.11). Two levels of language have been distinguished, for example, by Robert Dixon (1980; 33–40), the dialect or tribal language (Language 1) and groups of related dialects (Language 2). Dixon, among others, viewed the tribe as the principal political unit, being largely endogamous and operating along formal kinship lines. In Victoria, however, pan-tribal groupings (Language 2) also appear to have performed such functions – that is, as extended networks. Three 'super-networks' operated in southern Victoria: the central Kulin based in the Melbourne area, the eastern Kurnai in Gippsland, and the southwestern Mara (Manmeet) (Curr 1886–1887, III: 541; Smyth 1876, I: 136, 359; Howitt 1904; 70–77; Howitt and Fison 1880: 213; Lourandos 1977a)

The heartlands of these wider networks were demarcated by territorial corridors acknowledged through competition and tension (Lourandos 1977a; Smyth 1876, II: 4). The eastern Kulin, which encompassed a territory roughly the size of Tasmania, was composed of at least five or six of what Dixon would term 'tribal languages', and the Kurnai and Mara of five each. Each society was composed of groups of clans bound together through kinship that controlled

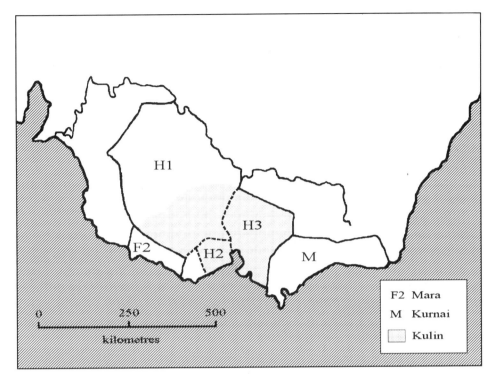

Figure 2.11 Extensive 'super networks' of central and southern Victoria. H1, H2, H3 are linguistic groupings. The largest of these groups is the central Kulin which is flanked by the Kurnai in Gippsland to the east and the Mara in the southwest (based on Dixon 1980 and Lourandos 1983a).

marriage and thus social interaction (Dawson 1881; Howitt 1904: 124–137). Clan elders, among whom polygyny was common, were often acknowledged as powerful and prestigious individuals (Robinson 1839–1849; Smyth 1876, II: 291; Lourandos 1977a: 211–212). Status and power also were acquired through the organisation of spectacular mass hunts (Lourandos 1977a), as well as through initiation into the hierarchical and elitist ceremonial life, shamanism, and participation in extensive exchange networks (see also below, this chapter).

Land and resource management
Southern Australia was considered for a long time to be relatively impoverished in plant resources (Cleland 1939). Recent research has significantly altered this misconception. Root plants, for example, were used widely in southern temperate Australia and this group of plants included rhizomes, corms, bulbs and tubers, which are rich in carbohydrates (Gott 1982, 1983). These foods can be regarded as staples because of their high calorific value, reduced seasonality and growth in dense clusters. During seasons of dormancy, carbohydrate storage was at a maximum (Gott 1982: 60, 65). In cost-benefit terms, these plants were selected

for their nutritional qualities, ease of access and processing. Root plants were obtained from both wet-land and dry-land habitats.

Maximum growth in wet-land plants occurred in summer and was lowest in winter. The most important wet-land plants, those most extensively used, were two species of *Typha* (*T. domingensis* Pers. and *T. orientalis* Pers.). Early European observers, such as Edward Eyre (1845: 269) and George Grey (1841: 292) noted that *Typha* was burned off by the Aborigines, the latter viewing this as 'a sort of cultivation'. Rhizomes of these plants were stored (Mitchell 1839: 60; Krefft 1865: 361; Hallam 1975: 14, 39), and in Western Australia the plant was beaten, following cooking, to extract the starch. It was extensively used also in the Murray Valley (Gott 1982: 61).

Tubers of salt-tolerant marsh clubrush (*Scirpus medianus*) and sea clubrush (*Scirpus calwellii*) were roasted and then pounded into cakes, and the seeds may also have been ground up (Gott 1982: 61–62). Eyre described the former plant as extending over 'immense tracts of country on the flats of the Murray ... six or seven feet high ... growing so closely together as to render it very difficult to penetrate far among them' (1845: 269). Waterribbons (*Triglochin procera*) were dug out of mud or the shallows of streams, lakes, swamps or flood-plains (Gott 1982: 62).

Dry-land plants generally sprout green leaves during the cooler autumn months. Orchids (Orchidaceae) were widely utilised, in particular the 'native potato' orchid (*Gastrodia sesamoides*). Lilies and plants of the related groups, such as Iridaceae, Araryllidaceae, Haemodaraceae and Hypoxidaceae, inhabit drier environments than orchids. These plants were also widely used, especially in Western Australia (Gott 1982: 62–63).

In Victoria the murrnong or yam-daisy served as a staple. This dandelion-like plant grew prolifically on the open plains, for example in southwestern Victoria where Robinson recorded 'millions of murnong all over the plain' (1840: 18). Large quantities of the plant were collected daily in baskets by Aboriginal women according to Robinson, and baked in earth-ovens, according to Dawson in 1881.

> Today the native women were spread out over the plain as far as I could see them, collecting *punimim, murnong*. I inspected their bags and baskets on their return and each had a load as much as she could carry. They burn the grass the better to see these roots. (Robinson 1841, 24th July)

Aboriginal burning would have promoted the growth and dispersal of murrnong by eliminating competing understorey vegetation. After European settlement sheep in their thousands and the spread of introduced species (for example, Cichorae) severely restricted the murrnong's habitat. Aboriginal burning would also have promoted the growth of the Austral bracken (*Pteridium esculentum*) and their numbers, and cyclic burning could therefore maintain relatively constant yields. *Pteridium* prefers forest clearings in high rainfall areas.

The starch, pounded by stone and baked as cakes, has 'a carbohydrate content higher than potato per 100 g. of edible portion' (Gott 1982: 65).

Plant and land management practices in southwestern Victoria and wider southern Australia have been seen as overlapping with procedures more commonly classified as 'cultivation' (Lourandos 1980a, 1980b; Gott 1982: 65; see also Hallam 1975). In this regard, Beth Gott has detailed the ecological effects of firing, gathering and digging up of plants:

> [firing . . .] returned nutrients to the soil, removed shading litter, formed clear areas where seed could germinate and grow, and maintained the open structure of the vegetation necessary for plants such as *Microseris* and *Pteridium* . . . Even wet-land plants were fired . . . Underground organs enabled plants to survive firing and to regenerate more rapidly than from seed. (1982: 65)

She states that gathering resulted in thinning out dense plant patches and thus eliminating intra-specific competition. The range over which plants were distributed was expanded; opportunistically as rhizomes capable of regeneration were transported, and by intentional planting. Digging up resulted in producing a mix of root plants out of shallow ground and from a sizeable area. The effect of the digging is to aerate the soil, loosen it for seed germination and root penetration, and to incorporate litter into it. Plants would be propagated by scattering and breaking-up of the underground parts (Gott 1982: 65). Gott assessed these Aboriginal plant and land management practices in the following way:

> This regime of firing, gathering and digging might well be regarded as a form of 'natural cultivation' on the part of the southern Australian Aborigines. It has important implications for the abundance and distribution of food plants, as well as for the general ecology. (Gott 1982: 6)

Temperate island Tasmania

The mountainous island of Tasmania (situated between southern latitudes 40 and 44 degrees) lies over 200 kilometres south of the Australian mainland. In size, Tasmania is around 67,900 square kilometres, that is, roughly the same size as the island of Hokkaido, Japan, and it is similarly positioned as regards latitude. Tasmania, a southern extension of the Australian Great Dividing Range, is elevated and rugged, with narrow coastal plains. The climate is temperate and marine, with mild winters and cool summers (Langford 1965). Rainfall is highest in the western half of the island, where annual averages of over 1,375 mm. are recorded, while in the east a rainshadow exists, especially in the southeast. Vegetation patterns follow this west–east dichotomy, and rainforest, composed of *Nothofagus* (southern beech), a southern Oceanic form, is extensive in the west. In contrast, in the east a mixture of dry and more humid sclerophyll forests of Australian form predominate. Along the northern coastline a narrow coastal fringe of heathland is found, with open moorland in exposed elevated regions, such as the southwest and Central Plateau (Jackson 1965).

This ecological diversity supports a rich Australian fauna, although reduced in species range as is common for islands. The highest terrestrial numbers are recorded from coastal heath environments, and the lowest in rainforest (Guiler 1965: 37). Huge numbers of migratory birds seasonally inhabit many of the islands such as those in Bass Strait, and freshwater habitats are extensive throughout the island, the Central Plateau being composed of thousands of lakes. Marine resources are also plentiful, including fish, molluscs, crustacea, and sea mammals such as seal.

Ethnohistorical information on the Tasmanian Aborigines has more recently included the important journals of George Augustus Robinson for the years 1829 to 1834 (Plomley 1966). Although linguistic information for the Tasmanians is sketchy, it appears that there were between eight and twelve languages on the island and the phonological system is of the Australian type (Dixon 1980: 229,232). Using Robinson's information, Jones calculated that there were nine socio-linguistic groups in Tasmania, composed of between 70 and 85 bands, or local groups, such bands being composed of about 40 to 50 people (1974: 327–329). From this information, Jones produced a general population estimate of between 3,000 and 5,000 people for the whole island (see also Ryan 1981: 19–20). While some groups were oriented more towards terrestrial foods, all appeared to have had access to coastal resources at some time during the year (Jones 1974: 329). In general, these social units were associated with the main ecological divisions of the island (see Figure 2.12).

Tasmanians exploited a wide range of terrestrial and marine resources, both plant and animal. Plants included bracken fern (*Pteridium*), and the pith of the grass tree (*Xanthorea*), and terrestrial resources, the large- to medium-sized mammals and reptiles. When compared with Victoria, a less varied number of root plants was used as food in Tasmania. Gott records 218 species, including 166 orchids, as being possibly used in Victoria, compared to 10 different plant species in Tasmania (1982: 60). Orchids were also widely used in Tasmania (Gott 1982: 63). While this discrepancy may in some way be attributable to the wider ecological range of Victorian environments, it may also highlight selectivity on the part of Tasmanians. For example, the yam-daisy, so popular in Victoria, does not appear to have been used by the Tasmanians.

Marine resources, as I have already observed, included shellfish, crustacea and marine mammals. One notable class of food, however – fish – was avoided altogether. The eating of fish appears to have been an island-wide taboo (Hiatt 1967), although fish are generally plentiful in Tasmanian waters. On the other hand, fire was used to create vegetation disclimaxes, forests became grasslands supporting large numbers of herbivores in the central midlands; and marginal closed forest – rainforest and wet sclerophyll – was reduced to productive

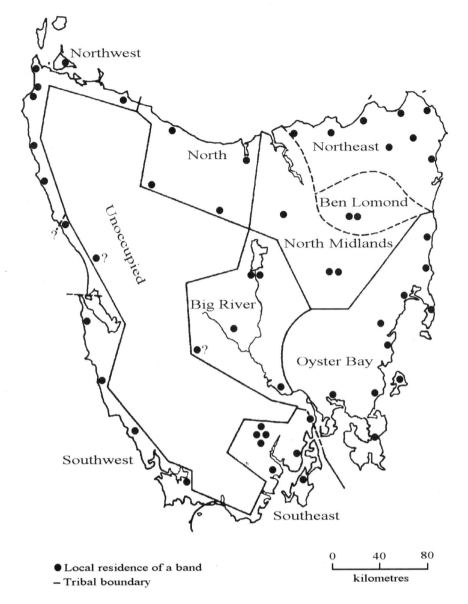

Figure 2.12 The 'tribes' and 'bands' of Tasmania as compiled by Jones, largely from the Tasmanian journals of George Augustus Robinson (based on Jones 1974).

heathland along the northwestern and northeastern coastlines. Economic advantages, therefore, were gained in both cases (Hiatt 1967: 219; Jones 1969; see also below).

Tasmanians inhabited most environments, excepting the denser rainforest, which was poor in animal and plant resources and difficult to penetrate. But some recent discussion and research would suggest that more extensive settlement of these parts of the island had taken place (see below). Tasmanians also occupied offshore islands year-round in the southeast, and in the northwest and southwest on a seasonal basis during the summer. People inhabited the exposed west coast all year, but retreated from the elevated Central Plateau during the worst storms of winter (Hiatt 1967).

I have argued that different settlement patterns existed in the two major contrasting environments of the island: that is to say, west and southeast Tasmania. Settlement of the west coast, including the northwestern and southwestern corners, was tightly coastal, to a large extent constrained by closed forest, including rainforest. 'Villages' of well-constructed conical huts were spaced at intervals at opportune locations for the length of the coast. In contrast to this semi-sedentary settlement pattern, in eastern and especially southeastern Tasmania, where the resources of coast and hinterland were more dispersed due to the drier open forests, settlement patterns also were more dispersed. Resource procurement in this region was more specialised and task-specific, and hut forms ephemeral. There also appears to have been a spatial and temporal distinction between the reaping of marine resources and the exploitation of terrestrial habitats and resources. In general a more mobile pattern pertained (Lourandos 1968, 1970, 1977b).

The Tasmanians employed a limited range of largely hand-held equipment; one form of wooden spear, club, digging-stick, net-bag and the like. One exception was a bag-snare for birds employed along the west coast (Lourandos 1970). A form of canoe, or float, constructed from bundles of reeds of *Typha* lashed together, also was used (Plomley 1966: 366; Gott 1982: 61), and one- or two-piece skin cloaks were worn against the cold.

Social networks in Tasmania appear to have been centred upon tribal language units (Language 1), rather than on groups of these (Language 2), as was the case in Victoria, on the mainland of southeastern Australia described earlier. To illustrate this distinction further, Tasmania is roughly the size of the eastern Kulin network, one of a number of such social systems operating in central Victoria. In Tasmania, some exchange networks also appear to have cross-cut these linguistic groups (Lourandos 1983a, 1985a). Knowledge of Tasmanian social structure, systems of descent and the like, is poor, but from the available evidence, in general marriage appears to have been monogamous, or at least not strictly controlled through male seniority as is usual in mainland Australia. There is much evidence in Tasmania of marriage of individuals of the same age grade (Jones 1974). There is also one instance of polygyny involving an older male (Rose 1960). While decimation of the population at contact would undoubtedly have disrupted marriage and other social interaction, if polygyny and male seniority in marriage had been more widespread on the island, as it was in parts of the Australian mainland, more historical references to these practices would be expected. Evidence of ceremonial activities involving large groups of people exists (Horton 1979; Jones 1977a), but there is no good parallel for the lengthy and large-scale events of the Australian mainland, which ran for months at a time and throughout the year. Once again, some reference to this could be expected to have remained, no matter how sketchy, even during the period of social disruption following European annexation of the island. A general interpretation of the Tasmanian evidence suggests that a broad-based hunting-gathering (but not fishing) economy was practised on the island, which cross-cut a large number of diverse terrestrial and marine environmental zones (Hiatt 1967).

The distinction in western and southeastern Tasmania settlement-economic patterns may be characterised in the following way. This settlement pattern dichotomy suggests, to me that in western Tasmania there was more of an emphasis upon 'logistical organisation', while in southeastern Tasmania 'residential' or 'mapping-on' strategies predominated. These distinctions can be explained to some extent by environmental factors, for example the differential distribution of resources in the two areas. In the west, resources were concentrated along the coastal fringe, while in the east, and southeast in particular, resources were generally more dispersed in coastal, estuarine and terrestrial environments. Other factors, however, also must be considered. I suggest that the patterns are also, to some extent, the product of cultural choice (Lourandos 1983a, 1985a). Had the aquatic and marine resources (for example, fish) been more extensively exploited, then it may be hypothesised that generally higher levels of sedentism would have been promoted in coastal and riverine areas of the island. The southeastern subsistence-settlement pattern, for example, may then have resembled more a 'logistical' one in these locales than was the case. An under-utilisation of certain resources, therefore, to some extent also may have produced these patterns (see also Chapter Seven).

The rudimentary range of largely portable equipment suggests that Tasmanian economies operated more along the lines of 'immediate-return' systems. This viewpoint is reinforced by the lack of fixed and communal facilities such as fish traps, weirs, large fishing and hunting nets, and storage technology as is found on the opposite side of Bass Strait, for example in southwestern Victoria, which I described earlier. The latter region shares marked environmental similarities, especially with the northern coast of Tasmania, which is well endowed in freshwater wetlands, rich volcanic soils and a complex and productive mosaic of floristic communities. The southwestern Victorian equipment approximates more closely with 'delayed-return' systems. The exception, of course, is in western Tasmania, where fixed 'villages' and one example of a fixed bird trap exist.

The evidence, although sparse, of social relations also approximates more closely to the 'immediate-return' end of the spectrum. The more 'open' social networks, and the reduced emphasis upon polygyny, ceremony, exchange, feasting and the like, in some ways suggests less complex intergroup social interaction than in environmentally comparable areas of the mainland, such as we have seen for southwestern Victoria. Tasmanian society, in general, may have approximated more closely with 'open' social networks than with the more 'closed' networks operating in Victoria at the time of contact. More open alliance networks would require less territorial or boundary maintenance, characterised by such behaviour as the ceremony, feasting exchange, and so forth discussed earlier. Given these generally more open social conditions, therefore, fewer opportunities for mediation by individuals and groups would have been available in Tasmania, at both the social and economic levels, than in the Victorian example. I am not arguing here for unilineal evolutionary comparisons, which smack of the nineteenth-century models by which the Tasmanians have long been judged by anthropologists. I am merely searching for ways to explain the varying socio-cultural patterns, without attributing cultural values to these.

Given the general richness and diversity of the Tasmanian environment and the avoidance of fishing, in what must be regarded as a potentially prime fishing province, these Tasmanian socio-economic patterns cannot be viewed as being determined solely by environmental factors. These conclusions are supported by reference to comparative population densities from Tasmania and southwestern Victoria. Comparison of population density of broadly equivalent regions, such as northwestern Tasmania and coastal southwestern Victoria, show the latter figures to be more than three times those of Tasmania (see Table 2.1, p.37). This suggests that relatively more complex socio-economic relations were at work in southwestern Victoria. While no one-to-one relationship between population size and extractive efficiency is being argued here, a general relationship can be upheld, given the magnitude of difference in population sizes between the two areas. Recent reconsideration of the Tasmanian evidence suggest that population sizes and densities may have been underestimated (Pardoe 1991; also Chapter Seven). The same can also be said, however, of the southwestern Victorian figures, which post-date introduced diseases (Butlin 1993a; see also above).

Hunters and horticulturalists

The idea that economic differences between north Australian hunter-gatherers and adjacent hunter-horticulturalists of Torres Strait are clinal, rather than dichotomous, has been discussed above. It now remains for us to extend this argument to include a more general comparison between the two socio-economic 'classes' – that is, hunter-gatherer and hunter-horticulturalist – in this case, between mainland Australia and parts of Papua New Guinea. As we have already seen, Australian population densities, at the highest end of the range, overlap with the lower end of the New Guinean cline (see Table 2.1, p.37). This comparison was between societies in roughly comparable environments. This evidence suggests comparable socio-demographic relations and levels of extractive efficiency. Both hunter-gatherers and hunter-horticulturalists had broad-spectrum economies, based to a large extent upon natural resources. The question of what may be termed domestication emerges in the degree to which they *managed* land and resources (Dwyer and Minnegal 1992).

From an ecological viewpoint, the two groups also share strong similarities. For example, detailed ethnographic studies of two Highland New Guinea societies, the Myanmin (Morren 1974) and the Gadio-Enga (Dornstreich 1973), indicate the following. Both societies are of low population density, and composed of small band-sized groups. Population density for the Myanmin is less than seven people per square kilometre, and for the Gadio-Enga, 85 persons per 4.7 square kilometres. Attempts were made by both groups to stabilise productivity by limiting their impact upon the local environment, restricting the form and intensity of procurement, and by creating disclimaxes and other forms of artificial habitat; this was to ensure the productivity of some prey populations (Morren 1974: 98). Population was continually in flux, with sedentism increasing at ecologically managed locations (Morren 1974: 36). Only during ceremonial periods was the camp continually occupied (Dornstreich 1973: 306–310). The Gadio-Enga strategy was to produce heterogeneous environments, as ecologically these are the most stable (Dornstreich 1973: 69). All of these basic characteristics of the Myanmin and Gadio-Enga find parallels in many of the Australian and Tasmanian case studies and examples mentioned above.

Socially, Australian hunter-gatherers and certain Melanesian hunter-horticulturalists also share characteristics. Social interaction in both groups is organised by kinship, with differential development of power structures controlling both production and reproduction. In many ways, for example, the polygynous, gerontocratic Tiwi fit this general pattern. Alliance systems also share similarities, with complex intergroup ritual, feasting and exchange. As we have seen in Chapter One, production is stimulated and intensified in Highland New Guinea to meet the demands of alliance (feasting, exchange) (Modjeska 1977, 1982; Brown 1978; Feil 1987), and this description may be extended also to Australia. Australian Aboriginal production, such as the creation of surpluses through processing and the storage of foods, was also intensified during or in anticipation of intergroup occasions such as rituals, feasts and exchange. This was the case in most regions of the continent (Lourandos 1988b). In both Highland New Guinea and Australia, alliance formation reflects aspects of inter- and intra-group competition, expressed in territorial behaviour which was often of a ritualised form.

The similarities in organisation of hunter-gatherer and hunter-horticultural society begs the question of why further horticultural practices were not adopted by people in north Australian societies such as those of northern Cape York, who were in close contact with Melanesians. One ecological explanation points to levels of energy expenditure. 'According to most ecological theoreticians, relatively greater amounts of energy are required to change the organisation of "diverse" systems' (Dornstreich 1973: 460). Increased specialisation within an economy results in greater expenditure of group effort. In the long term the process involved in this trend towards specialisation leads to increasing *instability* (Rappaport 1967; Dornstreich 1973: 82). Given this information, both hunter-horticulturalists and hunter-gatherers may be viewed as systems of low energy-expenditure and low growth rate and, therefore, more ecologically stable and less likely to change. In this context, the problem of a low level of adoption of horticultural practices in northeastern Australia is less difficult to unravel. If more complex 'artificial' economic strategies require greater expenditure of effort, and if extractive efficiency is already high (as broadly measured by population density) and comparable to that of small-scale hunter-horticulturalists, the adoption of more intensive food producing strategies would have provided few benefits for groups already practising a wide range of low-density land management practices (see also White and O'Connell 1979; Lourandos 1980b). Following this line of thought, Douglas Yen argued that the adoption of the yam, *Dioscorea alata* (a domesticated plant in Melanesia) in northern Australia indicated 'a receptivity to desirable species and a resistance to agricultural production' (1989: 59). In contrast, however, Matthew Spriggs more recently suggested that, 'It might, on the other hand, represent a relic of a previously agricultural system in northern Australia, transformed into a wild plant-food production or foraging system' (1993: 141). In any case, the situation in north Australia was more complex than Yen, for example, had allowed, for incentives to intensify production also were present, and these are discussed below (also in Chapter Nine).

Overview

The recent re-evaluation of Australian Aboriginal ethnography and ethnohistory indicates that Aboriginal Australia was more populous and culturally more varied and complex than had hitherto been appreciated. Population decline, largely brought about by introduced diseases and European aggression during the early stages of colonialism, have masked, in varying ways, the rich fabric of Australian Aboriginal society. The overall disruption or displacement of socio-demographic patterns, and the survival of fewer Aboriginal people, would have given an overall impression of a less complex society, one operating at a lower socio-economic threshold. This is also true of the Tasmanian information.

The evidence presented here also indicates that southeastern Australia, for example, was both richer in natural resources and more populous than previously considered. Complex use and manipulation of plant foods and fish in the southeast provided a strong economic base, with population densities, patterns of sedentism and social complexity at least equalling those along fertile tropical and sub-tropical coastlines.

Social networks criss-crossed the continent, with extensive and complex alliance systems developed in southeastern Australia, where there was an emphasis upon social 'closure' and the development of 'super' networks incorporating large numbers of people. Relatively more 'open' social networks formed in more environmentally stressful regions, such as arid areas. Leadership and power relations associated with intergroup mediation and access to ritual, land, resources, wives and the relations of production (to name but a few elements) were also more complex than previously appreciated, and especially (although not exclusively) so in more fertile regions. A close relationship was also discerned between the complexity of ceremony and ritual and the economic base, with production intensified at the intergroup level of social interaction where ritual and ceremony were expressed. Economic surpluses (including storage, and the processing of foods), were acquired for communal intergroup and ritual purposes and to meet seasonal subsistence needs in most major environments. Production was increased in many instances by expanding, or rearranging, the workforce and the socio-economic relations controlling it. Examples of this were the large polygynous households of the Tiwi, and co-operative procurement activities such as fishing (weirs, traps, drains), and hunting (nets, mass drives and the like), which were often linked to intergroup occasions.

Economic specialisation is apparent in tropical coastal areas, and on particular offshore islands, with an emphasis on exploiting marine resources, such as the hunting of dugong and turtle, offshore fishing, extensive fish traps, and specialised marine equipment, such as canoes and fishing gear (harpoons and fishhooks). Specialised coastal and inland fishing, including a wide variety of techniques and equipment (nets, weirs, traps, and large-scale artificial drainage systems) were employed in the better-watered stretches of the continent, including the tropical north, east and southeastern temperate Australia. Specialised net hunting (and birding) was also employed in some areas. Plant foods were intensively and extensively harvested, processed, and in some cases managed and stored, in all major environmental zones, including arid regions. These practices also were intensified at the intergroup level. Emphasis was placed on roots and tubers in tropical, sub-tropical and temperate zones, and seeds (including grass seeds) in more arid and semi-arid areas. In all, Aboriginal Australians possessed a very wide range of equipment and techniques.

Settlement appears to have been more sedentary in more fertile regions, such as the tropical and sub-tropical coastlines and in temperate southeastern Australia, correlating closely with increased Aboriginal population sizes and densities. Sedentism was also related to group and household size as evidenced in the case of the Tiwi. Aspects of territoriality also were expressed, especially in these regions, in terms of boundary maintenance and group cohesion (for example, communal ritual, ceremony and festivities). Territoriality is evident also in individual and group control of resources and resource areas, and in intergroup conflict (overt and formalised). It was not only in resource-rich areas that complex practices took place, however. Aspects of these social and economic practices were also observed in harsh arid environments, such as the Cooper Creek riverine corridor (see also Chapter Five).

The developmental or 'evolutionary' implications of the above, in light of arguments developed in the first chapter of the book, are the following. Of the five ecological 'avenues' where economic growth was possible, four appear to have been expanded on mainland Australia – grass seeds, roots and tubers, fishing and hunting of aquatic mammals (for example, dugong), and, to some extent, tree nuts. The patterns of sedentism and use of fixed economic facilities (weirs, traps, drains and the like) are indications of the development of more 'logistical' strategies; territorially located ceremonial and burial precincts are further examples. All these may also be equated in some ways with more 'delayed-return' systems.

This evidence also suggests that while Aboriginal patterns were closely associated with regional environmental factors they were *not determined* by them. For example, while specialised marine practices developed in northeastern Australia and its offshore islands, practices in the rich northwestern Australian islands were less specialised. Some northeastern islands and island groups were relatively intensively occupied (and had extensive fish trap systems), and others were not. The elaborate fishing practices of parts of the Australian mainland, in both marine and freshwater contexts, could also have been attuned to the broad range of resources available in Tasmania, but were not. In Tasmania also, while strong environmental distinctions exist between sectors of the island and were reflected in Aboriginal settlement and subsistence patterns, the emphasis upon 'mapping-on' strategies and 'immediate-return' systems, for example, is not fully explained in purely environmental terms. Each region had its own particular recent cultural 'signature' and history. We can expect changes, therefore, through time associated with, but *not directly controlled by*, environmental factors.

In support of these interpretations, Australian hunter-gatherers may be favourably compared, in many ways, with many Melanesian hunter-horticultural societies. For example, the management of many plant species (and fish) overlaps markedly with Melanesian practices. Australian Aboriginal land and resource practices are not generally labour-intensive, which was equally true of some Melanesian horticultural practices. Many of the hunter-gatherer-fisher practices are also common to both regions. Population densities, in some way, are also comparable – at least for the low-density hunter-horticultural populations of Papua New Guinea residing in roughly comparable environments to those of Australia. Subsistence strategies, settlement patterns, technology, social structure, ceremony and exchange also provide many parallels. For example, in both regions intergroup festivities, ceremonies and events served to integrate and regulate the socio-political and demographic relations between populations. This comparison serves to drive home the impression that the organisational or structural elements of both Australian and New Guinean social groups have more in common than material differences in technology – for example some horticultural practices – might at first suggest. In the past, too much emphasis has been placed upon these technological differences, upon the forces of production, and not enough upon the social relations of production that guide them. From an ecological point of view, also, both Australian (and Tasmanian) hunter-gatherers and Melanesian hunter-horticulturalists are small-scale, low-intensity, economic systems, with a low potential growth rate. Many of these issues will now be considered in light of the Australian archaeological evidence, with its long-term temporal dimension, in the following chapters.

CHAPTER 3

OUT OF ASIA: EARLIEST EVIDENCE AND PEOPLE

When was Greater Australia first colonised and by whom? And what impact did the arrival of people have upon an ancient continent unused to their presence? These questions are pursued here in some detail and we discuss theories of first colonisation; Southeast Asian cultural connections; the earliest archaeological evidence; interpretations of the human skeletal material; and, finally, environmental impact, with emphasis upon use of fire, and the extinction of Pleistocene fauna.

Deep-sea channels divide the continent of Greater Australia from the island world of Southeast Asia. Even during the lowest sea levels of the Pleistocene, at glacial maxima, the region of Wallacia provided a substantial watery barrier to human contact with Australia (Figure 3.1). Whenever it was that they first dry-landed, people had to cross the water to the southern continent by island-hopping. Detailed estimates were made by Birdsell (1977) of likely routes of

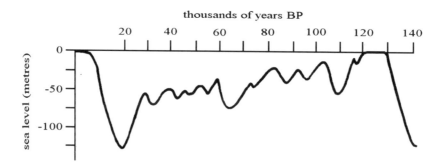

Figure 3.1 Sea levels of the last 140,000 years in Australasia (based on Chappell 1993).

passage from the Indonesian region to Greater Australia and he calculated two possible alternatives. The first was via Sulawesi across an island chain to New Guinea, and the second via Timor onto the northwestern shelf of the Australian mainland (Figure 3.2). Most of these islands were high, thereby assisting navigation in providing a visible route across the Sulawesi passage.

Whatever the mode of water transport, or the social relations that existed at the time of earliest colonisation, people maintained their connection with water transport, islands and the sea. Occupation of northeastern New Guinea took place from about 40,000 years ago, and of the large islands of the Bismarck Archipelago (New Ireland and New Britain) and Buku in the Solomons, from around 33,000–29,000 BP. Suggested here is a possible continuous use of islands of the tropical north of Greater Australia, with settlement extending out into the northeastern Pacific (see Chapter Four). Geoffrey Irwin argues that passage throughout the 'voyaging corridor', which extends from Sulawesi to the Solomons (Figure 3.3), presents 'predictable seasonal reversals of wind and current, a sheltered equatorial position between bands of cyclones and a large measure of intervisibility, which accommodates all islands but the Pleistocene outliers' (1992: 24). Easterly movement was easiest, he adds, from island Southeast Asia to New Guinea during the summer monsoon (Irwin 1992: 28). The tropical climate of the region would have provided no real barrier, as it was similar to island Southeast Asia. The Australian communities of plants and marine animals are to some extent shared with those of Southeast Asia (Golson 1971).

Various types of sea craft have been considered as likely original prototypes, including the most basic (Birdsell 1977); and also the question of the intentionality of the colonisation (White and O'Connell 1982: 46). Given the present evidence, however, there is no good reason to suggest otherwise. If even earlier settlement by earlier populations of *Homo sapiens* is detected, then the same argument would apply.

Links with Southeast Asia are also provided by forms of stone artefact. 'Waisted' axes are among the earliest types of artefact found, and have broader connections with Southeast Asia as well as more far-flung parts of Australia. The edge-ground axes found in northern Australia (at Malangangerr and Nawamoyn) dated at around 20,000 BP and earlier (Schrire 1982) are also known from Pleistocene sites in Japan (Blundell and Bleed 1974). Also, from southwestern Sulawesi (for example, Ulu Leang) high-angled scrapers, broadly resembling those of early Australian industries, have been found at least from terminal Pleistocene sites (Glover 1976), although further socio-economic details are not available. In general, however, archaeological material from Southeast Asia is no older than 40,000 years, and therefore roughly contemporary with that of Greater Australia. Pleistocene sites of this age and earlier have been found in Thailand, Sarawak (Niah Cave), southern Sulawesi, Palawan Island, the Malay Peninsula, island Malaysia and north Vietnam (Table 3.1). Bowdler (1993) has recently argued for a general morphological uniformity of Pleistocene stone

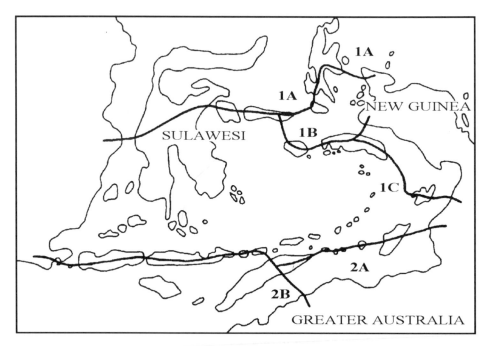

Figure 3.2 Two hypothetical sea crossings (1A-C, 2A-B) to the continent of Greater Australia along the island chain adjoining the Southeast Asian and Australian continents (based on Birdsell 1977).

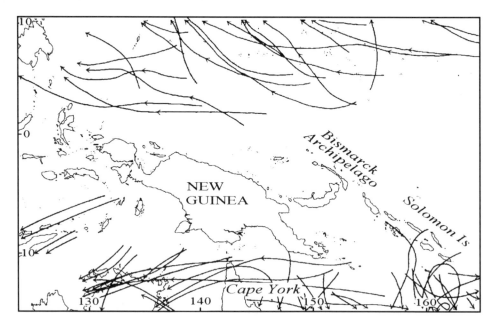

Figure 3.3 An alternative route of colonisation of the tropical north of Greater Australia and the Pacific islands lying further east. This 'voyaging corridor' is positioned in a sheltered zone between northern and southern tropical cyclonic activity, which is represented by thin directional lines (based on Irwin 1992: 24, Figure 10).

Table 3.1 Estimated basal dates from late Pleistocene caves and rock-shelters of Southeast Asia (after Bowdler 1993: 64–65).

Site	Date	Reference
Lang Rongrien, Thailand	c. 37,000 BP	(Anderson 1987)
Niah Cave, Sarawak, Malaysia	c. 40,000–35,000 BP	(Zuraina 1982)
Leang Burung 2, southern Sulawesi	c. 31,000 BP	(Glover 1981)
Tabon Cave, Palawan Island	c. 26,000 BP	(Fox 1970)
Kota Tampan, Perak, Malay Peninsula	c. 31,000 BP	(Zuraina 1990)
Tingkayu, Sabah, Malaysia	c. 28,000 BP	(Bellwood and Koon 1988: 48–9)
North Vietnam (four caves and rock-shelters)	c. 23,000–18,000 BP	(Hoang Xuan Chinh 1991)

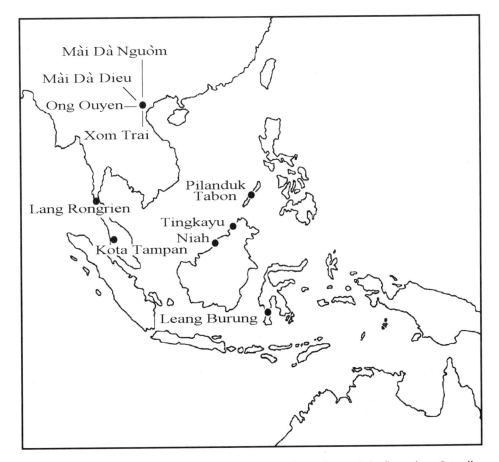

Figure 3.4 Late Pleistocene archaeological sites of Southeast Asia (based on Bowdler 1993: 64, Figure 2).

industries of this age in both the regions of Greater Southeast Asia and Greater Australia. This common tradition, she considers, may reflect the general spread of modern people *(Homo sapiens sapiens)* from China, across Southeast Asia and into Greater Australia between 50,000 and 40,000 years ago (Figure 3.4).Bowdler's model stands in contrast to the more traditional view that Java was the source of migration into Greater Australia (see further in this chapter and Chapter Ten).

Earliest sites

Papua New Guinea, the northern corridor of Greater Australia, and a likely point of entry for human colonists, has only recently provided more definite evidence of early human occupation. From the Bobongara area at the southern end of the Huon Peninsula, in the northeast of the island, archaeological evidence at least 40,000 years old has been found on a series of raised coral terraces (Groube et al. 1986; Figure 3.5). The terraces are the product of continual tectonic uplift of the coast during the upper Pleistocene, with each phase of reef formation including a coastal environment of lagoons and surrounding reefs. The terraces have been dated by several methods and correlated with deep-sea core records. The archaeological site is located on reef complex IIIa, in a stream gully which adjoined a small palaeo-lagoon. Stone artefacts are stratified within layers of strongly weathered tephra and are considered to be older than 40,000 years, and thermoluminescence (TL) dating of quartz particles within each unit supported these conclusions. Excavation took place along an ephemeral channel (Jo's Creek) and exposed three layers of tephra which rested upon basal tuff and limestone. The in situ artefacts included waisted axes, together with a stone core and flakes, and one excavated waisted axe was found in several pieces which indicated that little post-depositional displacement had occurred. A second excavated waisted axe had a distinct groove between the waisted notches and was made of raw material (andesite) still available in the nearby Masaweng River. Thin sectioning of the axe indicated that its external patina was the product of long-term burial in the tephric matrix.

More than a hundred waisted axes of similar form (but without hafting grooves) were found on the surface of the site and these are all unifacial, and made on rounded river boulders similar to the above notched axe. Two other axe forms were also reported, and the excavators drew wider cultural comparisons in the following way.

> Our waisted axes have similarities with artefacts discovered elsewhere. In highland New Guinea, waisted axes at 26,000 years are reported at Kosipe and occur from 6,000 to over 10,000 BP at Yuku. Pleistocene ages are inferred for waisted axes at Kangaroo Island in South Australia and at Mackay in north Queensland. Waisted axes of inferred Holocene age occur at Botal Tobago and Japan, in east Asia, although these appear to be smaller than the Huon Peninsula tools. (Groube et al. 1986: 455)

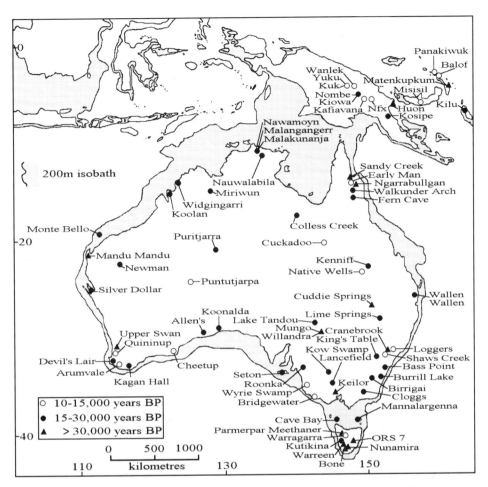

Figure 3.5 Pleistocene archaeological sites of Greater Australia discussed in the text.

Les Groube has also argued that these axes had the potential for forest clearance, and he hypothesised that such clearance may have led to forest management and further to forest horticulture in the late Pleistocene. In this way the dense rainforest canopy could be opened allowing for management of a range of plants including *Pandanus* and *Colocasia taro* (Groube 1989; see also Chapter Four).

Mainland Australia's demonstrably oldest site to date, Upper Swan, is located in riverine alluvium on an ancient flood plain of the Swan River, close to the present-day city of Perth (Pearce and Barbetti 1981). The site is now located about 27 kilometres from the coast, stratified in Quaternary sediments. This extensive open site was originally detected by a clay pit operation. The cultural horizon was stratified between 70 and 90 cm below the original surface, and consists of stone artefacts, charcoal and carbonised material, and possibly resin. Four dates were obtained from two different parts of the site, with an average age of around 38,000 years BP. Pearce and Barbetti argue that radiocarbon dates of such great antiquity may not be an accurate assessment of the site's true age. They suggest that dates approaching about 40,000 BP are likely to be even older for a variety of technical reasons associated with the processing of the datable material. They state, for example, that 'observed count-rates are very close to the lower limit of detection for our best counter' (Pearce and Barbetti 1981: 177). The estimate, therefore, of first colonisation of the continent at around this time might be just as much a product of dating methods as of archaeological evidence (also Allen and Holdaway 1995).

A few artefacts were also recovered higher up in the deposit between 40 and 60 cm from the surface, perhaps indicating more recent occupation. Exposures on the clay pit indicate that the site covered at least 250 square metres. The second excavation in 1981 of seven square metres contained 679 stone artefacts, of which 17 percent were flakes, 75 percent small chips, and 5.5 percent had retouch or edge-wear. Overall, the stratigraphy, sediments and artefacts suggest that the site is stratigraphically sound with no evidence of re-working.

Eighteen kilometres south of Upper Swan, a salvage excavation at the Helena River site produced a date of 29,400 ± 2,000 BP from the base of the cultural deposit at a level of between 123 and 143 cm. At this depth the lithic assemblage appears to bear similarities to that of Upper Swan. The site is situated on an old river terrace of the Helena Valley, and extends over an area of at least 2,975 square metres (Schwede 1983).

Some sixteen kilometres north of Melbourne, in southeastern Australia, the alluvial terraces of the Maribyrnong River close to Keilor have produced over the years an array of Pleistocene evidence. These investigations are the work of a number of researchers (Gill 1957, Gallus 1971, Marshall 1974, Bowler 1976). At Dry Creek, close to the Maribyrnong junction, a cross-section of the alluvial sediments indicate that archaeological evidence has come from two main stratigraphic units, the more recent Keilor Terrace and the underlying D clay (Mulvaney 1975; Bowler 1976: 59-64; see also Figure 3.6).

The Keilor Terrace has been radiocarbon dated to between c. 20,000–18,000 and c. 15,000 BP, and contains artefacts and human skeletal remains. The age of the D Clay has been estimated stratigraphically to lie between c. 36,000 and c. 26,000 BP, with a possible maximum age of c. 45,000 BP (Bowler 1976: 64). At various places throughout the D Clay, including the base of the unit, stone artefacts have been detected and extinct fauna also has been found in these layers (see further below).

Comparable evidence has been obtained from the alluvial Cranebrook Terrace, near Penrith, west of Sydney. Stone artefacts have been found in river gravels which are claimed to be older than 40,000 years (Nanson et al. 1987). Problems exist, however, in verifying the association between the dates and the artefacts as alluvial deposits of this kind are very much subject to redeposition and hence mixing of materials.

Firmer evidence comes from Ngarrabullgan (Nurrabullgin) Cave, on Mount

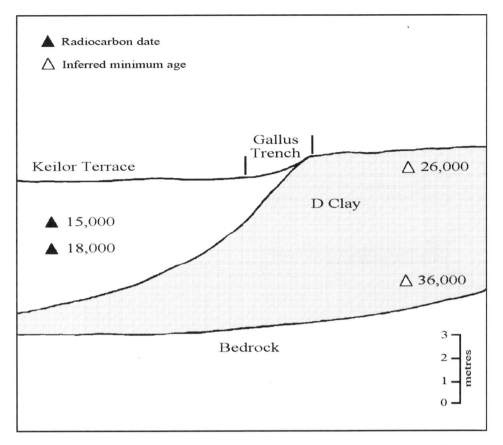

Figure 3.6 Cross-section through the Maribyrnong River Valley near Dry Creek, Keilor, indicating the Keilor Terrace and the underlying D Clay, in which archaeological remains have been found (based on Bowler 1976: 63, Figure 4).

Mulligan in Cape York Peninsula, northern Australia, which was first inhabited prior to 37,170 BP (Beta 45906) (David 1993). The relatively shallow deposit has well stratified evidence of a series of charcoal-rich hearths and stone artefacts up to about 30,000 years ago. This layer is capped by a more intensively occupied late Holocene level (see Chapter Four), and comparisons between radiocarbon and thermoluminescent (TL) dating of the site are presently under way (David personal communication 1995)(Figure 3.7). Dates of around 35,000 years BP also have been obtained from a number of sites across Greater Australia and these are discussed further in Chapters Four to Seven.

Earliest claims

Recent claims have been made of occupation between about 50,000 and 60,000 BP at the rock-shelter of Malakunanja 11, in Arnhem Land (Roberts et al. 1990a). These results, however, now require further support due to stratigraphic problems

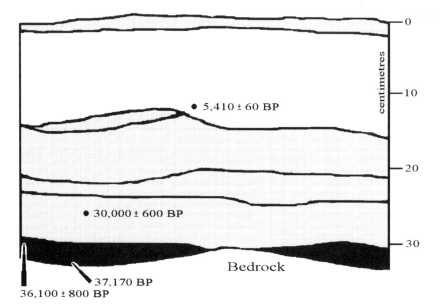

Figure 3.7 A diagrammatic representation of Ngarrabullgan (Nurrabullgin) Cave, northeastern Queensland; stratigraphic profile, east section of the test excavation (based on David 1993: 52, Figure 3).

in soft, sandy sites of this kind; there is also the difficulty of calibrating radiocarbon dates with those of thermoluminescence dating, the method employed at the site, as others also have pointed out (Bowdler 1990b, 1991; Hiscock 1990; Roberts et al. 1990b, 1990c; see also Chapter Four).

Earlier claims still for initial settlement of the continent have been derived from palynological evidence. For example, the deep pollen core from Lake George, near Canberra in southeastern Australia, has produced evidence of increased fire activity and expansion of fire-tolerant vegetation, supposedly from around 120,000 BP, which has been interpreted as an early appearance of people in Australia (Singh and Geissler 1985). Changes in climate were ruled out as providing the explanation of the data. This interpretation, however, has been challenged by Richard Wright (1986), who argued that the age of the shift in fire regime might only be half that estimated.

People

Where did the Australians come from? Is the morphological variation observable in ancient and modern populations the product of either more than one migration, or biological adaptation to Australian environments? These are the questions that have shaped the investigation of the biological origins of the Aboriginal people of Australia.

Prior to the discovery of firm evidence confirming the Pleistocene colonisation of Greater Australia, research had concentrated upon morphological variation

Figure 3.8 Ngarrabullgan (Nurrabullgin) Cave, 1991 (Photo: Lara Lamb).

among living Australian populations. Birdsell's trihybrid theory, for example, assumed a protracted colonisation by three waves of morphologically distinct groups (1949, 1967). (In this model, the three Aboriginal groups – of tropical and temperate Australia and Tasmania – came from Asia at different times; modern studies do not support Birdsell's hypothesis.) Later opinions viewed this phenotypic variation as related to genetic adaptation to varying Australian climatic factors (Bodmer and Cavalli-Storza 1976). Then there have been biological studies, for example those of blood genetics, which have dealt with the geographical spread of various gene frequencies (Curtain et al. 1976; Kirk 1976; Kirk and Thorne 1976; Simmons 1976; Mellars and Stringer 1989). These analyses have shown the close relationships between populations of the Australo-Melanesian region, and also have documented local population groupings (see also Kirk 1987). Problems, however, concern viewing this information in terms of long-term historical population trends. For example, geographical re-arrangements of peoples in the wider Southeast Asian and Australasian regions, among other things, may have affected these patterns.

Australasian skeletal evidence has long been viewed as reflecting a Southeast Asian, and in particular an Indonesian, connection. Australian fossils, such as the Talgai and Cohuna crania (which are discussed below) were seen in this light (Coon 1962; Thorne and Wolpoff 1981; Wolpoff et al. 1984). N. W. G. Macintosh (1965) for example, recognised 'the mark of ancient Java' on the

Australian material. Alan Thorne considered Australian connections with the main Southeast Asian fossils of Niah (c. 40,000 BP), Wajak and Tabon: 'Thus all these fossils are likely to point in the direction of the Lake Mungo–Keilor end of the Australian fossil morphological range' (1977: 197–198).

In these studies emphasis was placed, in the main, on 'cranial size and gross morphology' (Brown 1987: 41). The early debate revolved around a dichotomy – the observation of both 'gracile' and 'robust' morphological features. From a chronological perspective gracile characteristics were viewed as 'modern', and robust characteristics as 'archaic'. Thorne investigated this long-standing problem by introducing a wider range of fossil evidence (1975, 1976, 1977). His analysis was based upon the evidence of the Cohuna and Keilor crania, the isolated Mossgiel and Lake Nitchie skeletons, the three Lake Mungo individuals and the Kow Swamp skeletal series (1977: 189).

No comparable evidence is available from New Guinea. The Cohuna cranium was discovered in 1925 during the excavation of an irrigation channel towards the northern fringe of Kow Swamp and has more recently been placed firmly within the Kow Swamp population (Thorne 1975). The Keilor cranium was found in 1940, some 2 kilometres north of Keilor in Victoria, and a fragment of femur, which was found near the cranium, produced a bone collagen date of 12,000 ± 100 (NZ 1327) (Brown 1987: 43). The Lake Nitchie burial was brought to light by Bowler in 1969 (excavated by N. W. G. Macintosh and K. N. Smith in 1970), and dated by bone collagen to 6,820 ± 200 (Macintosh 1971). The cranium was classified as 'robust' by Thorne (1977; Thorne and Wilson 1977), and a pierced Tasmanian Devil *(Sarcophilus harrisii)* canine tooth necklace was found with the burial (Macintosh et al. 1970).

Lake Mungo I, a cranium, was found by Bowler in 1968 (Bowler et al. 1970) and dated to 24,500–26,500 BP from bone collagen and charcoal from a nearby hearth. Lake Mungo III, also discovered by Bowler (in 1974) is an extended burial and was dated stratigraphically to 28,000–32,000 BP (Bowler and Thorne 1976: 136-138), while Lake Mungo II is fragmentary, as were the fossil remains of over forty other individuals found in the Willandra Lakes region at the time (Brown 1987: 43; see Figure 3.9).

Kow Swamp is located some 10 kilometres southeast of Cohuna in the central Murray River Valley. This multiple burial site (Thorne 1975, 1976; Thorne and Macumber 1972) has been dated to between 13,000 ± 280 BP (ANU 1236) and 9,590 ± 130 BP (ANU 532). The remains of over twenty-two individuals were discovered, most of them in a fragmentary condition due to poor preservation and only two crania were relatively complete. In a multivariate study, the above group was compared with a series of 'near-contemporary' (that is, recent) Australian skeletal remains from northern Victoria (Thorne and Wilson 1977). The results isolated two separate groups of fossils. The first group included Lake Mungo I and Keilor (and by analogy, Lake Mungo III, which was not available for study) and the second group, the Kow Swamp population (together with the

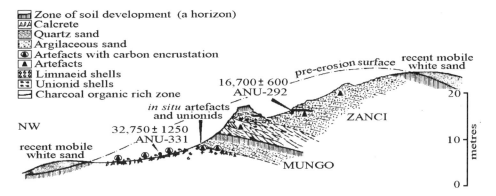

Figure 3.9 Lake Mungo, western New South Wales. Stratigraphic section through the southern end of the Walls of China lunette, indicating the Mungo and Zanci stratigraphic units (based on Bowler 1971: 60, Figure 5.6).

Cohuna cranium) as well as the Mossgiel and Lake Nitchie individuals. These two late Pleistocene groups were found to lie at the extreme ends of the range of the near-contemporary Australian crania, and beyond. The first group (which included the Lake Mungo individuals) was characterised by Thorne as gracile, and in the case of Lake Mungo I and III, 'of extreme gracility':

> The non-metrical features of the Keilor cranium appear to be consistent with near-contemporary forms of southeastern Australia. The same features in Lake Mungo I and III are unusual, when taken together, in that no single character lies outside the range observed in more recent samples. The combined incidence of non-metrical features in these two individuals creates a picture of extreme gracility and modernity . . . the female Lake Mungo I is ultra-feminine and, were it not for femoral and pelvic evidence, one could be tempted to diagnose Lake Mungo III as female. (Thorne 1977: 190)

According to Thorne, 'all the Lake Mungo individuals, including the fragmentary Lake Mungo I and II . . . possess very thin cranial vault bones' (1977: 191).

In contrast to these, the second group (which included the Kow Swamp population) was described by Thorne as 'robust' and 'archaic' in appearance. 'The Kow Swamp crania are large by more recent Aboriginal standards. They indicate a greater robustness or ruggedness, although this has to be seen as a feature of the population as a whole and not of all individuals' (1976: 105). The mean size of Kow Swamp molar teeth was larger than for recent Aboriginal populations. Kow Swamp crania generally displayed thick vault bones and mandibles, greater size in some individuals, and flattened frontal bones (Thorne 1976: 108–109).

The differences between the ancient morphologies and those of the recent Aboriginal sample were explained as indicating 'significant morphological change within Australia, certainly over the last 10,000 years' (Thorne 1976: 110). Thorne discounted alternative explanations of the Kow Swamp morphology (1976: 109–110). These explanations included pathology, artificial deformation and adaptive responses to environmental factors, for example those of nutrition. He also considered that the evidence was open to various interpretations. First, while it seemed to 'confirm and extend the contrast noted in earlier discoveries of Australian prehistoric remains', it also did 'not resolve the problem of two late Pleistocene morphologies, or even indicate whether they are really elements, or extremes, from within a broader range of Pleistocene skeletal forms' (1976: 111). He therefore proposed three possible explanatory models for this information (Thorne 1977: 193–196).

The first two models assumed that two morphologically disparate populations, one more 'gracile', the other more 'robust', entered the Australian continent some time during the Pleistocene. Both groups lay outside the morphological range of near-recent late Holocene crania. In the first model, the two populations entered Australia at different times, the sequence of chronological events being difficult to untangle. In contrast, in the second model, the two populations entered the continent at approximately the same time from different geographical homelands. In both models the two migrating populations merge within Australia to form the homogeneous modern, or recent, population. The third model assumed a single founding population with a more restricted morphological range than Thorne had detected in his 'gracile' and 'robust' dichotomy.

> The skeletal variation of the founding population cannot be known but given the relatively restricted ranges of tropical environments from which the crossing was made it might be expected to have been narrow, compared to contemporary Australian continental variation. The late Pleistocene fossil evidence, indicating greater variability than in Holocene times, would imply that the spread of populations around and across the continent involved a series of physical adaptations, in addition to a complex of genetic effects. (Thorne 1977: 195)

Although Thorne was unable to favour one of the above three possible interpretations, he suggested that the narrower morphological range evident in Holocene populations was largely the product of post-glacial environmental changes such as sea level rises, terrestrial environmental changes, and the like. He viewed this process as beginning some time towards the start of the Holocene period (Thorne 1977: 195–196). In essence, therefore, Thorne's interpretations of the Australian Pleistocene skeletal evidence depended upon the veracity of his 'gracile-robust' morphological dichotomy. The discovery of new material such as an archaic cranium in Western Australia, in a Holocene context (Freedman and Lofgren 1979), appeared to support Thorne's theories.

Thorne's research was continued by his student, Peter Brown. First, Brown demonstrated that certain of the morphological features of the archaic (including Kow Swamp) individuals were the result of artificial deformation (1981).

Comparative ethnographic and cranial studies of Melanesian material led Brown to suggest that 'The probable method of deformation was repetitive pressure by the mother's hands on the front and back of the infant's cranium' (1981: 166).

Brown's (1987, 1989) analysis included most of the skeletal material employed by Thorne (1977), together with Pleistocene and comparative Holocene material. The latter included the Coobool Creek crania, collected in 1950 from a site near 'Doherty's Hut' at Coobool Crossing on the Wakool River between Swan Hill and Deniliquin, in the Murray River region by G. M. Black and as yet the material is undated. Morphologically and metrically, however, the Coobool collection is close to the Kow Swamp material, and unlike more recent Holocene remains from sites such as Swanport, Roonka and Chowilla. On the strength of the latter, Brown suggests that Coobool Creek is at least early Holocene in age. A date of 12,500 ± 400 BP was obtained on bone from Coobool Creek 65 (Brown 1987: 42). The Coobool Creek collection included 126 individuals, all heavily mineralised, of whom 24 males and nine females were included in Brown's analysis. Brown also included the undated Talgai cranium which was discovered on the Darling Downs, near Warwick in southeastern Queensland, in 1884, and has been termed 'archaic', due to both the size of the palate and the canine teeth (Macintosh 1952).

Comparative skeletal evidence from three Holocene sites (Broadbeach, Swanport and Roonka) was also included by Brown in his study. The Broadbeach burial ground is located 1.5 kilometres inland from Mermaid Beach in southeastern Queensland; over 100 individuals were unearthed between 1965 and 1968 and were mostly poorly preserved, with eighteen adult crania in reasonable condition (Haglund 1976). The burial ground was in use from around 1,290 BP until the contact period. Roonka is another burial ground, situated on the Murray River some five kilometres south of Blanchetown, in South Australia, and the site dates from 7,000 BP and was also in use until the contact period (Pretty 1977). Remains representing more than 120 individuals were obtained from Trench A at Roonka but due to poor preservation of the skeletal material only eight male crania from Phase II (7,000–4,000 BP) were included in Brown's analysis. Swanport is located 10 kilometres southeast of Murray Bridge in South Australia and the skeletal material was collected in 1911 (Stirling 1911) and is considered to date to around contact times. Comparison with recent burials and artefacts from Roonka support this relative dating of the site, as does a comparison of the skeletal remains (Pietrusewsky 1984). Finally, the Murray Valley collection consisted of 100 crania, all obtained from the region between Chowilla and Coobool by G. M. Black between 1943 and 1950. Although this group is undated and not clearly provenanced, on comparative grounds it appears to be of late Holocene age.

Brown's statistical analysis was based upon tooth size, cranial vault thickness and facial skeletons. His results did not support Thorne's (1977) distinction between two discrete human Pleistocene populations, 'gracile' and 'robust'.

In contrast to Thorne (1977), a combination of the craniometric, tooth size and vault thickness results suggest a single, homogeneous Pleistocene population ... With the exception of Lake Mungo I, the most obvious shared feature is increased size. This involves the structure of the dentition and the entire cranium, although there are more marked proportional increases for some anatomical regions (facial skeleton and cranial vault thickness). Associated with this general size increase is a consistent Australian Pleistocene morphology. (Brown 1987: 61)

The latter, Brown described as 'a general enlargement in cranial size and robusticity' (1987: 61).

Specifically, Brown reclassified the Keilor cranium as 'robust', along with other Coobool Creek crania, instead of 'gracile' as Thorne (1977) had considered it. The Lake Mungo 3 individual was also reclassified by Brown (1987: 61) as lying within the modern Murray Valley male range, rather than as 'gracile', as classified by Thorne. Only Lake Mungo 1 retained the classification of 'gracile' that Thorne had assigned to it, lying outside the modern female range.

Brown's assessment, therefore, removed the necessity to argue for two distinct Australian Pleistocene populations, the varying chronologies of the arrival of the two populations on the continent, and the separation of the two populations within Australia. One Pleistocene population with both 'robust' (archaic) and 'gracile' (modern) characteristics could now be modelled, irrespective of when the ancestral population first made landfall. Phil Habgood's multivariate analyses came to similar conclusions, and he argued that morphological variations may be a product of environmental and other changes within Australia throughout the Pleistocene and Holocene periods (1986, 1989).

Colin Pardoe's (1988) research also concluded that the terminal Pleistocene-early Holocene populations of the Murray River Valley region were more than likely the product of local regional morphological developments. The emergence of territorial behaviour in the region at this time and its effect on intermarriage and gene flow is central to his arguments (see also Chapter Six). Pardoe states: 'Kow Swamp is not an archaic relict Pleistocene population, but the forerunner of a modern, socially complex, dynamic system' (1988; 14).

Stephen Webb's analysis of the remains of over 130 individuals from the Willandra Lakes region arrived at somewhat different conclusions (Webb 1989). These fragmentary skeletal remains were mainly surface collections made between 1974 and 1982 and are largely undated. Given that most of this material was found on the lunette dunes of the region, Webb assigned the collection to the period 40,000–15,000 BP, that is, to the period of lunette formation. Basing his assessment upon detailed analyses, Webb supported the general dichotomy of the distinct morphologies, robust and gracile. Essentially Webb viewed the evidence as the results of a series of migrations covering the full span of Australian prehistory. He argued that the older the initial occupation of the continent, the more robust or archaic would have been the appearance of earliest immigrants. In this way they would have reflected continuing old-world trends in morphology, from robusticity towards gracility. Some time towards 35,000 BP more gracile characteristics, he suggested, would be evident among Australian populations. But whether this represented a 'second population' or another 'link in the chain' of migrations was unclear (Webb 1989: 76–77).

Webb's scenario is persuasive in that it incorporates the vast time span involved, presents a chronology of events, and links this to morphological trends taking place outside Australia. Just how the model fits the archaeological data which are so poorly dated, and in some cases so fragmentary, is another problem. It is a problem, however, also shared by most of the explanations outlined above. A further difficulty lies with the classification of the fossils, which, as we have seen, goes beyond a straightforward division into one or two groups.

In conclusion, therefore, the evidence at the present time points more in the direction of a single Australian population with a broad morphological range. The historical details of the process of immigration, covering such a great stretch of time, and of the subsequent morphological patterns formed within Australia, are at present unclear. As to connections with Southeast Asian populations, Thorne and Wolpoff (1981; Wolpoff 1989) argue for regional continuity within the Australasian region during the Pleistocene, and link the Australian populations with those of Java (Sangiran, Solo-Ngandong). Regional continuity assumes a development of modern people from earlier regional populations (including *Homo erectus*). These arguments, linking the morphologies of Java to the archaic populations of Pleistocene Australia, parallel the earlier hypotheses referred to above. Further analyses of the Australian material are now needed, however, not only to avoid sampling problems but also to eliminate bias introduced by individual researchers.

Environmental impact

The role of people in producing changes to the natural environment and its fauna and flora in both present and past contexts is now considered. We first discuss the role of fire within Aboriginal society and its long-term and short-term effects upon vegetation, followed by an assessment of Pleistocene faunal extinctions.

Fire

Fire is acknowledged as a key agent in the propagation and evolution of many of the Australian vegetation communities (Gill et al. 1981). Rhys Jones (1969) also pointed out the significant role played by people in the process. He coined the term 'fire stick farming' to describe Aboriginal management of flora and fauna of particular biomes. Drawing upon the Tasmanian botanical work of Jackson (1965), Jones indicated that fire could be used to produce ecological disclimaxes by arresting natural environmental trends which affected vegetation communities. Rainforest, for example, was transformed by fire to more open-canopied or mixed forest, woodland was opened up to savanna, and further still to grassland. In this way the natural productivity of particular environments (and their plant and animal resources) could be regulated or increased. Herbivores, for example, congregated in grassy savanna where pasture had been rejuvenated following a burn. Jones pointed to parts of northwestern Tasmania, the Hampshire Hills, where open vegetation conditions were increasingly giving way to encroaching rainforest in the 150 years since Aboriginal burning had ceased.

Jones' observations have been supported by a range of Australian ethnographic and ethnohistorical studies. Gould reported the complex and subtle range of Aboriginal uses of fire for hunting, as well as its being used as a tool of ecological management in the Western Desert (1971b). For example, Gould suggests that the secondary succession produced by firing spinifex is more productive than the climax spinifex itself (1971: 23). Tindale (1974) wrote of similar examples from the Western Desert as well as Arnhem Land and Cape York. Jones' (1980) ethnographic work among the Gidgingali of northeastern Arnhem Land reported in detail on their annual burning strategies. The Gidgingali regarded these practices as 'cleaning up' their country. Kimber's ethnographic and ethnohistorical studies found likewise:

> ... the Aborigines of the Central and Western Deserts ... are as one with the Eternal Ones of the Dream in their present and recent past fire-practices. I examine early European records to indicate the nature and extent of fires, and to suggest that large Aboriginal fires were not accidental, random or otherwise uncontrolled ... records from 1970-81 will show that Western Desert Aborigines still perceive fire as an important tool which can be used to improve their country. (Kimber 1983a: 38)

Detailed ethnohistorical coverage of the literature of southwestern Australian on Aboriginal burning practices by Sylvia Hallam (1975) also found agreement on the matter. Hallam details the opening up of the southwestern Jarrah forests, and the impact upon the mallee (1975: 51, 54). She also discussed the way burning practices were timed to coincide with fish runs (1975: 30–31), and the management of beds of yams upon which large Aboriginal populations subsisted (1975: 73).

> Aboriginal groups *did* modify the structure and distribution of floral and faunal communities. For the more generalised but highly skilled and tightly regulated Aboriginal usages, Rhys Jones' phrase 'fire stick farming' is exactly apposite. The Aborigines had indeed 'worked' for their crop of grass and their stock of herbivores. (Hallam 1975: 111)

Some of the clearest statements of the effects of Aboriginal burning regimes are found in early historical accounts. Many observers wrote of open park-like landscapes managed by fire and operating as hunting and gathering domains (Hallam 1975). The explorer Ludwig Leichhardt, while en route to Port Essington in Arnhem Land, recorded:

The natives seem to have burned the grass systematically along every watercourse, and round every waterhole, in order to have them surrounded with young grass as soon as the rain sets in. Long strips of lately burnt grass were frequently observed extending for many miles along the creeks. The banks of small isolated waterholes in the forests were equally attended to, although water had not been in either for a considerable time. (1847: 354)

Thomas Mitchell's observations were similar:

Fire is necessary to burn the grass and form those open forests in which we find the large forest-kangaroo; the native applies that fire to the grass at certain seasons; in order that a young green crop may subsequently spring up, and so attract and enable him to kill and take the kangaroo with nets. In summer, the burning of long grass also discloses vermin, birds' nests etc., on which the females and children, who chiefly burn the grass, feed. (1848: 412)

Complementary ethnohistorical studies on North American hunter-gatherers (for example, Mellars 1976) also generally substantiate the claims made for Australia. Mellars argued that by firing woodland a complex mosaic of microenvironments was produced, and a more ecologically diverse and productive environment thus created. Herbivore populations, for example, may have been increased, and as well, less energy may have been exerted in hunting with less travel, and the uncertainty factor of the chase being reduced. More complex relationships, therefore, between people and animals may have emerged, which more closely resemble those traditionally termed 'pastoralist' or 'herding' economies.

Research on fire ecology also generally supports these observations. At the same time these studies point out the subtle range of influences upon vegetation communities, of which burning is but one. However, one critic of the 'fire stick farming' model, David Horton, challenged the degree of impact Aboriginal burning may have had upon vegetation, arguing that it was generally minimal (1982). He reasoned that there is a natural potential fire regime in Australia, with its own processes of ignition. While Aboriginal firing practices provided an alternative source of ignition, Horton argued that they did not change the natural fire regime; as an economic tool, firing indeed may have been detrimental to certain species of fauna and flora. In relation to short-term processes, however, Horton's viewpoint is not necessarily incompatible with most of the above evidence. Aboriginal burning practices may have been closely tied to natural fire regimes and perturbations in ecological stages of succession. At the same time, Aboriginal intervention in these ecological processes appears to have been both profitable and productive in an economic sense, as is indicated by most of the available evidence. My main objection to Horton, however, is that he assumes a passive role for people in these ecological events, largely ignoring their economic and broader socio-cultural roles. The long-term effects of Aboriginal burning upon vegetation are discussed below.

Faunal changes, megafaunal extinctions

EVIDENCE

The problem of the extinction of the Australian Pleistocene megafauna has had a long history, but archaeological interest was revived independently by Merrillees (1968) and Jones (1968). They argued the case for human intervention in the process of the extinction of these megafauna which included kangaroos (two genera, one species) *(Sthenurus; Procoptodon; Protemnodon* sp.); wombat (several species) *(Phascolonus* spp.; *Vombatus* spp.); the family *Diprotodontidae*; one flightless bird *(Genyornis)*; and a predator-scavenger *(Thylacoleo)* (Figure 3.10). Dwarfed species included koalas *(Phascolarctos)*, wombats *(Phascolomys)*, dasyurids *(Sarcophilus laniarius)*, and three varieties of macropod (Wells 1978). A further predator *(Thylacinus)*, and scavenger *(Sarcophilus)*, became extinct during the Holocene period on the Australian mainland.

In recent years a number of archaeological sites have been excavated which throw a brighter light on the chronology of the extinct megafaunal species and the possible association between humans and the extinct fauna.

In southwestern Australia, at Mammoth Cave, were found significant quantities of megafauna, including *Sthenurus* sp., *Zygomaturus, Zaglossus* and *Thylacoleo.* The bones exhibited signs of breakage, damage, burning and 'notching', some of which has been attributed to humans (Archer et al. 1980). Further indications of human use of the cave, however, could not be demonstrated. Although charcoal was present, dating of the deposits appeared to be outside the range of radiocarbon techniques, in this case older than 37,000 BP. In the same general region, the limestone cave of Devil's Lair produced evidence of *Sthenurus* (two species), *Protemnodon, Zygomaturus,* and *Vombatus hacketti* (Balme et al. 1978). These remains were obtained from levels 30–39, which generally date to 31,000 BP and older; but as only ambiguous evidence of humans was found here, their association with the extinct species has been dismissed (Balme 1980; Dortch 1979b). In contrast, above level 30 indisputable evidence existed of the presence of humans in association with modern fauna (see also Chapter Six).

At Cloggs Cave in southeastern Victoria, a mandible of *Sthenurus orientalis* has been dated to 22,980 ± 2,000 BP (ANU 1220), while the evidence for human occupation at the site begins higher up in the deposit, around 17,720 ± 840 BP (Flood 1980: 260). Further evidence of extinct species, including *Diprotodon, Macropus titan* and *Thylacoleo* have come from the D Clay layer at Keilor in southern Victoria. While evidence for the presence of humans also exists in these deposits, their connection with the megafauna is disputable.

In the Florentine Valley of central Tasmania, Titan's Shelter has produced evidence of *Macropus titan* and *Sthenurus occidentalis* in contexts perhaps less than 20,000 years old. No evidence of humans, however, were detected in these deposits (Goede and Murray 1979). From a cave near Montagu in northwestern

Figure 3.10 Extinct late Pleistocene fauna. Silhouettes of most of the extinct animals, with the Aboriginal hunter providing the scale (based on Murray 1984: 622, Figure 27.21).

Row A: left to right: *Palorchestes azeal, Zygomaturus trilobus, Diprotodon optatum, Diprotodon minor, Euowenia grata.*

Row B: *Thylacoleo carnifex, Ramsayia curvirostris, Phascolonus gigas, Phascolomys major, Phascolomys medius, Vombatus hacketti, Phascolarctos stirtoni, Propleopus oscillans.*

Row C: *Procoptodon goliath, Procoptodon rapha, Procoptodon pusio, Sthenurus maddocki, Sthenurus brownei, Sthenurus occidentalis.*

Row D: *Sthenurus gilli, Sthenurus atlas, Sthenurus tindalei, Sthenurus pales, Sthenurus oreas, Sthenurus andersoni, Troposodon minor, Wallabia indra.*

Row E: *Protemnodon roechus, Protemnodon anak, Protemnodon brehus, Macropus ferragus, Macropus (Osphranter) birdselli, Macropus siva, Macropus titan.*

Row F: *Macropus rama, Macropus thor, Macropus piltonensis, Macropus gouldi, Macropus stirtoni, Sarcophilus laniarius, Zaglossus hacketti, Zaglossus ramsayi.*

Row G: *Progura naracoortensis, Progura gallinacea, Genyornis newtoni, Megalania prisca, Wonambi naracoortensis.*

Tasmania, a date of 10,000 BP was reported for extinct fauna (Goede and Murray 1977).

A few sites do indicate a closer association between humans and megafauna. In the Florentine Valley of central Tasmania, and close to Titan's Shelter, the cave of Beginners Luck produced evidence of *Macropus titan*. A single cuboid (bone) of the species was found together with good evidence for human occupation (stone artefacts, food remains) in a level dated to 20,650 ± 1,790 BP (GaK 7081) (Murray et al. 1980; see also Chapter Two). These deposits have also been reworked by water action. On Kangaroo Island, at the Seton rock-shelter, *Sthenurus* (3 fragments of molar) were dated to 16,110 ± 100 BP (ANU 1221) in a level signifying the presence of humans. *Sarcophilus* also appears to have been associated with the breakage patterns in the bone of this layer, but the extinct fauna does not appear to have been reworked from older deposits (Hope et al. 1977). At the site of Rocky River, also on Kangaroo Island, the bones of extinct animals have been sorted into small piles around the edge of the swamp, suggesting to the excavators that humans may have been associated. The site is thought to date to around 19,000 BP, and included the extinct *Sthenurus* sp., *Diprotodon, Protemnodon* and *Zygomaturus* (Hope et al. 1977).

At the Nombe rock-shelter in the Mount Elimbari Region of the New Guinea Highlands, two extinct macropods, *Protemnodon* sp. and *Dendrolagus* sp., together with the extinct thylacine, were found in stratum C, dated to between 16,500 ± 200 BP (ANU 2580) and 10,200 ± 120 BP (ANU 2576). The excavators also claim that these species existed in the earlier stratum D, which has an approximate basal date of 24,000 years. The presence of humans was increasingly evident at the site throughout this sequence (Gillieson and Mountain 1983: 56, 59, 60–61).

In general, the above archaeological evidence indicates that certain of the extinct species were still extant at the end of the Pleistocene, between 20,000 and 10,000 BP, at least in New Guinea and southeastern Australia. Extinction may already have taken place in southwestern Australia (see more on this below). Where the dating is strongest, it is suggested that *Sthenurus* cf *gilli* was extant on Kangaroo Island as recently as 16,000 BP, and *Protemnodon* sp. and *Dendrolagus* sp. in the New Guinea Highlands between 16,000 and 10,000 BP. The evidence for direct association between megafauna and people, however, is less clear. The strongest evidence for a temporal overlap between people and the extinct fauna is found at Nombe, in Highland New Guinea, and Seton, on Kangaroo Island. The slender evidence from Beginners Luck, in central Tasmania, lends some further support. From the above evidence, there appears to be no unambiguous example of megafauna having served as the object of human predation.

These issues have been investigated more fully recently at four main archaeological sites: Lancefield, Lake Tandou, Lime Springs and Cuddie Springs. Lancefield is a small swamp located north of Melbourne. An extensive bone bed

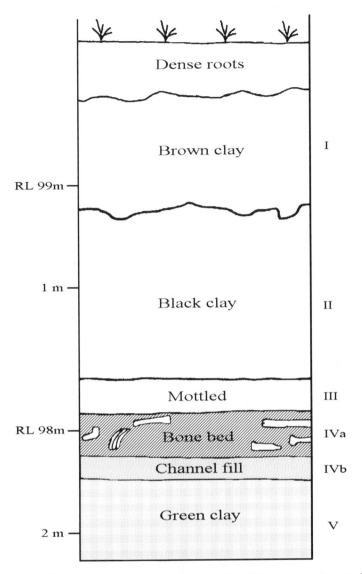

Figure 3.11 Lancefield, Victoria. Stratigraphic profile of the excavation at the site, indicating the bone-bed layer and channel fill from which the radiocarbon date was obtained (based on Gillespie et al. 1978: Figure 1).

0.2 metres in thickness, it is stratified 1.5 metres below the surface (Gillespie et al. 1978; Figure 3.11). The well preserved remains of six extinct megafaunal species were identified from the bone-bed deposits, which formed some time after 26,000 BP. Two charcoal samples were taken for purposes of dating from the infill of a narrow water channel which underlies the bone-bed layer: the results were 26,600 ± 650 BP (SUA 538) and 25,200 ± 800 BP (SUA 685). Both channel and bone bed sat upon an underlying basal green clay. 'The bones interlock as a horizontal network' and are located within an area of some 2,000 square metres (Gillespie et al. 1978: 1045). Spring-fed water appears to have controlled the local distribution of the bones, preservation of which also was assisted by constant saturation, together with the alkaline nature of the water. Palynological samples taken from the deposits indicate that during the time a treeless plain surrounded the site. Some five square metres of excavated deposit yielded around 3,000 bones, with an estimated minimum number of 72 individuals. Based upon these figures, it was estimated that the swamp as a whole contained some 10,000 individual animals.

Macropus titan comprised around 90 percent of the species sampled. The remaining frequencies were *Protemnodon anak* (7 percent), and one percent each of *Protemnodon* cf *brehus, Sthenurus occidentalis, Protemnodon* sp., cf *Genyornis* and *Dromaius* sp. (emu).

> Except for *Dromaius,* they are all extinct. They are all large species; *M. titan* is twice the mass of the living grey kangaroo *(M. giganteus)* and the smallest *(S. occidentalis)* is about the size of a modern kangaroo . . . This remarkably restricted species list, of large species only, shows that some special selective event was causing death . . . Eighty percent of the *M. titan* sample was over 7 years old, and 92 percent more than 2 years old. (Gillespie et al. 1978: 1046)

The excavators viewed this age range as representing either a drought-affected population, with few immature individuals, or the selective deaths of only mature animals from a normal population (Gillespie et al. 1978: 1046).

Around 7.5 percent of the bones indicated disease, the most common being 'lumpy jaw', which is found in modern wild animals under drought conditions. A broader range of species, including smaller species, were found in the channel fill, indicating a different process of selection from that of the bone-bed. Three explanations were offered by the researchers: recurrent droughts, or predation by *Thylacoleo* or people (Gillespie et al. 1978: 1047).

Droughts may have forced relatively large numbers of megafaunal species to sources of permanent water, where the increasingly diminishing supplies of food would have hastened the death of the animals. Cut marks on some of the bones had been attributed to *Thylacoleo.* While people, it was thought, may have driven animals into the swamp, or ambushed them there before dispatching the carcasses.

One stone artefact had been found in the bone-bed layer; a 20-centimetre-long quartzite blade, and a small 3-centimetre-square piece of similar material was detected also in the channel fill. In comparison with this sparse evidence, 191 artefacts, including geometric microliths, had been found in the overlying black clay layer, and attributable to a mid-late Holocene age. A later detailed examination of a large sample of bones with cut marks from the bone bed indicated that the *Thylacoleo carnifex* was the cause, rather than human beings (Horton and Wright 1981).

Evidence for human predation, or involvement, at Lancefield, therefore, appears to be slight and, given the verified presence of *Thylacoleo,* inconclusive. Indeed, this information served to strengthen the drought hypothesis. Also, Lancefield indicated that people and megafauna had coexisted for at least 14,000–12,000 years, or much longer if dates in excess of 40,000 years for the occupation of Australia are accepted. 'Such a prolonged coexistence calls into question the model of rapid overkill proposed by Jones . . . for Australia, a model which is analogous to that proposed by Martin . . . for the Americas' (Gillespie et al. 1978: 1047).

Horton argued further, using evidence from Lancefield and other Australian archaeological sites (1980: 94). He considered that people and megafauna had coexisted for a lengthy period of time 'before man began to have an effect on the megafauna', around 26,000 BP, as illustrated by the Lancefield evidence. Extinction took even longer, he postulated, until around 15,000 BP on the mainland, and 11,000 BP in Tasmania. Horton linked the period of extinction to the onset of the last major arid phase for southern Australia (26,000–15,000 BP), as described by Bowler (1976). Similar sentiments had been earlier expressed also by Calaby (1976). Horton, however, outlined the more difficult question of the selective process that, in his view, contributed to faunal extinctions, using the Lancefield evidence for support.

> If in fact . . . mature animals were dying in disproportionally high numbers, then this would make it very difficult for the population to sustain itself. One possible response to this situation would be for breeding to take place in younger and younger animals. This response could lead to a form of neoteny (that is, a species in which the mature animals had characteristics which would have been those of immature animals in the original species). This change is precisely what has been suggested for the post-Pleistocene 'dwarfing' in a number of species, e.g. *Macropus titan – M. giganteus,* in which the modern species is smaller in size and has simpler teeth. Species which were unable to make such a response would simply have become extinct. (Horton 1980: 94–95)

Broadly similar explanations were provided by Main.

> . . . attention is drawn to the size reduction of some Pleistocene forms which persisted and the marked sexual dimorphism in the extant large kangaroo. It is suggested that these are adaptive responses in an oscillating environment when periods favourable for recruitment to the population are short. It is inferred that the large extinct fauna were unable to evolve smaller, earlier maturing, females and hence lacked the capacity to recruit to their populations and that this led to their extinction. (1978: 169)

As Horton himself pointed out, however, apart from hypothesised problems of water balance and food supplies, the nature of the environmental stress which produced the selective processes outlined above has not been demonstrated in either his or Main's model. Horton suggested that:

... after ten thousand years, all parts of Australia had been affected by the oscillations of aridity which Bowler had found evidence for at Mungo. By 15,000 BP, only small species (which did not need free water) and those megafaunal species which had evolved smaller descendants had survived. (1980: 95)

The Tandou lunette in western New South Wales and its geomorphology and archaeology (Hope et al. 1983) are covered in more detail in Chapter Five. What concerns us here is the strong contrast which was found to exist between the evidence for the presence of humans and those of extinct animals at the site. Human occupation was apparent in levels younger than 27,000 years, and extinct species in strata older than this. For example megafaunal remains were (except for a few instances) absent from the Bootingee unit, suggesting that most of the extinct Pleistocene species had disappeared from the region prior to 27,000 years BP (Hope et al. 1983: 51–52).

Preservation does not appear to be a problem as bone was well preserved at the site in the three major units – Parker, Tandou and Bootingee. In contrast, conditions unfavourable to preservation may have contributed to the dearth of extinct fauna at the roughly contemporary Willandra Lakes sites (Hope 1978). Supporting evidence at Tandou strengthens the case that major changes in fauna had taken place during the late Pleistocene period. For example:

A size reduction in the Tasmanian devil, *Sarcophilus,* parallels the decrease in megafaunal fossils. *Sarcophilus* remains from the Tandou unit are very large in size, equivalent to the giant Pleistocene form *Sarcophilus laniarius* from elsewhere in eastern Australia, while fossils from the Bootingee unit, at least one of which was recovered *in situ* from immediately above the Bootingee-Tandou contact, are all extremely small. The apparent lack of intermediate-sized specimens of *Sarcophilus* from any known fossil locality in western New South Wales suggests that we may be dealing with geographic shifts in population of different body sizes rather than the dwarfing of a population *in situ* ... (Hope et al. 1983: 52)

Similar evidence relating to *Sarcophilus* has also been found by these excavators at the Willandra Lakes sites.

Another parallel between Tandou and Willandra concerns *Procoptodon* and *Sthenurus*. At Tandou the latter appear to come from stratigraphic contexts of the post-27,000 BP period, although problems of admixture also have not been ruled out. At Willandra most *Procoptodon* remains appear to be of Lower Mungo age, with one individual from the Mungo–Zanci interface (Hope et al. 1983: 52). The Willandra evidence, therefore, appears to be roughly synchronous with that from Tandou. Fossil evidence from other sites of the Darling region also appear to correspond. For example, extinct fauna from the northeastern end of Lake Menindee appear to come from contexts older than 18,000–26,000 BP, and this also may be the case at Lake Cawndilla and Kangaroo Lake (Hope et al. 1983: 52).

On the strength of the above evidence, the excavators concluded that in western New South Wales most megafaunal extinctions had occurred before 27,000 BP, a period of high lake levels and regionally high watertables, with some possible faunal survivals, including *Procoptodon* and *Sthenurus,* following this period (Hope et al. 1983: 52). They argued, therefore, that their evidence contradicted the earlier hypothesis of Gillespie et al. (1978), that is that extinctions were principally caused by the onset of arid conditions between 25,000 and 15,000 BP.

The dearth of evidence for the presence of humans at Tandou prior to 27,000 BP, however, leaves open the question concerning their role in the process of faunal extinction. 'Until we know the extent of human settlement in the region before this time, it is premature to speculate on the possible effects of human behaviour on the environment or fauna', Hope stated in 1983 and this is still the case, broadly speaking (Hope et al. 1983: 52).

Lime Springs is a spring-fed swamp on the Liverpool Plains of northeastern New South Wales researched by Pawl Gorecki and others (1984). This well-watered region receives reliable winter and summer rainfall; a contrast to semi-arid western New South Wales. A 7-metre-long trench was excavated in the swamp, which is 100 metres in diameter, and around 1.3 metres of archaeological deposit was unearthed. The deposit rested upon a basal horizon two metres below the present surface (unit 4). Unit 3, the earliest depositional stratigraphical unit, is composed of 1.2 metres of black sandy clays. The latter is capped in places by a shallow 0.1 metres of yellow aeolian fine sands (unit 2). Above units 2 and 3 is 0.6 metres of black sandy clays dating to the European period. A radiocarbon date of 19,300 ± 500 BP (SUA 915) was obtained from an organic-rich band (unit 3b) in the middle of unit 3.

Fragmentary bone and teeth are distributed throughout units 3 and 2, and over 36 percent of the 5,218 fragments of bone were burnt. Identification of the bone was restricted to fragments of enamel from teeth, with around 10 percent of all tooth fragments coming from extinct species. The latter included *Diprotodon, Macropus* cf *titan,* cf *Protemnodon,* cf *Procoptodon,* cf *Sthenurus.* 'There is no indication in any of these data that the representation of extinct species decreases through time – on the contrary, remains of *Diprotodon* and the others are relatively more common in the upper layers' (Gorecki et al. 1984: 118).

Flaked stone artefacts also were distributed throughout the deposits, and debitage indicates that flaking took place on site. Typologically two styles of industry were found in unit 3; for example in the lower two-thirds, flakes were generally small and undiagnostic. In contrast, in the upper third of unit 3, large horse-hoof cores and scrapers of quarried tabula tuff were found, and almost half the flakes are of tuff, compared with only ten percent in the lower deposits. (For more explanation of stone artefact styles, see Chapter Five). The excavators argued that this sequence of stone artefact styles and percentages of raw materials lends support to the stratigraphic integrity of the site, meaning it had been little disturbed. The thin capped aeolian sand (unit 2) also contained stone artefacts, and appears to represent increasing aridity, followed by a cessation of swamp sediment with groundwater remaining low until the water table was raised by European farming practices.

Lime Springs, therefore, suggests a long-term stratigraphic association between humans (stone artefacts) and megafauna.

> It is important to point out that the Liverpool Plains cannot be seen as an isolated refugium in which there was an idiosyncratic late survival of megafauna, nor do we have a site where there is simply a survival of a *Sthenurus* species (as at Clogg's Cave and Seton). Rather, the area, given its locale, can be more reasonably thought of as a core area for megafaunal distribution, and we have evidence that the broad spectrum of megafauna has survived. We suggest, moreover, that it is precisely in such stable and well-watered core areas that answers must be obtained to the question of what caused extinction. (Gorecki et al. 1984: 119)

The excavators explained the differences between the evidence from Tandou and that from Lime Springs as environmental; Tandou and wider western New South Wales being arid, with low rainfall predictability, and therefore less stable than the well-watered Liverpool Plains, where rainfall is spread evenly throughout the year. Megafaunal extinctions, they argued, would have been hastened in the more arid region.

> ... there is no reason to think that extinctions were synchronous over Australia ... and given the survival of the megafauna to a date more recent than 19,300 BP at Lime Springs, we can say with confidence that continent-wide extinctions were not caused by initial human impact. Explanations, whether involving human or climatic causes, will need to be more complex than has previously been supposed. (Gorecki et al. 1984: 119)

At Cuddie Springs there is the chance of the clearest association between people and megafauna so far discovered. Cuddie Springs today is a shallow ephemeral lake located in semi-arid northwestern New South Wales (Figure 3.12). Excavation took place across the clay pan on the lake floor, and reached a depth of three metres or so. The sediments are of aeolian origin and consist of lake muds, silts and clays, and fossil bone was found throughout the stratigraphic sequence. The minimum age of the site has been estimated at about 30,000 BP, based upon a radiocarbon date of 29,570 ± 280 BP (Beta 46171), and much of the deposit is beyond radiocarbon dating. Stone artefacts and increased quantities of charcoal appear after 30,000 BP, in clear association with megafaunal remains, and have a continuous presence until about 19,000 BP.

Pollen is well preserved and indicates that shrubland, with scattered *Acacia* and *Casuarina,* was replaced by more open vegetation with a reduction in taxa by 19,000 BP as the glacial maximum drew near. During this time the site changed from a freshwater lake to a more ephemeral water source situated within the arid zone, indicating an expansion of Australia's arid core by at least 150

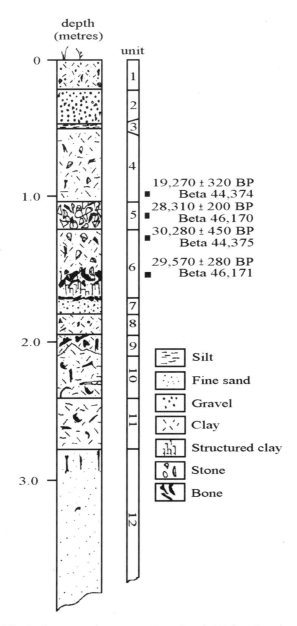

Figure 3.12 Cuddie Springs, northwestern New South Wales. Stratigraphic section of the excavation, indicating position of the remains of extinct fauna, with radiocarbon dates (based on Furby et al. 1993: 205, Figure 2).

kilometres. Much of the bone is very fragmented, but indicates a diverse assemblage of mammals, birds and reptiles, and the following megafauna: *Diprotodon, Sthenurus, Protemnodon* and *Megalia*. The well-preserved pollen and charcoal, together with numbers of intact small bones, argue against the material having been redeposited naturally in the lake sediments. These issues now require further investigation. Hypotheses currently being investigated are that large animals became bogged in the marshy landscape and either perished naturally or were preyed upon by people.

The artefacts allow these scenarios to be expanded even further. At a depth of 1.0–1.2 metres a concentration of artefacts, bone, charcoal and burnt wood together with horse-hoof cores occurs. A wide range of artefacts is present, including flakes, cores and scrapers, mainly of silcrete. Use of other raw materials, such as quartzite and chert, changes with depth. Some of the stone artefacts bear evidence of animal tissue, red blood cells and mammalian hair, suggestive of butchering; woodworking is also indicated. Grindstone fragments here have flat polished surfaces and evidence of starch grain residues The latter may indicate the use of grass seeds, *Acacia* seeds or tubers, such as *Typha* spp., but as yet these issues remain unresolved. The polish on these artefacts resembles that of Holocene grindstones, and this association is to be investigated further. In all, the evidence recorded suggests a range of activities rather than a special purpose site. Included also are hardened clay balls, close to hearths and perhaps serving the purpose of oven 'stones'; ochre and a weathered conical stone (suggesting to the excavators a connection with ritual) (Dodson et al. 1993; Furby et al. 1993). To what extent some of these artefacts indicate admixture with more recent material also remains a problem.

Again, at all the above four sites, Lancefield, Lake Tandou, Lime Springs and Cuddie Springs, several key issues remain largely unresolved. These include the chronological and stratigraphic integrity of the deposits; this is a perennial problem in large open sites, of vast time depth and considerable antiquity. Unresolved also is the all-important question of the nature of the association between the extinct fauna and people, which is dependent to a large extent upon the first issue.

EXPLANATIONS

Interpretations of this information concerning the demise of the megafauna largely fall under three broad categories: that is to say, causality has been attributed to climate, human predation, and the alteration of the environment through the use of fire.

Horton, as we have seen, attributed the faunal extinctions and dwarfing to the period of major aridity between 25,000 and 15,000 BP (1980). This interpretation, however, has been challenged by Hope, Dare-Edwards and McIntyre, who argued that the evidence from Lake Tandou indicated that the extinctions had already taken place in western New South Wales by 27,000 BP, that is, during a less stressful time of high lake levels (1983). In reply, Horton,

Wright, Gorecki and Stern considered that the extinctions were not synchronous throughout the continent, nor unicausal, basing their argument upon new evidence derived from northeastern New South Wales (Gorecki et al. 1984). Indeed, if the present archaeological evidence is accepted as indicating the timing of the extinctions, then these events appear to have taken place in southwestern Australia by 30,000 BP, by 27,000 BP in arid western New South Wales, and more recently, perhaps between 20,000 and 10,000 BP, in southeastern Australia, in areas of more reliable rainfall.

If a broader perspective is taken, then Calaby's suggestion of twenty-five years ago may well provide the overriding explanation. Calaby hypothesised that the animals may not have been capable of adapting to the post-Pleistocene changes, having become well adapted to the preceding environment, which was a relatively stable one (1976). That would mean that during the late and terminal Pleistocene, we may be observing the tail-end of a long-term ecological process involving climate, environment and biological adaptation.

While human predation has long been considered a central or related factor in producing the faunal extinctions, the archaeological record has provided little support of this. As we have seen, archaeological sites indicating a chronological association between people and megafauna are few, and the data to explain the relationship between people and the animals is slight and ambiguous. A clear demonstration of human predation of the fauna has yet to be found; and nowhere is evidence of extinct animals and the presence of humans found in any quantity.

The evidence we have, therefore, is weighted heavily against theories favouring significant human impact upon the extinct Pleistocene fauna such as proposed by Jones (1968), and this is reinforced by the complete absence of 'kill sites', such as are found on other continents, for example in North America. Several explanations have been offered for the striking dearth of evidence of human predation. Bowdler has suggested that 'big game' hunting was a more recent Australian strategy, and that only medium-to-small animals were hunted during the Pleistocene (1977). More recently reported evidence from Pleistocene sites such as Devil's Lair, however, where the larger extant macropods appear to have been hunted, counters this viewpoint. White and O'Connell point to bias in the archaeological record (1982: 92). They suggest that sites where the larger extinct animals were butchered have yet to be found. Notwithstanding this suggestion, the argument would not necessarily apply to the smaller-sized of the extinct animals (including immature individuals), whose size range overlaps with the modern fauna found in Pleistocene archaeological sites.

The implications of the archaeological evidence, therefore, are that in parts of Australia, people and some surviving megafaunal species co-existed for many thousands of years. A period of between 20,000 and 30,000 years (and longer, if more recent dates are accepted) is indicated in parts of southeastern Australia. While the apparent paucity of evidence for human predation of the extinct fauna can have a variety of explanations, one implication is that the members of the surviving species already may have been thin on the ground. This evidence would also fit a model of Pleistocene human population as small in size and density, with transient economies, as has been proposed (see Chapter Nine). Presumably the latter subsistence-settlement pattern would have been ecologically of low impact and therefore have produced fewer immediate changes to flora and fauna.

The artificial transformation of the natural distribution of vegetation by fire has been viewed by some as the main cause of faunal extinctions. Merrilees (1968) considered the long-term effects of such an ecological process, whereas Jones (1973), on the other hand, conceived of the process as principally occurring a short time before 30,000 BP. The complex issue of the long-term effects of fire have been taken up by Horton (1982), who argued, as discussed earlier in this chapter, that the role of humans was minimal. He pointed out discrepancies of pollen sequences from key Australian palynological sites, such as Lake George, and Lashmar's Lagoon in southeastern Australia, and Lynch's Crater on the Cape York Peninsula (Singh, Kershaw and Clark 1981). For example, increased rates of deposition of charcoal through time were interpreted, in some instances, as due to both the presence and the absence of humans and their burning practices. Horton concluded that climate was the main cause of change in both fire regimes and vegetation complexes through time. Clark also was in agreement, and pointed out the problems in scale of attempting to compare relatively short-term observations of burning with the long-term pollen record, stating that 'The complex interaction and interdependence of fire, climate, soils and vegetation, make it extremely difficult to distinguish effects of Aboriginal burning' (1983: 35). The most recent explanation, by Flannery, presents a more sophisticated combination model of 'overkill' plus habitat modification by firing (Flannery 1990; see also accompanying comments by others). But as many of these commentators also point out, the archaeological data do not necessarily fit Flannery's scenario, and the difficulty still remains: how to distinguish between the effects of climate and those of people upon vegetation and fire regimes of the past.

If the chronology of the archaeological evidence is accepted, then at present it appears as if faunal extinctions, together with dwarfing of species, took place differentially across the Australian continent. These processes appear to have occurred by 30,000 BP and 27,000 BP in southwestern Australia and western New South Wales respectively (but see also the discussion of Cuddie Springs, above). In areas of more reliable rainfall, such as New Guinea and southeastern Australia (including Kangaroo Island, northwestern New South Wales and perhaps southern Victoria and Tasmania), remnant extinct species may have survived until more recently, that is, between 20,000 and 10,000 BP.

The causes behind these events are complex and open to dispute. Although climatic factors are undoubtedly of prime importance, the environmental variables involved are not clearly defined. For example, while the arid climates of between 25,000 and 15,000 BP have been identified as likely times of great stress, this explanation does not fit the full sequence of events for extinctions also may have occurred prior to the latter arid phase in some regions. There is little evidence for direct human predation of extinct fauna. Long-term co-existence of humans and extinct fauna is apparent, for at least some 10,000 to 30,000 years. Human fire regimes, however, may have had both long- and short-term effects on vegetation and therefore on fauna. Until stronger evidence is produced for the direct or indirect involvement of humans in the extinction and diminution of fauna, I suggest the human role would appear to be only one of many involved in the final stages of the process during the late and terminal Pleistocene.

Analogous faunal extinctions on other continents and islands have also been the subject of wide debate and are seen as the product of a variety of causes, including climate and, in some cases, people (Martin and Klein 1984; see also Flannery 1990, and comments: 45–67; Schrire 1980). At any rate, given the present archaeological evidence from the Pleistocene, there seems no good reason to suggest that the colonisation of Greater Australia by people produced an immediate and long-term destabilisation of ecological conditions, seriously affecting both plants and animals, as suggested by some. More subtle effects, however, upon a continent unused to human beings and their firing practices, especially in the long term, cannot be ruled out.

The following four chapters examine the Australian archaeological data regionally in order to provide as detailed a picture as possible of both Pleistocene and Holocene Australia and its inhabitants.

CHAPTER 4

THE TROPICAL NORTH

As we have already seen, the tropical north of Greater Australia forms, in many ways, an extension of the island world of Southeast Asia, from where the original Aboriginal settlers came. These similarities, however, must also be tempered by the more arid conditions of continental Australia along its tropical northern fringe. Discussed here in some detail are the archaeology and prehistory of the Pleistocene and Holocene periods of the region, which includes Papua New Guinea, the Bismarck Archipelago, tropical northern Australia and sub-tropical southeastern Queensland.

PLEISTOCENE SETTLEMENT

Palaeoenvironment

In northern Australia the climate of the Pleistocene was generally dry, with low precipitation and temperatures below those of today. Palaeoenvironmental information, obtained mainly from pollen studies, has come largely from four main lake sites: Lynch's Crater and Strenekoff's Crater on the Atherton Tableland in north Queensland (Kershaw 1973, 1986; Kershaw et al. 1991), Lake Carpentaria, which once filled the present Gulf of Carpentaria (Torgensen et al. 1988; McCulloch et al. 1989), and Lake Woods (Jones and Bowler 1980; Bowler 1986).

Conditions drier than those of today are reflected in the distribution and type of vegetation. Around the shores of Lake Carpentaria, for example, and the Atherton Tableland was open savanna. While rainforest appears to have been reduced in area, large stretches of wetlands and grasslands surrounded the Gulf of Carpentaria.

Drier conditions existed from about 80,000 years ago, and at around 38,000 years BP there is the suggestion of even drier climate on the Atherton Tableland, with a shift in vegetation from vineforest (araucarian) to savanna woodland, and a lowering of lake levels. Lake levels were also lower in Lake Carpentaria following this period. As an indication of regional variation in climate, however, levels at Lake Woods were much higher than today's. Very dry conditions existed about 25,000 years ago, and these were generally maintained by the marked continentality, and thus lower precipitation, of northeastern Australia. On the Atherton Tableland the driest phase appears to have been between 15,000 and 11,000 years ago, while in Lake Carpentaria there is an indication that precipitation was beginning to increase at this time (Hiscock and Kershaw 1992).

From Papua New Guinea, geomorphological evidence indicates that around 2,000 square kilometres were glaciated during the maximum phase, when compared with 8 square kilometres today (Mt Carstensz, Irian Jaya). Pollen studies show that much of the highland region was clothed in a herbfield vegetation (Hope and Hope 1976). By inference, average temperatures at the time were at least 6 degrees centigrade below those of the present. A number of sources of evidence, including pollen sequences from Sirunki (Enga district), Mount Wilhelm (Chimbu district) and other sites, indicate that glacial retreat had begun by about 15,000–14,000 years ago, and was largely completed by around 9,000 years. Forests, including rainforest, began to colonise highland areas during this period (Hope and Hope 1976; Swadling and Hope 1992; Haberle 1993).

Late Pleistocene: c. 40,000–15,000 BP

Northern Greater Australia (New Guinea, New Ireland, New Britain and the Solomons)

The very earliest signs of the presence of people in this region come from the Huon Terraces in northeastern New Guinea (see also Chapter Three). Further evidence, more recent in time, is found in other parts of the New Guinea Highlands and offshore islands, like New Ireland and New Britain, and even further afield on the Solomon Islands (Figure 4.1; see also Figure 3.5, p. 85).

In the New Guinea Highlands are two important Pleistocene sites, Kosipe and Nombe. Kosipe is an open site featuring a scatter of artefacts and carbon stratified within datable layers of volcanic ash. It has a maximum age of around 26,000 BP, and it has been suggested that the site may have been visited seasonally for collection of pandanus from a nearby swamp (White et al. 1970; White and O'Connell 1982: 56). Nombe, an extensive limestone rock-shelter, is located in the Mount Elimbari region of the highland Simbu (Chimbu) Province. A preliminary report on the geomorphology and archaeology of the site indicates that its initial use began after about 25,000 BP (Gillieson and Mountain 1983). Two Pleistocene units (strata C and D) were distinguished from the four occupation units of the deposit, which extends to a depth of 2 metres. Evidence for human activity is most ephemeral in the earliest unit, which is dated to between c. 25,000 and 16,000 BP, and increases in the succeeding phase from between c. 16,000 and 10,000 BP. Most conspicuous human presence, however, is in the Holocene unit (stratum B), which begins around 10,000 BP. This phase has the largest number of animal species and highest densities of bone. These trends were measured by the quantity of burnt and charred animal bone, stone artefacts and rate of sedimentation.

In the Pleistocene strata there is clear evidence of non-human predators such as the now-extinct thylacine, *Thylacinus cynocephalus*, the New Guinean marsupial cat, *Dasyurus albopunctatus*, and predatory birds. There is also contemporary evidence here of extinct macropodids, *Protemnodon* sp. and *Dendrolagus* sp.; and an increase in the smaller animals in these Pleistocene levels, although the medium-to-small body-size groups still predominate. The widest range of species also occurs between about 16,000 and 10,000 BP. This trend is not easy to interpret and may indicate either environmental change or increasing human predation, or both of these factors. Other evidence of increased human presence during this phase (C) includes burnt bone, burnt soil and pieces of charcoal and ochre.

In summary, at Nombe there is evidence of increasing use of the site by humans throughout the Pleistocene after about 25,000 BP. At this time there is evidence for hunting, mainly of medium-to-small animals and use of the site accelerates from the start of the Holocene period. Mary Jane Mountain's recent analyses indicate more complex changes in fauna through time, including a reduction in the numbers of large animals between 25,000 and 10,000 BP (Mountain 1993). The problem still remains, however, of distinguishing between the amelioration of climate, with increasing forestation culminating in the early Holocene, and increasing human presence in the area. The latter would include both use of the site and local resources, and a trend towards deforestation through increased firing practices, related first to hunting and later to agriculture. The clearing of forests would be a further trend associated with more farming.

New Ireland is one of a group of islands off the northeastern coast of New Guinea which was separated by deep sea channels from the New Guinea mainland during the Pleistocene, although the distances were not great (Figure 4.1). The cave site, Matenkupkum, which is one of a series of uplifted coral limestone caverns, was initially inhabited by people from around 32,500 ± 800 BP (ANU 5065) (Allen et al. 1988), and a range of radiocarbon dates supports this chronology (Figure 4.2). Today the cave is located only 50 metres from the littoral at an elevation of 15 metres, but the steeply sloping shoreline in front of the cave indicates that throughout the Pleistocene the sea may never have been very far away.

Around 1.4 metres of cultural deposit rests upon sterile beach sand and bedrock. The basal cultural layer is described as 'a dense marine shell midden' containing over 200 flaked stone artefacts, together with terrestrial animal bones

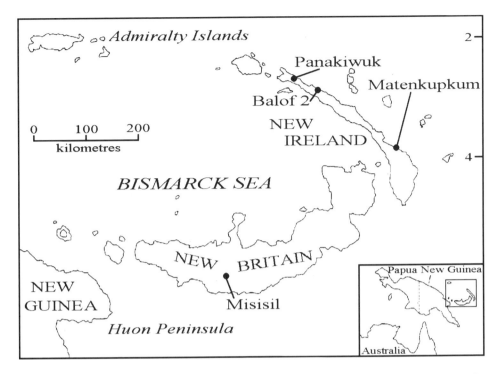

Figure 4.1 Location of late Pleistocene and early Holocene sites on New Britain and New Ireland (based on Allen et al. 1988: 707, Figure 1).

(Allen et al. 1988: 708). The earliest shell midden was clearly distinguishable from the underlying beach sand levels and all the shell (which was also used for radiocarbon dating) was of a single species of gastropod (*Turbo argyrostoma*). The overall impression is 'of intermittent occupation and gradual accumulation of these lowest deposits' (Allen et al. 1988: 708). The site received little use during the period of maximum glaciation, and was most intensively inhabited during the terminal Pleistocene, from around 12,000 BP. During the glacial maximum, however, occupation appears to have taken place nearby at the coastal cave of Matenbek, some 70 metres away, where shellfish, fish, as well as obsidian, are present. The nearest source of obsidian was possibly New Britain, some 350 kilometres away (Allen et al. 1989; Enright and Gosden 1992: 173–174).

East of New Ireland, and at the northern end of the Solomon chain of islands, is located the island of Buku. Here, the site of Kilu Cave was first inhabited about 28,740 ± 280 years ago (Wickler and Spriggs 1988). As sea levels were low at the time, it is considered that no great sea voyages were needed to settle the far-flung islands of this group. What this indicates, however, is the continuing use of islands all along the northern fringe of the continent of Greater Australia – a practice begun at least 40,000 years ago, and this includes the colonisation of Greater Australia itself. Spriggs (1993) also speculated on the possibility that

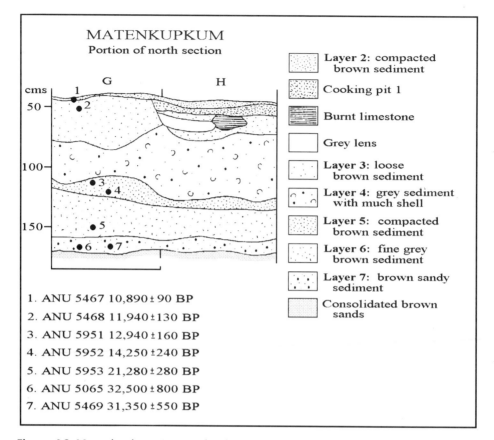

MATENKUPKUM
Portion of north section

Layer 2: compacted brown sediment
Cooking pit 1
Burnt limestone
Grey lens
Layer 3: loose brown sediment
Layer 4: grey sediment with much shell
Layer 5: compacted brown sediment
Layer 6: fine grey brown sediment
Layer 7: brown sandy sediment
Consolidated brown sands

1. ANU 5467 10,890 ± 90 BP
2. ANU 5468 11,940 ± 130 BP
3. ANU 5951 12,940 ± 160 BP
4. ANU 5952 14,250 ± 240 BP
5. ANU 5953 21,280 ± 280 BP
6. ANU 5065 32,500 ± 800 BP
7. ANU 5469 31,350 ± 550 BP

Figure 4.2 Matenkupkum, New Ireland. Stratigraphic section of squares G and H of the site (based on Allen et al. 1988: 708, Figure 2).

agriculture or cultivation may have been practised on these islands in Pleistocene times. The evidence, although slight, is of starch-full taro (*Colocasia esculenta*) residues on artefacts from Kilu Cave dating from the time of earliest settlement. A second example is of *Canarium* almond, which appears in the Bismarcks and Solomons (including Kilu Cave), and Pamwak on Manus Island during the terminal Pleistocene, and may have been introduced from New Guinea (Fredericksen et al. 1993).

Northern Australia
The East Alligator River region of Arnhem Land today is a rich, coastal tropical belt of lush swamplands, forests and savannas. In the period between about 25,000 and 18,000 BP, however, this region was becoming increasingly dry and was located some 400 kilometres from the sea. Pleistocene occupation has been found at four sandstone rock-shelters. Malangangerr was sparsely inhabited between 22,900 ± 100 BP and 18,000 ± 400 BP, and Nawamoyn from 21,450 ± 380 BP (Schrire 1982). No upper date, however, has been determined for the

termination of this Pleistocene phase at Nawamoyn. Stone artefacts comprised the main finds, the most important discovery being of a number of edge-ground axes from dated contexts of around 20,000 BP (White 1967; see further below). Faunal remains were not preserved here. There is also a hiatus in occupation at both sites between the Pleistocene levels and later Holocene material. A third site, Malakunanja, was inhabited prior to 18,040 ± 300 BP, but apparently not intensively (Kamminga and Allen 1973: 45–52; see Chapter Three). Here too faunal remains are absent, with stone artefacts the main cultural markers.

Seventy kilometres to the south of these sites in Deaf Adder Gorge, the Lindner site (Nauwalabila I) is a deeply stratified rock-shelter with almost three metres of cultural deposit. The earliest date obtained so far is that of 19,975 ± 365 BP, which is from a level located less than two metres below the surface of the site. Stone artefacts were found even within the rubble layer at the very base of the excavations. This layer rests upon large rocks which may have formed an ancient apron at the edge of the escarpment. Given these stratigraphic details therefore, the initial occupation of the site is thought to be considerably earlier. The frequency of deposition of stone artefacts throughout the site indicate that Nauwalabila I was continuously, rather than intensively, occupied. Faunal evidence is not preserved at this site either. Unlike both Malangangerr and Nawamoyn, however, Nauwalabila I was occupied throughout the most arid phase of the Pleistocene, between about 18,000 and 15,000 BP (Kamminga and Allen 1973; Jones and Johnson 1985b: 165–227). A number of grindstones also were found at both Malakunanja and Nauwalabila I and they have been dated to c. 18,000 BP. The processing of plant foods and use of ochre is indicated from these examples, but this form of equipment is not considered now to be synonymous with millstones, which are used for processing grass seeds (see more on stone tools in Chapter Five).

In Cape York, sites of Pleistocene age are continually being discovered. For example, apart from Ngarrabullgan (discussed in Chapter Three), Sandy Creek 1 was first inhabited prior to 31,900 ± 690 BP (Morwood 1989) as was Mushroom Rock West (Morwood and Hobbs 1995); and Yam Creek, with a non-basal date of 17,000 BP, may be as old (Morwood 1993: 175). Fern Cave also has a sub-basal date of 26,010 ± 410 BP (Beta 30403) (David 1991) and appears to have been relatively more intensively utilised during the glacial maximum (Lamb 1993). A limestone cave near Chillagoe, Walkunder Arch, was occupied from before about 18,000 BP (Campbell 1982). All these Pleistocene sites were sparsely utilised, indicating intermittent habitation. Regular, systematic use of Sandy Creek 1, for example, only begins in the terminal Pleistocene, after about 13,000 years ago (Morwood 1993: 176).

Parts of more elevated regions, such as those of the Great Dividing Range in eastern Australia, also were occupied at this time. Kenniff Cave, which is located in the central Queensland highlands at an altitude of 701 metres, was inhabited first prior to 18,800 ± 480 BP (Mulvaney and Joyce 1965). This was the first

Australian site to be firmly dated to the Pleistocene period. Ephemeral Pleistocene occupation is indicated by the lithic assemblages and sediments and by comparison with the deeper Holocene deposits of the site. The cave appears to have been inhabited more intensively during the Holocene and, while faunal remains have not been preserved, pellets of ochre are found throughout the deposit.

Northwestern and coastal central Western Australia

Recently excavated rock-shelters in this very broad region bear evidence of Pleistocene coastal occupation. Koolan Island Shelter 2 (O'Connor 1989) is a large rock-shelter on the coastal west Kimberley, and today, the site is situated on an island only about one kilometre from the mainland. The initial occupation of the shelter appears to have been prior to 27,300 ± 1,100 BP, at a time when mangrove-dwelling bivalves (*Geloina coaxans*) were in close proximity to the site. After about 24,600 BP, however, the site appears to have been abandoned, and not reoccupied until the start of the Holocene when seas rose and the region began to form part of the Buccaneer Archipelago (see Chapter Four). The rock-shelters Widgingarri 1 and 2 were occupied from about 28,000 BP, and at the time were located some 100 kilometres from the coast. Evidence of baler shell (*Melo* sp.), however, indicates a coastal connection, perhaps even exchange. These sites were also abandoned about 18,500 BP, during the height of the glacial maximum.

The limestone rock-shelter, Mandu Mandu Creek (Morse 1988, 1993), also produced evidence of Pleistocene coastal exploitation. Today, this small shelter is located on the tip of a narrow peninsula, North-West Cape, on the coast of central Western Australia. This projection of the Australian continent is nearest to the edge of the continental shelf, and at the time the site was initially inhabited it was situated some 4–5 kilometres from the coast. The rock-shelter is presently located about one kilometre from the seashore.

An upper Holocene unit and a lower Pleistocene unit were detected. More recent excavations at the site have resulted in a revised time for first occupation as at around 32,000 years ago, based upon the dating of baler shell samples (Morse 1993). (The original basal date of 25,200 ± 250 BP (SUA 2354) had come from a depth of around 80 cm, and located immediately above basal rock.) A date of 19,590 ± 440 BP (SUA 2614) was obtained close to the top of the Pleistocene unit, and Pleistocene occupation of the site was indicated by small quantities of shell and bone, together with stone artefacts, including one horse-hoof core. No charcoal was detected. While preservation of material presents some problems, a broad range of resources appear to have been exploited. These comprised fish, reef-dwelling shellfish, crab, together with terrestrial fauna, which included medium-sized mammals (for example, rock wallaby, *Petrogale*) and large mammals (red kangaroo, *Megaleia rufa*; or Euro, *Macropus robustus*). A wider variety of species was present in the late Holocene levels of the site. There is also evidence of shell 'beads' (*Conus* sp.) from the earliest levels, and ochres which may have been transported some 300 kilometres to the northeast from the Hamersley Plateau or even further. Mandu Mandu Creek was most intensively occupied after about 22,000 BP and abandoned towards the peak of glacial aridity, c. 19,000 BP. During this most intensive phase of occupation it may have been part of a coastal refuge area (Morse 1993: 163). The site was not reoccupied, however, until the late Holocene. Mandu Mandu, the Widgingarri sites and Koolan Island Shelter 2, therefore, may have been abandoned as the sea fell to its lowermost levels, and the climate was coldest and driest, around the time of the glacial maximum, effectively stranding the shelters inland.

A second rock-shelter, Pilgonaman Creek, is situated near Mandu Mandu and also may have been occupied beginning roughly at the same time. Pilgonaman and a third rock-shelter in the same region, Yardie Well, were both somewhat ephemerally inhabited throughout the Holocene. All three sites were most intensively utilised in the late Holocene (Morse 1993).

The Monte Bello Islands are now situated some 120 kilometres from the Pilbara coast. On Campbell Island, the limestone Noala Cave was inhabited from about 27,000 years ago, when it was located close to the Pleistocene coastline of the mainland. The site indicates the exploitation of marine and terrestrial resources, including shellfish and macropods. Following the Holocene rise in sea levels about 8,000 years ago, Noala and two nearby sites (Haynes and Morgan's Caves) were occupied quite intensively. Mangrove-dwelling shellfish, fish and terrestrial game were utilised at this time. All the sites were abandoned after about 7,500 years ago, and by the mid-Holocene the islands were located some 50 kilometres from the mainland and no longer inhabited (Veth forthcoming; Flood 1995: 101).

The Ord River Valley is located in the East Kimberley region of northwestern Australia. A local quartzite rock-shelter, Miriwun, was shown to have been utilised during the Pleistocene from about 17,980 +1,370/ −1,170 BP (Dortch 1977: 108–113). Judging from the depth of sediments displayed in section drawings of the site, the Pleistocene occupation layers appear not to be as extensive as more recent Holocene levels. A preliminary assessment of the fauna from the site indicates that a broad range of species is to be found in both Pleistocene and Holocene levels. 'These include terrestrial animals such as wallabies, possums, bandicoots, lizards and rodents and a number of lacustrine and riverine forms including molluscs, reptiles, catfish and goose eggs' (Dortch 1977: 111). Dortch suggests that there is continuity in the presence of fauna throughout the site. A detailed faunal analysis now is required to substantiate these impressions. Taphonomic studies may still help to distinguish between the human and non-human contribution to the faunal assemblage.

SOUTHEASTERN QUEENSLAND

On the west coast of North Stradbroke Island, in sub-tropical southeastern Queensland, is the open site of Wallen Wallen Creek. This unique site appears to have had continuous occupation from before 20,560 ± 250 BP to the present day (Neal and Stock 1986), the lowest date obtained from a hearth. The archaeological site itself is stratified within a well-vegetated dune (termed relict parabolic) close to an extensive freshwater swamp. Stone artefacts occur throughout the 2.5 metres of archaeological deposit, but high quality stone materials only are found in the Pleistocene levels. Fourteen radiocarbon dates have been obtained, and there is strong agreement between the dates from the original test excavation and the one square metre of deposit from subsequent excavation.

Terminal Pleistocene: c. 15,000–10,000 BP

Northern Greater Australia (New Guinea, New Ireland, New Britain)
Terminal Pleistocene sites in highland New Guinea include the open sites of Wanlek (Bulmer 1977) and NFX (Watson and Cole 1977) and three rock-shelters, Kiowa and Yuku (older than 12,000 BP) (Bulmer 1975) and Kafiavana (White 1972). The pattern observed here may indicate increasingly intensive use of highland regions as climate improved during the terminal Pleistocene. It has also been suggested that the rising treeline caused a contraction in grasslands (environments considered important for hunting), thus producing considerable economic stress during this period (Hope and Hope 1976). Given the magnitude of climatic changes throughout the Pleistocene in the region, the alternative idea of a uniform Pleistocene occupation (White and O'Connell 1982: 59; also Haberle 1993) would be difficult to sustain.

On New Ireland, four cave sites were occupied during the terminal Pleistocene (Allen et al. 1988, 1989). Apart from Matenkupkum (which was used more intensively at this time) and Matenbek (see above), Balof 2 was inhabited from about 14,240 ± 400 BP (ANU 4848) until around 10,000 BP. The lower date comes from a hearth at the base of the 1.8 metres of cultural layers which rest upon sterile clay. Occupation appears to have been episodic, but with quantities of marine shell, stone artefacts and animal bones. The site is now located about one kilometre from the coast.

A fourth cave, Panakiwuk, was initially occupied around 15,140 ± 160 BP (RIDDL 531). The cultural deposit is 1.6 metres in depth, resting upon sterile clay, and occupation appears to have been ephemeral, represented by stone artefacts and animal bones. The mention of large quantities of small rat bones by the excavators also may indicate the presence of predators other than humans. The site was used more systematically around the early Holocene and abandoned around 8,000 BP, until it was reinhabited 2,000 years ago.

Both Balof and Panakiwuk are situated away from the coast and within rainforest and, together with Matenkupkum and Matenbek, suggest a change in the pattern of settlement and resource use at this time. A more extensive use of the island is indicated; the earlier, largely coastal use changing to more intensive use of the coast together with parts of the rainforest. There is also evidence that resources were being transported to the island – obsidian and cuscus, an animal not found in earlier deposits. There appears, therefore, to have been a change in strategy; rather than people moving to resources, as before the glacial maximum, resources were moved to people (Enright and Gosden 1992: 173–175). On the nearby island of New Britain, the Missisil Cave was also first inhabited at this time from about 11,400 ± 1,200 BP (Specht et al. 1983).

Pleistocene rock art

The dating of rock art remains a difficult and controversial issue, and only a few securely dated examples exist of Pleistocene rock art from within a far greater number of possibilities. Here we consider the main examples, not only of the north but throughout Greater Australia, as these are of more than regional interest; and also the problems involved with dating of other cases. I have largely followed Andrée Rosenfeld's (1993) recent review of the topic (see also Layton 1992).

The dating of rock art (also known as petroglyphs) has been a major preoccupation, and early successful attempts include those of Mulvaney (1975: 185) at Ingaladdi, the Mount Cameron West site in Tasmania (1975: 170), and the Early Man site in north Queensland. Lesley Maynard suggested that Australian rock art may be divided into two major phases – an earlier (presumably Pleistocene) homogeneous phase of rock engravings, and a later (presumably Holocene) phase, including the rich range of figurative (or representational) art (1977, 1979; see also Edwards 1971). Maynard termed the earlier petroglyphs the 'Panaramitee' style or tradition, and she considered it to have an Australia-wide distribution. This tradition was composed predominantly of geometric, non-figurative motifs. Tasmanian rock art was thought to be associated with the earlier phase and preserved, to some extent, in isolation on the island. These general issues have served, among others, as the basis for recent rock art studies. One such study by Franklin (1991), for example, of the Panaramitee style, essentially confirms Maynard's general model of a geographically dispersed but relatively homogeneous rock art tradition. Franklin also was able to distinguish variation within this broad style.

The strongest evidence of dated rock art comes from the terminal Pleistocene –early Holocene period. Radiocarbon dating of deposits immediately overlying deeply weathered engravings at the Early Man rock-shelter in North Queensland, studied by Percy Trezise, produced a date of approximately 13,000 BP (Rosenfeld 1981). At Eight-Mile Creek, Sturts Meadows, in arid western New South Wales, engravings of roughly similar age have been examined. Radiocarbon (AMS) dating of carbonate concretion overlying the 'desert varnish' which covers the engravings has produced dates older than 10,000 BP (Dragovich 1986). In northeast Queensland, Morwood has also recently dated material overlying engravings at the site named Mickey Springs 34 to the start of the Holocene (Morwood 1992). As well, from Gum Tree Valley on the Burrup Peninsula, near Dampier in Western Australia, similar claims have recently been made by Lorblanchet (1992).

Other examples, which are covered below, are not as conclusive as the above, which, as I have observed, were not free of problems either. Dating of art pigments themselves has also been attempted with varying success. Radiocarbon (AMS) dating of what is believed to be blood haemoglobin from Judd's Cavern in southwestern Tasmania and Laurie Creek in the Northern Territory have produced dates of around 10,000–9,000 BP and 20,000–23,000 BP respectively (Loy et al. 1990). Hand stencils were dated at the Tasmanian site and an 'ochreous encrustation' at Laurie Creek.

Finger markings drawn across the soft rock surface of limestone caves on the southern coast of Australia, also have been assigned a Pleistocene antiquity. Of these, the most authenticated is Koonalda Cave in South Australia (Wright 1971; see also Chapter Six). The markings are partially covered by rockfall, but they have only been dated relatively in relation to the time the site was utilised, between 22,000 and 15,000 BP. At Koongine Cave near the South Australia–Victoria border, occupation dates to two relatively short episodes, about 10,000–9,000 BP and post-700 BP, and the markings on the cave wall might be related to one or both of these periods. Interpretations of this evidence, however, vary considerably (Frankel 1986, 1990; Bednarik 1984). At nearby Malangine Cave, markings appear to be older than about 5,500 BP (Bednarik 1984).

The dating of patina or 'skins' that have formed over engravings presents a potentially important direction in rock art studies but is not a straightforward matter. Radiocarbon (AMS) dates have been obtained in this way by Watchman from sites in the Kakadu National Park of the Northern Territory, and have produced dates of 8,800 BP (Watchman 1991). Problems with the technique, however, have not yet been overcome. Difficulties also exist with the cation-ratio dating method which has been applied to engravings in the Olary district of South Australia (Krinsley et al. 1990). A range of dates stretching from the late Holocene back to about 31,000 BP have been obtained in this way and have been extended also to other arid-zone engraving sites, even though problems with the methods remain. Apart from these examples, recent dating of oxalate skins from a rock-shelter near Laura, similar to those covering haematite traces on the nearby rock wall, have been dated to about 26,000 BP, and therefore may date the 'painting' (Watchman 1992; see also Morwood and Hobbs 1995).

George Chaloupka's work on the paintings of west Arnhem Land is perhaps the key example of an attempt to date the art by its content or iconography. Styles of art were distinguished on the basis of their faunal content: a recent X-ray style associated with wetland and estuarine fauna, varied intermediate styles, and an earlier style, termed 'Dynamic', linked to terrestrial and freshwater fauna. Sites of the Dynamic style are also spatially separated from those of the more recent styles, being found in shelters on higher ground, while recent styles and sites fringe the lowlands. Chaloupka considered that the Dynamic style predated present environmental conditions, and was older than about 6,500 BP (Chaloupka 1984; but see also Taçon 1987; Lewis 1988; Haskovec 1992).

Chaloupka and Murray also associated art sites of this general region with the Pleistocene period by attempting to identify extinct fauna, including *Zaglossus*, *Sthenurus* and *Thylacoleo*, among the painted motifs (Murray and Chaloupka 1984). As with all efforts to interpret the iconography of rock art, whether in recent or very ancient contexts, without supporting evidence the interpretations remain impressionistic; or in these cases, as elegant models waiting to be tested in the light of harder chronological data.

In conclusion, Rosenfeld's evaluation of the general chronological patterns in Australian rock art, no matter how tentative the present information, was 'that structured visual systems on rock' date largely to the terminal Pleistocene–early Holocene, and, in her words, indicate 'Corporate territorial expression through the indelible marking of place with a stylistic graphic system may have been a powerful means of asserting corporate rights and relationships'. She considered this process to be 'entirely consistent with a model of tightened social and territorial organisation at the close of the Pleistocene', a time of rapidly changing environment. Rosenfeld hypothesised that prior to this period, 'less constrained social systems' operated (1993: 76–77). In general, Rosenfeld's evaluation is in accord with those of others, including Morwood and David, both working in northeastern Queensland, although chronological details vary (see below, this chapter, for a discussion on rock art of the Holocene). Her assessment also finds support, in some ways (although not necessarily the temporal details), with the general socio-demographic models of Australian prehistory developed in this book, on which there is further discussion in Chapters Nine and Ten.

Overview: Pleistocene settlement

Northern Greater Australia, including the present-day islands of New Guinea, New Ireland, and Buku (now one of the northern Solomon Islands), has some of the earliest archaeological evidence of settlement of the continent. This is not surprising, in some ways, given the closeness of this area to the Southeast Asian islands of today's Indonesia, and the assumed homeland of the earliest Australian immigrants. The earliest archaeological site of Huon, on the northeastern New Guinea coast, at about 40,000 years is among the very oldest Australian sites. At this time the region was forested. About 33,000 years ago, offshore islands such as New Ireland were also occupied and, by 29,000 years, Buku. Use of coastal resources is evident at both sites. No great sea voyages had to be undertaken by people to reach these islands and the process might be viewed, in some ways, as a geographical extension of use of tropical islands, beginning with those of Southeast Asia and eventually spreading east into Australasia and beyond.

By about 25,000 years ago settlement is apparent in the New Guinea Highlands, and around the humid belt of northern Australia. Settlement in Arnhem Land and Cape York might be as old, or older, than at Huon (see Chapter Three), and is clearly evident in Cape York by 37,000 BP and in northwestern Australia by 32,000 years. Coastal resources, including mangrove species, were exploited in northwestern Australia from this time.

The onset of increasing aridity after about 25,000 years ago, which peaked at the glacial maximum about 18,000 BP, reveals a range of archaeological patterns. Some sites were first occupied at this time, others more intensively utilised, and others still, abandoned. In Arnhem Land sites such as Nauwalabila I and Malakunanja II, although at this time located far inland, appear to have been occupied throughout the glacial maximum. Colless and Louie Creek in drier southwestern Queensland were most intensively utilised at this time, as was Fern Cave in Cape York. The two former sites indicate the contraction of population around refuges of permanent water as increasing aridity set in, and this may also be so for Fern Cave (see also chapter Five). In northwestern Australia, Koolan Island 1, Widgingarri 1 and 2 and Mandu Mandu Creek were abandoned at this time and left stranded far inland in dry country following the lowering of sea levels. In contrast, Miriwun was first occupied in this period. These complex patterns of site and land use, in both time and space, may reflect the concentration of people within refuge areas throughout this increasingly dry period.

On New Ireland, Matenkupkum also appears to have been abandoned during this dry phase, although a further site Matenbek is occupied for the first time. In southeastern Queensland also, Wallen Wallen Creek is first utilised at this time.

In contrast to this earlier period, however, after about 15,000 years ago, during the terminal Pleistocene, there is both an increase in the use of sites and in the appearance of new sites. This is so generally throughout the humid northern zone of Australia, in the New Guinea Highlands and New Ireland. In Highland New Guinea a broader range of sites appears; for instance, at Nombe a wider range of animal species is represented, while on New Ireland there appears to have been a more intensive use of marine and rainforest areas and changes in strategies of resource use. The difficulty here is to clearly distinguish between the effects of changing climate, such as vegetation and faunal alterations, and shifts in human behaviour.

A general overview would suggest that population levels and densities, judging from the numbers of sites and the intensity of their use, were rather low until after the glacial maximum. For example, at the time of high lake levels (before about 25,000 years ago) there is little evidence of dense settlement in any of the environments studied, including the most fertile of areas. It has been argued also, more recently, that in some areas, such as the northwest and the central-west (including the coast), sites indicate more substantial occupation prior to about

22,000 BP. This has given rise to suggestions that populations may have been increasing throughout this period, with a decline experienced during the glacial maximum (22,000–18,000 BP). In arid refuge areas this may have resulted in higher residential mobility, and lower population density (O'Connor et al. 1993; see also Chapter Nine). After about 15,000 years ago, however, settlement appears to intensify somewhat in all the above regions, which suggests that Aboriginal populations (as indicated by the above archaeological signs) may have risen at this time. In some cases this may have been associated partly with the improving, more humid climate and the reforestation of, for example, highland areas; this would suggest overall increasing levels in bioproductivity.

Evidence of cultural behaviour, including patterns of settlement and subsistence, would generally support the above scenario. Use of sites seems to have been rather intermittent, implying infrequent occupation prior to about 15,000 years ago. Use of resources also suggests neither an extensive or intensive emphasis. There is evidence, perhaps, of extensive exchange from before 30,000 years in parts of western Australia. But apart fom this, only in the terminal Pleistocene is there some suggestion of more complex use of sites, resources and landscapes, for example on New Ireland, the New Guinea Highlands and northeastern Queensland. In general the available rock art evidence, although poorly dated, lends support to these socio-cultural and demographic patterns.

HOLOCENE SETTLEMENT

Palaeoenvironment

In northern Australia, amelioration of climate, with rises in temperature and rainfall as well as a strengthened monsoon, took place during the early Holocene after about 10,000 years ago. Palaeoenvironmental evidence comes largely from two sources, lake sites of the Atherton Tableland and several coastal areas.

On the Atherton Tableland a series of lake deposits, including Lynch's Crater, has produced the general sequence described below (Walker and Chen 1987; Chen 1988; Hiscock and Kershaw 1992: 54–58). Effective precipitation continued to increase from about 10,000 years until about 7,000 years ago, and increasing reforestation of the region saw a gradual replacement of savanna woodland by rainforest during this period. Rainforests reached their maximum extent between about 6,500 and 5,900 years ago. About 3,000 years BP, however, the climate became markedly drier, with a contraction in rainforest, and this may have continued until as recently as 1,400 years ago, after which conditions were more humid. In northwestern Australia also, the evidence is broadly in agreement with wetter climates in the early Holocene between about 8,500 and 6,500 years ago (Wyrwoll et al. 1986; Ross et al. 1992: 87).

Rises in sea level continued from the time of the glacial maximum, stabilising about 6,000 years ago, and these were followed by a relatively dynamic sequence of largely local changes in coastal environments (Chappell and Grindrod 1984; Chappell and Thom 1986). Evidence for coastal environmental histories have come from a number of northern and northeastern coastal areas (see further, this chapter). For example, on the South Alligator River plain, in Arnhem Land, estuarine conditions are evident from about 7,000 years ago, with mangrove communities reaching their maximum extent between 6,800 and 5,300 years. Following this phase, mangroves were replaced by a succession of varied and productive environments including freshwater wetlands (Woodroffe et al. 1988).

Princess Charlotte Bay, north Queensland

Three sandstone rock-shelters and thirteen shell mounds were sampled in this region which includes Princess Charlotte Bay on the mainland and the offshore Stanley Island (Beaton 1985) (Figure 4.3). From this information, and the accompanying geomorphological data, John Beaton obtained the following chronological sequence. While sea levels stabilised around 6,000 years ago, evidence of human occupation only begins around 4,700 BP, that is, 1,500 years after the cessation of the marine transgression. The earliest date for occupation comes from the Walaemini rock-shelter, which is located close to the headland facing the offshore islands. The first of the chenier ridges formed around 4,000 BP, and a second rock-shelter, Alkaline Hill, was inhabited from about 3,500 BP. The first evidence of occupation of the islands is from around 2,500 BP at the Endaen rock-shelter on Stanley Island, and of the chenier ridges around 2,000 BP. The latter event took place some two thousand years after the first of the cheniers was formed in Princess Charlotte Bay.

The oldest of the shell mounds, which are discrete, heaped up shell structures atop chenier ridges, begin from around 1,700 BP. The most numerous and largest mounds occur, however, between about 1,200 and 800 BP, and by about 600–500 BP both the large cheniers and anadara shell middens and mounds had ceased to be accumulated. Evidence from the excavated sites in some cases indicates changes through time. The small rock-shelter of Walaemini is located some 400 metres behind the present beach, and close to the headland opposite the islands (Beaton 1985: 6–7). Nearby is an estuarine swamp. The compact shell midden within the shelter has a basal date of 4,760 ± 90 BP (ANU 3041), and, by weight, sixty percent is composed of *A. granosa* shell in the lower layers. Other shellfish species at this time include those from mudflats, mangroves and the rocky shore. Small quantities of animal, bird and fish bone were also present in these layers. The middle and upper levels of the site include an additional nine species of shellfish, which Beaton explains as due either to a widening of Aboriginal shellfish practices or the increasing productivity of mudflat shellfish communities (1985: 7). Twenty centimetres of sterile sand underlie the midden deposit, indicating to the excavator a dearth of prior occupation of the site.

The Alkaline Hill rock-shelter is located close to the edge of the chenier plain and was inhabited from around 3,440 ± 80 BP (ANU 3041) (Beaton 1985: 7).

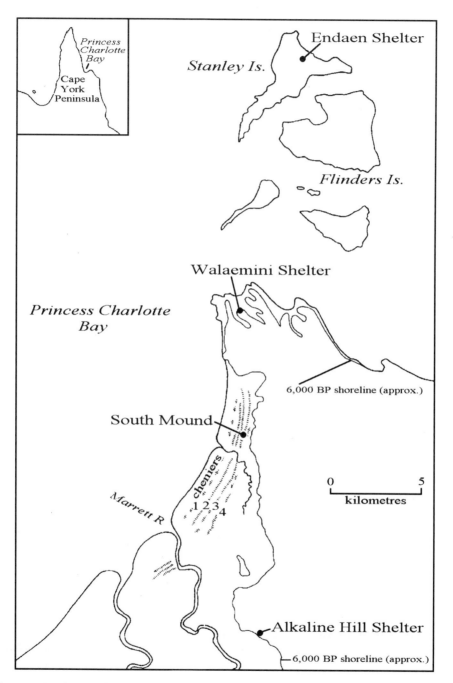

Figure 4.3 Princess Charlotte Bay, north Queensland (based on Beaton 1985: 2, Figure 1).

Two depositional units have been distinguished, both of which are dominated by *A. granosa*. The upper unit has greater quantities of ash and bone and fewer mangrove-dwelling shellfish species represented by *Terebralia* and *Telescopium*, also evidence of *Macropus agilis*, in both stratigraphic units. At the three rock-shelters of Alkaline Hill, Walaemini and Endaen, there is no flaked stone, apart from three edge-ground axes on the surface of Alkaline Hill. Stone appears to have been replaced by shell, mainly of *Geloina coaxans*, in the form of 'flaked scrapers'. Underlying the midden is 2.5 metres of sterile sand and rubble.

A detailed excavation was carried out at one of the shell mounds, the South Mound, which is located on top of one of the chenier ridges (Beaton 1985: 7–8). The mound was deposited about 1,700 BP – 1,100 BP, and this sizeable structure appears to have been largely an *A. granosa* dump with ninety-six per cent of the shell remains being of the latter species. Small quantities of bone, including fish, were also present together with lenses of burnt wood, but no evidence of structures or living floors was found.

On Stanley Island, the large Endaen rock-shelter has 0.5 metres of deposit and a basal date of 2,370 ± 100 BP (ANU 3379) (Beaton 1985: 6), and appears to have been used until the present. Below this dense shell midden unit was 100 cms of sterile yellow sand. In the upper level of the site the dominant shell species is the mangrove gastropod, *Terebralia palistris*, together with reef shellfish, and fragments of sea turtle and small quantities of fish. In the lower levels (2, 3 and 4), an identical range of shellfish was found, together with three species of wallaby, which are no longer found on the island. The large sea mammal, the dugong, appears in all levels, and shell artefacts were detected, as well as one bone tool (see also Cribb and Minnegal 1989). No shell fish hooks, however, were found. While Beaton argues that no significant economic changes can be detected through time at the site, the greater percentage of mangrove shell species in the upper level may have an economic as well as an ecological explanation. Beaton attributes the presence of this shellfish species to recent expansion of mangrove communities, but no explanation is offered for this supposed environmental trend. In contrast, a decline in mangrove species was found in the upper levels of the Alkaline Hill shelter.

Beaton's interpretation of this information from Princess Charlotte Bay is largely environmentally based, dependent principally upon the stabilisation of sea levels and subsequent productivity of coastal resources. While Beaton points out that these environmental events and his archaeological sequence are not synchronous, it can be noted that thousands of years have lapsed between the stabilisation of sea levels around 6,000 BP and the archaeological events that followed. For example, 1,300 years pass before the first signs of coastal occupation occur (at the Walaemini shelter); 3,500 years go by until the islands are first inhabited (at the Endaen shelter); and it is some 5,000 years before the largest and most numerous of the shell mounds, including the South Mound, are constructed. Beaton attributes these lengthy gaps in time to what he calls a 'time lag'. Although this concept is not specifically defined, presumably it refers to an ecological process whereby optimal productivity levels of certain coastal resources lag significantly behind the stabilisation of mid-Holocene sea levels, and the creation of favourable environmental conditions. Beaton argues, in general, that late Pleistocene and early Holocene coastal environments were not as productive as those of the late Holocene (1985: 12–13; also Beaton 1995).

Beaton's explanation can be questioned in a number of ways. For instance, Chappell and Thom (1977: 287) have argued that a transgressive tropical coastal environment is not necessarily resource-poor, but highly productive with extensive mangrove habitats and a rich array of biotic communities. Presumably therefore, exploitation of coastal resources could have taken place in the early Holocene and prior to the period of mid-Holocene sea level stabilisation (see also McInnes 1988).

A similar argument could be proposed for the mid-Holocene. If marine resources were available throughout most of the Holocene, why then is the archaeological evidence of their use so late? Beaton provides some evidence for the fluctuation in availability of only one resource, *Anadara granosa*, throughout the late Holocene. This information, however, has been derived from archaeological data which are a cultural artefact. Independent information is required also of changes in *Anadara*, and other resources, to substantiate Beaton's impressions (also Nolan 1986).The chenier ridges were composed of shellfish derived from the product of wave action on nearby mudflats (Beaton 1985: 5). As the earliest chenier ridges date to about 4,500 BP, presumably the availability of shellfish also extends back that far, and further still to around 5,000 BP, as is indicated by evidence of *Anadara* from the Walaemini rock-shelter (see also Cribb 1986). The availability of *Anadara*, therefore, fails to explain the evidence of more intensive marine exploitation and settlement of the region only in the last 2,000 years or less. An explanation based upon the *stabilisation* of sea levels and general coastal ecological conditions leading to more productive shell beds (Beaton 1985: 12) can also be questioned. Instead, in this example we have a *dynamic* scenario of shoreline progradation, and as no other environmental evidence is provided by Beaton, room is left also for other explanations.

As a solution to this problem, Beaton turned to demography and identified the causal factor as increasing population (1985: 16–18). Although acknowledging that environmental and socio-economic factors may be related in the process, Beaton concludes that 'Growth of population also may be quite *independent* of either environmental enrichment (via climatic change) or socio-technic change' (1985: 17, my emphasis). Given the complex nature of human demography and its close tie with cultural factors (see Chapter One), this last statement would be difficult to uphold. I suggest that if no overriding environmental cause (such as increasing enrichment of coastal resources) can be pinpointed, as appears to be the case, then a more plausible explanation might involve an interrelationship of demographic and socio-economic factors. As Woodroffe et al. have suggested, Beaton's evidence may indicate 'a time-lag between the availability of coastal resources and their exploitation' (1988: 101). Given these objections to Beaton's explanation, it might be suggested that together these data suggest a progressive cultural change or expansion *throughout* the late Holocene. The data also allow for cultural changes, such as the expansion of economic niches involving (a) more intensive and recent use of the mainland coastal fringe and its resources (the large shell mounds); (b) recent use of the offshore islands and reefs; (c) the introduction of more efficient marine technology (for example, outrigger canoes), which would have allowed a wider range of marine exploitation (for example, dugong). Rather than explain this evidence as a passive adaptation to changing environmental conditions, it can also be viewed as a positive response to changing circumstances, both environmental and cultural. This trend appears to have peaked some 5,000 years after the stabilisation of Holocene sea levels and may have been halted by local environmental events, as Beaton suggests (Lourandos 1985b: 38). Viewed in this way, the recent trends would suggest the development of relatively specialised marine-oriented economies, in a more territorial context placing emphasis upon the coast and islands. This settlement–subsistence pattern reflects the ethnographic picture (see Chapter Two) of the area quite well, and suggests its relatively recent origin.

Beaton's final assessment of the Princess Charlotte Bay material in some ways expresses broadly similar sentiments:

> One recurrent theme of Holocene archaeology has been the demonstration that some environments were first incorporated into the foraging domain only within the last 4,000 years or so ... In these terms it is possible to view the increasingly dense coastal occupation of the late Holocene also as an expression of the incorporation of yet another class of resource community into the total foraging economy of Australia. (1985: 18)

Southeast Cape York Peninsula

Both Mike Morwood and Bruno David have independently synthesised general archaeological sequences of this region. All available excavated data from southeastern Cape York were drawn together by David (1994: 140–158; personal communication 1994), who arrived at the temporal trends I now summarise. The sites, all rock-shelters, are located mainly in the elevated hinterland of the peninsula together with the above-mentioned Princess Charlotte Bay material. From a sample of 13 excavated rock-shelters from the region with 'basal' dates the pattern indicates that while sites have been occupied since around 37,000 BP, there were significant increases in the number of occupied sites after about 5,000–4,000 BP, with occupation continuing to increase markedly up to recent times (Figure 4.4; Table 4.1). Many of the sites are only first occupied during the latter period. Increases occur in deposition rates of a number of factors

Table 4.1 Dates when deposition rates begin to increase significantly in north-eastern Queensland. Sites are listed along a north–south axis (after David 1994: 142, Table 47).

Sub-region	Site	Years BP
Koolburra Plateau	Green Ant rock-shelter	2,200–1,800
Koolburra Plateau	Echidna Shelter	1,400
Laura	Mushroom Rock	3,000
Laura	Early Man rock-shelter	1,800–950
Laura	Yam Camp	1,000
Laura	Sandy Creek 1	1,900–1,200
Palmer River	Hearth Cave	3,500
Mitchell River	Mitchell River Cave	3,800
Ngarrabullgan	Ngarrabullgan Cave	5,400
Mungana	Echidna's Rest	c. 3,000
Chillagoe	Walkunder Arch Cave	3,700

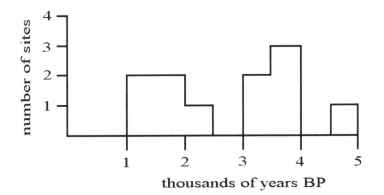

Figure 4.4 Temporal trends indicating the time of increase in deposition rates at a number of northeastern Queensland rock-shelters over the last 5,000 years (based on information from David 1994, see Table 4.1).

including cultural material such as stone artefacts, bone, charcoal and ochre as well as sedimentation rates. 'Blade' technologies and 'burren adzes' were also introduced during this period, and the specialised hunting of rock wallabies at two sites (Echidna's Rest and Walkunder Arch Cave) also detected. Increases in deposition rates of similar magnitude, however, were not observed in earlier periods. Of sites with Pleistocene deposits, only Fern Cave indicates a major change in deposition rate during the late Pleistocene, towards the glacial maximum. At Ngarrabullgan Cave, where the Pleistocene levels are well stratified (back to 37,000 years BP), major changes are also only evident from about 5,000 BP. David broadly explains the temporal patterns as indicating an intensification of use of the region in late Holocene times.

David's results are supported by more recent data of long-term trends covering the last 37,000 years in the region (David and Lourandos, in press.). Use was made of a large data base of 33 archaeological sites (including 26 rock-shelters) and 178 radiocarbon dates, and three different methods – radiocarbon dates, number of sites occupied and rate of site establishment. These archaeological data were then compared to long-term climatic trends. The results showed that for a very long time – 37,000 until c. 4,000 BP – the archaeological trends followed the environmental trends more closely. After about 4,000 BP, however, the archaeological and environmental trends diverged significantly.

Morwood's results are generally in agreement (Morwood 1993; Morwood and Hobbs 1995). Based upon research in the Quinkan reserve region, this extensive project incorporated excavation of a range of rock-shelters, many of them containing rock art, together with palaeoenvironmental investigation. While occupation of sites was generally ephemeral during the Pleistocene, as already noted, the terminal Pleistocene and early Holocene is characterised by an increase in the number of occupied rock-shelters and changing patterns of use of stone materials. Further major changes take place after about 4,000 years ago. More sites were now utilised more intensively, and the use of adzes increased. These changes appear to occur in a somewhat staggered fashion throughout the period and to suggest that they are a continuation of earlier trends. Artefact discard rates increase during this period together with a wider range of artefact types, including burren adzes. Evidence of labour-intensive plant processing occurs also with the appearance of cycads and large increases in the number of grindstones in the uppermost levels of one site. Evidence of increased burning of vegetation also appears in the last few thousand years. Morwood and Hobbs link this sequence of cultural changes to alterations in climate and thus bioproduction. The first major climatic change they see as having occurred in the terminal Pleistocene and early Holocene, with further increases after about 2,700 BP. These increases in bioproduction they associate with corresponding rises in Aboriginal population, and subsequent demographic restructuring, including territorial rearrangements. I would argue, however, that the post-2,700 BP environmental evidence they present is inconclusive, with the possibility of loss of prior data. General climatic curves from the late Holocene in the region (above) indicate climatic reversals in this period.

North Queensland highlands

Further supporting evidence for the Cape York results comes from the neighbouring Upper Flinders River region of the North Queensland highlands (Morwood 1990, 1992). Preliminary results indicate that Mickey Springs 34 has a continuous chronological sequence spanning 11,000 years, with noticeable increases in deposition rates of artefacts after about 8,000 years. The site was most intensively occupied, however, after 3,400 years ago with marked increases in deposition rates of stone artefacts and ochre, new artefact types, large dense hearth deposits, and a broadening of the resource base. New artefact types include backed blades, burren and tula adzes, edge-ground axes and 'grindstones' (see

Chapter Five for further discussion of grindstones). From Quippenburra Cave comes similar evidence from a 3,300-year sequence. Mention is also made of a third site – Mickey Springs 31 – and roughly comparable sequence. Morwood (1990) interprets the changes as indicating more regular use of the sites, a broader range of activities, including seed processing, and possibly increases in local population and productivity.

North Queensland rainforest, Mulgrave River region

Little archaeological work has been carried out in the rich and complex rainforests of north Queensland, the Mulgrave River study (Horsfall 1987) being one of the few. Archaeological sequences at Jiyer Cave and Mulgrave II extend back to about 5,100 years, but evidence of cultural occupation remains slight until more recently; 1,800–1,000 BP at Mulgrave II and 650–850 BP at Jiyer cave. Other rock-shelters and open sites examined in the forest also appeared to reflect this general chronological pattern. The evidence from plant materials, which were plentiful, indicates that toxic plant foods also were used only in these more recent phases; from around 2,000 BP at Mulgrave II and 1,000 BP at Jiyer Cave. While organic materials, including plants, have been poorly preserved in the lower levels of the sites, this temporal pattern is reinforced somewhat by artefactual evidence. Stone artefacts, such as 'grindstones' resembling ethnographic examples known to have been used for processing toxic plants, appear only in the more recent levels and in increasing numbers. In contrast, in older levels only the occasional 'expedient' grindstone is found (see Chapter Five). The overall impression obtained, therefore, is that intensive exploitation of toxic plants is a fairly recent practice in the area.

Notwithstanding the preliminary nature of these results, and the small sample size, this evidence suggests that this region of tropical rainforest was largely unoccupied until around the mid-Holocene (c. 5,000 BP), and most intensively utilised only in the last 2,000–1,000 years or so, together with increasing evidence of use of toxic plants, which require considerable processing time. This archaeological pattern, however, does not fit a directly environmental explanation. Rainforests had reached their maximum extent in this region (including the Atherton Tableland and Mulgrave River estuary) in the early Holocene with increased levels of precipitation, and thus would have provided attractive habitats. They do not appear to have been used, however, until some 2,000 years later, and not intensively until quite recently, with neither pattern fitting the climatic and floral chronological trend. This temporal pattern has also been detected in two neighbouring areas. For example, Peter Hiscock and Peter Kershaw have suggested that on the Atherton Tableland, 'Increased representation of pollen from successional plants may be an indication of increased burning at forest margins and in patches of open sclerophyll vegetation within the forest massif, perhaps to maintain and extend route-ways through the forest' (1992: 64). Swamp forest at Lynch's Crater, they argue, appears also to

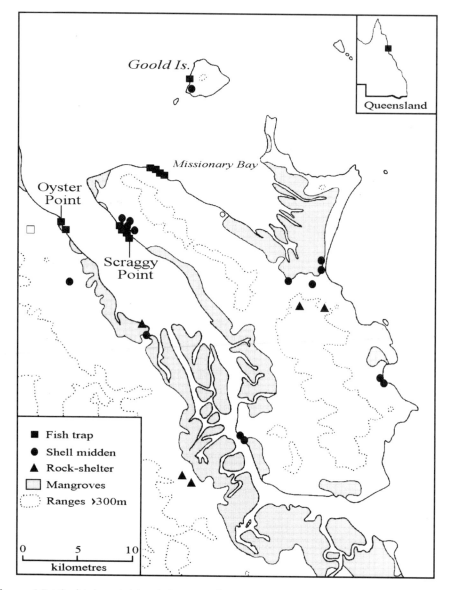

Figure 4.5 Hinchinbrook Island sites, northeastern Queensland (based on Campbell 1982: 97, Figure 1).

have been reduced at this time, perhaps as part of Aboriginal fire management strategies. The crater was visited annually by coastal peoples to collect taro (*Colocasia esculenta*) according to ethnographic reports.

Islands of north Queensland
Here we consider the archaeology of Hinchinbrook Island, the Whitsundays and the Keppel Islands. Hinchinbrook Island, for example, has evidence of intensive

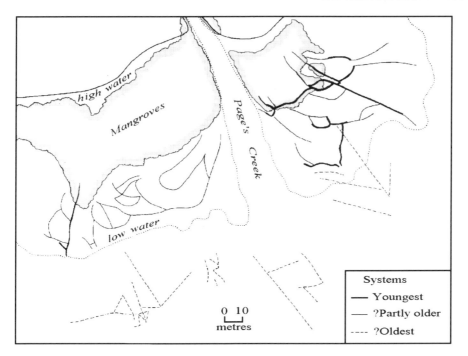

Figure 4.6 Stone fish trap complexes, Scraggy Point, Hinchinbrook Island, Queensland (based on Campbell 1982: 101, Figure 2).

use of marine resources. This large, elevated island, which hugs the tropical coastline between Townsville and Cairns, is today heavily vegetated with a substantial percentage of rainforest and extensive mangrove communities around its coastline. Preliminary archaeological investigation indicates many tidal fish traps of stone, and shell middens, especially in the north and west of the island (Campbell 1982) (Figure 4.5). At Scraggy Point investigations revealed a complex of fish trap systems which covers an estimated total area of 21,600 square metres. These systems varied in size, form and complexity, and may belong to different time periods (Figure 4.6).

All the systems are sub-divided into many different sorts of components: raceways, loops, pools, funnels, breakwaters and 'arrowheads' with various connecting walls. The best preserved walls in the youngest system are usually about 0.5–0.8 metres high, with a few spots standing even higher than that (Campbell 1982: 101). The estimated volume of these trapping systems suggest that they ' . . . would have held or retrieved very substantial quantities of seafood, especially during the best seasons' (Campbell 1982: 102). Molluscs and mud crabs are perennially retrievable from the traps. Today, the youngest system continues to operate *automatically*, and seems to stand out quite clearly as an *automatic seafood retrieval system*. When the fish-trap system was more complete (in the past) it would have been even more effective and capable of

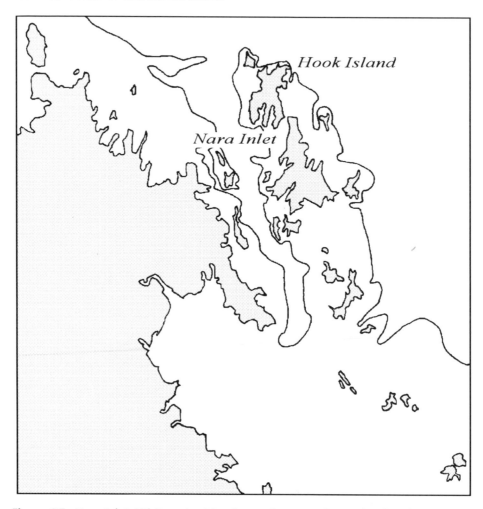

Figure 4.7 Nara Inlet, Whitsunday Islands, northeastern Queensland, indicating the early Holocene coastline about 8,000 years ago and the present coastline and islands dating from about 6,000–5,000 years ago (grey) (based on Barker 1995).

feeding substantial groups of people for extended periods of time (Campbell 1982: 102).

Excavations of a nearby midden at Scraggy Point revealed a rich array of marine resources: a range of molluscs, and smaller quantities of crab, shark and other fish, and possibly turtle. A recent date of about 500 BP was obtained from the site, which has an estimated basal date of around 1,000 BP. Campbell considered these fish trap systems as comparable in 'their levels of ecological diversity, productivity and management' to inland fishing systems, such as those of southwestern Victoria (1982: 106) which I go into further below. He further raised the possibility that the Aboriginal population of the island was much larger than previously considered, as a separate social unit resided there (Tindale 1974:

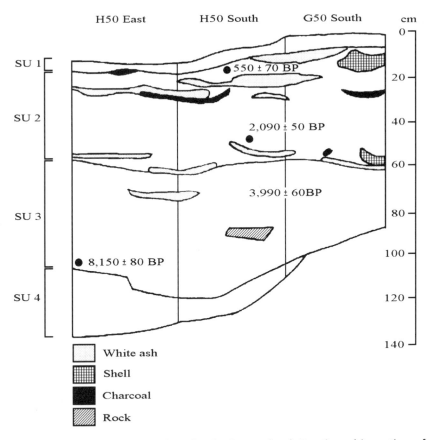

H50 East   H50 South   G50 South   cm

- 550 ± 70 BP
- 2,090 ± 50 BP
- 3,990 ± 60BP
- 8,150 ± 80 BP

White ash
Shell
Charcoal
Rock

Figure 4.8 Nara Inlet 1, Whitsunday Islands, Queensland. Stratigraphic section of squares G and H (based on Barker 1995).

165). Campbell speculated that 'If it were … then elaborate systems of ecological control would have been necessary to maintain it' (1982: 106). In support of such a proposal is evidence that much of the vegetation of the island was also the product of human intervention, for example through the use of fire.

Nara Inlet I (Barker 1989, 1991, 1995) (see also Chapter One) is a large coastal rock-shelter on Hook Island, one of the Whitsundays, with excellent preservation of organic remains (including plants) throughout its deposits (Figures 4.7, 4.8). The site has been continuously occupied for most of the Holocene period, or from sometime before 8,150 ± 80 BP. By around 6,500 BP, the peninsula on which the site was located had been transformed into a series of islands (the Whitsundays), but the rising sea levels appear to have had little effect upon marine resources. Fishing, including large species (which were perhaps speared), shellfishing, and hunting of terrestrial animals continued from the time of initial occupation. After about 2,500 BP, however, the site appears to have been more intensively utilised with increases in sediment rates, shell and charcoal, and economic remains, such as fish and plant foods.

A wide variety of artefacts manufactured from bone, wood, shell and turtle shell as well as stone was introduced at this time. In general, this change is seen to represent a broadening of the resource base, a greater degree of marine resource specialisation and an increase in human activity at the site (Barker 1989: 24). The range of plant foods, including highly processed species such as toxic cycads, also had increased in the last 600 years.

Bryce Barker has now excavated five rock-shelters within the island group, all of which support the chronological and cultural sequence originally obtained at Nara Inlet I (Barker 1995). Occupation of two of the five sites (including Nara Inlet I) commences around 8,000 years, and the remaining three in the last 3,000–2,500 years, coinciding with the period of more intensive occupation at the latter two sites. All five sites also indicate still more complex and intensive habitation during the last 1,000 years. The upper levels, therefore, at all five sites appear to reflect the more specialised island-based marine economies present in the ethnographic record (see Chapter Two). The timing of the late Holocene changes on the Whitsunday Islands is comparable also to evidence from other tropical islands (including those of Princess Charlotte Bay, discussed earlier).

Archaeological investigation of the Keppel Islands, which lie off the Queensland coast just north of Rockhampton, has been conducted by Mike Rowland (1980, 1981, 1982a, 1982b). South or Great Keppel Island, which is the least remote of the island group, is situated some 13 kilometres from the mainland. An open site, Mazie Bay, on North Keppel Island, has an archaeological sequence which extends back to around 4,000 BP. In contrast, excavation of seven open sites on South Keppel Island indicated that all were of the last 700 years. Excavation continued below the occupation units at all these sites in order to search for the possibility of earlier deposits. As well, a comprehensive survey of all likely site locations on the island was carried out. In general the sites included shellfish, for example oyster, *Crassostrea amasa*, and evidence of marine exploitation. Fish hooks also appear in the last 1,000 years (see below).

Rowland considered that the ethnographically distinct population which inhabited the Keppel Islands had been the product, to some extent, of both cultural and genetic isolation. He speculated, however, that:

> . . . the period of isolation need not be great. On the other hand, present sea levels in this area were established by 5,000 BP . . . so the Keppel Islanders could have been isolated just prior to this. (1980: 12)

Rowland's later interpretation of the archaeological evidence from North and South Keppel Islands suggested to him that:

Figure 4.9 Nara Inlet 1 rock-shelter, Whitsunday Islands, north Queensland, during excavation (Photo: Bryce Barker. Courtesy of the North Queensland Land Council.)

... North Keppel at least was visited on an occasional basis from 4,000 BP. However from about 700 BP a permanent population occupied both North and South Keppel Island, forming a distinct group as indicated in the historical records. (1982: 47)

The ethnographic picture of island use, therefore, would appear to be the product only of the last 1,000 years or so. Given the proximity of the Keppel Islands to the mainland, the degree of isolation, both genetic and cultural, remains problematical.

Islands of Northwest Kimberley, Western Australia

High Cliffy Island is a rocky islet and part of the small Montgomery group of islands in the Buccaneer Archipelago. The island lies some 10 kilometres from the mainland, and is 1 kilometre long and 300 metres wide. This island group is surrounded by an extensive coral reef system and many of the islands are connected at low tide. Heavy monsoonal rains lash this area during the summer months and at high tide the island group covers less than 20 square kilometres. Even so, during recent times, these islands were the domain of a discrete dialectal group, the Jaudibaia, who were island-based, and without a mainland territory. Archaeological reconnaissance was conducted in this region by Sue O'Connor, who recorded hundreds of stone structures on one section of High Cliffy Island. A variety of structures had been built, some of which appeared to be small,

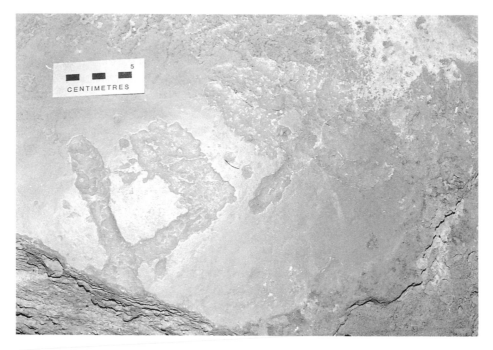

Figure 4.10 Patinated peckings reminiscent of 'early' Australian rock art forms from the Mitchell–Palmer limestone belt, north Queensland (Photo: Bruno David. Courtesy of the North Queensland Land Council).

circular hut bases. 'These structures are roughly circular with a small entrance ... The walls stand up to 1 metre high and may be up to 50 cms wide at their base. Inside the structure is a maximum of nine square metres of useable space' (O'Connor 1987: 33). Stone artefacts were scattered in quantity inside and at the entrance of these structures, and two of the houses contained grindstones, and one a broken baler shell (*Melo* sp.).

O'Connor compared the structures to similar forms from the Mitchell Plateau, also in the Kimberley region, and to those from Lake Condah in southwestern Victoria (see below). 'They utilise the same walling technique and are approximately the same size and cluster in the same way. Like the High Cliffy houses they are located immediately adjacent to a resource rich zone' (O'Connor 1987: 33). Excavation of one of the structures revealed large quantities of stone artefacts, fish bone and turtle carapace. This confirmed the Aboriginal origin of the structure and its domestic use. Radiocarbon dating of shell from this site produced a modern (post-European contact) date.

Using ethnographic analogies of comparable hut forms from the nearby regions of the Mitchell Plateau and the Bardi country to the south, O'Connor considered that these structures were wet-season huts with organic superstructures (made, for example, of spinifex and clay). This interpretation was reinforced by evidence from the Bonaparte Archipelago where stone structures occurred and offshore islands were used mainly in the wet season when water was available. O'Connor argued that rocky islets, such as High Cliffy, may have been used in the wet season and the larger sandy islands of the group, which had perennial fresh water, during the dry season. Further, she considered that of the many islands of the Kimberley region, the Montgomery group were unique because of, first, the large productive reef system; second, the large quantities of good quality stone (chert) on High Cliffy island which is not available on other islands (or the adjacent mainland); and, third, their occupation by a discrete social group.

> Like the inhabitants of the Lake Condah stone houses and the Victorian mounds, the Jaudibaia could have maintained a viable sedentary or semi-sedentary population which concentrated on an extremely productive resource zone. In the case of the Lake Condah fishtraps it was necessary to modify the landsurface to maximise or regularise the resource. In the case of the Jaudibaia, no modification was necessary as natural fishtraps are formed by holes in the reef and each new tide replenishes the traps. (O'Connor 1987: 36)

O'Connor considered, however, that this island population could not have been economically self-sufficient.

> If, as has been proposed, the Jaudibaia were a discrete dialectal unit moving back and forward between the sandy and rocky islands of the group they would not have been able to sustain their population on this tiny group of islands without an extremely well developed trading system. While direct subsistence needs could be met entirely from the reef and surrounding waters and the plant foods of the island, suitable wood for spear making is not available on these islands and it is likely that many other raw materials would have been absent. I suggest that what we are possibly witnessing at this high density living site is the Australian equivalent of Motupore and the island trading centres of Melanesia (cf. Allen 1985, Irwin 1978).
> High grade chert could be traded with the mainland for other raw materials not available on this small island group. The large quantities of artefactual material found all over the High Cliffy Island testify to a level of stone working not seen in any of the mainland rockshelters and open sites. Such an interpretation receives support from the type and quantity of material in the excavated rockshelter site. This shelter is not a quarry; material is being transported from elsewhere on the island, and yet, the density of material is unrivalled at any of the other north west Kimberley sites investigated. (O'Connor 1987: 37)

To what extent the island operated in regional exchange patterns remains a matter of interpretation; at the very least, however, it is yet another indication of relatively intensive recent use of tropical coastal islands perhaps by a more territorially discrete social group, as the ethnography suggests.

South central Queensland uplands

Archaeological research was conducted in this region by Mulvaney (1964; Mulvaney and Joyce 1965), and later by Beaton (1977) and Morwood (1979, 1981, 1984). Situated in the Carnarvon Ranges, Kenniff Cave is the oldest of the nine sites (all caves and rock-shelters), and is dated to around 19,000 BP. Three of the sites were first occupied during the terminal Pleistocene–early Holocene juncture – Native Wells I and II, and the Tombs. All of these sites, however, were more intensively inhabited during the time of the Australian Small Tool tradition, which dates in this region from around 4,300 BP. The remaining sites were all *first* occupied within the last 4,500 years, and these include Wanderer's Cave, Rainbow Cave, Cathedral Cave, Turtle Rock, Ken's Cave and Goat Rock 2. Beaton argued from the results of his research for 'a marked intensification of Aboriginal use of the region beginning about 4000 to 5000 years ago' (1977: abstract). He also noted that 'This increase is not a gradual one but occurs abruptly, at the temporal boundary of the two major tool traditions' (Beaton 1977: 192).

Morwood's results are generally in agreement with those of Beaton: 'It may be more relevant to ask why shelters appear to have been intensively used later, during the period of the Small Tool Tradition' (1981: 42). Morwood is also more precise about the timing of the introduction of the lithic tradition in this area: 'Thus the period 4,300–4,100 BP seems to be a reasonable estimate for the introduction of the Small Tool Industry to this region' (1981: 42). At Ken's Cave, which is dated to the last 2,000 years, Morwood reports abundant plant, as well as faunal, remains. His results indicate that the most intensive period of occupation of his sites 'as expressed by rates of implement, ochre, and sediment deposition' (1981: 42) occur prior to about 2,000 BP, and that after this date decreases in use are indicated. This last point is discussed below.

Beaton demonstrated that cycads, *Macrozamia moorei*, were found in large quantities in his rock-shelter sites (1977: 70, 83, 87, 190). This botanical information, dated from around 4,300 BP, and densities of husks, shells and seeds of between 400–600 per cubic metre were recorded at the sites of Rainbow Cave, Cathedral Cave, and Wanderer's Cave. He attributed the introduction of the labour-intensive leaching, drying and fermenting techniques associated with these plants from ethnographic evidence (see Chapter One) to this period, and he viewed the supposed new technology in the following way:

> The leaching tool if added to the [tool] kit, would open up as many possibilities for expanding the economic base as there were appropriate plants. [It] would have population, adaptation and survival value ... Its presence in prehistory could mark an intensification of habitat use that would have parallels in other major shifts in extractive economy, such as the adoption of horticulture. (1982: 56)

Beaton linked the introduction of cycad use, together with its appropriate technology, to the development of intergroup ceremonial gatherings and the spread of the Australian Small Tool tradition. 'The use of cycads in the uplands may be an archaeological expression of an emerging pattern of important Aboriginal social interactions that were widespread at the time of European contact and which are still practised in some areas today' (Beaton 1982: 57). He based this assessment on ethnographic evidence from Arnhem Land (Harvey 1945) where large-scale and populous ceremonies are supported by the processing of cycads. Regarding the production of cycads as *communion food*, Beaton adds ' . . . the investment of energy is high, and production time is long. Crops are not annual, but may be synchronised by firing the grove. If this is done, productivity may ensue that would embarrass a single band of Aborigines' (1982: 57). Beaton assumed, however, that the laborious leaching techniques were indispensable in the use of cycads. He states that 'without it, no cycad food of any kind is possible' (1982: 58). Cycads, however, also are leached by natural processes, such as through the weathering of fallen nuts, therefore they may have been in use long before the leaching techniques were adopted. The time-consuming processing methods thus would have to be viewed as a clear indication of an intensification of production.

Claims have also been made by Moya Smith (1982) of late Pleistocene use of cycads at the southwestern Australian site of Cheetup. A small quantity of uncharred, but carbonised, nuts and kernels of *Macrozamia riedlei* came from a shallow pit which was sealed by a layer dated to about 13,000 BP. The pit and date are stratigraphically separated from upper levels (less than 20 cms in depth) which contain artefacts of the Australian Small Tool tradition. Smith suggested that the pit and plant remains indicate that processing (leaching) had taken place at the site, and she provided ethnographic information to support her arguments. Smith distinguished the Cheetup plant remains, however, from those of Beaton's southern-central Queensland sites, which she described as 'the only clear archaeological evidence of extraordinary intensive exploitation of zamia' (Moya Smith 1982: 120). From her review of both ethnographic and archaeological evidence, Smith concluded that:

> The role of zamia in Aboriginal society would appear to vary greatly in different regions. Generally three functions of zamia in traditional Aboriginal diet have been recognised: starvation food when preferred sources are unavailable; staple food exploited as part of the daily diet during seasons of availability; and 'communion' food as an integral part of large ceremonies . . . For southern WA, the quantity of nuts, pit size, and ethnohistorical observations on zamia use, imply a more casual use of zamia as a dietary staple by the Cheetup occupants than is implicit in archaeological deposits in the south central Queensland uplands after 4300 BP. (1982: 120)

If the examples of both Beaton and Smith are drawn together, and accepting Smith's chronology, I suggest that the use of cycads and leaching methods may date from around the terminal Pleistocene, and the intensification of cycad use from about 4,300 BP, at least in the south-central Queensland uplands.

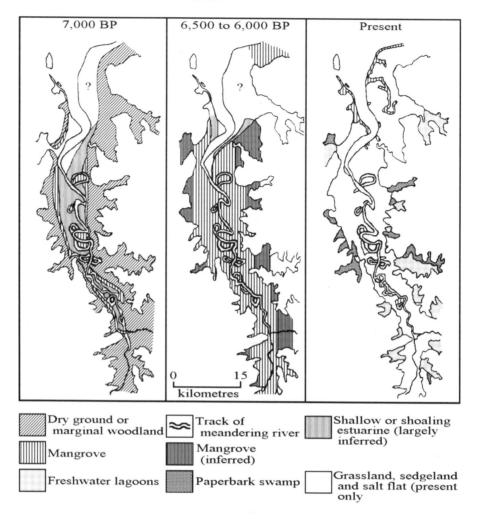

Figure 4.11 Stages in the development of Holocene estuarine environments in the South Alligator River, Arnhem Land (based on Hiscock and Kershaw 1992: 56, Figure 4.3; see also Woodroffe et al. 1988: 99)

Alligator Rivers region, Arnhem Land

Palaeoenvironmental and archaeological studies from this varied tropical estuarine region allow us to consider the complex relationships between people and environments, both natural and sociocultural.

A geomorphological study of the South Alligator River catchment undertaken by Woodroffe, Chappell and Thom (1988) throws considerable light on the archaeological evidence and their interpretations are discussed below. This palaeoecological study was based upon stratigraphical analysis, together with pollen analyses and radiocarbon dating. Four phases in the development of the riverine plain were distinguished; Figure 4.11 summarises these phases.

(i) Transgressive phase (8,000–6,800 BP). The sea rose from around 12 metres below its present level, drowning the South Alligator River valley, and attained its modern level around 6,000 BP.

(ii) Big Swamp phase (6,800–5,300 BP). Mangroves covered most of the present estuarine plain which is an area greater than 80,000 hectares. This was 30 times the area of present mangrove stands in the estuary. The disappearance of mangroves at the end of this phase was rapid, and most had vanished by 4,000 BP.

The next two phases refer to the establishment of freshwater conditions (from 4,000 BP or before) and the changing contours of the river.

(iii) Sinuous phase (5,300–2,500 BP). (iv) Cuspate phase (2,500 BP and after). Little change in the distribution of mangrove and wetland habitats took place between these last two phases. A similar evolutionary sequence has been predicted for other northern Australia estuaries (Woodroffe et al. 1988: 98). The authors pointed out the richness of mangrove forests in terms of molluscs, fish and crustacea (Woodroffe et al. 1988: 101). Small shell middens, of which fourteen were reported and radiocarbon dated, were found in four locations: on the coast, surface mounds on the plain, on palaeochannels and as surface scatters. The oldest midden was 6,240 ± 100 BP (ANU 4915), surface mounds ranged between 4,600 and 1,950 BP, while the palaeochannel middens were around 2,000 years younger than the channels themselves. The coastal middens, which date to between 800 and 430 BP, are also considerably younger than the ridges on which they are located.

The indication is that shell middens were established from around 6,000 BP, with earlier evidence perhaps buried by later siltation. The surface mounds appeared once mangroves had gone from the plain, and palaeochannel middens may indicate a late mangrove-bearing stage of channel infill. Woodroffe and his fellow researchers pointed out, however, that:

> A disproportionate number of middens on the coastal and estuarine plains of the South Alligator River were deposited in the last 1000 years . . . It is not clear whether more abundant recent middens indicate *increased resource exploitation*, or preferential preservation of the younger material. (1988: 101; my emphasis.)

SOUTH ALLIGATOR RIVER

The above palaeoecological interpretation differs in some important respects from earlier assessments of the archaeology of the South Alligator River region. Freshwater wetlands may have existed for 4,000 years over much of the study area, and were extensive by about 2,500 years (Woodroffe et al. 1988: 101), and prior mangrove forests were highly productive in terms of useable resources. A rich complex of estuarine environments, therefore, had been established in the region for at least 7,000 years. Although rearrangements in the distribution of resources took place throughout this period, it is not clear whether the catchment area as a whole has become more productive through time as Jones (1985), for example, has argued. If rises in general productivity are to be associated with

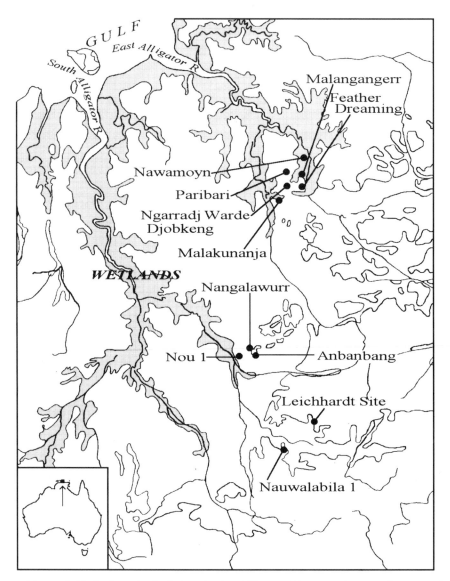

Figure 4.12 Archaeological sites in the Alligator Rivers region, Arnhem Land (based on Jones 1985a).

freshwater wetlands, as Jones considered, then this would have begun by around 4,000 BP and not around 1,500 BP.

The archaeological sequence was obtained from seven rock-shelters and one main open site (Figure 4.12). The Pleistocene Lindner site, Nauwalabila I (see Chapter Three), contained the oldest and most detailed evidence. Faunal remains were not preserved in the site, but the distribution of charcoal and stone artefacts indicate continuous use up to the present time. If the temporal distribution of these variables can be taken as a rough indication of overall intensity of site use, then a gradual increase through time is indicated. Fluctuations in the density of both charcoal and artefacts also occurs through time, but the highest concentration of material, which perhaps indicates the most intensive occupation, occurs between about 3,000 and 1,000 years ago, peaking around 2,500–2,000 BP. There is a general decrease of remains in the last 1,000 years (Jones and Johnson 1985b: 183). Introduction of elements of the Australian Small Tool tradition appear to have taken place independently; for example, the excavators argue that bifacial stone points and their technology were introduced at least by about 5,500 BP (some 1,500–1,000 years earlier than at other Arnhem Land sites). At this time the site does not appear to have been intensively occupied. In contrast however, adze/chisels are introduced around 3,500 years ago, which marks the start of the most intensive phase of stone tool discard and possibly of site use (Jones 1985: 296).

The other sites excavated during this field project support and expand upon the sequence derived from Nauwalabila I. Four of these rock-shelters are located in the region of the Nourlangie Rock outlier, some 10 kilometres or so from the rich wetlands regions. Anbanbang I (Jones and Johnson 1985a: 39–76) was occupied initially sometime before c. 6,000 BP (black silt levels) and very intensively between about 1,200 and 700 BP. A plentiful array of organic materials are found in the 'intensive' upper unit.

Nearby, the Spirit Cave in some ways reflects the Anbanbang I sequence. Very sparse occupation in lower levels was succeeded by a dense upper unit of plentiful stone artefacts, including two edge-ground axes, which has a basal date of about 2,500 BP. From atop Mount Brockman, some 16 kilometres away, the Yiboiog rock-shelter has a rich upper unit with a basal date of around 1,100 BP. Plant and faunal preservation is excellent and includes shellfish, macropodid, possum, lizard and goanna. Stone artefacts reflect those of the upper levels of Anbanbang I, and the deposit extends a further two metres to basal rubble, but is as yet undated.

Jones associated this recent intensive phase of the last 1,000 years or so, in his suite of sites, to the creation of the highly productive wetlands, which were considered to have come into being between about 1,500 and 1,000 years ago (1985b: 291–292). Around these marshlands were found extensive open sites, composed of thousands of stone artefacts, which included adze/chisel slugs, stone points, edge-grounds axes and grinding mortars and pestles. Jones suggested that these sites were for the exploitation of plants, such as *Eleocharis* spike rush corms, as well as geese and other water birds. On a transect of 16 kilometres on the east bank of the South Alligator River, six large open sites were studied, and one of these, Ki'na, was excavated. Ki'na was an extensive flat mound of earth (perhaps constructed from parts of termite mounds and used as earth ovens) which also included mussel shells. The site had a basal date of c. 280 ± 140 BP. From this largely surface evidence Jones speculated that this complex of wetland sites was about 1,000–500 years old (1985b: 291). He argued that seasonal (dry season) use of the wetlands may have drawn people from far-flung sites such as Nauwalabila I, which is some 40 kilometres away, and where a decrease in occupation was indicated during the last 1,000 years.

Interpreting this archaeological sequence largely from an environmental perspective, Jones viewed economic and demographic changes as the product of two main environmental events: the arrival of the post-glacial sea, and the recent formation of the freshwater wetlands. He considered that it was only about one thousand years ago, with the transformation of the wetland landscape and the appearance of the freshwater swamps, that the population density increased dramatically and the Aboriginal economy was reorganised to take advantage of the new food resources which abounded in the swamps (Jones 1985b: 293).

Jones viewed the population density of the area, prior to the formation of wetlands, as low. He considered this earlier occupation as ephemeral and seasonal, much like the Aboriginal settlement pattern of the dry inland areas of Arnhem Land in recent times. Jones suggested that wetlands were used during the dry season, and that the contemporary outlier sites, some 15–25 kilometres away, were occupied mainly during the wet season. He extended this model to other productive estuarine environments of the tropical coastline of north Australia, and suggested that these also might be of recent origin. For example, he cited the unpublished work by Betty Meehan on the Blyth River plains, where sites older than 1,500 years are yet to be found. In all, these recent environmental changes in the South Alligator River region were viewed by Jones as having 'profound economic and probably social consequences for the Aboriginal populations' (1985b: 294).

This interpretation of Rhys Jones', however, is essentially environmentally deterministic. He did not explore possible alternative human responses to changing environmental conditions. Nor did he consider the significant cultural and environmental changes that *pre-date* the last thousand years. As has been shown above, freshwater wetlands first formed in the area around 4,000 years ago and rich estuarine conditions up to 8,000 years ago. Bifacial points are first introduced about 6,000–5,000 BP and adze/chisels from around 3,000 BP (at Nauwalabila 1). Nauwalabila I indicates maximum use from about 3,000 BP, the outlier site of Spirit Cave about 2,500 BP, and Anbanbang I and Yiboiog in the last thousand years. Also, the wetland site of Ki'na is unusual in that it has a build-up of deposit unlike most other wetland sites (Jones 1985a: 103; also Hiscock and Kershaw 1992: 68–69) and has a very recent basal date which post-dates wetland formation by thousands of years. Important changes, therefore, in the introduction of stone technology and intensity of site use (which are analogous in some ways to those Jones associated with recent transformations in demography) economic and broader social factors, took place up to *6,000–3,000 years ago*. These cultural changes occurred also at sites which are not directly connected with the recent wetlands, that is in drier, less productive locales.

It could be argued, therefore, that a dynamic sequence of cultural events appears to have taken place from around 6,000–5,000 years BP, and to have continued more or less throughout the late Holocene right up to the time of colonial contact. Environmental changes, overall, cannot be viewed as the controlling factor, and in some cases their relationship is unclear. As well, the issue of siltation of the plain may be connected to these events, and it appears to be related to human impact on the landscape, in particular the long-term firing of vegetation. It has been argued that this process led to 'major erosion of the soft mantle of deposit on the escarpment, and the accumulation of the sands at its foot and on the floors of the inland river valleys' (Jones 1985b: 297). Presumably wetland formation also is associated with these events. This evidence may point to increasing human impact upon the natural environment and thus indirectly indicates increasingly changing cultural practices, demographic changes, or both, *pre-dating* the last one thousand years. The sequence of events beginning around 6,000 years BP, if not before, and including cultural and environmental changes, is more complex, therefore, than present models allow.

EAST ALLIGATOR RIVER

The paleoenvironmental information for this region published by Woodroffe et al. (1988) in general is consistent with the reassessment of the South Alligator material. A broadly similar palaeoenvironmental sequence was also obtained from the East Alligator River plain by Clark and Guppy (1988). This new evidence also fits the archaeological pattern of this region, which I discuss below. For example, estuarine middens occur from about 7,000–6,000 BP at the sites known as Nawamoyn, Malakunanja II, Malangangerr (see also Woodroffe et al. 1988: 102), with substantial use of aquatic and terrestrial resources recorded at sites throughout this period. (It is suggested also that freshwater resources were employed at Nourlangie I long before 1,500 BP.)

The archaeological evidence from the East Alligator River studies of Carmel Schrire (1982) and Jo Kamminga and Harry Allen (1973) are now considered in light of the above interpretations. Schrire excavated five rock-shelters, three on the estuarine plain (Paribari, Malangangerr and Nawamoyn), and two some 30 kilometres away on the elevated plateau (Jimeri I and II). Kamminga and Allen excavated a total of eight rock-shelters. Ngarradj Warde Djobkeng, Malakunanja II and Feather Dreaming are situated in close proximity to Schrire's plain sites, while the remainder lie further to the south and include the Burial Cave (Nou I, Nourlangie), Nangalawurr, and the Lindner site (see above), together with the Leichhardt site and the Disturbed site in the Deaf Adder Gorge. For the sake of brevity I will consider all these sites as one group.

Estuarine conditions existed on the plains some time between about 7,000 and 6,000 BP, as is indicated by the basal dates of shell middens within the sites of Malangangerr (5,980 ± 140 BP), Nawamoyn (7,110 ± 130 BP) and Malakunanja II (6,355 ± 250 BP). In contrast to these, the estuarine shell middens at Paribari (3,120 ± 100 BP) and Ngarradj (3,450 ± 125 BP) appear up to 3,000 years later. Schrire (1982) attributes this to the proximity of the sites to estuarine resources, but we cannot rule out also differential cultural use of the sites through time as a likely contributing factor. Variations also were detected in the proportions of estuarine shellfish through time at both Malangangerr and Nawamoyn (Schrire 1982: 89, 122). The suggestion, therefore, is of quite a dynamic sequence of environmental or economic change, or both of these possibilities.

These estuarine shell middens contain a broad range of aquatic and terrestrial fauna, which includes mammals (kangaroo, wallaby, possum, bandicoot, rat), fish (barramundi, catfish), reptiles (python, goanna), birds (geese), and crabs. Similarly, from their preliminary analysis of Ngarradj, Kamminga and Allen noted a larger proportion of terrestrial fauna in the levels underlying the shell midden, followed by increasingly greater quantities of aquatic resources in upper levels. In the uppermost layers only aquatic resources were found. They tentatively interpreted this sequence as representing the establishment of estuarine conditions (Kamminga and Allen 1973: 30).

In contrast, a casual inspection of the tables of faunal remains from Malangangerr and Nawamoyn suggests that there was a greater range and number of terrestrial species in the upper midden levels (Schrire 1982: 90 table 31, 123 table 53). These observations may be misleading, however, unless they are supported by a broader range of radiocarbon dates and sedimentary analyses to document the rates of deposition of these assemblages. Until such detailed studies of these sites have been conducted, basic questions such as the intensity of site and resource use and the distinction between environmental and economic changes must remain unanswered (also Schrire 1982: 235, 258).

The question of the appearance of freshwater wetlands in this East Alligator River region now needs to be discussed. The Burial Cave (Nourlangie, Nou I) has a 40-cm deep shell-midden in its upper layers, composed predominantly of freshwater mussel, *Velesunio angaasi*, together with mixed aquatic and terrestrial resources. The site is thought to document the existence of a freshwater billabong located some 100 metres away. Unfortunately the midden layer is undated, although at a depth of 80 cms a basal date of 8,630 ± 310 BP for the site was obtained from an underlying sand layer (Kamminga and Allen 1973: 64–66). Whether the freshwater midden of Nourlangie I correlates with the chronology of freshwater wetland formation, described by Woodroffe et al. (above) for the South Alligator River region, is an open question. As no estuarine deposits are indicated at the site, and given the basal date, the freshwater midden at Nourlangie I may be considerably older.

Partial resolution of this question can be obtained from Paribari, Malangangerr and Nawamoyn. At these sites sparse deposits of freshwater mussel, *V. angaasi*, are recorded from the most recent levels (Schrire 1982: 52, 89, 122). The stratigraphic location of freshwater mussel in all three sites suggests a recent date, and therefore generally correlates with Jones' findings from the South Alligator River region. But the sparseness of the material at Schrire's sites, when compared with the density of evidence in the underlying estuarine midden layers, does not support Jones' model of an intensification of site and resource use in association with the formation of freshwater wetlands. At these three sites (Paribari, Malangangerr and Nawamoyn) more intensive use of the sites and resources had taken place *long before* the period of freshwater wetland formation (also Allen and Barton 1989).

Holocene occupation is visible on the plains here from around 8,000 years ago (Ngarradj and Nourlangie I), and estuarine shell middens were established perhaps by about 6,000 BP, if not before. Cultural changes, which included the introduction of stone artefact forms, however, appear well *after* the beginning of this estuarine phase and by a considerable period of time, as Schrire pointed out. Bifacial stone points, in particular, appeared between about 5,000 and 4,000 BP at Paribari, Malangangerr, Nawamoyn, Malakunanja II, Ngarardj and Nourlangie I (Schrire 1982: 238). Further inland, at the plateau sites of Jimeri I and II, the introduction of stone points occurred at $3,820 \pm 100$ BP and $4,770 \pm 150$ BP respectively (Schrire 1982: 239). In Deaf Adder Gorge stone points appeared well after about 5,000 BP, judging from stratigraphic evidence, and at the Leichhardt site, as well as the Lindner site (Nauwalabila I), from around 3,000 BP (Kamminga and Allen 1973: 87, 96). As we saw earlier, Jones (1985) argued strongly for an earlier date for the introduction of stone points at the Lindner site.

Data from other sites in northern Australia reinforce the late Holocene date for the introduction of stone points. At Ingaladdi they appeared at $2,890 \pm 73$ BP (ANU 57) (Mulvaney 1975: 291), and at Yarar around $3,350 \pm 90$ BP (V 72) (Flood 1970: 30–31; Schrire 1982: 239). There appears to be no coincidence, therefore, between the establishment of estuarine conditions and changes in stone artefact technology, as also pointed out by Schrire.

SUMMARY: ALLIGATOR RIVERS REGION

The examination of the research of the East Alligator River area appears to support the re-evaluation of the findings from the South Alligator River region as argued above. If we combine the evidence from both regions and their surrounding outliers, some broad conclusions may be drawn.

While the region as a whole displays widespread evidence of earlier Pleistocene occupation, the most obvious signs of Holocene habitation of the plains occurred around the time of estuarine development about 6,000 years ago. Analogous environmental changes in the East Alligator River region, that is the formation of wetlands, do not appear to be as dramatic as those of the South Alligator River region. In contrast, the richness of archaeological deposits is associated with the earlier *estuarine* phases of the mid–late Holocene which continue in this region up until the present.

Environmental changes, therefore, represented by the establishment of estuarine conditions and later freshwater wetlands, do not fully explain the archaeological patterns. The sequence of archaeological changes does not coincide completely with the above environmental events. As well, comparable archaeological changes also took place at sites further inland in areas not directly connected with either estuarine or freshwater locales. The question of differential cultural responses to both natural and socio-cultural environmental changes needs to be pursued more carefully at these sites. We cannot assume, therefore, that socio-cultural and demographic changes evident in this region merely reflected changes in local environmental factors.

If we are to try to answer questions about possible demographic and socio-economic changes, as both Jones and Schrire have suggested (above), the first archaeological indications are that these took place with the onset of estuarine conditions by around 6,000 BP. Further indication of these trends may be argued from around 3,000 BP to about 2,000 BP (by which time freshwater wetlands were forming); these involved greater use of sites, the establishment of new sites and the introduction of new stone technology. Following this phase, further changes more or less continued up to the present. This final phase involved the presumed association of freshwater wetlands with intensive site use, continued and perhaps more intensive use of estuarine middens, together with possibly less use of some inland sites.

If these archaeological impressions can be associated with demographic and economic changes, two alternative explanatory models may be proposed. The first is that fairly steady socio-cultural and demographic changes (including possible increases in population) took place from around 6,000 BP and continued more or less up to the historical period. The second model is that while changes in demography and society may have occurred from about 6,000 BP, the process appears to peak between about 3,000 and 2,000 BP. This phase was followed by substantial demographic and socio-cultural rearrangements, including a greater emphasis on freshwater wetlands, and, possibly, a reduction in the use of some inland areas.

At present I believe the first model appears to accommodate better the information from both study areas and their apparent contradictions (see also Allen and Barton 1989).

Art and social networks of northern Australia

Further clues regarding the spatial and temporal complexity of Australian Aboriginal social interaction can be obtained from rock art studies, which, as already observed, are presently receiving much attention. Morwood, for example, has documented a shift from non-figurative engravings to figurative paintings in the central Queensland highlands, some time around 5,000–4,000 BP (1979, 1980, 1981, 1984). Stratified ochres were used to infer the dating of the art. Morwood interpreted the change as a move from esoteric and restricted symbolic art to more public art. Inasmuch as non-figurative art was produced up to the present in the form of sacred art, it could be proposed that a development of dual social spheres may be observed – the esoteric (sacred) and the public (secular).

A broadly comparable case study comes from northwestern Queensland (David 1991, 1994; David and Cole 1990), although interpretations are somewhat different. Bruno David and Noelene Cole compared ethnohistorical evidence of two separate exchange networks in northwestern and northern Queensland (Cape York), with evidence of separate – stylistically distinctive – rock art provinces in the same two areas (see Figure 4.13). An extensive, more open social and exchange network operated in the west, and a more regionalised, less open system, based upon short-distance exchange, in the north. For the western province, a more homogeneous set of rock art styles is documented, while in Cape York differing regional rock art styles are found (see Figure 4.14). In Cape York, two main rock art provinces are located lying to the north and south of the Mitchell and Walsh Rivers; a mainly figurative northern tradition and a southern non-figurative. Each of these is further sub-divided into regionalised styles, and the southern region also shows similarities to rock art of northwestern Queensland. These spatial patterns in art styles were substantiated by a detailed statistical study (David 1994). David argued that both these social (exchange) networks and painted art styles developed in the late Holocene (especially during the last thousand years or so), and were preceded by an earlier and more homogeneous rock engraving style which is found in both areas (1991, 1994; David and Cole 1990). Archaeological evidence, mainly of stratified ochres similar to those used in the paintings, and excavated within rock-shelters and caves containing paintings, supports this chronological scheme to a large extent.

Demographic changes, including increases in Aboriginal populations, may have led to the development of the two regional networks. The more open network may have operated as a cultural buffer to the harsher semi-arid conditions of the northwest, and the more regionalised (more 'closed') network developed in the more fertile environment of Cape York. Archaeological information of site use in the region also lends further support, indicating that most sites (including rock-shelters) were mainly occupied in the late Holocene (as observed earlier in this chapter). David (1994), following the European Palaeolithic studies of Jochim (1983) and Gamble (1986a), views the so-called recent, spatially varied rock art styles as indicating more regionalised territorial networks, the result of more dynamic, increasingly intensive land use and ownership. He found no direct relationship between these patterns and climatic change, which may have, for example, led to a rise in bioproduction followed by an increase in Aboriginal populations.

Morwood's research in southeast Cape York has produced broadly similar conclusions (Morwood 1993; Morwood and Hobbs 1995) (see also above, this chapter). The earliest rock engravings in the region date to the terminal Pleistocene–early Holocene period and are composed of pecked panels of non-figurative (geometric) and track motifs. Morwood and Hobbs suggest that this

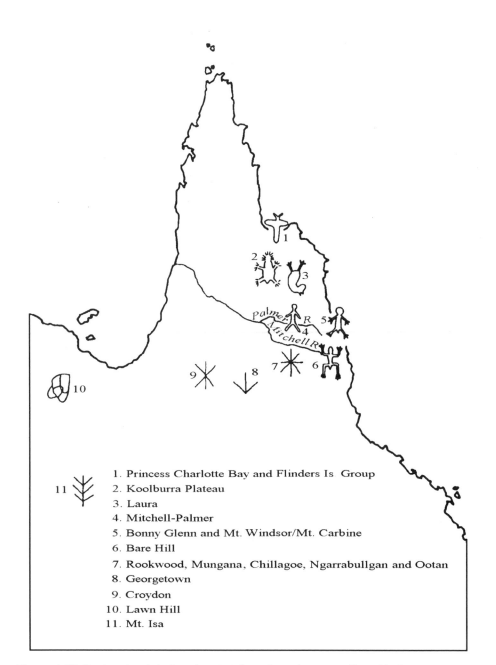

Figure 4.13 Regional painted rock art styles of northeastern Cape York, Queensland, and northwestern Queensland (based on David 1994: 291, Figure 148).

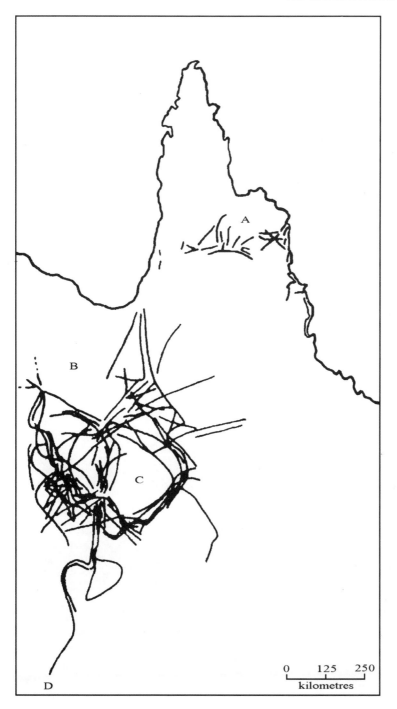

Figure 4.14 Social interaction (groups A, B, C, D) in northern and western Queensland, as documented by Roth (1897–1910) (based on David 1994: 303, Figure 149; compare with Morwood 1987). Two distinct patterns of social interaction within and between groups are indicated; short-distance interaction in the north (short lines) and long-distance interaction in the southwest (longer lines).

Figure 4.15 Garnawala 1, Wardaman country, northern Australia, 1990 (Photo: Bruno David. David et al. 1994. Courtesy of the Binjari Association, Wardaman community).

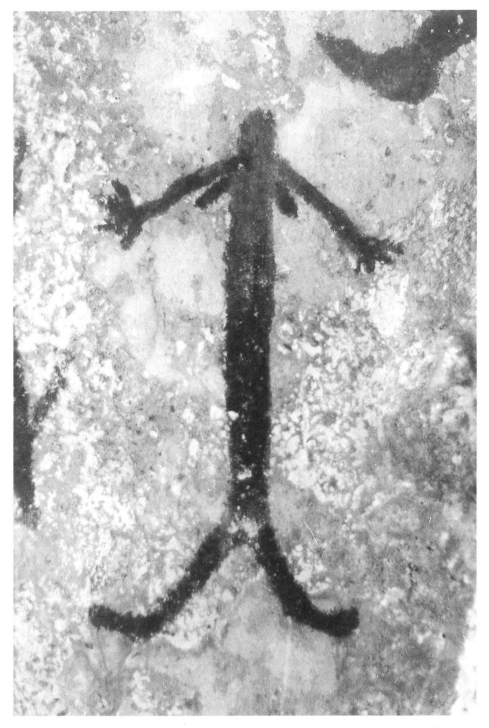

Figure 4.16 An example of mid–late Holocene rock art from the Mitchell–Palmer region, north Queensland (Photo: Bruno David. Courtesy of the North Queensland Land Council).

Figure 4.17 Another example of mid–late Holocene rock art from the Mitchell–Palmer region of north Queensland (Photo: Bruno David).

relatively homogeneous rock art tradition may have served to align a social network of low population density. In contrast, they argue that the Quinkan painted figurative tradition begins around the mid-Holocene in the area. They view these two traditions as signifying basic restructuring of Aboriginal patterns of land use. Aboriginal populations continued to increase from the terminal Pleistocene, and more so in the late Holocene, as the result of increased bio-production. This process resulted in increased territoriality in the region, which is reflected in the two different rock art traditions.

Similar recent changes in rock art towards more regionalised patterns have also been detected in Arnhem Land and further west. In the Alligator Rivers region of east Arnhem Land, broadly similar patterns have been documented for the last thousand years or so and these have been linked to the recent develop-ment of rich freshwater wetlands during that time. It has been suggested that smaller Aboriginal territorial units may have been viable in these conditions, which were then reflected linguistically (on ethnographic evidence) and in recent regionalised rock art (Taçon 1993; see also Layton 1991, 1992). As we have already seen, however, freshwater wetlands in this region extend back to about 4,000 years and rich estuarine conditions to between 8,000 and 7,000 years BP. It becomes difficult to imagine, therefore, why more territorial, regionalised pop-ulations had not arisen before. Given this problem, I would suggest that expla-nations more in line with those of David, and of Morwood and Hobbs, for the development of regionalised patterns of rock art patterns in Cape York would best fit the Arnhem Land evidence also, although details can be expected to differ somewhat (also McDonald 1994).

The post-contact period also produced major reorganisation in traditional Abo-riginal society, and this is indicated also by significant change in the rock art in northern Australia. At Yiwarlarlay I in the Northern Territory, for example, which is an important Dreaming place of the Wardaman people, the myth of the Lightning Brothers is clearly depicted. This religious cult appears at the site only in the last 150 years (as demonstrated by the presence of stratified ochres), although evidence of occupation extends back some 700 years (David et al. 1994).

Southeastern Queensland

A large number of researchers have contributed to the archaeology of this sub-tropical region (see Figure 4.18), and a number of syntheses and explanatory models have appeared (Hall 1982; Hall and Robins 1984; Morwood 1987; Walters 1987, 1989; Hall and Hiscock 1988). Sites of the region extend back beyond about 20,000 BP, which is a date obtained from Wallen Wallen Creek (Neal and Stock 1986; see Chapter Two). In his synthesis Morwood considered a sample of twenty-five archaeological sites (1987: 343–348). Apart from Wallen Wallen Creek, which appears to have been continuously occupied into fairly recent times, sites were constantly established from the time of the post-glacial

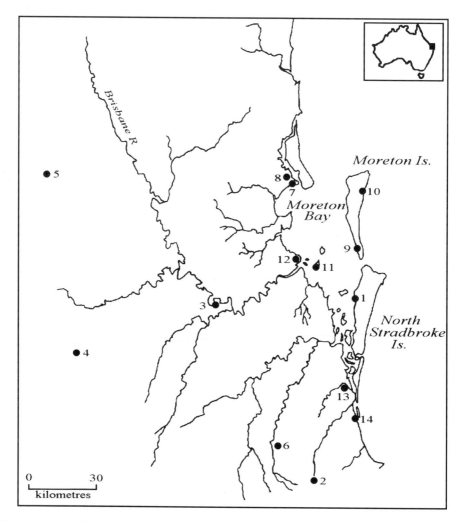

Figure 4.18 Archaeological sites of southeastern Queensland (based on Hall and Hiscock 1988: 5, Figure 1).The numbered sites are:

1. Wallen Wallen Creek
2. Bushrangers Shelter
3. Platypus Rock-shelter
4. Gatton Shelter
5. Maidenwell Shelter
6. Bishop's Peak
7. Sandstone Point
8. Brown's Road
9. Toulkerrie
10. First Ridge
11. St. Helena
12. Brisbane Airport
13. Hope Island
14. Broadbeach

stabilisation of sea levels, and especially after about 4,000 BP. He considered that most sites, however, were inhabited in the last 2,500 years, and this trend continued more or less up to the present (Figure 4.19). This increase took place in all principal environments of the region. Suggested are changes in site and resource use in both coastal and hinterland areas, including offshore islands and forested locales, for example peripheral rainforest. As well, offshore islands of Moreton Bay, such as St. Helena (Alfredson 1983: 83) and Moreton, appear to have been more intensively utilised during the last 2,500 years. Jay Hall has

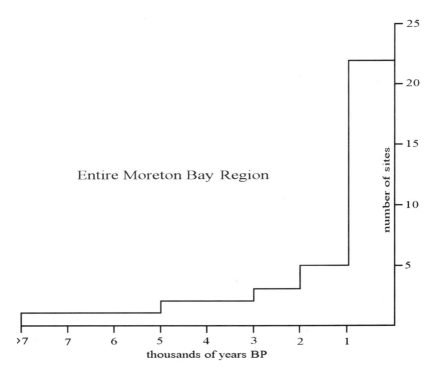

Figure 4.19 Temporal trends in the rates at which archaeological sites are first occupied in the Moreton Bay region, southeastern Queensland (based on Hall and Hiscock 1988: 12, Figure 2; compare with Morwood 1987).

cautioned, however, that many of the coastal sites in this sample may not be a true indication of the age of coastal occupation, due to changes in coastal geomorphology (1982; Hall and Robins 1984).

Wallen Wallen Creek, which is located on North Stradbroke Island, also indicates a similar sequence and 'gives evidence of a major increase in occupation of the offshore islands of Moreton Bay only during the past few millennia' (Neal and Stock 1986: 618). At this site the shell midden from this recent period indicates that:

> The inhabitants initially hunted terrestrial and aquatic vertebrate fauna, including dugong (*Dugon dugon*), pademelon (*Thylogale* sp.) and snake (*Python spilates*). This was later replaced by an exclusively coastal economy based on the littoral and marine resources of fish and shellfish, with limited dugong hunting. (Neal and Stock 1986: 618)

The suggestion here is of a more specialised and broad-based coastal emphasis in the economy of the most recent phase. Evidence from other later Holocene middens on the island support these conclusions (Neal personal communication).

The occurrence of dugong in the basal levels of the Wallen Wallen midden

and shellfish in the basal levels of the Hope Island midden indicates that biologically productive, estuarine environments had developed and were being
exploited by 4,300 BP in some sections of Moreton Bay. However, it has also
been suggested that intensive and specialised use of marine foods did not occur
until much later (Morwood 1987: 346). Subsequent excavations at the Airport
site (Hall 1988), which is located on the spur of a prior coastline, also indicate
coastal occupation around 4,000 BP.

Ian Walters has argued also that the fishery of Moreton Bay was largely the
product of the last 2,000 years, even though coastal resources had been available
in the bay since about 6,000 BP (1987, 1989). Walters considered that marine
exploitation had expanded from the mainland to the offshore islands, with a
general increase in these practices in the last thousand years or so. His findings
were exemplified best at the midden complex at Sandstone Point, which is
located at the northern end of the bay, and which indicates an intensification of
fishing and shellfishing during the last 1,000–800 years (see also Nolan 1986).

These broad archaeological trends are also apparent in a number of hinterland
rock-shelters in the region, which are all first occupied between about 6,000 and
3,000 BP. These sites include Bushranger's Cave, Platypus Shelter, Maidenwell,
Gatton and Bishop's Peak. Rock art is also found at the last three rock-shelters,
which date from about 4,000 BP, thereby associating them in some way with
the intergroup and territorial behaviour discussed above. The chronological trend
is clearly represented at Gatton (Morwood 1987: 346–347), which is situated
upon a natural passage between coast and ranges known to have been used in
the 1840s by Aboriginal groups on their way to the Bunya Mountains. In the
earlier levels of the site, which date from about 3,800 BP, an emphasis was
placed upon two species (*Macropus dorsalis* and *Thylogale* sp.) from ecotonal
areas between wet sclerophyll forest and rainforest. In the recent levels a more
diverse range of smaller-bodied species was included; this had been taken from
'canopy and hollow tree locations in dry and wet sclerophyll forests (for example,
arboreals, goannas, pythons)' (Morwood 1987: 347). Morwood interpreted this
trend as an indication of 'a broadening of the resource base with more intensive
exploitation of wider habitat and species ranges' (1987: 347).

A taphonomic study of the faunal remains from Gatton was also conducted.
Throughout the period of occupation increased rates in the deposition of fauna,
charcoal and sediments indicate more intensive use of the site.

> Through time there was a reduction in … stone artefact densities, range of knapping
> debris, and number of stone artefact types … *If* changes in the artefactual and faunal
> sequences are functionally related, then general changes in the technology of predation
> are indicated. These possibly involved a change in emphasis from 'individual pursuit
> strategies' (ambush, tracking, stalking), in which both spears and macropods featured
> prominently, to use of both individual pursuit and cooperative hunting strategies and
> nets. Certainly many of the species represented which occupy dense undergrowth
> scrub are most readily captured in communal drives using hunting nets, and Petrie

(1904, 86) notes that this was the method used by Aborigines in the general Brisbane area for hunting wallabies, kangaroo rats, 'paddymelons' and bandicoots. (Morwood 1987: 347)

Morwood's speculations led him to conclude:

Economic diversification to emphasise use of abundant small-bodied species at Gatton, Sandstone Point and Wallen Wallen, and the development of appropriate extractive technologies and techniques, imply periodic resource stress ... by historic times high population densities and social demands on production seem to have been the principal factors involved ... Increased emphasis late in the regional sequence upon use of communal extractive techniques, such as large drives, nets and stone wall fishtraps, also has implications for organisational complexity and resource management ... (1987: 347)

In this explanation (that there was increasing population and social complexity) Morwood viewed population as increasing from around 6,000 BP, initially as a response to a rise in coastal bioproduction following the stabilisation of mid-Holocene sea levels. He attributed later increases in population, which appear to be registered archaeologically especially in the last 2,000 years, to socio-demographic factors. The archaeological evidence that Morwood drew upon for support included increases in the establishment and use of sites, and the employment of a broader range of resources and microenvironments (marine, island and terrestrial) during the most recent phase. He associated increases in social complexity and interaction with a range of recent sites of symbolic-ceremonial significance (rock art, bora rings), the appearance of exotic materials and new lithic types. Morwood also suggested that the reduced occupation of certain sites in the most recent phase is due to the development of increasing social differentiation, as exemplified by differential access to symbolic knowledge and to specific sites of ritual significance.

In Morwood's view, local population networks were centred around locations of seasonal resource abundance, such as the inland bunya nut harvests in summer and the coastal mullet fish runs during winter (see also above, Chapter Two). He argued that the establishment of reciprocal access to these centres, together with the general bioproductivity of the area, would have promoted 'the development of finely-honed, demographic flexibility and the required reciprocity network' (1987: 348). Morwood argued further that these circumstances may have led to even higher population levels and more complex patterns of social interaction (for example, exchange). He speculated that bountiful areas such as southeastern Queensland may have acted as centres of diffusion of demographic, social and technological changes, especially after about 4,000 BP on the Australian mainland.

Critical of Morwood's model were Hall and Hiscock (1988; see also Hall 1982; Hall and Robins 1984), who questioned the chronological details. They argued instead that following mid-Holocene stabilisation of sea levels, Aboriginal populations increased and gradually 'fissioned' into a number of new social groups. This development they placed in the last thousand years or so, basing their assessment on archaeological evidence. They could find no *earlier* evidence for the regionalised social groups of the area that existed during the ethnographic period (Hall and Hiscock 1988: 15). In support of this interpretation they considered the following: (i) considerable increases in sizeable coastal shell middens from around 1,000 BP; (ii) use of plant processing equipment ('bevelled pounders' associated with staple fern root) since about 1,500 BP; and (iii) the establishment of a large cemetery (Broadbeach) about 1,200 BP, indicative of territorial social identity. Further support was obtained from linguistic evidence indicating the divergence of the Gnugi language (of the Gnugi people of Moreton Island) from neighbouring languages about 1,000 years ago.

From the Cooloola area, just north of Moreton Bay, Ian McNiven has produced broadly comparable evidence of increasingly regionalised habitation in the late Holocene, based largely upon open site survey (1990, 1991; personal communication). He suggested changes in subsistence-settlement patterns, including increases in faunal resources and use of local stone over the last 900 years. A rock-shelter near Gympie, which was also excavated by McNiven, has an archaeological sequence similar to that of other rock-shelters of Moreton Bay and indicates substantial occupation only during the last 2,000 to 1,000 years. McNiven argues that the territorially coastal social networks extant in the ethnographic period may have developed during this recent period; and that prior networks were more open and extensive, incorporating both coastal and hinterland environments.

Discussion also has centred upon the question of the establishment of marine resources in the Moreton Bay area and the extent to which this has influenced the archaeological socio-economic patterns (Nolan 1986: 24, 29–30; Walters 1987: 212, 1989). By about 6,000 BP, evidence exists in Moreton Bay of *Anadara trapezia* shell beds (Flood 1980, 1981, 1984) and coral reefs (Hekel et al. 1979: 17). Shallow waters around coral reefs provide favourable conditions for fishing (Alfredson 1984: 81). Regarding the Brisbane River estuary, which flows out into Moreton Bay, optimal productivity of the area may have been between 4,000 and 3,000 years ago (Alfredson 1984: 83). Evidence existed also of mangrove communities (which provide vital sources of nutrients) in southeastern Queensland (Scarborough, Maroochydore) from the mid-Holocene (Hekel et al. 1979: 9; Bell 1979: 29; Walters 1987: 212). Research shows that mature mangrove stands can be established rapidly under favourable conditions (Quinn and Beumer 1984: 248), which arguably have existed in parts of Moreton Bay also since the mid-Holocene (Nolan 1986: 30).

When all this evidence is drawn together, the indication is that favourable conditions for the production of marine resources (fish, shellfish and the like) have existed in Moreton Bay since around 6,000 BP, and that optimal conditions, at least in parts of the bay, may have occurred between about 4,000 and 3,000 years ago. This environmental information, therefore, does not fit the archaeo-logical patterns which indicate relatively more recent exploitation (the last 2,000–1,000 years or so) and in some cases intensification of marine resources, as some other researchers have also argued.

Occupation of hinterland rock-shelters from around 6,000 to 3,000 BP coin-cides with a drier climatic phase, on evidence generally derived from other parts of eastern Australia (as no local sequences are available), and this may have facilitated the opening up of forests by fire. But the apparent increasing trend in use of these shelters throughout the last 2,000 years or so runs counter to the general climatic trend, which indicates slightly more humid conditions at this time. This suggests that once forests were opened, the process was maintained if not accelerated into recent times. Evidence of changing hunting patterns from the Gatton shelter (above), indicating shifts from closed (wet) to open (dry) forest species, may in some ways be associated with these events.

In all, a general pattern of increasingly complex socio-demographic conditions are indicated from around 6,000–3,000 BP and peaking in the last 2,000–1,000 years; perhaps initially stimulated by environmental events (changing sea levels and drier climates), but then running counter to climatic and environmental events. The evidence suggests that involved in the process were probable increases in population sizes and densities, trends towards regionalisation and territoriality, and changes in patterns of mobility and sedentism, in land and resource use (including specialisation and intensification), and intergroup social relations. These spatio-temporal patterns cannot *solely* be explained as being products of increased bioproduction followed by rises in Aboriginal population, as they do not entirely fit the environmental details, in particular those of the last 3,000 years. Also unexplained is the dearth in occupation of hinterland rock-shelters during the early Holocene, as this was a more humid period and therefore one of high bioproductivity. While expansion of forests at this time may have provided some obstacle to settlement of these areas, it does not explain the avoidance of the sites altogether. Forests are resource-rich landscapes and thereby attractive habitats. Socio-demographic explanations, therefore, also should be sought, as discussed in Chapter One (see also Chapter Nine).

Overview: Holoclene settlement

As we have seen marked changes occurred in climate and coastal landscape in northern Australia during the early Holocene period, a trend begun in the terminal Pleistocene. Warmer, more humid climate produced rises in sea levels drowning huge stretches of the north, creating the present Arafura Sea, and severing the connection with New Guinea between 8,000 and 7,000 years ago. Sea levels stabilised about 6,000–5,000 years ago, and islands were created sometime after this. Estuaries (such as those in the Alligator Rivers region), however, have more dynamic histories, starting in the early Holocene and continuing up to the present.

Effective rainfall appears to have peaked in the early Holocene, and so too the maximum extent of the expansion of forest. In contrast, the late Holocene was slightly drier, with fluctuating, more humid climates in the last two thousand years.

Archaeological records are available from a number of north Australian study areas, and there is some strong agreement in the sequence of events in these places, although the interpretations of this material vary considerably. I argue, however, that general socio-cultural and demographic trends are apparent in most parts of the north. A brief summary of the main case studies follows.

While the early Holocene experienced rather dramatic climatic changes, in contrast the archaeological record of northern Australia at present indicates a relatively steady, low-level trend in cultural shifts. There is little evidence of marked changes in demography at this time or of other major cultural changes. A steady trend in the establishment and use of sites, however, generally is evident from the terminal Pleistocene. Evidence for more significant socio-cultural and demographic changes appears during the late Holocene, from around 4,000 or so years ago, increasing after about 3,000 years, and particularly in the last 1,500 years or so.

These general trends are apparent in most study areas. These regions include Cape York and the coastal Princess Charlotte Bay area, the related rainforest belt of northeast Queensland and north Queensland highlands, the offshore islands of the Queensland coast (including the Whitsundays and Keppel Islands), the coastal and hinterland region of southeast Queensland, the Alligator Rivers region of Arnhem Land, and the Kimberley region of northwestern Australia. There are changes in patterns of settlement and resource use, in the use of more peripheral environments (such as islands, forests and wetlands), in technology, as well as in rock art. These socio-cultural changes include an increase in numbers and use of sites, the appearance of new sites, such as large shell and earth mounds (Cape York and Arnhem Land, for example), alterations in and intensification of use of resources (for example, labour-intensive plants such as cycads, grass seeds, fern root and those of the rainforest as well as marine resources), the introduction of new stone, bone and marine technology (for example, new artefact types, some associated with plant processing), as well as a domesticated animal – the dingo – together with new regionalised styles of rock art.

While individual interpretations of this information vary, it is clear that these socio-cultural changes do not *only* reflect reactions to alterations in climate and, therefore, in the general distribution of resources. For example, there is no evidence of *marked* change in demography – an indication perhaps of population increase – during the early Holocene when climate was most humid and bio-production high; rather, this appears to occur in the late Holocene, when climate was relatively more stressful, with a corresponding effect upon resources. Similarly, coastal cultural changes (including those of estuaries) do not correspond to the time of sea level stabilisation around the mid-Holocene, but several thousand years later, during the last 3,500 years or so. And while the spread of closed forests may have been checked somewhat about 3,000 years ago by the relatively drier climate, archaeological trends towards increasing Aboriginal use of these environments continue largely up to the present. This is in spite of increased humidity and corresponding increased distribution of forest in the last few thousand years. Examples of this are found in northeastern and southeastern Queensland.

My own interpretation of this material is that Aboriginal settlement, as reflected in demographic and socio-cultural patterns, generally follows the environmental trends from the terminal Pleistocene and early Holocene periods, diverging significantly from these in the late Holocene. Since the terminal Pleistocene, climatic amelioration may have increased bioproduction, which was followed by some increases in Aboriginal population. This trend continues throughout the early Holocene. In the late Holocene, however, and especially since about 3,500 years ago, more significant changes are apparent in Aboriginal demography, society and economy. The suggestion here is of relative increases in Aboriginal population together with shifts towards an increased use of sites and locales. These trends are apparent in a wide range of environments, including coastal areas, estuaries, wetlands, and uplands. More peripheral environments, such as offshore islands and forests, are also involved. Changes in technology and resource use also reflect, to some extent, these shifts towards more intensive and complex patterns of land use. Transformations and regionalisation in styles of rock art during this period in Cape York (and Arnhem Land) reinforce this interpretation to some extent. These have been interpreted as shifts from more 'open' towards relatively more 'closed' social relations and territorial patterns. Greater formalisation of social relations is reflected here. Reversals in these general trends, however, are also evident in the central Queensland uplands. Indeed, the entire process could be best characterised as one of greater dynamism involving a variety of socio-cultural and demographic patterns, which I return to in Chapter Nine.

Overview

As might be predicted, some of the earliest evidence from Greater Australia is found in the north of the continent, in this case from the raised Huon Terraces of New Guinea around 40,000 years ago and northern Queensland not long after. More of the earliest evidence of coastal deposits and use of coastal resources is also found close to the Pleistocene coast on the islands of New Ireland and New Britain from about 33,000 years, indicating clearly that use of islands was part of the earliest foraging practices. Island use may indeed be part of a long-standing tradition, stretching back to the time when the islands of northern Greater Australia first became incorporated into the world of the original Australian migrants from Southeast Asia.

Other early coastal sites are also found in northwestern and central western Australia from about 32,000 years, and occupation of parts of Highland New Guinea, Arnhem Land and Cape York is increasingly evident also throughout the last 32,000 years. At this time, climate, although cold and dry, supported large inland bodies of fresh water, and more forested environments; sea levels were lower, exposing large stretches of coastal plain, especially in northern Australia. Compared with the succeeding period, this was a time of relatively abundant resources.

With the onset of increasingly dry conditions after about 25,000 years, which reached a low point around 18,000 years – the time of the glacial maximum – there is evidence that a contraction of populations took place in 'refuge' areas fringing the more arid regions. This is so in parts of Cape York (Fern Cave), and Arnhem Land (Alligator Rivers), and in northwestern and central coast western Australia. Sites in the latter two regions were also abandoned towards the end of this dry phase (for example Koolan Island 2, Widgingarri 1 and 2 and Mandu Mandu Creek). Broadly similar trends took place in semi-arid and arid areas of the north (for instance, Colless Creek; see also Chapter Five).

During the terminal Pleistocene, after about 15,000 years, there is a slight general increase in numbers and use of sites, as well as the suggestion of relatively more intensive, and extensive, use of some resources and landscapes (for example, in highland New Guinea and New Ireland; also parts of northeastern Queensland). The implication here is of increasing population sizes and densities, although their relationship to improving climates is as yet unclear.

Climatic changes in mainland Australia were dramatic during the early Holocene (for example, higher rainfall), and there is evidence of some demographic changes, such as increases in or redistribution of Aboriginal populations. Still stronger evidence of these does exist, however, in highland New Guinea, but there is little evidence in north Australia (as yet) of marked cultural changes at this time. Neither do significant demographic or cultural changes take place at the time of sea level stabilisation during the mid-Holocene.

More important cultural, and possibly demographic, changes are evident, however, after about 4,000–3,500 years ago. Changes continue to occur, and often in increased magnitude, during the last 1,500 years or so. At this time, there are alterations in stone artefacts (that is, new types), fishing equipment, use of processed plants (for example, cycads), regional art styles, and in settlement patterns with the establishment of new sites (and new site types) and increased occupation of older sites. As well, offshore islands are now either utilised for the first time or more intensively occupied.

These patterns are apparent in a wide range of regions and ecological zones, including the coastal, upland and rainforest sectors of Cape York, the offshore islands of the lengthy Queensland coastline, the coast and hinterland of southeastern Queensland, as well as in northwestern Australia. The archaeological patterns are also evident, although perhaps not as clearly, in the Alligator Rivers regions of Arnhem Land.

Changes in rock art styles (largely from schematic peckings to paintings) during the late Holocene also are generally in support of this hypothesis. In Cape York these changes towards regionalised rock art styles have been linked to demographic rearrangements, in particular to territorial shifts towards more regionalised, more 'closed' social entities. Similar changes in rock art styles towards regionalised groupings of paintings have been reported from Arnhem Land and from further west. Only in the central Queensland highlands is there a notable alteration in pattern. Here late Holocene cultural changes are followed by apparent reversals in site use after about 2,000 years ago.

Overall, therefore, there appears to be a closer relationship between the archaeological and environmental trends in the terminal Pleistocene and early Holocene periods, and strong differences in both these trends in the late Holocene, after about 4,000 years ago. In some ways these general archaeological patterns reflect those of the arid and semi-arid areas which border the humid tropical belt of northern and northeastern Australia. We now turn to a discussion of these in the following chapter.

CHAPTER 5

ARID AND SEMI-ARID AUSTRALIA

Together the arid and semi-arid regions make up two-thirds of the present continent of Australia, and in the past they were even more extensive. This chapter considers the archaeology and prehistory of these harsh areas during the Pleistocene and Holocene periods.

PLEISTOCENE SETTLEMENT

Palaeoenvironment

For arid and semi-arid regions of Australia, palaeoenvironmental information has been obtained mainly from lake and dune sites. For arid Australia, sequences come from Lake Frome, at the southern end of the Strzelecki dunefield (Bowler and Wasson 1984; Bowler and Magee 1990), and also Lake Eyre (Ross et al. 1992); while for the semi-arid belt, evidence has been derived from the Willandra Lakes (Bowler and Wasson 1984) and also Lake Tyrrel in northwestern Victoria (Bowler and Teller 1986) (Figure 5.1). In general, this information points to high lake levels prior to 25,000 years ago, which is an indication that while climate was dry, evaporation rates were low due to depressed temperatures. Colder, drier climate followed until the glacial maximum around 18,000 years, and continued somewhat until about 15,000 years ago. During this phase lake levels fluctuated. This more stressful phase was followed by a general climatic amelioration towards the start of the Holocene period around 10,000 years ago.

The arid zone

The timing of settlement of the Australian arid zone has been the cornerstone of many of the most influential models in Australia prehistory. Birdsell (as I have

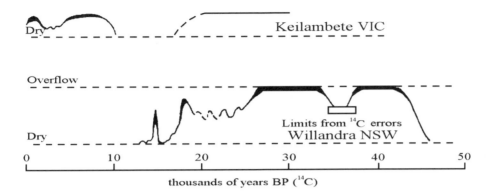

Figure 5.1 Lake levels from the Willandra Lakes (semi-arid zone) during the late Pleistocene, and from Lake Keilambete, southwestern Victoria, during the Late Pleistocene and Holocene periods (based on Bowler et al. 1976: 377, Figure 6: see also Ross et al. 1992: 78, Figure 5.1).

already discussed) considered that occupation of arid Australia took place relatively soon after initial colonisation, within a matter of millennia (1953, 1957). Until about a decade ago, however, archaeological evidence pointed to a terminal Pleistocene–early Holocene settlement. Richard Gould, for example, argued for long-term cultural stability or equilibrium in the Australian arid zone, basing his argument upon the key excavated rock-shelter of Puntutjarpa (1977a,b). Gould developed the concept of the 'Australian desert culture', largely from ethnographic information and his own ethnoarchaeological investigations. He viewed this cultural adaptation as being largely unchanged, at least for the length of the Holocene period, basing his ideas upon the apparently continuous 10,000-year-old archaeological sequence at Puntutjarpa.

The notion of long-term cultural stability in the Australian arid zone has developed along several lines of enquiry. Most explanations have taken into consideration the peculiar resource base of the region, in particular the plant species. Golson, largely following Sauer's hypothesis, suggested that seeds may have replaced tropical plants in the diet of arid-region dwellers (Golson 1971). Archaeological investigation has continued to highlight seed use and its introduction as the key to understanding the cultural adaptations to arid and semi-arid zones and their long-term stability. Bowdler (1977), for example, considered that the arid zone was not effectively settled until the development of seed-grinding in the terminal Pleistocene, basing her assessment upon the estimation of the time of introduction of grindstones (Allen 1974; see below), and the Puntutjarpa archaeological sequence (Gould 1968). Others have viewed seed use largely as a prerequisite to the occupation of these harsh environments (for example, O'Connell and Hawkes 1981: 114–116).

More recently, it has been considered that Australia's arid zone, or parts of it,

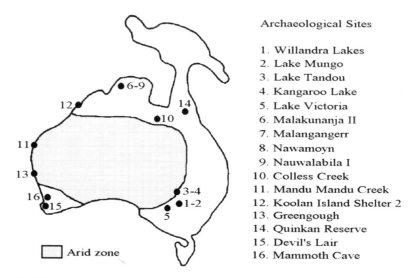

Archaeological Sites

1. Willandra Lakes
2. Lake Mungo
3. Lake Tandou
4. Kangaroo Lake
5. Lake Victoria
6. Malakunanja II
7. Malangangerr
8. Nawamoyn
9. Nauwalabila I
10. Colless Creek
11. Mandu Mandu Creek
12. Koolan Island Shelter 2
13. Greengough
14. Quinkan Reserve
15. Devil's Lair
16. Mammoth Cave

Figure 5.2 Pleistocene archaeological sites surrounding the arid zone prior to about 25,000 years ago (based on Ross et al. 1992: 99, Figure 5.17a).

had been inhabited earlier during the Pleistocene (Hughes and Lampert 1980; Hiscock 1984; Lourandos 1985a, 1987a). New evidence now has been found to confirm this with the discovery of the central Australian site of Puritjarra which has been dated to about 22,000 BP (and which is covered below). Some would argue, however, that even earlier signs of use of relatively arid lands also exist. Because of this, I begin with a general examination of archaeological evidence from the periphery of the arid core and predating about 22,000 BP.

Pre-c. 22,000 BP

Increasingly dry conditions began around Australia sometime after 30,000 BP, but even before this, back to 37,000 BP, there is evidence of settlement of regions encircling today's arid core (Figure 5.2). The oldest sites are located in semi-arid New South Wales and include the Willandra Lakes (Lake Mungo), Lake Tandou and Lake Victoria. For the open site of Greenough on the Murchison River in southwestern Australia dates of 37,000 BP are claimed (Wyrwoll and Dortch 1978), while on the central coast of Western Australia the Mandu Mandu Creek rock-shelter abutted the desert around 25,000 years ago (see Chapter Four). And along the northern arid fringe of the continent we have the sites of Koolan Island Shelter 2, dating from 27,000 BP, in the northwest, and in north Queensland the sites of Ngarrabullgan, Sandy Creek 1 (Quinkan Reserve) and Fern Cave respectively from 37,000 BP, 32,000 BP and 26,000 BP. Evidence of increasing aridity is found at many of these sites, and in these regions, and this has been viewed as reflecting human adaptation to drier climates – the precursors of people adapted to true desert occupation (Ross et al. 1992: 97).

c. 22,000–10,000 BP

Indisputable archaeological evidence for settlement of central arid Australia occurs from about 22,000 BP, a time of increasingly dry climate which reached its nadir around 18,000 BP – the glacial maximum. During this driest of periods signs of settlement appear throughout the arid core that now also included the semi-arid zone (see Figure 5.3). The central Australian site of Puritjarra was first occupied from between 21,950 ± 270 BP (Beta 19901) and 22,440 ± 1370 BP(Beta 18884), if not earlier as the stratigraphic evidence suggests (Smith 1987). This sandstone rock-shelter is located in the Cleland Hills, west of the MacDonnell Ranges. The Pleistocene levels contain stone artefacts, including large flakes and large flake implements, charcoal, plus a small piece of red pigment. The site was inhabited intermittently from about 22,000 until 12,000 BP, that is to say during the most arid phase of the Pleistocene. From around 6,000 BP the rock-shelter was occupied more frequently and most intensively after about 1,900 BP (see below).

Some would argue that evidence already existed of arid zone Pleistocene occupation. Koonalda, a deep limestone sinkhole and cave system on the broad Nullarbor Plain, served principally as a flint quarry from about 24,000 until 15,000 BP (Wright 1971a). Today the site is located on the southern margins of Australia's great arid belt, and is relatively close to the coast. During the Pleistocene, however, it was situated up to 180 kilometres inland, and there is evidence of prehistoric quarrying some 75 metres or more below the surface of the plain, and deep within the cave system. Archaeological excavations of around six metres in depth produced evidence of specialised flint quarrying, such as flakes, charcoal and hearths. Raw materials appear to have been transported elsewhere for further use, but there is no evidence that the site was inhabited as a camping spot. In the deeper recesses of the cave system were found various panels of wall engravings which cover an extensive area. The engravings consist largely of finger markings and incised lines on the soft limestone walls, and the evidence suggests that the art is of considerable antiquity (see below).

Allen's Cave is located some 80 kilometres west of Koonalda, and appears to have been abandoned sometime between 20,200 ± 1,000 BP and 11,950 ± 250 BP (Marun 1974). In the Flinders Ranges there is some evidence of occupation around 14,770 ± 270 BP in a dune deposit at Hawker Lagoon, where 'Kartan' artefacts were also found (Lampert and Hughes 1988: Table 9).

By about 18,000 BP in western New South Wales, truly arid conditions had set in, but occupation continued at Lake Tandou and Kangaroo Lake (Balme and Hope 1990), as well as at the Willandra Lakes and Lake Victoria (see sites which are discussed further below).

On the other side of the continent, in the arid Pilbara region of northwestern Australia, the Mount Newman rock-shelter (PO187), is located on the Hamersley Plateau. The site presently is situated 360 kilometres inland, but during the Pleistocene its distance from the coast was nearer 500 kilometres. Today the region has been classified as a 'mountain and piedmont desert' (Mabbutt 1971: 75). The sediments within the site appear to have been dammed by an enormous boulder which is located at the mouth of the shelter. The earliest occupation of the site took place before 20,740 ± 345 BP (Maynard 1980; Troilett 1982). Nearby, a second rock-shelter, PO2055.2, has a basal date of 26,300 ± 500 BP (S. Brown 1987: 24). Both these sites appear to have been inhabited intermittently and possibly abandoned during the glacial maximum (Veth 1989a: 86). Two recently excavated limestone rock-shelters, Mandu Mandu Creek and Koolan Island 2, were located close to the edge of the Australian continental shelf. Both appear to have been stranded far inland and abandoned as the seas dropped to their lowest limits around the glacial maximum (see Chapter Four).

Colless Creek is a dolomite rock-shelter located within a rich system of gorges in the now semi-arid Lawn Hill region of the Barkly Tablelands, northwestern Queensland. It appears to have been first occupied before 20,000 BP, and was utilised most intensively during the arid glacial maximum, after about 17,000 BP (Hughes and Lampert 1980; Hiscock 1984, 1988). During this arid phase the site was up to 900 kilometres inland, and may have acted as an oasis in a progressively arid environment. In this way, the more intensive occupation has been explained partly by the concentration of population at a permanent water source, within the gorges, during a time of increasing desiccation. Hiscock also discounted the possibilities of either increases or decreases in population at this time. Fauna has not been preserved in the lower levels, and stone artefacts constitute the primary evidence. A similar archaeological sequence was found also in the same region at the site of Louie Creek (Hiscock 1988).

Further sites lie beyond the arid belt itself in the north and northwest of Australia, but were close enough to be affected by encroaching aridity. As the glacial maximum approached, Arnhem Land rock-shelters such as Malakunanja II were now positioned far inland. Even so, the latter site appears to have continued to be occupied at this time, as was the Lindner Site, Nauwalabila I, from 19,975 ± 365 BP. Further west in Cape York, Queensland, increasing aridity appears to have had a more marked affect; Fern Cave is most intensively utilised around the glacial maximum and perhaps also Quinkan Reserve and Walkunderarch Cave (see Chapter Four).

Overview: Pleistocene arid Australia

The spread of archaeological evidence, both spatially and chronologically, suggests that settlement ringed the arid core of Australia from at least 37,000 BP and increasing aridity set in sometime after 30,000 BP. By 22,000 BP signs of occupation appear at the very centre of the continent, the 'dead heart'; and occupation continued throughout the dry glacial maximum in various sites and regions of what was the now considerably expanded arid zone, although abandonment of other sites is also indicated. Some sites, within and around the arid core, were more intensively occupied at this time, perhaps indicating a concentration of population around better-watered centres of refuge. In all, however, settlement appears to have been somewhat ephemeral in all the regions surveyed.

Research has expanded in the past decade or two in arid Australia, and interpretations of the archaeological patterns vary considerably. Smith (1988, 1989a, 1989b), for example, considered that the arid zone was initially settled sometime prior to 22,000 BP, as the site of Puritjarra suggests, when climate was milder and fresh water more widespread. He considered special adaptations, such as seed-grinding technology, to be unnecessary as fully arid conditions had not yet developed. In contrast, he saw settlement during the glacial maximum as restricted largely to areas of springs and permanent waterholes, such as existed in the ranges. Smith argued that the repeated use of Puritjarra between 22,000 and 13,000 BP:

> . . . together with its location away from any natural corridor for travel into the region, indicates the presence of a resident local population . . . there is no a *priori* reason for expecting the region to have been totally abandoned during the last glacial maximum. (1989b: 93)

More widespread settlement of arid areas, he argued, took place following the glacial maximum in the terminal Pleistocene and early Holocene.

Peter Hiscock also came to broadly similar conclusions: '. . . whilst people occupied the interior under good conditions they were not adjusted to life in fully arid conditions' (n.d.: 3).

From his research, Hiscock suggested that the complex, extensive social networks of recent times may not have existed during the Pleistocene and that this may have inhibited the occupation of more arid regions. Overall, Hiscock and others (Lampert and Hughes 1987; Veth 1987, 1989a, 1989b) pointed to the ephemeral nature of Pleistocene settlement of the arid zone, and that it may not have been continuous throughout this very long period as the evidence indicated that abandonment of sites and sub-regions had taken place.

Peter Veth (1987, 1989a, 1989b) is another writer who has pointed out just how environmentally diverse the Australian arid zone was, even during the Pleistocene, and he suggested that:

> . . . the occupation of the arid zone from the late Pleistocene on is likely to have been a highly dynamic process. The notion of a stable human adaptation to the diverse landforms and environments of the arid zone finds little support in the archaeological record (1989b: 81).

The general model of arid zone settlement offered by Veth (1989a, 1989b) is based on the argument that the arid and semi-arid regions of the continent are composed largely of three climatic tracts: (a) refuges or 'islands' of better-

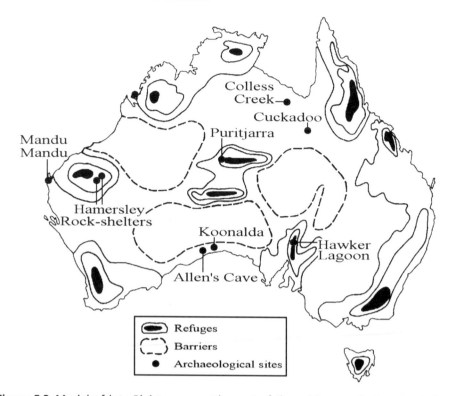

Figure 5.3 Model of late Pleistocene settlement of the arid zone. Archaeological sites are located within the expanded arid zone (based on Veth 1989a: 85, Figure 2).

watered land (including the range country); (b) intermediate, relatively arid corridors; and (c) the harsh, arid sandy deserts (Figure 5.3). The archaeological evidence, he suggested, indicates that the more humid belts were first occupied (including the Puritjarra Region) while the drier corridors witnessed more transient occupation, being abandoned during the dry glacial maximum and largely resettled later during the terminal Pleistocene and early Holocene periods. Finally, the harsh sandy deserts were occupied only in the mid–late-Holocene period. Given the existing archaeological evidence presented here, Veth's stadial model appears to be the most plausible explanation and, together with more recent assessments (Ross et al. 1992) somewhat modified, largely forms the basis of my own account.

Indeed, the assumption that conditions were milder in arid Australia prior to the glacial maximum, that is before about 22,000 BP, has been questioned by Ross et al., who argued that 'The arid interior has always been dry, in geomorphic terms' (1992: 102); thus effectively undermining the environmental basis of most previous models of colonisation of the arid zone.

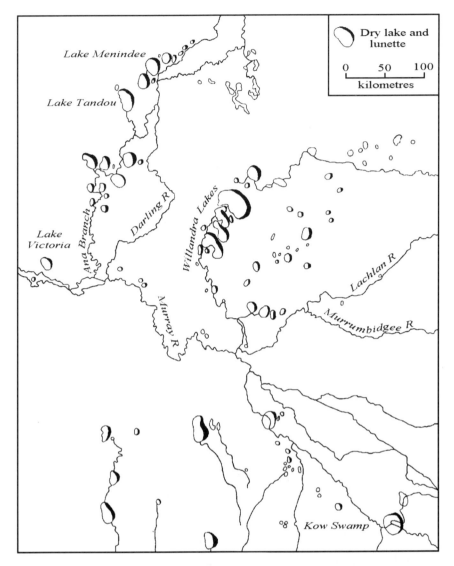

Figure 5.4 Southwestern New South Wales and northern Victoria, showing location of the Willandra and Menindee Lakes, Lake Victoria, the Murray and Darling Rivers and Kow Swamp (based on Bowler 1971: 56, Figure 5:3).

The semi-arid zone

Willandra Lakes

Parts of semi-arid southeastern Australia have produced some of the most plentiful evidence of Pleistocene occupation of the continent. The best known region is that of the Willandra Lakes, a system of now dry lake basins located in western New South Wales (Figures 5.4, 5.5). Complex hydrological and

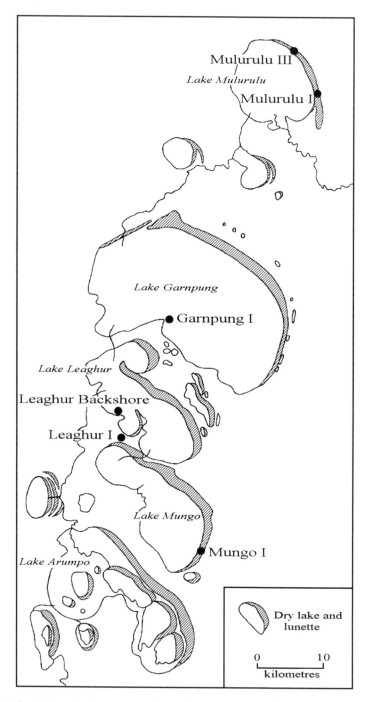

Figure 5.5 The Willandra Lakes showing Lake Mungo and sites mentioned in the text (based on Bowler 1971: 57, Figure 5:4).

sedimentological histories have been obtained from this area, mainly from aeolian deposits, furnishing information on the climate of the late Pleistocene period.

Surrounding the eastern margins of the lake basins are high, crescent-shaped dunes, referred to as lunettes. These lunettes were formed either when the lakes were full and containing fresh water, or when they were drying up and becoming increasingly saline. A three-part stratigraphic sequence from these Willandra lunettes was recognised by geomorphologist Jim Bowler (1971, 1976, 1980; see also Figure 3.7, p. 88 above).

A basal unit, Golgol, which is thought to be dated between about 120,000 and 70,000 BP, was deposited during ancient lake-full conditions, and appears not to house evidence of human occupation. Overlying the Golgol levels was a second stratigraphic unit, Mungo, which was also deposited at a time when the lakes were full. This Mungo lacustral phase has been dated to between 50,000 and 25,000 BP, and this interpretation is supported by evidence of aquatic fauna from dune deposits, such as the remains of mollusc, fish, crustacea and the like. This stage is followed by a trend towards increasing aridity and a lowering of lake levels. Quartz sands, which indicate fresh full lake phases, were now increasingly replaced by a higher clay component, indicating increasingly drier and more saline conditions. From about 26,000 to 23,000 BP, Lake Mungo appears to have been an ephemeral body of water, and after about 22,000 BP there is evidence of increasing aridity with a corresponding lowering of lake levels (Bowler 1976: 70). The final stage of dune building is associated with the Zanci unit, which is dated to between about 18,000 and 15,000 BP. Alternatively, the lakes may have been dry between 22,000 and 17,000 BP (Hope 1993: 191). Zanci appears to represent the final lake-full phase at Willandra. By about 17,000 BP aridity was again on the increase, and by about 14,000 BP the entire lake system was dry. This drying-out process began first with the lakes furthest downstream; for example, Lake Mulurulu appears to have undergone a short freshwater phase between about 15,000 and 14,000 BP.

Archaeological evidence has been found in the eroding lunettes of the Willandra system. Two chronological groups of sites come from the Pleistocene period. The first group is linked to the Mungo lake-full stage, and the second to the final drying-up of the lakes towards the terminal Pleistocene. The first group of sites has been consistently dated to between about 32,000 and 25,000 BP (Barbetti and Allen 1972; Allen 1972; Bowler 1976, 1980). The archaeological material consists of patches of shell midden, hearths, ovens and stone artefacts predominantly. One shallow oven, with several lumps of baked clay, was dated to about 31,000 BP (Barbetti and Allen 1972). A 'concentration of disarticulated shells along a horizontal bedding plane', in association with fragments of charcoal near Lake Mungo, yielded a date of at least 35,000 BP (Bowler 1976: 59). A similar date was obtained from mussel shell, together with ash and charcoal, in an excavation undertaken by Isabel McBryde on Lake Outer Arumpo

Figure 5.6 Lake Mungo, western New South Wales, in 1969 (Photo: H. Lourandos).

(Mulvaney 1979). Much of the archaeology reported has been from opportunistic finds detected by erosion of the aeolian deposits. Today there is more careful monitoring of these deposits than was the case in the past.

The most complex archaeological site to date is that of Mungo I, which is located on the Lake Mungo lunette and is referred to locally as 'the Walls of China'. Mungo I is an important site and we need to carefully consider its initial interpretation as a short-term seasonal camping spot. As stratigraphic and taphonomic issues have yet to be resolved, it is not clear whether it represents a discrete entity rather than an amalgamation of task-specific sites. As much of the site was exposed through erosion rather than controlled excavation, stratigraphic admixture of separate lenses may have taken place. Most of the other sites of this period are of the latter type, composed predominantly of a single variable such as mussel shell, hearths or stone artefacts. Leaghur I, for example, also an eroded deposit, consisted of a thin lens of mussel shell, *Velesunio ambiguus*, scattered over an area of 925 square metres and dated to 27,160 ± 900 BP. A hearth, seven flakes and a small proportion of other fauna complete the assemblage, which was interpreted by Allen (1972: 283–284) as a specialised shell midden. Several other shell middens have been dated to between about 32,000 and 30,000 BP (Hope et al. 1983: 51). Another site, located at the southern end of Lake Mungo, is composed of a group of five fireplaces or ovens, the oldest of which has a date of 30,780 BP, but no fauna or artefacts accompanied these finds (Barbetti and Allen 1972).

More recent research in the Willandra–Darling area generally supports the impression of small, task-specific sites (Balme 1995, personal communication). Analysis of many of these sites was carried out before taphonomic techniques were well developed. Taphonomic analysis of material such as this would help clarify stratigraphic problems and also isolate more carefully the human contribution to the assemblage.

The second group of sites from the Willandra Lakes has been dated to between about 16,000 and 13,000 years BP. Originally these were viewed as being related to the Zanci high-water phase, and therefore are in some ways reminiscent of the earlier occupation during the Mungo lacustrine period (Allen 1972: 318–320). Interpretations of the climatic sequence during this terminal phase of the Pleistocene are now seen to be more complex than previously believed (Clark and Hope 1985). This second site grouping, therefore, may be linked generally to the final drying phase of the lakes.

The sites of this period are also more numerous and larger than earlier Willandra sites (Allen 1972; M. McIntyre and J. Hope, personal communication 1979, 1985; Hope 1993). Most sites are shell middens with an emphasis on aquatic resources, and include the following examples (Allen 1972: 280–320). Leaghur Backshore II is an extensive site composed of a continuous thin layer of mussel shell (*V. ambiguus*) and is dated to 15,690 ± 235 BP. Garnpung I, which is dated to around 15,480 ± 210 BP, consists of mussel shell, fish, crayfish and some land mammal. There is also, however, admixture with more recent evidence, for example stone artefacts. Mulurulu I is dated to around 15,000 BP and is composed of a series of small mussel shell middens and is similar to Leaghur Backshore I but twice its size. Fish and mammal bone are plentiful at this site and some of the bone is burnt. The faunal suite is comparable to that of Mungo I and there are few stone artefacts. Mulurulu IIIA is a group of twelve small shell middens, and there is a higher percentage of mammal bone here but fewer fish than at Mulurulu I.

As with the earlier Willandra and Tandou sites (including Mungo I) there is evidence here of admixture with more recent material (stone artefacts, bone, and material of earlier dates) at three of the above four sites, excluding perhaps Mulurulu I. Interpretations of site use, economy and the like, therefore, need to be cautious. While the aquatic fauna may plausibly be linked to sites of this age (as lakes dried during this phase and appear not to have revived), other fauna also may have come from more recent contexts. As well, sites may include evidence from more than one phase of this last series of lacustrine episodes. Taphonomic issues also have yet to be addressed.

Johnston's recent surveys of the Willandra Lakes indicate that generally Willandra middens are very small, especially when compared to those of riverine regions such as the Murray and Darling Rivers. '...[t]he small average size of middens is not due to slow erosion of the original sites but generally reflects the scale of Pleistocene shell collecting behaviour' (1993: 202). In general, the middens appear much smaller than those recorded by Allen (1972) over twenty years ago. He suggests that lacustrine resources may have played only a small role in economies of the region, which in all may have had a more terrestrial emphasis. 'In contrast to the Willandra middens, the Murray River middens may be up to 1 km in length and from 10 cm to 100 cm thick' (Johnston 1993: 202). Large, local concentrations of river mussel (*Alanthyria jacksoni*) may account for the size of these middens, compared to the sparse lake-dwelling *Velesunio* which makes up the bulk of the Willandra middens. Murray River middens fringe the present river, its ancient course and lake shores nearby (Johnston 1993: 202).

The question of cereals

In his original interpretations of the Willandra–Tandou Pleistocene sequence, Allen suggested that one human response to the desiccation of the lakes was an economic shift to cereals in this and the wider Darling Region, during the terminal Pleistocene (1972, 1974). He proposed that as the region became increasingly drier, grasses may have proliferated and their exploitation by humans thus may have become more profitable (1972: 339). Supporting archaeological evidence came in the form of lithic processing equipment, that is grindstones, indicating the use of plants. Allen argued that evidence of these cereal-related artefacts could be found in many of the middens and other sites of this terminal Pleistocene phase from between 13,000 and 15,000 BP. For example, grindstones were shown to exist on the sites of Leaghur Backshore II and Mulurulu I and IIIA. Most of this evidence, however, was from surface finds and not hard and fast stratified material, with the exception of one example. The one stratified example was of six broken pieces of grindstone, all appearing to be from the same tool, which came from the Tandou lunette (Tandou I). A date of 12,530 +1,630/ −1,350 BP (ANU 705) was obtained from 'charred collagen' from a human cremation in the site (1972: 234). Carbonate-encrusted grindstones also suggested to Allen a great antiquity.

Given the paucity of stratified evidence and the problems of admixture at these sites, it still remains to be demonstrated whether cereals were first introduced – or their use intensified – at this time. We also might ask whether these supposed terminal Pleistocene practices were equivalent to the intensive and sophisticated techniques recorded in the ethnographic period discussed in Chapter Two. More recent evidence from arid or semi-arid zones indicates that intensive use of cereals may have been a relatively recent practice of the last few thousand years (below). The identification of the grindstone equipment has also been questioned of late.

Lake Tandou and the Murray-Darling basin

Less than 200 kilometres northwest of the Willandra Lakes are located Lake Tandou and the Menindee Lakes (see Figure 5.4, p. 177). While earlier work was initiated at Tandou by Allen (1972) and Merrilees (1973), more recently detailed stratigraphic and archaeological surveys were enacted as part of a broader investigation of the palaeoenvironments of the Lower Darling (Hope 1981; Hope et al.1983). With over a decade of investigation of these semi-arid aeolian deposits to draw upon, this recent investigation of the Tandou lunette has been able to clarify, to a large extent, the complexities of these large, eroded sites and their stratigraphic and taphonomic problems.

The Tandou lunette is 25 kilometres in length, with a maximum height of around 25 metres towards the dune's centre. The uppermost stratigraphic unit of the lunette is the Bootingee, dated to between about 27,000 and 15,000 BP, and it appears to correspond to the Upper Mungo and Zanci units at the Willandra Lakes. Unlike Willandra, however, the high quartz sand component throughout the rather uniform Bootingee unit, together with evidence of aquatic fauna from the deposit, suggest that freshwater conditions prevailed throughout this period. Included among this aquatic fauna were mussels, fish, crustaceans, amphibians, and platypus. Major sedimentation also may not have ceased at Tandou by about 15,000 years ago, as it appears to have at the Willandra Lakes.

Archaeological material is found throughout the Bootingee unit, and for sampling purposes the lunette was subdivided into 124 localities. Forty midden sites have been identified from 22 different localities. It was possible to distinguish between scatters of archaeological material and discrete features such as hearths, burials and middens. 'Some of these sites are simple discrete accumulations of shell, while others are complexes of shell midden, hearths and scatters of animal bone, fish otoliths, and crustacean gastroliths' (Hope et al. 1983: 48). Admixture of evidence, however, through deflation of surface material and the like, remains a problem at the site, and '*in situ* material at different levels even within one stratigraphic unit is unlikely to be contemporary' (Hope et al. 1983: 47). As with Mungo I, therefore, it becomes extremely difficult to disentangle discrete task-specific sites (shell, hearths, burials and the like) from more complex sites such as this, which may be the product of admixture. Taphonomic issues also remain to be resolved once again.

Radiocarbon dates were obtained from eleven of the 40 stratigraphically controlled sites from samples of freshwater mussel, *V. ambiguus*. Dates cluster between about 27,000 and 22,000 BP, supported by the majority of undated sites which also lie close to the basal Bootingee unit, and therefore the earliest phase. Erosion, however, cannot be ruled out in affecting this assessment. A smaller number of shell middens are stratified higher up in the Bootingee unit, implying more recent occupation. In support, four of the latter sites were dated to between about 16,000 to 15,000 BP (Hope et al. 1983: 48, 51). The matter of chronology of occupation at Tandou, therefore, remains unresolved.

Unlike the Willandra Lake region, at the Lake Tandou lunette there appears to be less evidence of occupation than in the prior lacustrine period, that is, before about 27,000 BP. A small number of shell middens are located high in the Bootingee Unit, some three metres above its base. Shell middens from four of these sites lie between about 16,000 and 15,000 BP (Hope et al. 1983: 49).

Major sedimentation, however, may not have ceased at this time as happened at the Willandra Lakes. As well, there is an indication of more recent evidence at Lake Tandou as the date of about 12,000 BP (above) illustrates. More in line with the Willandra Lakes evidence is the chronology of shell middens from the anabranch channels of the Lower Darling system which cluster around 13,000 BP (Clark and Hope 1985: 84).

The evidence from Lake Victoria, which is located further to the south of the Willandra Lakes, is also broadly in agreement with the Willandra sequence. At Lake Victoria shell middens are concentrated between about 18,000 and 15,000 years BP (Gill 1973; Kephous 1981).

Extensive recent work in the Murray-Darling region (Balme and Hope 1990; Hope 1993) has produced a wealth of data. Generally middens cluster in two main groups: before and after the glacial maximum. 'The two groups are distinct in the absolute number of sites dated, their geographic spread and the variety of landforms presented' (Hope 1993: 190). The second group, 18,000 to 8,000 BP, appears to be the most numerous, and overlaps with similar concentrations of middens in the Willandra of the period 16,000–15,000 BP. Indeed, most of the better preserved and numerous evidence from this entire region, which includes the Murray-Darling and Willandra, comes from this terminal Pleistocene. Little is in fact known of the time before the glacial maximum, when it has been hypothesised by many archaeologists that climate was more benign and resources plentiful (Hope 1993: 183).

HOLOCENE SETTLEMENT

Palaeoenvironment

Evidence from Lake Frome, in the Strzelecki Desert, indicates that in general the early Holocene was a more humid period, and the vegetation composed of eucalypt woodland, with the highest levels of precipitation between about 7,000 and 4,000 years ago. A drier phase followed until about 2,200 years ago, with vegetation dominated by shrubland. Since this time, conditions have been relatively more humid, and the sequence from Lake Tyrrell is broadly in agreement.

The arid zone

Explanations that have viewed the Holocene settlement of the Australian arid zone as a direct response to changes in climate are not generally supported by the existing archaeological data. The evidence strongly demonstrates that settlement was both more widespread and intensive during the late Holocene, especially after about 3,000 BP, and more so in the last thousand years. During the last few thousand years also, significant changes occur in the use of resources, equipment, sites and settlement patterns. The implication here is of demographic shifts (including population increase) and transformations in social and economic relations.

Smith, for example, considered that climate improved significantly in the early Holocene, with increased availability of water, and that this was followed by rises in Aboriginal population and expansion of settlement in arid areas (1986, 1988, 1989b; see also Horton 1981; Lampert and Hughes 1987, 1988). He argued that this growth in population was later checked by a reversal in climate between 4,000 and 2,000 BP, which in turn resulted in changes to technology and economy, including an emphasis upon the use of grass seeds. In this way, initial population growth in the early Holocene was seen as triggering later economic changes (see below).

The archaeological evidence, however, does not lend support to this scenario. First, there appears to be no sign of population increase during the early Holocene. Rather, evidence of this kind appears later, during the last 3,000, and especially the last 1,000 years – that is, either coinciding with, or following, the time of climatic reversal. As well, the assumed magnitude of climatic improvement during the early Holocene also has been questioned (Veth 1989b; Ross et al. 1992: 102; see also above). A more detailed discussion of these issues, and the archaeological evidence, now follows.

Archaeological sites

A wide range of sites and study areas of the Holocene period has now been reported (Figure 5.7). For example, in central Australia there are some fifteen sites which were all occupied within the last 3,500–3,000 years, most of them in the last 1,000 years. There is a marked increase in rates of deposition and, since about 850 BP, also in quantities of stone artefacts, bone, charcoal and ochre. Increases also occur in the range of artefact types, amount of retouch and raw materials (Smith 1988). In various parts of the Simpson Desert numbers of sites appear to be no older than 4,000–3,000 years, from dated and associated contexts (Davidson 1983; Davidson et al. 1993; Hercus and Clark 1986; Wasson 1986). Sites in the Strzelecki Desert are assessed as being of similar age (Hughes and Lampert 1980). Investigations in the Coongie Lakes region of the Cooper Creek district (Williams 1988b) arrived at similar conclusions; apart from one Pleistocene occupation, the bulk of evidence is of late Holocene age.

In the Sandy Desert region of northwestern Australia, Veth excavated five rock-shelters. Three of these are located in the McKay Range, and appear to date from about 5,000–3,000 years ago, and 'A marked increase in the density of artefacts and charcoal occurs in the upper spits' (Veth 1987: 186). The Karlamilyi rock-shelter, from Rudall River, has a basal date of 3,200 BP (WK 1093) and a significant increase in the rate of discard in the upper levels. An increase in the density of artefacts in the upper spits was common to all five excavations. A preliminary depth–age curve from Karlamilyi shows a doubling in the rate of deposition over the last 1,000 years in comparison to the preceding 2,000 years.

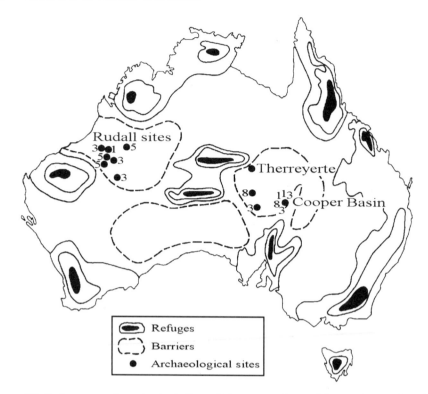

Figure 5.7 Holocene archaeological sites of the Australian arid zone located within and close to 'barrier' deserts (based on Veth 1989a: 89, Figure 4). (The figures refer to initial dates of occupation of the sites in thousands of years BP: e.g., 3 = 3,000 years BP.)

The large increase in the numbers of artefacts after 1,000 BP is, therefore, even more pronounced (Veth 1987: 106–107). Depth–age curves from two other sites produced similar results; increasing rates of artefact discard accelerate between 1,400 and 800 BP (Veth 1989a: 175). Veth's results, therefore, were strikingly similar to those of Smith (1988: 325) as regards timing and rates of discard of cultural material including stone artefacts, grindstones, charcoal and bone.

Veth contrasted the ethnographically derived subsistence-settlement patterns of his study area with those reported by Gould (1969, 1980) for the Gibson Desert in central Australia (see also Chapter One). Veth's field reconnaissance appears to bear out his interpretations; that settlement was predictable and that more intensive encampments were associated with permanent springs and soaks (1987: 104–106). These sites were the largest, with the greatest quantities of artefacts and diversity of artefact types. There was also abundant evidence of the use of grindstones and tulas. At ephemeral water sources sites were smaller and artefact assemblages less varied. These dichotomous patterns are well represented by the Kadaru site, located at a permanent well, and the Wantili site, which is situated at an ephemeral water source. Broadly comparable results in terms of settlement patterns and mid-late Holocene chronology of occupation also have been obtained by Cane (1984) from the western Desert.

On the Nullarbor Plain, three caves, Madura, Norina and Allen's, are all more intensively occupied in the last 4,000 years, with increases in stone artefacts and faunal remains. Occupation began around 8,000 BP in the two former sites (Wright 1971a; Martin 1973; Milham and Thompson 1976). Hawker Lagoon in the Flinders Ranges also indicates increased usage, with large numbers of stone artefacts, including grindstones (Lampert and Hughes 1987). In the region of Lake Frome and Lake Eyre, sites around the Mound Springs appear to be mainly of the last 5,000 years (Smith 1986). In Western Australia at Walga Rock in the Murchison Basin, occupation begins around 9,000 BP, and site use is intensified after 1,000 BP.

It is only by 6,000 BP at Puritjarra that the artefact discard rate increases significantly, that is to say 30-fold: from three to 105 pieces per thousand years. During the last 1,500 years the artefact discard rate increases to 330 pieces per thousand years (100 times that at 6,000 BP)(Smith 1986). Similarly, over 60 percent of *all implements* from the 10,000-year occupation at Puntutjarpa come from spits encompassing the last 500 years (Gould 1980: Figure 6). These increases are often accompanied by increases in other economic remains such as charcoal, fauna and grinding material (Smith 1986; Veth 1987: 108; see also Lourandos 1985a).

At most sites there is a significant increase in the rate of artefact discard over the last 1,500 years. At Puntutjarpa also a reanalysis of the micro-adzes indicates that 'an adzing toolkit similar to that observed ethnographically appears less than 6,000 years ago, and possibly as recently as 1,000 years BP' (Hiscock and Veth 1991: 342).

One of the few early Holocene sites is Balcoracana Creek, which was originally inhabited around 10,000 BP (Lampert and Hughes 1988). As well, archaeological visibility is generally relatively good in arid and semi-arid areas (more so than in other parts of the continent), and therefore a large number of surface sites are included in the data bases from many sub-regions. Many surface sites have been dated relatively by their association with recognisable artefact types (such as those of the 'Australian Small Tool tradition', or by geomorphological means.

Broadly similar archaeological trends in site use and settlement patterns have also been obtained from the semi-arid Mallee region of northwestern Victoria (see Chapter Seven). In the Darling River region marked increases were noted in the number of sites during the late Holocene period, especially in the last 3,000 years or so. Most of the dates came from fire places (also a recent site type) (Allen 1972; Hughes and Lampert 1982).

Grass seed use and intensification

The introduction, and intensification, of use of grass seeds in arid and semi-arid Australia is a key example of prehistoric economic change and has distinct parallels in other parts of the world. Shifts towards use and increased reliance upon grass seeds in hunter-gatherer economies is documented archaeologically on all occupied continents at various points in time. In some cases these shifts or trends culminated in the development of agricultural societies, in others to complex systems of land management, the difference between the two in some ways being a matter of conjecture (as covered in Chapter One). A closer examination of this process in Australia, therefore, helps to cast considerable light upon transformations within Aboriginal society and relationships with the land. The Australian example also can help our understanding of broadly similar events elsewhere and at other points in time.

The problem of just when shifts towards use, and possible intensification in use, of grass seeds took place has been studied recently by Smith (1985, 1986). He first examined grindstones, presumed to have been used in processing of grass seeds, from Pleistocene contexts in the Willandra Lakes of the Darling Basin and other regions. These sites included Malakunanja II, Malangangerr and Nawamoyn in Arnhem Land, Quininup Brook in southwestern Western Australia, Miriwun in northwestern Australia, and Kenniff Cave in northern Queensland. Smith demonstrated that these tools had been wrongly identified. Rather than being specialised seed-grinding equipment comparable to ethnographic examples, they appeared to be 'expedient grindstones', used for a range of other purposes. These uses include the processing of a range of plants, such as hard-coated seeds, fibrous roots, as well as animal bone and the preparation of pigments and resin, together with the sharpening of wooden artefacts. They stand in contrast, therefore, to highly curated instruments, such as *millstones*, which are used for the wet milling of a variety of soft-coated seeds, and seeds initially dry-ground on a mortar.

These practices have been observed ethnographically (Horne and Aiston 1924: 53–56; O'Connell 1977: 274). 'Millstones are large flat- surfaced slabs with one or more shallow grooves worn into the surface' (Smith 1986: 32). Use-wear is distinctive, often indicating a fine 'silica polish'. Millstones are used together with hand-sized *mullers* which sometimes are also carefully manufactured and display 'silica polish' (Smith 1986: 32–33; 1985: 95–99) (Figure 5.8). Millstones and mullers can be clearly distinguished from other seed-processing equipment, such as pestles and mortars (Figure 5.9), which are used in central Australia for hard-coated seeds, such as those of the acacia, prior to wet-milling, and also for a wide range of other purposes (Smith 1986: 33).

Grindstones from five key excavated archaeological sites of Holocene age were examined by Smith: Puntutjarpa (Gould 1971a) and James Range East (Gould 1978; Smith 1986), both in arid Central Australia; Native Wells I (Morwood 1979, 1981), in central Queensland; and Graman B1 and B4

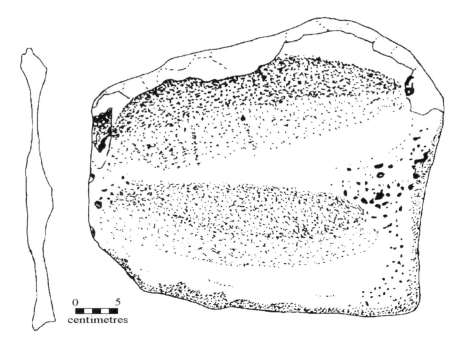

0 ___ 5
centimetres

Figure 5.8 Millstones from central Australia (based on Smith 1986: 32, Figure 2).

(McBryde 1974, 1977) in the New England region of New South Wales. Smith also considered evidence from Burkes Cave (Allen 1972) in western New South Wales, Hawker Lagoon (Lampert 1983) in South Australia, and Mickey Springs 34 (Morwood and Godwin 1982) in central northern Queensland. Notwithstanding the large geographical area involved and the small size of the sample, this evidence suggested that use of seed-grinding implements was a late Holocene development of the last 3,500 years or so. Some of these sites (for example, James Range East, Hawker Lagoon and Mickey Springs 34) indicated that seed grinding took place very recently, that is within the last 1,000 years.

This equipment was considered by Smith to be an outgrowth of existing grindstone technology whose antecedents lay firmly in the Pleistocene, rather than a major innovation, as some had supposed (Bowdler 1977; O'Connell and Hawkes 1981). The introduction of new technology, therefore, did not appear to be the answer to the problem of the origins of seed-grinding. Smith explained the development of seed-gathering economies – those placing an emphasis upon seeds analogous with ethnographic practices – as essentially due to climatic and demographic changes (Smith 1986: 37–38). He saw the shift to the use of grass seeds as a broadening of the hunter-gatherer resource base, a move towards more labour-intensive foods (see Chapters One, Two), and he argued that environmental changes alone cannot explain this shift in dietary emphasis.

Smith explained that the late Holocene climate of the arid zone was generally more stressful than in the early-mid-Holocene. The fact that no seed grinders

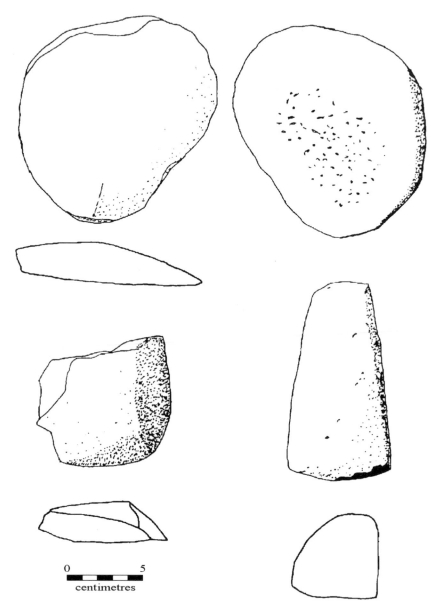

Figure 5.9 Mullers from central Australia (based on Smith 1986: 32, Figure 3).

were detected in even earlier dry phases, for example between about 8,000 and 7,000 BP and the lengthier late Pleistocene period between about 18,000 and 12,000 BP, weighed heavily against an environmental stimulus for change. Smith proposed that prior to around 4,000–3,000 years ago population densities were lower and so too would have been pressure upon resources. This explains why earlier, drier climatic phases, did not force people to intensify the use of existing resources. He argued that the development of seed-grinding economies was the result of increasing populations during the early-mid Holocene, coupled with drier conditions and resource stress in the late Holocene. 'In other words, Aboriginal groups had no option but to intensify their use of the land in this fashion' (1986: 38).

It was also Smith's view that intergroup occasions were central to the process that led to the intensification of seed use. 'The pressure upon resources, whatever its cause, would initially be felt during large gatherings for ceremonies' (1986: 37).

By placing emphasis on population increase as the major causal factor, however, Smith's argument is open to critique. To Smith, demographic pressure appears as the alternative to some environmental stimulus. But is this so, and is demographic change an independent variable as is suggested here? First, as I have shown above, there is no archaeological evidence to suggest population growth during the early-mid Holocene period. Second, Smith assumes that intensification of resources towards more costly or high-ranking foods, such as seeds, is predetermined by population increase in the face of climatic reversals, '... rather than stabilise at a lower level of population, human groups would intensify their use of resources and their management of the land' (1986: 38). He does not explain, however, why the first option was not selected, that is, to maintain existing economic practices and experience a subsequent decline in population during drier phases of the late Holocene. The latter option does not appear to have been taken in central Australia, and this would indicate that factors other than population increase (for which, as I have observed, there is no evidence) were at work.

Third, demographic pressure at these times is not just a measurement of numbers of people in relation to certain quantities of resources. The socio-cultural context, in many ways, will influence people's perceptions of whether pressure exists in relation to resources, and the way a social group will react to this problem. People may choose to congregate for lengthy periods of time, increasing 'carrying capacity', and to offset the problem of resource scarcity by intensifying their resource strategy. This possibility does not require the biological increase of a population in a given region, but rather a rise in population density through socio-cultural structures that emphasise lengthier periods of aggregation or increasingly larger numbers of participants, or both.

I would argue, therefore, that the stimulus for change, or in this case intensification of seed use, also may have come from another source – from within the society itself (see Chapter One). The changing social context, therefore, may have provided the *incentive* to intensify resource use, which would not necessarily have been a negative pressure, as Smith implied. Intergroup gatherings would provide such a social context and it could be argued that these events would also influence the changes in demographic patterns and therefore density-dependent relationships between people and resources. The duration and size of these intergroup events may have been underwritten by resources, but the choice and level of production of resources was largely determined by the social relations of the participants (see Chapter One). If this line of argument is followed, pressure upon resources can be seen as largely socially determined, with demography as a dependent variable.

Is there archaeological evidence from central Australia for population increase? The more intensive use of sites and increasing numbers of sites of the late Holocene is suggestive of demographic change, and therefore change in the dispersal, density and size of populations. The timing of events also needs to be clearly defined. For example, a general increase in site use takes place about 3,000 BP and not before, that is, around the same time, or after, seed use is introduced. The James Range East site, in contrast, is intensively used only in the last seven hundred years. If population increase occurred, therefore, it may have post-dated or coincided with seed use rather than preceded it. If the latter is the case, then population increases may be the consequence rather than the cause of shifts in resource use. Further intensification of seed use may have led to still further demographic changes, as exemplified, perhaps, during the last seven hundred years at James Range East and other sites.

The sequence of events and pattern of causality, therefore, are as yet unclear in this example. Rather than a case of increasing population size (the product of the more humid climate of the early Holocene) and pressure on resources in the drier late Holocene, leading to an intensification of resource use, as Smith argues, we have here a complex interrelationship of factors. These include environmental decline, possible demographic changes (including population dispersal and growth), and changes in the socio-cultural environment (specifically associated with intergroup relationships). The latter two factors – demography and socio-cultural relationships – are not as easily distinguished as Smith and others suppose, and it is not legitimate, therefore, to argue that changes in one automatically lead to changes in the other.

Use of grass seeds, however, was not only restricted to arid and semi-arid areas. These practices existed also, for example, in the more humid tablelands region of New South Wales (see above). Smith's explanation (1986) that here grass seeds helped shore up a diet low in available plant resources cannot be fully sustained. Specialisation and intensification of grass seed use, therefore, should not merely be viewed in terms of the Aboriginal settlement of arid areas. As this example shows, it is clearly linked to historical processes taking place within a very wide range of Australian societies and natural environments (see also Chapter Four).

Overview: Holocene arid Australia

Veth considered that significant differences existed between mid-late Holocene patterns of site use and those of the Pleistocene in the arid zone. Pleistocene sites indicated only intermittent use when compared with mid-late Holocene sites (see also Chapter Two). New technologies were introduced between about 5,000 and 3,000 BP (including microliths, hafted adzes and grindstones), and there is evidence of increased site use in the last 1,500 years. Areas with less defined drainage, he suggested, such as the harsh sandy deserts, may not have been occupied until mid-Holocene times.

> It seems reasonable to argue that changes in social structure and economy were necessary before the arid zone could be occupied on a permanent basis and that the timing of permanent occupation of different regions varied. (1987: 109)

In conclusion, Veth offered an explanatory model for the settlement of the Australian arid zone. According to this, first a permanent arid adaptation was established by the early Holocene, possibly featuring large tribal/dialectal boundaries and extended social networks, providing reciprocal access to vital resources in marginal environments. Second, a mid-to-late Holocene increase in the number of people and sites on the landscape is noted. This may be a result of greater permanency at major sites (perhaps in the form of ceremonial gatherings), more intensive use of resources and the utilisation of a wider range of desert habitats. Finally, a late Holocene increase in the intensity of occupation at sites can be demonstrated and possibly reflects an elaboration of previously established social relations. (1987: 109)

Overview

Aboriginal use of some arid regions of Australia, therefore, appears to be of great antiquity, stretching back well beyond 22,000 years, and the time of the glacial maximum. Settlement of semi-arid zones extends back even further, to around 35,000 years ago. Aboriginal society appears to have become well attuned to the forces of aridity by this time. Clear signs, however, of settlement of Australia's arid centre are not evident before this period.

As dry climates increased, reaching their peak about 18,000 years ago, settlement continued to take place in parts of central Australia. But at this time occupation appears to have been concentrated in areas of more reliable sources of water, such as the range country and riverine corridors (for example, the Darling Basin and wider Willandra region).

With the easing of drier conditions, as the Pleistocene drew to a close sometime after about 15,000 years ago, Aboriginal settlement increased, spreading out from prior centres of refuge into surrounding drylands. Archaeological evidence of settlement is more conspicuous and widespread throughout arid Australia at this time and during the early Holocene period, until about 5,000 years ago.

Although climate improved after about 10,000 years ago and during the early Holocene, recent evaluations suggest that this was not as dramatic a change as previously thought. While early Holocene climate was relatively more humid, arid zones retained their character as regions of unpredictable rainfall. And even though settlement expanded, there is no indication of major increases in Aboriginal population at this time.

In the last few thousand years, however, during the late Holocene, relatively marked changes in Aboriginal settlement and society took place. After about 5,000 years ago, Aboriginal settlement spread throughout arid Australia even into the driest of areas, the harsh sandy deserts. Archaelogical signs of occupation of all desert regions, and of individual sites, increase dramatically after this time. The implication here is of an increase in both the size and density of Aboriginal populations.

Between 5,000 and 3,000 years ago also, changes in technology occurred with the appearance of new implement types, including stone grinders for processing grass seed – the desert staple of ethnographic times. In the last 1,500 years, further changes still are indicated, including the increased use of sites, and the intensified use of grass seeds. Suggested here are important economic shifts towards use of grass seeds, and more recently an intensification of these practices, associated with perhaps increased permanency of residence. Some have suggested that the extensive social networks of the ethhnographic period, that acted as elaborate support systems in these harsh environments, had not developed until Holocene times.

I have argued here that these late Holocene changes in use of sites and resources cannot be satisfactorily explained by assuming a marked growth in Aboriginal population during the early Holocene which placed increasing pressure upon land and resources. There is no archaeological evidence for significant population growth preceding these events. Evidence for population growth either coincides with or follows the changes. A complex set of relationships is, therefore, involved during the last few thousand years, and in particular the last thousand years or so. I suggest that stronger explanations lie in the relationship between society and demography, and these issues are discussed in greater detail below in Chapter Nine.

There are advantages for the archaeologist in studying arid regions. In some ways arid and semi-arid landscapes allow fairly good visibility of archaeological sites, and their relatively sparse ecological outlines also have allowed us to sharpen our focus on the possible and probable historical events that took place there. In the following chapter, however, which focuses on more varied and fertile environments, the historical sequence of cultural and natural events is less easy to unravel, as we have seen was the case also for some parts of northern Australia.

CHAPTER 6

TEMPERATE SOUTHERN AUSTRALIA

The temperate southern portions of the Australian mainland include some of the most fertile tracts of any on the continent; although this was not always recognised as regards studies of its Aboriginal people. Models, even stereotypes, of Australian Aborigines derived from observations of these people in arid or tropical parts of the continent, but information from the temperate region adds a new dimension to their history. In this chapter we consider the archaeology and prehistory of the area during the Pleistocene period, and of southeastern Australia in particular, during the Holocene. (This does not include Tasmania, which is covered in Chapter Seven.)

PLEISTOCENE SETTLEMENT

Palaeoenvironment

Information on past climates from the vast and ecologically complex region of temperate southern Australia is relatively abundant, especially in the southeast, when compared to other parts of the continent. A fairly clear picture, therefore, emerges, one which is based upon pollen and sedimentary studies, among others, of lake deposits and other sites.

Lake levels were high prior to 30,000 years ago, and forested areas, including rainforest, were extensive, perhaps even more so than today due to lower rates of evaporation (Dodson et al. 1992: 117). This more humid period was followed by an increasing trend towards aridity, which reached a climax around the glacial maximum (about 18,000 years ago). These trends are clearly visible in sequences, for example, from the Willandra Lakes (Bowler and Wasson 1984), and Lake

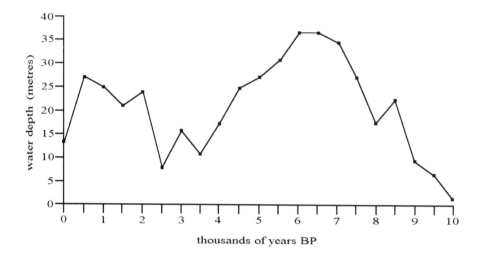

Figure 6.1 Lake levels of the last 10,000 years from Lake Keilambete in southwestern Victoria (based on Ross et al. 1992: 83, Figure 5.9: also Lourandos and Ross 1985).

Keilambete in Victoria (Dodson 1974a; Bowler 1981) (Figure 6.1). Dunefields at this time are found even in coastal areas (Bowler 1982). At the same time also, there was a contraction in the distribution of eucalypt and more closed forest communities which were increasingly replaced by more open woodlands, grasslands, and alpine vegetation in upland areas. Extensive areas of southern Australia were vegetated by a semi-arid grassland-steppe plant community that no longer exists (Figure 6.2). Pollen sequences illustrating these trends have been obtained in South Australia at Lake Leake (Dodson 1975) and the Wyrie Swamp (Dodson 1977), at Lancefield Swamp in Victoria (Gillespie et al. 1978), and Lake George (Singh and Geissler 1985) and Ulungra Springs in New South Wales (Dodson and Wright 1989; Dodson et al. 1992). At this time also, glaciers were more extensive in the southern highlands, and snowfalls common along the Great Dividing Range of the east coast (Galloway 1986).

The sea fell to its lowest limits during this period, exposing large stretches of Bass Strait which formed a substantial land bridge with Tasmania (Chappell and Thom 1977; Chappell 1983; Chappell and Shackleton 1986; see also Chapter Seven). During the last few thousand years of the Pleistocene, sometime after about 15,000 years ago, sea levels continued to rise, together with increasing temperatures, once again flooding the Bass Strait and creating a cluster of islands including Tasmania, as well as Kangaroo Island further to the northwest. Large parts of southern Australia, including the highlands, began to be reforested towards the end of this phase as the Pleistocene drew to an end.

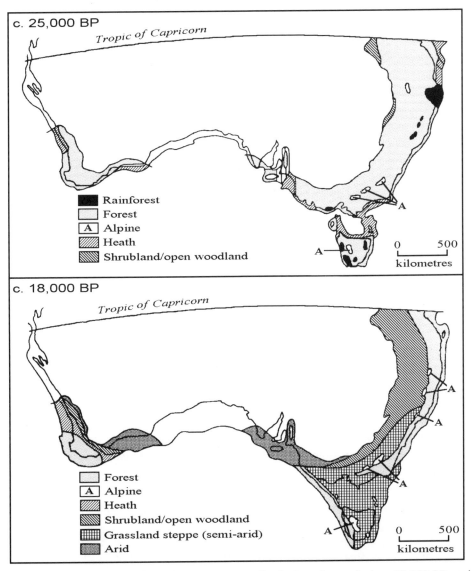

Figure 6.2 Vegetation of southeastern Australia during the periods c. 25,000 BP and c. 18,000 BP (based on Dodson et al. 1992: 121, Figure 6.1).

Pleistocene sites: c. 30,000–20,000 BP

Southwestern Australia

In this corner of the continent are some of Australia's oldest sites. The oldest site, Upper Swan, has already been discussed in Chapter Three.

Just under 300 kilometres to the south of Upper Swan is located the small limestone cave of Devil's Lair (Dortch 1979a, 1979b). The deep sediments of the cave have been excavated to depths exceeding 5 metres and some 30 radiocarbon dates have been obtained, ranging from basal dates of about 37,000 to about 300 BP, at the top of the deposit. Sparse Aboriginal occupation of the cave appears to begin, however, around 27,700 ± 700 BP, and earlier (more conjectural) dates of around 30,000 BP also have been proposed. The cave appears to have been intermittently used by people up until between about 12,000 and 6,000 years ago, with the most intensive period of human occupation between about 23,000 and 13,000 BP. Small quantities of bone and stone artefacts occur in many layers, together with occasional mollusc shells and fragments of emu eggshell, as well as other archaeological features such as hearths and pits. The earliest bone tools appear about 25,000 BP.

Most layers contain plentiful fragmented and occasionally charred bone, which represents a wide range of animal species. Balme's (1980) taphonomic study attempted to distinguish between animal bone deposited by humans as distinct from bone which had been left by other predators. A strong correlation existed between the number of stone artefacts and the amount of charred bone in individual layers. There was a further correlation between the percentage of charred remains of individual animals and the size of the animal. It was found that the highest percentages of charred bone were associated with the largest animals, and from this evidence Balme concluded that the largest species of animals were related to human predation. (The latter species included *Macropus fuliginosus*, *M. irma*, *M. eugenii*, *Petrogale*, *Bettongia penicillata* and *B. leseuer*).

The cave appears to have been continually occupied even during the driest, coldest phase of the Pleistocene when the sea was furthest away. Between about 23,000 and 13,000 BP (including the glacial maximum), the time of maximum human occupation, the sea was between 40 and 30 kilometres away from the cave. At this time it is suggested that a well developed terrestrial economy was operating at Devil's Lair. In contrast today, the sea is only about five kilometres from the site. In support of this explanation the oldest levels, that is prior to human occupation, included few large animals and have been interpreted as the product of owl predation (Balme et al. 1978).

More recent palaeoenvironmental data from this southwestern region, however, indicates that the climate during that the period 18,000–12,000 BP was colder but more humid than today. Increased use of Devil's Lair and other sites (Kalgan Hall, Quininup Brook and Arumvale) at this time, therefore, has been interpreted as indicating an amelioration in climate (more humid) and resources and reduced levels of mobility (O'Connor et al. 1993; see also Chapter Nine).

Southeastern Australia

On the other side of the continent, and equally distant from the Southeast Asian frontier of likely colonisation, early evidence of human occupation again has been found in alluvial riverine deposits. Potentially the oldest of these, Keilor and the Cranebrook Terraces, have already been discussed (see Chapter Three). Evidence of Pleistocene habitation also has been detected at isolated sites along the eastern, southeastern and southern seaboards, the southeastern highlands and sections of the Great Dividing Range of eastern Australia. Most of the sites that have been discovered are caves or rock-shelters, no doubt because these are more conspicuous in this region than sites within, for example, aeolian or alluvial deposits.

Southeastern highlands

Cloggs Cave, a limestone cavern, is located in the foothills of the southern highlands close to the Snowy River, which drained the meltwaters of some of mainland Australia's highest country (Flood 1980). Intermittent occupation is indicated from around 17,720 ± 840 BP until 8,720 ± 230 BP in an inner chamber of the cave. The cultural deposit, which extends to nearly two metres in depth, is composed mainly of hearths and a small percentage of stone artefacts together with some bone tools. Although the deposit is rich in faunal remains, the great majority of these can be attributed to non-human predators, such as owls. From just below the lowest cultural level of the site was found a mandible of the extinct megafaunal macropodid, *Sthenurus orientalis*. No megafaunal remains, however, came from the culture-bearing layer.

More recently a Pleistocene site also has been found higher up on the tablelands and ranges of the southeastern ranges (Flood et al. 1987). Birrigai is a small granite rock-shelter located within a group of large boulders, and has a cultural deposit of around 80 cms in depth, and a basal date of 21,000 ± 220 BP. There is no evidence of occupation by people in the underlying levels which, on stratigraphic grounds, are thought to stretch back to about 32,000 BP. A detailed sedimentary analysis was carried out which, together with the cultural remains, indicated a very low and perhaps constant rate of Aboriginal occupation throughout the Pleistocene and early Holocene periods. In contrast, dramatic increases in the rate of occupation took place in the late Holocene. In the Pleistocene levels, there are low frequencies of stone artefacts and charcoal (including one hearth); no faunal remains are preserved. The nature of the Pleistocene occupation, therefore, appears to be highly ephemeral (Figure 6.3).

Southeastern coast and tablelands

The first early site to be discovered in this region was the rock-shelter of Burrill Lake, which is located on a coastal lagoon in southern New South Wales. Two consistent radiocarbon dates have established its initial occupation at around 20,000 BP (20,760 ± 800 BP and 20,830 ± 810 BP) (Lampert 1971). The Pleistocene units of the site indicate a constant, although comparatively low, level of occupation when compared with the more recent late Holocene habitation layers (Hughes and Lampert 1982). Stone artefacts (a series of 'scrapers') comprise the cultural assemblage but faunal remains were not preserved. At the time of its initial occupation Burrill Lake was situated some 16–13 kilometres inland.

North of Burrill Lake is the coastal peninsula and archaeological site of Bass

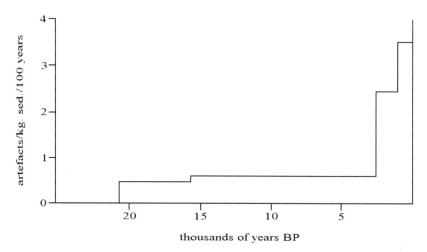

Figure 6.3 Temporal trends showing increasing rates in discard of artefacts at Birrigai, southern highlands (based on Flood et al. 1987: 18, Figure 9).

Point. This open shell midden is located above the rocky foreshore, and has a cultural deposit of around 1.15 metres in depth. Below recent Holocene levels, composed of shell, was a 60-cm-deep stratigraphic unit of white sand; this lower unit, which rested on rock and sand, had a basal date of 17,010 ± 650 years (Bowdler 1976: 254). Organic remains were not preserved in the Pleistocene levels which contained an assemblage of stone artefacts. Further inland, in the Blue Mountains west of Sydney and at an altitude of 884 metres, the rock-shelter of King's Table was inhabited very intermittently from about 22,000 BP (Stockton and Holland 1974).

Pleistocene sites: c. 20,000–10,000 BP

Southwestern Australia
Two or three kilometres south of Devil's Lair is the stratified open site of Arumvale, which contained chert and quartz artefacts. The site has been dated to 18,400 ± 540 BP (SUA 456), and 9,220 ± 136 BP (SUA 455) (Dortch 1979a, 1979b). Another site, Minim Cove, near Perth, also appears to be of Pleistocene origin, with a date of 9,930 ± 130 BP (SUA 454), which was obtained 90 cms above the lowest stone artefact.

The Quininup Brook site complex, on the southwestern coast of Western Australia, is a group of six open sites covering an area 500 by 800 metres, which appear to have been stratified within siliceous sands. The horizon in which the sites are located is dated between 18,500 ± 1,700 BP (SUA 687) and 10,800 ± 300 BP (SUA 688), that is covering the glacial maximum and terminal Pleistocene periods (Ferguson 1981). This complex is composed of clusters of stone artefacts, and appears to represent a set of inland domestic camp sites once located on a ridge above an extensive coastal plain, which are now being eroded by the sea. Ferguson suggested that the site complex was abandoned during the early Holocene because of changing environmental circumstances (1981: 609, 631–633). He argued that increasing forestation of the region brought about by a wetter climate, together with rising sea levels, would have effectively reduced the area of exploitable resources. Other sites were also occupied during the terminal Pleistocene. Cheetup in southwestern Australia, for example, is inhabited from about 13,000 BP (Moya Smith 1982).

Kangaroo Island

Kangaroo Island, a large land mass, now lies around 14.5 kilometres off the South Australian coast, close to the present-day city of Adelaide. During much of the Pleistocene, the island was a peninsula of the southern coastline of Greater Australia, and close to the mouth of its largest river, the ancestral Murray River. The island was severed from the Australian mainland with the post-glacial sea rise which occurred around 9,000 years ago.

Lampert's extensive reconnaissance of the island produced one Pleistocene site, Seton, although he also found abundant evidence of later Holocene occupation (1981). The limestone cave of Seton is located today above a freshwater lagoon and has close to two metres of cultural deposit. There are two main periods of occupation dated to 16,110 ± 100 BP and 10,940 ± 60 BP, respectively. During the earlier occupation phase, ephemeral use of the site is indicated by the sparse archaeological remains, which include flint (from stone quarries some 16 kilometres away), hearths and land animals. Taphonomic and economic analyses of the site indicate the hunting of the larger animals; these include the red kangaroo, *Megaleia rufa*, now an arid zone dweller and no longer found in this region, and the extinct megafaunal species *Sthenurus*.

Some five thousand years intervened between the initial period of occupation, during which Seton served principally as a carnivore's den, and a relatively intensive phase of habitation around 11,000 BP. Flint and quartz were now used and hunting appears to have focused upon the large grey kangaroo, *Macropus fuliginosus*, a forest dweller and still found in the region today. Other animals were also included, together with emu egg, an indicator of cold weather. The upper layers of the site appear to have been truncated.

SOUTHWESTERN VICTORIA

The limestone Bridgewater caves are located southwest of Seton, on the present-day coast of southwestern Victoria (Lourandos 1980a, 1980b, 1983a). The southern cavern (South Cave) has deposits reaching a depth of three metres outside the present lip of the shelter. Of the two main cultural units, the lower has been dated to between about 11,500 and 7,500 BP, and the recent upper unit to the late Holocene (see below). The early phase is somewhat reminiscent of the contemporary lower unit at Seton. This level at Bridgewater suggests an ephemeral use of the site as a hunting bivouac, with an emphasis on the larger land mammals, including the grey kangaroo and the wombat, as well as pademelon, potoroo, brush and ring-tail possum (Lourandos 1983a: 85). A taphonomic study of the faunal suite carried out by Luke Godwin supported these findings, as well as distinguishing between the food remains of humans and of other predators, which included the Tasmanian Devil, *Sarcophilus harrisii* (Godwin 1980). The increasing presence of small quantities of marine fauna may point to contact with the approaching post-glacial sea which, even earlier in the Pleistocene, was never more than 25 kilometres away. A palynological study of the sediments from the excavation indicated that the area must have been increasingly warmer and wetter with the onset of Holocene climatic conditions (Head 1983).

Further terminal Pleistocene occupation has been detected some 150 kilometres northeast of Bridgewater, at the inland Lake Bolac lunette. Evidence of hunting of large land mammals (macropodids) around 12,500 years ago is indicated at the site (Crowley 1981). Over the present South Australian border, northwest of Bridgewater, is the unique Wyrie Swamp site which is stratified within a peat bog and was detected during quarrying operations. Ephemeral use of the margins of the swamp as a short-term camping spot is indicated by stone artefacts and debitage which have been dated to between 10,200 ± 150 BP and 8,990 ± 120 BP (Luebbers 1975, 1978).

Southeastern highlands (New South Wales)

As climates improved during the terminal Pleistocene, highland regions may have become more hospitable, at least seasonally. At this time sites were occupied in a number of highland areas in southeastern Australia, for example in New South Wales. A rock-shelter, Noola, was inhabited sporadically from around 12,550 ± 185 BP (Tindale 1961; Bermingham 1966; Johnson 1979), and another rock-shelter, Lyrebird Dell, in the Blue Mountains near Sydney, around 12,500 ± 145 BP (Stockton and Holland 1974). At lower altitudes and closer to the coastal plain, a third rock-shelter, Shaws Creek K II, was also inhabited intermittently sometime before 12,980 ± 480 BP (Kohen et al. 1984) and ephemeral occupation is first recorded at Logger's Shelter in the Upper Mangrove Creek region around 11,000 BP (Attenbrow 1982: 198; see also below).

Overview: Pleistocene settlement

Southern Australia has evidence approximating the oldest settlement of the continent. Upper Swan, Keilor, perhaps the Cranebrook terraces, as well as the nearby Willandra lakes and southwestern Tasmanian sites, all are dated between about 40,000 and 35,000 years ago (see discussion in Chapters Three and Seven). During this early phase, however, signs of Aboriginal occupation remain slight, although much of the region was forested and better watered with higher lake levels. This pattern is reflected to some extent also at Willandra and wider Darling regions (Chapter Five) as well as in southwestern Tasmania. On the

Figure 6.4 The Bass Point shell midden on the south coast of New South Wales during excavation in 1969 by Sandra Bowdler (Photo: H. Lourandos).

whole, however, Pleistocene evidence is fragmentary and what we have is based mainly upon rock-shelters and caves – the forested nature of much of the environment today also inhibiting visibility. With increasingly drier conditions after about 30,000 years ago, reaching a low point at the glacial maximum, landscapes were becoming increasingly more semi-arid. The southern highlands were glaciated and arid landscapes stretched south to the Victorian coastline.

Why does the evidence for this lengthy period of Pleistocene settlement remain so slight? If refugia were more intensively inhabited during the glacial maximum, then evidence for this should be apparent in the better-watered sectors of the south of the continent, including coastal areas. Some does exist. For example, in the general coastal area of southwestern Australia, Devil's Lair is most intensively occupied during the glacial maximum and terminal Pleistocene, and Quininup Brook and Cheetup are also inhabited at this time. In southeastern Australia, Birrigai in the southeastern highlands, Kings Table in the eastern highlands, and Bass Point on the eastern coastal plain, were first occupied as the glacial maximum approached. Other sites first appear as climate improves more or less immediately following the latter cold period. These sites include Cloggs Cave, Bass Point and Seton. More sites still are first inhabited towards the close of the Pleistocene, including the eastern highlands, the Murray Valley and the coastal plain of southwestern Victoria.

Between about 20,000 and 11,000 years ago, therefore, sites appeared in all major environments including the eastern and southeastern highlands, the southern coastlines of New South Wales and Victoria, Kangaroo Island, the Murray River region and southwestern Australia. During this time more sites were established and were more intensively occupied throughout these regions, and cemeteries also first appeared in the Murray River region. Increasingly more favourable climates of the terminal Pleistocene period (together with rising sea levels) undoubtedly influenced these trends which took place in highland, forested and coastal areas. The open semi-arid landscapes of the late Pleistocene were giving way to more humid, forested conditions, and the approaching sea was exerting an influence upon Aboriginal settlement in near-coastal areas.

Although this archaeological information is slight and may be altered by the availability of more or new evidence, the indications here are of low and dispersed Aboriginal populations, in some ways influenced by the semi-arid conditions and their dispersed resources. Broadly comparable patterns which support this picture were obtained from the arid and semi-arid zones, including the nearby wider Darling–Willandra region discussed in the previous chapter. Amelioration of climate in the terminal Pleistocene may have produced some increases in, and expansion of, Aboriginal populations, leading to changing patterns of dispersal and aggregation (for example, in the regions of the Murray and Darling Rivers). Specialised hunting of the larger macropodids occurs at both Seton and Bridgewater between about 16,000 and 11,000 years ago, and in some ways may compare with the specialised targeting of wallaby in southwestern Tasmania (see Chapter Seven).

The southern highlands appear also to have been sparsely settled in Pleistocene times, and in this way stand in contrast to the southwestern Tasmanian demographic patterns, which are also related to elevated areas. Differences in climate, and resource structure, between these two areas may provide an explanation to some extent. The southern Australian highlands after about 30,000 BP were open, periglacial landscapes with restricted access to coastal valleys and their lower temperatures and more abundant resources. On the other hand, southwestern Tasmanian periglacial environments were closely connected to such valley systems and to a much more extensive, and rich, coastal system. The ratio of coastline to terrestrial environments in Tasmania is much greater today than that of the southeastern corner of Australia and presumably would have been equally as great, if not more so, during the Pleistocene (see further on this in Chapter Seven).

HOLOCENE SETTLEMENT

Palaeoenvironment

The early Holocene witnessed rises in temperature and precipitation which in general appear to have reached their highest levels between about 8,000 and 6,000 years ago. Much of the region was reforested during this period with forests, including rainforests, reaching their maximum extent at the expense of more open vegetation communities such as grasslands. Forests also spread upslope into previously alpine habitats. Generally, the late Holocene was relatively drier and cooler with a lowering of lake levels about 3,000 years ago (although details vary regionally). Forests, including rainforests, began to contract during this period, expanding somewhat once more during the last two thousand years or so, as climate fluctuated and became slightly more humid (Dodson et al. 1992; see Figure 6.1).

Most of this information has been derived from sites, including lakes, that have been mentioned already in this chapter. For this period some information is also available from southwestern Australia, and this suggests a somewhat different pattern to that for southeastern Australia. While forest-dwelling species appear at the archaeological site of Devil's Lair from about 8,000 years ago and throughout the Holocene, more recent environmental evidence suggests that the mid-late Holocene was dry with more humid conditions appearing in the last few thousand years (Ross et al. 1992: 88). While sea levels stabilised about 6,000–5,000 years ago, coastal environments have remained relatively dynamic, being influenced by a wide range of local factors (Chappell 1983; Head 1987; also Chapter Four, above).

Southeastern Australia

South coast New South Wales

Undoubtedly because of its proximity to Sydney and Canberra, this region archaeologically is one of the best known in Australia and the synthesis of archaeological material undertaken by Hughes and Lampert (1982) has been influential and is relevant to issues raised in this chapter (Figure 6.5). They discussed increasing site establishment and use through time, based upon earlier work (Lampert and Hughes 1974) and including the pioneering geo-morphological work of Hughes (1977, 1978). In order to measure the rate of intensity of site use they correlated the rate of accumulation of sediment (roof-fall in rock-shelters and wind-blown sand on open sites) and that of artefacts, in this case stone implements. An investigation of trends in these variables was initiated at five important sites in the region: the estuarine rock-shelters of Burrill Lake and Currarong 1 and 2; the inland rock-shelter of Sassafras 1; and the open coastal shell midden of Bass Point. A close relationship was detected at the first three sites; in the last two sites, where the relationship was found to be less close, the investigators recorded the trend more generally. At Burrill Lake and Bass Point, Pleistocene occupation was relatively low when compared with the period following the establishment of present sea levels around 7,000 BP. At all the sites, including the inland Sassafras shelter, the intensity of occupation increased dramatically after sea levels had stabilised. A general six- to tenfold increase is

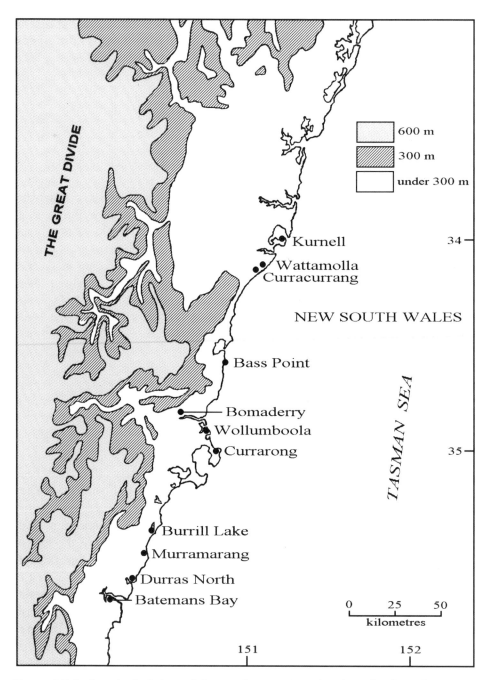

Figure 6.5 Archaeological sites of the south coast, New South Wales (based on Poiner 1976).

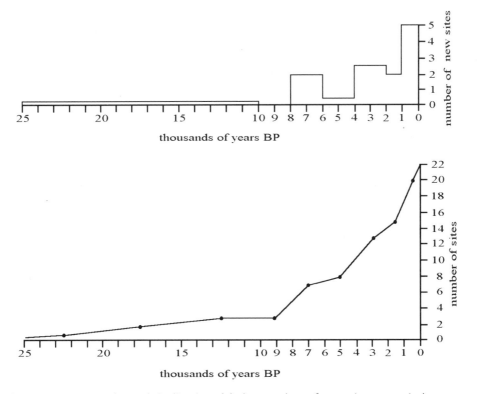

Figure 6.6 Temporal trends indicating: (a) the number of new sites occupied per thousand years and (b) the number of sites occupied per thousand years on the south coast of New South Wales (based on Hughes and Lampert 1982: 21, Figures 6, 7).

recorded during this intensive phase and this trend continues at all the sites, with varying patterns of site use indicated in the most recent 2,000–1,500 years.

Hughes and Lampert applied the results of this detailed analysis to a broader sample, which included a total of twenty archaeological sites from the region. Seventeen of these sites are rock-shelters and three are open sites which are located on headlands or hillslopes. The latter landforms are situated on stable land surfaces which were formed over a period of 30,000 years or so. Care was taken to eliminate problematic factors, such as the destruction or obliteration of earlier sites, and the establishment of sites on 'newly formed sandy landforms' (Hughes and Lampert 1982: 20), for example beach dune systems. Their results are presented on Figure 6.6 (see also Hughes and Lampert 1982: 22–23, Table 1.2). The trends observed indicate that few sites were occupied in the region before sea levels began to reach their mid-Holocene maxima, that is before about 8,000 BP. Once sea levels had risen, however, that is after about 5,000 BP, there was a two- to threefold occupation of sites. As well, during this last 5,000-year period the intensity of occupation of those sites which had been already utilised by humans increased six- to tenfold. 'In other words there was a progressive increase in intensity of occupation of a wide range of site locations along the coast: shelter and open estuarine, protected and exposed rocky shore' (Hughes and Lampert 1982: 20).

A number of alternative hypotheses were entertained by Hughes and Lampert, and these included: differential rates of destruction of sites principally due to environmental factors; loss of earlier site and land use patterns; and increasing use of lithic material per head of population. All of these propositions were rejected, as was the direct association of the trends with sea level rises around 6,000 BP. They argued that intensity of occupation continued to increase long after 6,000 BP, and that some of their results show these trends continuing up to the present time. They observed that similar trends were detected at the Sassafras site which is now situated approximately 35 kilometres inland. The trends therefore did not occur synchronously with the rising of sea levels, nor were they limited to coastal areas.

They concluded by attributing the observed archaeological changes to increases in Aboriginal population. While they had originally associated population increase with rises in marine productivity around 6,000–5,000 BP (Hughes and Lampert 1974), they now discounted this possibility when considering the more marked increases that occurred after 3,000 BP, arguing that coastline formation would have already taken place by this time. They preferred instead to link the trends to 'changes in resource use, in particular an intensification of land use practices' (Hughes and Lampert 1982: 26). They suggested the possibility of increases in Aboriginal burning during the late Holocene (also Hughes and Sullivan 1981). Finally they linked these general trends to comparable, widespread archaeological changes in other areas of Australia, both inland as well as coastal, and more tentatively with the introduction of new stone technology and possibly related cultural changes (see also Boot, in press; and Lourandos, in press).

Upper Mangrove Creek

Located some 30 kilometres inland, the rugged and elevated Upper Mangrove Creek catchment is a complex of narrow river valleys and creeks, steep ridges and more extensive ridge-top plateaux (Figure 6.7). This forested region, which has been incised in the Upper Hawkesbury sandstone, is around 60 kilometres northwest of the city of Sydney. In size the study area is a rough square of around 101 square kilometres. Val Attenbrow's research was originally a salvage project within the storage area of the proposed Mangrove Creek dam (1982, 1987). This detailed study involved an intensive archaeological survey of the area, the study area divided into six environmental zones, and ten percent of each zone was sampled.

Attenbrow's results have produced a sample of thirty-five excavated archaeological sites, which is by far the largest single analysed sample from a comparable study area in Australia (1987: 189–190). Of these sites, thirty-one

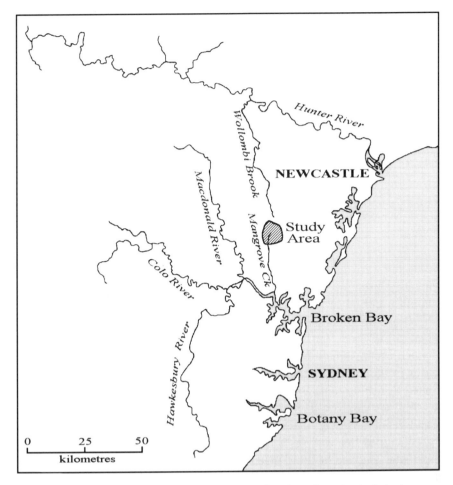

Figure 6.7 The location of the Upper Mangrove Creek archaeological study area, New South Wales (based on Attenbrow 1982: 68, Map 1).

were datable, and dates were obtained from twenty-seven rock-shelters and one open site. The age of these twenty-eight sites was evaluated relatively by stone artefacts and eleven of the rock-shelters were radiocarbon-dated. The age of the remaining three open sites was inferred by other criteria. The oldest of the sites was Loggers Shelter, at 11,050 ± 135 BP (SUA 931), which was rich in stone artefacts.

Four main factors were considered in her analysis which spanned around 11,000 years: (a) distribution of sites; (b) rate of site establishment; (c) number of sites used per unit of time; (d) rate of artefact accumulation (1987: 252). She found that very few shelters were occupied before 5,000 years ago, and 'between 2,750 and 1,200 years ago there may have been a greater number of shelters first occupied' (1982: 76). Her later conclusions were similar, indicating '. . . that the most dramatic increase occurred after 1,600 BP' (1987: 197; Figure 6.8).

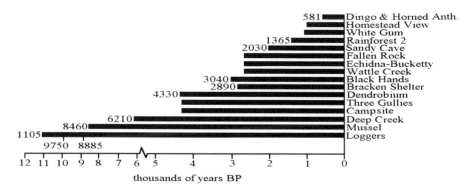

Figure 6.8 Temporal trends indicating rates of occupation of archaeological sites in the Upper Mangrove Creek region, New South Wales (based on Attenbrow 1982:75, Table 2).

Once sites were inhabited, Attenbrow demonstrated, they were more or less continuously used up to the present (1987: 199), and also, after 1,600 BP 'habitation occurred in topographic zones which were not previously inhabited' (1987: 201). This process, she explained, 'could be viewed as "movement into marginal areas" or "an intensification of land use"'. There was also an accelerated establishment of use of sites during the last 5,000 years with further increases in the last few thousand years. The rate of artefact accumulation also continued to rise up until about 1,000 BP, after which decreases are indicated at some sites (Attenbrow 1987: 217–218, 202). Faunal remains older than a thousand years, however, were not well preserved.

She concluded that there is a more complex interrelationship of variables, for example sites and use of lithic materials (1987: 385–386), and that the changing climate of the late Holocene may have played a key role in producing the archaeological patterns perceived.

> I suggest that the climatic change may have promoted cultural changes, but the nature of the changes in the cultural process, which led to changes in different aspects of the archaeological record taking apparently different directions, were dependent on behavioural variables. (Attenbrow 1987: 257)

In the last thousand years also indications of changes in fishing gear, and perhaps fishing practices, are apparent along the eastern coastline of Australia. For example, shell fish hooks appear as far south as the south coast of New South Wales at Durras North, around 700 BP (Lampert 1971), and Bass Point at around 600 BP (Bowdler 1976; Figure 6.9). During this same period shell fish hooks are found at Mazie Bay on North Keppel Island along the south Queensland coast (Rowland 1981). Indications of the introduction of turtle shell artefacts, which in the ethnography of the area include fish hooks, also appear on the Whitsunday Islands at Nara Inlet I during the last 800 years (Barker 1991). In general, the morphology of the shell fish hooks (and their production) have

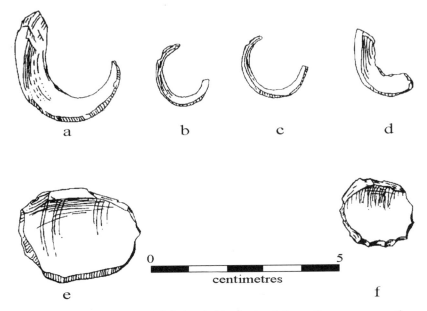

Figure 6.9 Fish hooks (a–d) and fish hook blanks (e, f) from Currarong, south coast, New South Wales (based on Lampert 1971: 55, Figure 15).

Melanesian and Oceanic parallels (see also Chapter Four). Bowdler (1976) has argued that the introduction of shell fish hooks in south coast New South Wales indicated changes in the sexual division of labour, and Walters (1987) has argued in a similar vein for the Moreton Bay region of southeastern Queensland, where fish hooks apparently were not used according to both ethnographic and archaeological records (see also Sullivan 1987; Mackay and White 1987, for an alternative explanation). Lampert also has argued that the appearance of bone points in the coastal sites of this recent period (such as Durras North) are associated with fishing, perhaps as fishing barbs (1971). Many of the sites along the south coast of New South Wales of the last thousand years or so indicate rather specialised marine exploitation, with an emphasis on fishing.

Most offshore islands from this region also were occupied recently, that is to say in the last two thousand years (Sullivan 1982; Blackwell 1982). On the north coast of New South Wales, however, Hiscock (1986) has also detected decreases in site use in the last 1,000 years in the Hunter Valley.

Southwestern Victoria

Palaeoenvironmental sequences have been obtained from the numerous lakes and swamps of this region (for example, Lake Keilambete) (Figure 6.10). The general Holocene sequence indicates higher lake levels and therefore increased humidity in the early Holocene, which decreases somewhat in the late Holocene (including a dry phase around 3,000 BP), followed by fluctuations in humidity (see Figure 6.1) (Bowler 1982). My original archaeological model for the region (Lourandos

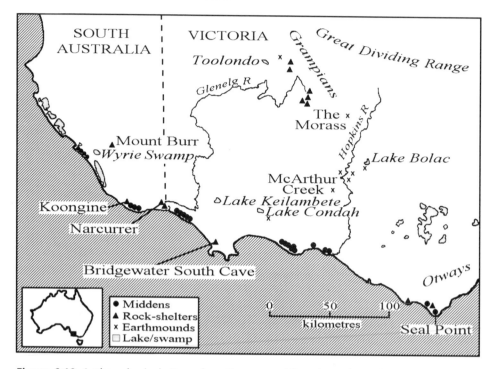

Figure 6.10 Archaeological sites of southwestern Victoria and southeastern South Australia (information from Lourandos 1983a, Williams 1987, Bird and Frankel 1991a).

1980a: 416–417; also 1976, 1977a, 1977b, 1980a, 1980b; Coutts et al. 1977) was based on ethnohistorical research (see Chapter Two). I argued that the high population density, semi-sedentism and complex economy and social relations of the region could be explained not only by the high bioproductivity of the area, but also by the development of these features through time, in particular during the Holocene period.

This last point was reinforced by comparisons made with Tasmanian ethnohistory (in particular with the environmentally comparable north coast), and the fact that both Tasmania and Victoria, once connected during the Pleistocene, had developed in isolation throughout the Holocene period. Southwestern Victorian population densities were over three times higher than those along the north coast of Tasmania, and Tasmanian settlement patterns were generally more mobile and subsistence practices more restricted (for example, no fishing was performed, as discussed in Chapter Two). I linked the southwestern Victorian archaeological, settlement and subsistence patterns, which broadly conform to the above description for the region, with artefacts of the Australian Small Tool tradition of the last 4,000–3,000 years rather than those of earlier times. I also speculated that the economic 'pathways' that had been intensified during this period were mainly those of fishing (especially eeling and the development of intensive swamp management practices), and of indigenous roots and tubers. Fire also may have been used to produce vegetation disclimaxes, as well as being employed in the management of the plants, roots and tubers.

This model was expanded by integrating further archaeological information from the region (Lourandos 1983a). A sample of nineteen archaeological sites was examined, which included shell middens, rock-shelters, caves, open sites (including earth mounds and lunettes) and artificial drainage systems. Shell middens ranged from complex sites to shell dumps. The oldest shell midden was around 7,300 BP at Thunder Point (Gill 1972). Earth mounds are artificial structures serving as habitation sites, with evidence of hearths, burials, stone artefacts and terrestrial and aquatic fauna (Coutts and Witter 1977), and correspond to ethnographic examples of important settlement markers (see also Chapter Two). Rock-shelters of the forested Grampian Range are associated with rock art (perhaps linking them with intergroup relations) and contain stone artefacts, mammalian animal bone, emu eggshell and freshwater mussel shell. The earliest Grampian shelter is dated to 3,330 BP (BR/2) (Coutts and Witter 1977), and microliths of the Australian Small Tool tradition are found at most of these sites.

Basal dates from this sample of nineteen excavated archaeological sites indicate that while sites had been established from around the terminal Pleistocene (about 12,500 BP), most sites date to the last 4,000–3,000 years. The most intensive phase of site establishment was the last 2,000 years, and the overall impression of this temporal sequence was of increasing site establishment through time. As well, the most complex sites (in relation to their size and economic details) appear in the last part of the sequence. 'For example, all the earth mounds are less than 2,500 years old together with some of the larger shell middens and open sites' (Lourandos 1983a: 86). The original nineteen sites are included in Figure 6.11. A wide range of unexcavated surface sites can be added to this list, many of which are associated with the Australian Small Tool tradition and thus generally of the last 4,000–3,000 years. The list does not include sites established for the first time on newly formed land surfaces and this is true of most shell middens and earth mounds (see also Williams 1987). Overall, from a geomorphological point of view, this sample appears to be relatively sound.

This information generally supported the interpretation which had been obtained from the three excavated sites referred to earlier, Bridgewater South Cave, Seal Point and Toolondo. At Bridgewater, the ephemeral terminal Pleistocene-early Holocene phase of occupation, from c. 11,500 to 7,500 BP, is followed by a more intensive occupation in the last 500 years or so. During this time there appears to be an overall broadening of the resource base, together with the range and number of artefacts employed. This analysis has been based upon faunal and lithic remains together with charcoal concentrations (Godwin 1980; Lourandos 1983a).

The extensive shell midden of Seal Point at Cape Otway is around 400 metres

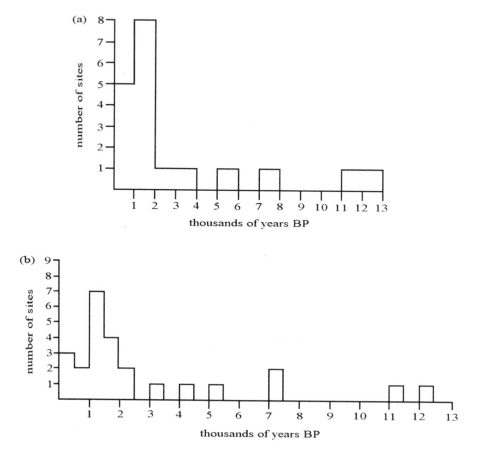

Figure 6.11 Temporal trends in the establishment of archaeological sites over the last 12,000 years in southwestern Victoria: (a) Lourandos 1983a; (b) Williams 1987.

long, 100 metres wide and about one metre in depth. A cluster of ten or more circular depressions at its eastern margin conform to descriptions from ethnohistorical sources of hut-pit structures (see Chapter One). The site appears to have been intensively occupied with a rich marine-terrestrial economy. It was first established, however, only about 1,500 years ago, and there is no evidence of prior occupation despite deep auguring of the dune beneath the site. Dietary emphasis was on seal, *Mirounga leonina*, and *Arctocephalus pusillus doriferus*, fish, medium-to-small-sized land mammals, such as possums, and macropodids, as well as shellfish and crustaceans. Presumptive evidence also exists of the heavy use of bracken fern, *Pteridum esculentum*.

More recent analysis of this site shows that it was most intensively occupied from around 500 BP and increasingly so more or less into recent times, with increments in fauna, stone artefacts, charcoal and sediments (Lourandos and Mitchell in prep; Mitchell 1988; Yap 1992). This recent intensive phase of the

Figure 6.12 Bridgewater South Cave, southwestern Victoria (Photo: H. Lourandos).

last 500 years is also found in other sites on Cape Otway, such as the rock-shelters of Glen Aire (Mulvaney 1962) and Moonlight Head (Zobel et al. 1984). As with Bridgewater and Seal Point, the extensive Toolondo drainage system (see below) also can be associated with recent contexts.

This model is examined further below, in light of new evidence and research. I undertook more recent excavations at Narcurrer, which is a large limestone rock-shelter within an extensive sinkhole, some 10 kilometres over the southwestern Victorian border in South Australia (Lourandos and Barker in prep; Barker 1987). The general results from this site support the chronological trends observed for southwestern Victoria. The one metre of cultural deposit indicated that the site was first occupied about 3,000 BP, and more intensively from 800 BP. No further evidence of human occupation was detected in the deep sediments which underlay the cultural levels. This site was selected for examination as there was little chance of loss of sediments in such a sinkhole environment. These trends were analysed by the following variables: faunal remains, stone artefacts, charcoal and sediments. Distinct charcoal lenses are evident in the most recent levels. The taphonomic study of the site's faunal remains indicate that medium-to-small land animals were the main prey throughout, although larger animals were also included. The most recent occupation unit also indicates a broader range in activities, as determined from both faunal and lithic studies. My general interpretation of the southwestern Victorian evidence is presented below.

EARTH MOUNDS

Elizabeth Williams (1985, 1987, 1988) tackled the difficult task of dating the introduction of earth mounds in central southwestern Victoria, and for this she built upon earlier research. Basing her analysis on ethnohistorical records, Williams chose three areas recorded as places where 'villages', complex fish-trap systems, and intergroup congregational sites, were located. The three areas are Caramut (Figure 6.13), Bessiebelle and the foot of Mount William. Williams confirmed the results obtained from ethnohistorical sources concerning the mounds, together with their distribution and connection with natural resources and semi-sedentism (see also Lourandos 1980a, 1980b). She found that large clusters of mounds (in excess of six mounds) were located on high ground, and close to a network of creeks and swamps, that is areas of high bioproduction. The largest mound clusters, the Ovens and Plover sites, cover 3.9 hectares and one hectare respectively, the former composed of twenty-eight, and the latter of seven mounds. These sites are associated with an ethnohistorical description of a 'village' of between twenty and thirty well-built huts (Williams 1985) and are situated close to a congregational site where up to 2,500 participants were recorded. The larger mound clusters, for example the excavated McArthur Creek cluster near Caramut (Figure 6.14), appear to be base camps.

The excavations, together with analyses of texture and particle composition of mound and off-mound sediments, indicated that the mounds are artificial structures, and these appear to have been habitually resurfaced. The mounds served a variety of functions: as hut foundations, general camping places and as ovens. Unfortunately, poor faunal preservation limited the analysis of the economic aspects of the site. The basal dates obtained from the mounds (Figure 6.10b, above) indicated that all the mounds that had been excavated were less than 2,500 years old (see also above).

At the Morass site near Mount William, which is located on the margins of an old lake, stratigraphic and sedimentary analyses showed that the mounds here had a basal date of only 300 years. Occupation of this site, however, continued beneath the mound structures as was evidenced by flaked stone artefacts. A basal date was retrieved for this site of 4,990 ± 260 BP (ANU 3883). The sequence here indicates that while the site was initially occupied at least 5,000 years ago, when lake levels were higher than in the late Holocene, the appearance of mounds is quite recent (Williams 1987: 317).

Williams also points out that many of the mounds of southwestern Victoria are located directly upon Pleistocene sediments which had been derived from weathered basalt flows. 'If mounds *had* first appeared during the early Holocene then dates older than 2,500 BP should have been obtained from the basal units of sites' (1987: 317). She was able to define more closely the chronology of changes in southwestern Victorian prehistory, and she argued that it was not until after 2,500 BP, that is coinciding with the introduction of mounds, that most sites are established in the region. Prior to mound building, camp sites

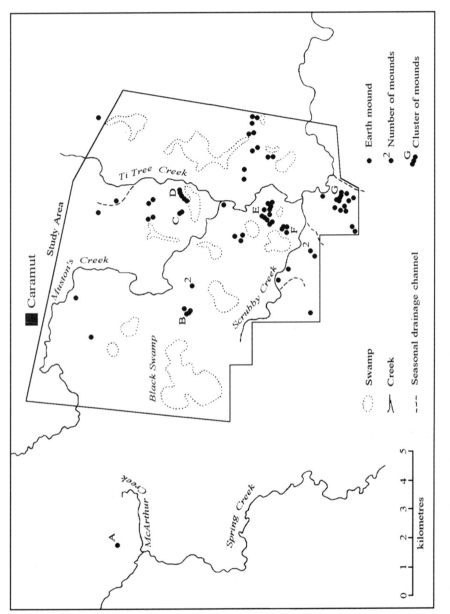

Figure 6.13 Archaeological earth mound sites in the Caramut region, southwestern Victoria (based on Williams 1987).

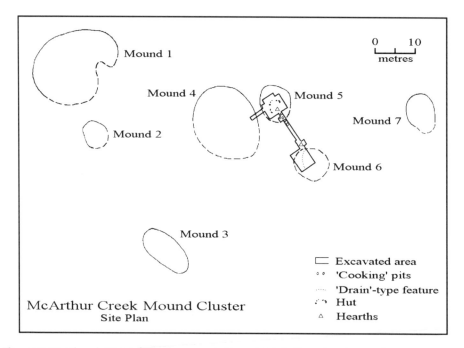

Figure 6.14 The cluster of earth mound sites at McArthur Creek, southwestern Victoria (based on Williams 1987).

mainly appear to have been restricted to well drained sandy deposits, such as lunettes, which are associated with lakes and swamps (1987: 318). She also considered the appearance of earth mounds as an indication of a reorganisation of labour and settlement towards a more sedentary use of sites. Clusters of sites indicated population aggregation, with an overall impression of a more intensive settlement of the region, and Williams (1987: 319) interpreted this material as indicating changes in alliance networks after about 3,000 BP, as we have discussed earlier.

Generally comparable chronological results have been obtained from complexes of earth mounds in the Murray River region (Berryman and Frankel 1984). The same is true of excavations of mound sites in other parts of Victoria (Williams 1988). Geomorphological studies have been carried out by Head (1987, 1989) and, in general, support the above archaeological interpretations. For example, Head demonstrated that the Lake Condah fish traps could only have operated during lake levels similar to those of the present time, and not lower or higher levels as existed in the past.

LARGE-SCALE DRAINAGE SYSTEMS

Archaeological examples of artificial drainage systems have been found at Toolondo, a site which is located between the Mallee and southwestern Victoria (Lourandos 1976, 1980a, 1980b, 1985a). These structures are comparable in scale to drainage systems observed in this region (for example, at Mount William) by

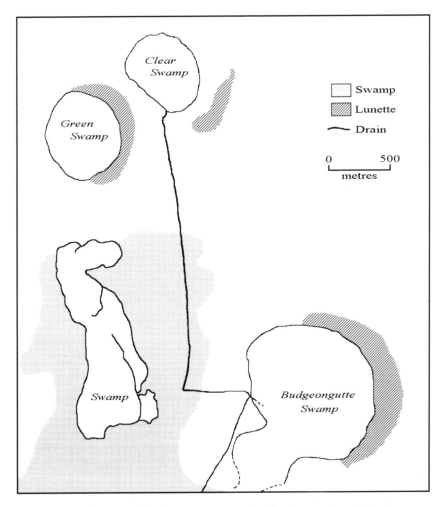

Figure 6.15 The Aboriginal drainage system at Toolondo, western Victoria, connecting a series of swamps and marshy ground (based on Lourandos 1980a).

the ethnographer Robinson in 1841 (see Chapter Two). The structures at Toolondo extend over an area well in excess of three kilometres, and their maximum area is unknown (Figure 6.15). A series of large artificial channels had been excavated so as to drain an extensive patch of swampy ground which lies between two natural morasses, the Clear and Budgeongutte Swamps. The main channel measured a maximum of 2.5 metres wide and over one metre deep (Figure 6.16), and was linked to a complex of lesser drains. A radiocarbon date of 210 ± 120 BP (GX 4785) was obtained from sediments at the base of the main channel, and perhaps indicates the termination of the operation of the drain. The channels had been constructed so as to take full advantage of the natural hydraulic system, and create a fast current by funnelling run-off and seepage water via the drains into both natural swamps. The autumn rains would have

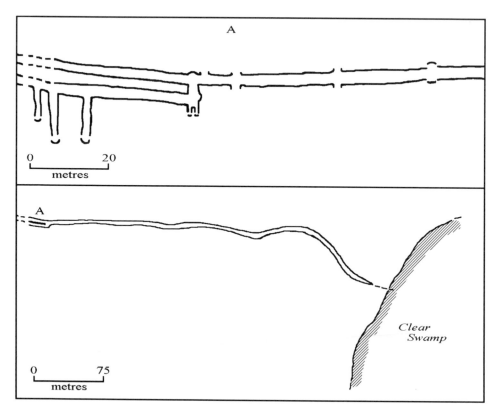

Figure 6.16 The northern section of the Toolondo Aboriginal drainage system connecting the Clear Swamp. Section A is enlarged (above) and shows dual main channels and a series of smaller connecting drains (based on Lourandos 1980a).

resulted in flushing eels and other fish out of the swampy ground and down into the drains, where a complex of traps appear to have been constructed close to the Clear Swamp (see Figure 6.16).

Archaeological excavations took place at a number of locations along the drains to verify their antiquity. The results indicated that the stratigraphic location of the drains, together with abundant evidence of stone artefacts in their infill, were the product of Aboriginal labour prior to European settlement. This evidence gave support to the testimony of the local land owners, descendants of the original European family to farm the area, of the Aboriginal origin of the drains.

Toolondo is situated at the northern margins of the natural distribution of eels, and only a few kilometres to the north of the divide between the major coastal and inland river systems. The southern Budgeongutte Swamp is linked to the coastal river system, while the northern Clear Swamp is not (see Figure 6.15). As these two swamps are not connected by natural means, the artificial drains would have provided eels, which live in the coastal river systems, with a route into adjacent swamplands to the north. The ethnographic example from Mount William has a comparable location, and together with Toolondo, these are the only two places in the area where the major drainage systems are close enough to be artificially connected (see Figure 6.15).

The size and construction of these drains points to their operation as more than eel-harvesting devices. As artificial water controls, the drainage systems operated as a form of swamp management, coping with excess water during floods and retaining water in times of drought. This would have served to counteract the effect of variation in water availability on the distribution, and therefore the availability, of eels in these marginal areas of their range. An extension of the eel range, by providing access to further inland swamps and waterways, would have led to an increase in the annual production of eels (Lourandos 1980a: 254). The drainage systems were labour-intensive in both their construction and maintenance. Using present-day ethnographic information from the New Guinea Highlands, it was calculated that the Toolondo system represented 13,000 hours of human labour (Lourandos 1980b: 381). The development of systems of this kind 'would have allowed for greater control over the local environment, certain of its resources, and by implication their yield. It can be seen as a form of artificial niche expansion' (Lourandos 1980a: 255).

Several factors can be associated plausibly with the development of these labour-intensive devices. These involve climatic change, competition between local populations and possibly demographic change. The gradual desiccation of marginal inland environments throughout the last 3,000 years or so (Bowler et al. 1976) would have increasingly endangered aquatic resources. Intensification of eel harvesting and management methods, partly in response to climatic shifts, appears to have been an attempt to comply with techniques used to the south along natural drainage systems that formed the economic basis for the main autumn ceremonial gatherings common to the whole of southwestern Victoria. Intensification is viewed here as being fuelled by the demands of social relations and merely stimulated by environmental factors. This argument is reinforced if a simplified cost–benefit explanation is offered. As the productivity of eels (and other aquatic resources) dwindled due to less humid conditions, presumably the cost of procurement would have increased and eeling would have become a less competitive strategy in scheduling terms (Flannery 1968). Daily consumption generally operated at the band level, and it would be difficult to conceive of the scale of the Toolondo drainage system being a profitable venture without back-up preservation and storage techniques, for which there is no evidence. Consumption of the great quantities of eels produced in this way was relatively immediate and thus necessitated the participation of fairly large groups of people (for example, a thousand or more were observed). Profitability, thus, can only be seen in terms of large groups of people – that is, at the intergroup level (Lourandos 1985a: 408).

Demographic change, it may be presumed, would have aggravated this competitive situation even further. The relatively sedentary people of the fertile coastal plain of southwestern Victoria may have experienced change of this kind periodically. Toolondo and Mount William are both situated on the border between the well-watered coastal strip and the drier inland plains, where groups had more mobile subsistence economies. 'The latter situation resembles Binford's "population frontier or adaptive tension zone" (1968: 332) where he predicts that more rapid cultural changes could be expected' (Lourandos 1980a: 255).

The evidence from Lake Condah in southwestern Victoria is comparable in some ways to that of Toolondo. Archaeological research in this marshy region largely confirms the ethnohistorical accounts (Coutts et al. 1978), as discussed in Chapter Two. A complex system of stone fish-traps, together with channels excavated in the local basalt, were situated at intervals extending over an area of several hundred metres. At least four individual sets of traps appear to have operated, each one attuned to variations in the depth of water levels. Flood levels would have been most variable during the autumn and winter seasons. It was calculated that up to eight traps could have operated at the one time. Around the stone traps, on higher ground, were the remains of large numbers of stone-walled, semi-circular hut structures or foundations and these conformed to ethnohistorical descriptions of similar habitations from the area. The accompanying artefacts indicated that these stone-walled structures may have been from the period of European contact.

Southeastern South Australia

Adjacent to southwestern Victoria is the equally fertile coastal and estuarine province of southeastern South Australia (see Figure 6.9, above). Two field projects were carried out by Luebbers (1978, 1981, 1984) in this broad area, which stretches northwest along the extensive Coorong estuary, to the mouth of the Murray River, and the nearby city of Adelaide. Luebbers (1978) conducted an extensive site survey of 600 square kilometres between Robe and Cape Banks. His archaeological sequence spans the whole of the Holocene period, which begins with rather ephemeral occupation along the margins of the Wyrie Swamp at about 10,000 BP. Use of inland swamps, as well as the coast, appears to have continued in a similar fashion until around 6,000 BP. In contrast to this early period, the mid-late Holocene is divided into two phases (Luebbers 1978: 108–109, 210–212). The first phase (c. 5,800–1,300 BP) consists of small discrete shell lenses, which are composed mainly of one shell species (the sand dweller, *Plebidonax*, or the small rock mussel, *Brachidontes*). Sparse numbers of stone artefacts (including microliths) also are associated. Similar sites are distributed from the coast up to two kilometres inland.

From about 1,300 BP until the present, however, more numerous and larger, deeply stratified shell middens appear which are composed of a wider range of marine resources. Shell species are reef gastropods, and the amounts of shellfish appear to increase tenfold. Raw materials also appear to have been transported from afar, and overall a wider range of economic activities are represented. Few microliths are evident and the locations of these sites differ from the earlier period, extending up to twelve kilometres inland.

Luebbers argued that this most recent archaeological pattern indicates more intensive occupation of the area and he described it as a diversification of the overall economic strategy on a larger scale than before. The pattern indicates more regular and sedentary settlement, together with wider communication and trade networks (Luebbers 1978: 209–211, 1984: 34–35). Luebbers linked these changing archaeological patterns to environmental changes, although he did not view these as determining the behavioural patterns (1978: 302–303). He argued that increasing climatic desiccation of the region as a whole was reducing the productivity of the wetlands and other areas, after about 3,000 BP, and especially between about 2,000 and 500 BP. Prior to this dry phase, conditions had been more humid, and he speculated that population and settlement would have been more widespread (306). More recent drier conditions, however, may have forced populations toward riverine and coastal areas. This may have led to a population increase, or to an increase in visitation in these zones, that is, a demographic rearrangement within the district as a whole (215–216, 307). He considered that intensification of resource procurement also may have been involved and that the economic rearrangements may have included the extensive fish weirs in South Australia, as well as the eel traps and earth mounds of southwestern Victoria (307).

While Luebbers' explanations correspond with those of southwestern Victoria to some degree, he does not explain why population sizes remained high once drier conditions set in after about 3,000 BP, therefore necessitating further economic, settlement and demographic rearrangements. Another possible solution was for population sizes and densities to be reduced as bioproduction diminished, much as Birdsell had proposed (see Chapter One). These issues are discussed further below. Also, the last two thousand years were not so dry; more humid conditions had taken place following the dry phase around 3,000 BP.

The second group of studies by Luebbers comes from further north – the Younghusband Peninsula and the Southern and Northern Coorong (1981, 1984). Extensive surveys were followed by excavation, as in the prior project, and he isolated three main chronological phases (1981: 32–33, 40–43; 1984: 3–4, 91–93). His general results, however, are not too dissimilar to those of the prior study:

(i) c. 6,000–4,500 BP. Sites are composed of small lenses of shellfish (mainly mussel) with few stone artefacts and emphasis is upon estuarine locations and resources. At this time the peninsula on which the sites were located was a chain of islands.

(ii) c. 4,500–2,000 BP. Sites are larger shell middens with a mixed marine-terrestrial fauna and although the sites were located on the estuary, there is a decline in estuarine resources.

(iii) c. 2,000 BP to the present. Sites include very large mounds and shell middens with a heavy emphasis upon marine resources, lesser quantities of terrestrial fauna, and no estuarine fauna. Long-distance transportation of resources is evident and the sites are located along the ocean forefront, especially during the last thousand years.

Luebbers explained this sequence mainly in environmental terms. After about 6,000 BP, bioproductivity declined in the Coorong estuary, and the Young-husband Peninsula was formed from a prior chain of islands, effectively closing off the mouth of the Murray River. Over time people turned their attention from estuarine to marine foods (Luebbers 1981: 3, 32–33). As with the prior explanation, however, while environmental changes may have influenced a shift from estuarine to marine resources, the reason for the relatively intense and spatially confined settlement of the most recent phase is not adequately explained. Following my prior criticism, a reduction in bioproduction, as proposed by Luebbers, also could have resulted in a reduction in the human population. If such a thing had occurred, then the expected settlement-subsistence patterns in the marine zone should have been much more like those of the earlier estuarine phase (i) – that is, small, sparse archaeological deposits. The evidence, therefore, of more intensive recent settlement of the area is the *reverse* of the climatic trend.

Summary: southwestern Victoria and southeastern South Australia

Recently all available radiocarbon dates from archaeological sites from both southwestern Victoria and southeastern South Australia have been drawn together (Figure 6.17). While the data set has grown by over four times the number of sites (over eighty) and ten times the number of dates, the *general* chronological trends, however, have remained essentially the same as those of the original model (Lourandos 1983a; for a contrary view see Bird and Frankel 1991a, 1991b; see also above, Figure 6.11a, b). Sites are first established from about 12,000 years ago, and show significant increases in their use and establishment from around 3,500 years ago, the general upward trend continuing more or less up to the present. All three main site types demonstrate the pattern – rock-shelters and caves, earth mounds and coastal shell middens. All mounds are about 2,500 years or less, as also predicted in the original model. In spite of this, Caroline Bird and David Frankel argue against the general temporal trend, preferring to see it as a series of small-scale events. They present, however, no satisfactory alternative explanation of these events, viewing the process as a series of adjustments to local conditions. My objections to their arguments follow, together with my interpretation of the regional temporal trends and patterns (also Lourandos 1993; Lourandos and Ross 1994).

Firstly, all *general* models are composed of small-scale events. Bird and Frankel's explanations of the latter are largely generalisations, essentially

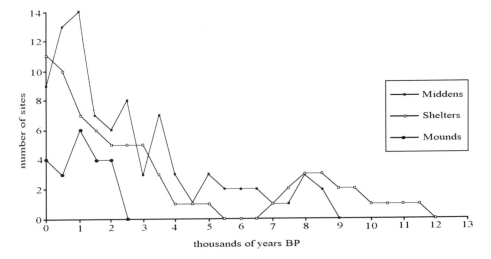

Figure 6.17 Archaeological sites of southwestern Victoria and southeastern South Australia, occupied in each 500-year period throughout the last 12,000 years. Indicated are rock-shelters, shell middens and earth mounds (compiled from information in Bird and Frankel 1991a: 9, Figure 5; see also Lourandos 1993; Lourandos and Ross 1995).

environmentally deterministic, and lack further detail. The general chronological trend is also the *opposite* of the general climatic trend (see Figure 6.1, above) for the area, thus arguing against a positive causal connection between the two, as Bird and Frankel suggest. A perceived decline in the use of shelters between 7,000 and 5,000 BP, as indicated by Bird and Frankel, is explained by the demonstrable truncation or loss of sediments at these sites (Bridgewater, Mount Burr and possibly Koongine also). Even though the southwestern Victorian coast is a prograded landscape, shell middens still follow the general chronological trend. Indeed, recent late Holocene middens are more endangered in this regard than older middens (Head 1983; and compare Godfrey 1989).

I would suggest that the temporal trends can be interpreted in terms of Aboriginal patterns of land use in the following way. Sites become visible in this region towards the terminal Pleistocene, along with general increases in bioproduction. Prior to this, climate had been drier, landscapes open and semi-arid, and resources more dispersed. Aboriginal populations may have been less dense and dispersed at this time also, a characteristic reflected in the low visibility of site use. During the more humid early Holocene, however, and presumably when bioproduction was greatest, there is no evidence of an emphasis upon wetlands, although ephemeral wetland sites occur (for example, Wyrie Swamp). Also, rock-shelters indicate relatively low levels of use when compared with the late Holocene. Expansion of forests at this time (post-8,000 BP) may have inhibited occupation of some of the rock-shelters to some extent (also rainforested areas like Cape Otway), but not all. On the other hand, increases in establishment and use of all three site types (rock-shelters, mounds and middens) during the last 3,500–2,500 years or so *run counter* to contemporary environmental trends as regards the productivity of forests, wetlands and coastal environments (see above, this chapter).

Climatic trends for the region, as we have seen, indicate a less humid late Holocene, and presumably lower productive levels, with a relatively dry phase about 3,000 years ago, followed by fluctuations in more humid conditions (see Figure 6.1, above). An increasing use of rock-shelters during the late Holocene, therefore, suggests increasing use of forested areas (including rainforest) where the sites are located. Similarly, the appearance of and increase in earth mounds since about 2,500 BP, in association with ephemeral and perennial wetlands, also suggests more intensive use of these environments, as no equivalent sites existed in prior times. Although the timing of the introduction of earth mounds appears to coincide with a phase of increasing humidity, this cannot be viewed as a response controlled directly by environmental factors as wetlands appear to have been largely avoided during the more humid early Holocene when they were most extensive. Also, earth mounds continue to have been increasingly established and used during the succeeding period of fluctuating humidity. The general temporal trends, therefore, for both shelters and mounds show marked increases in establishment and use *throughout* the last 2,500 years, thus cutting across the fluctuating climatic trends.

There is also evidence of more intensive use of shell middens in estuaries (for example, the Coorong) and coastal areas (for example, Cape Otway). However, more intensive use of the Coorong estuary coincides with a *decline* in local bioproductivity (that is, drier climate), and there appears to be no perceived change in resource availability in the Cape Otway area in recent times. Once forests have been contained in the Otway area, settlement continues to increase throughout the last 2,000–1,000 years.

More 'logistical' strategies are represented by the appearance and spread of earth mounds, serving as wetland bases, and increased use of rock-shelters, caves and certain shell middens (Coorong, Cape Otway). Further examples are complexes of stone fish-traps (Lake Condah) related to recent lake levels, and the 'recent' Toolondo drainage systems, which can also be viewed as 'delayed-return' systems. Changes in settlement patterns also suggest demographic changes, including patterns of population dispersal such as reduced mobility, and a more sedentary emphasis. Increase in population is suggested, for example, by increasing establishment of sites and use of particular sites and environments (for example, wetlands, forests, estuaries, and parts of the coast). One plausible general explanation, therefore, of this cultural sequence would be of more complex demographic patterns, including population increase, together with a more sedentary emphasis (that is, increased aggregation), during the last 3,000 years or so.

I maintain that these data indicate the emergence, during the last few thousand years, of the subsistence-settlement pattern observed ethnohistorically, with its semi-sedentary and populous features (as discussed in Chapter Two). In some ways these demographic-subsistence patterns are associated with complex social networks, the chronology of which is at present inferred by rock-shelters containing painted rock art (dated to this recent period) and evidence of extensive green-stone axe exchange (including stratified axe debitage), all roughly dating to within the last few thousand years (McBryde 1984). I will return to this later in this chapter.

Northwestern Victoria

The arguments developed for southwestern Victoria were tested in some ways by Anne Ross (1981, 1985), who carried out a detailed archaeological and geomorphological project in the adjacent semi-arid Mallee country of northwestern Victoria. Ross surveyed this extensive region using random transects as well as geomorphological methods and in this way she intensively surveyed over 70 percent of areas containing water resources. Considerably less area was covered in the waterless dune country. All the archaeological sites which were located were surface scatters found on dune blowouts, in lakeside sediments, or on aeolian ridges. Ross found that the history of settlement of the region did not fit her expected environmental model, which had predicted an expansion of population throughout the district during wet phases, followed by a contraction or withdrawal of populations during drier periods. The archaeological evidence, however, indicated that during the wet phase of the early Holocene, from about 12,000 to 7,000 BP, the only obvious signs of Aboriginal occupation were in the north of the district, along the Murray River and at Raak Plains (Figure 6.18). Radiocarbon dates from both these regions reinforced this impression. As well, the artefacts from the Raak Plains sites 'are of the large core tool and scraper tradition, with small horse-hoof cores, large flake scrapers and large utilized flakes' (Ross 1981: 149).

The southern portion of the Mallee region, which is largely composed of the lake country from Lake Hindmarsh to Pine Plains, appears to have been occupied from less than 4,500 years ago and is associated with recent stone industries. The latter consist of small flakes (which are often heavily retouched), geometric microliths, together with hatchet heads and grindstones. The latter artefacts indicate seed use. Raw materials (for example, chert) also appear to have been imported. Artefacts of the earlier industry are not found in this region. The available radiocarbon dates from these southern sites all fall between c. 2,500–1,500 BP. Anne Ross points out that although burial of earlier archaeological evidence cannot be ruled out in some locations, exposure of sediments (including Pleistocene deposits) has also been detected elsewhere. In the latter deposits, however, only recent artefacts (for example, microliths) have been found. As well, 'Nearly all the geomorphic activity in the Mallee since the early Holocene appears to have been largely restricted to deflation of dune surfaces, so that the *revealing* of sites is in fact more likely than their obscuring' (1981: 151). Ross

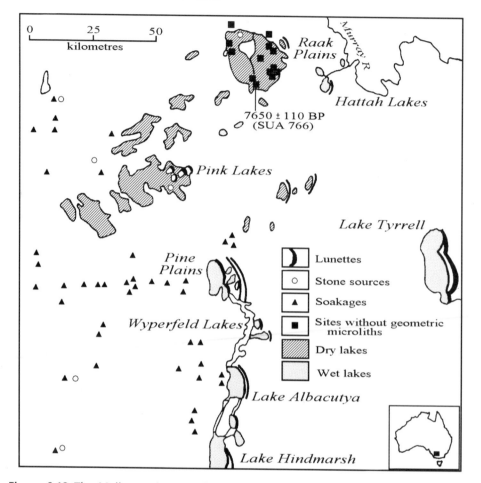

Figure 6.18 The Mallee region, northwestern Victoria, showing some of its natural features and archaeological sites (based on Ross 1981: 150, Figure 4).

did not rule out the possibility of earlier occupation in these southern areas: 'on archaeological and geomorphological evidence, therefore, it would appear that if occupation of the Mallee and Raak Plains had occurred prior to 4,500 BP, it was most probably a small-scale event, which is not now archaeologically visible' (1981: 151).

Ross explained this sequence of occupation in relation to the southwestern Victorian information. She considered two possibilities: first, population pressure triggered by a combination of increasing aridity after about 3,500 BP and, partly as a reaction to this, the development of the extensive water controls in the Toolondo area of southwestern Victoria, already referred to; and, second, general population increase in southwestern Victoria in the late Holocene. In either case Ross considered population increase, between c. 2,500 and 1,500 years ago, as the main cause and envisaged an overspill in expanding populations from southwestern Victoria, first into the Grampian Ranges and from there further north into the Mallee, presumably via the Wimmera River.

In support of her case, Ross introduced linguistic evidence which indicates that at European contact the Mallee languages were more closely related to those of southwestern Victoria than to those of the Murray River. If we are to accept Ross' archaeological evidence, we can also modify her explanation to some extent. Given the approximate nature of her chronological evidence (based mainly upon stone artefacts), the supposed expansion of population may have been even more recent, for example between about 1,500 and 1,000 years ago, or even less. Population growth also may have taken place from within the Wimmera district itself. As well, the linguistic connection may indicate closer social interaction with southwestern Victoria, rather than a direct migratory route. These modifications, however, do not alter the basic thrust of Ross's explanation.

Lower Murray Valley, South Australia

Of the four main sites excavated in this area, Devon Downs, Fromms Landing 2 and 6, and Tartanga, the first three (which are all rock-shelters) are briefly considered here. Devon Downs was the site originally excavated by Hale and Tindale (1930), from which they developed their chronological models for Australian prehistory (see Chapter One). The site was reanalysed by Michael Smith. Over six metres of deposit covers a period of occupation about 6,000–5,000 BP. Using stone artefact frequency as an indicator of intensity of site use, the rock-shelter appears to have been at its peak occupation about 4,000–2,000 BP, after which artefact accumulation rates decrease (Smith 1982: 114).

Similarly, Fromms Landing 2 (Mulvaney 1960; Smith 1982), which is located some 18 kilometres from the former site, appears to have been most intensively occupied after about 4,000 BP, being first established less than 1,000 years before. Smith notes 'no marked decline in the amount of occupational debris' (1982: 114). He associates the increased site use after about 4,000 BP at both sites with increasing population, and he explains the supposed decline in use of Devon Downs after about 2,000 BP as due to local environmental changes. A few years later, Attenbrow (1987: 310) also reconsidered another of Mulvaney's (1964) sites, Fromms Landing 6, which is located around 400 metres from Fromms Landing 2. The site has a basal date of about 3,450 BP (Mulvaney 1964: 490), and Attenbrow suggests (following Mulvaney 1964: Table I) that a decline in artefact accumulation also may have taken place after about 2,000 BP at this site. It should be borne in mind, however, that a decline in stone artefacts does not necessarily indicate a decline in site use, as I have discussed in the case of Attenbrow's Mangrove Creek study.

Exchange and social networks of Victoria

Detailed petrological studies of recent prehistoric exchange patterns in southeastern Australia have been conducted by Isabel McBryde (1978a, 1979, 1984; Binns and McBryde 1972). These studies were based upon artefact

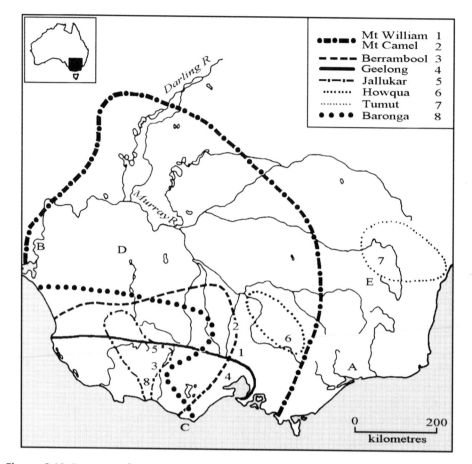

Figure 6.19 Patterns of stone axe exchange, from specific quarries, in southeastern Australia. Sub-regions: A (southeastern Victoria), B (Adelaide Plains), C (Otway Ranges), D (northwestern Victoria), E (southern highlands) (based on McBryde 1984: 268, Figure 1).

collections, and a range of quarry sites. Apart from other raw materials, emphasis was placed upon hatchet heads made of greenstone (altered volcanic rocks of Cambrian age). Ethnohistorical information indicates that these artefacts were highly prized, often prestigious, and exchanged widely throughout the region. Exchange appears to have had a strongly social motivation, for often items were exchanged by participants having access to similar raw materials (McBryde 1984: 268).

Seven quarry sites were investigated in Victoria, one in the southern Australian highlands, and a further three in northeastern New South Wales (Figure 6.19). Clear geographical patterns were detected indicating directional trends in the distribution of greenstone. This is particularly evident in Victoria. A sample of over seven hundred greenstone artefacts yielded four conclusions. They were, first, that greenstone artefacts are sparsely distributed or absent from southeastern

Victoria, the Otway Ranges, and in the distant Adelaide Plains area (A, B, C on Figure 6.19); second, that artefacts from southwestern Victoria (Berrambool quarry, Hopkins River) are absent from adjacent northwestern Victoria (D on Figure 6.19); but third, in contrast, that central Victorian greenstone artefacts are common in northwestern Victoria, but not found in the southern Australian highlands (E on Figure 6.19); and finally, that central Victorian greenstone artefacts are dispersed widely from their source, with 29 percent from the Mount William quarry, located more than 300 kilometres from the quarry. Distance decay curves for Mount William artefacts suggest that redistribution centres also existed. Mount William artefacts are also distributed widely in a southwestern direction (the coastal belt of southwestern Victoria and southern South Australia) (McBryde 1984).

McBryde argued that these patterns cannot be explained as due solely to the distribution of geological resources, for equivalent raw materials were often available in areas to which Mount William greenstone had been distributed. Nor do these patterns merely document the geographical distribution and density of Aboriginal populations (1984: 268–270, 277). She concluded that 'one could hypothesise the operation of social factors determining the direction of the flow of goods and providing for the redistribution ...' (1984: 270). The Mount William artefacts showed no size reduction in relation to distance from the quarry, which McBryde considered an indication of their valued status (1984: 278).

She explained the above patterns by reference to ethnohistorical evidence of socio-political influences in the region. It was reported that strong antagonism existed between the Kulin (central Victoria) and Kurnai (southeastern Victoria) groups. The latter appeared to be particularly insular, and also in opposition to the peoples of the southeastern Australian highlands (see Chapter One).

Secondly, relations between southwestern Victoria populations and groups in the drier regions of northwestern Victoria were also tense and socially restricted; in contrast, contact between central and northwestern Victoria groups was extensive, but this was not so for the southern Australian highlands.

Finally, indirect contact existed between the patrilineal Kulin of central Victoria and the culturally distinct, matrilineal coastal Mara peoples of southwestern Victoria. Complex social and ceremonial interaction took place along the border region, between southwestern Victoria and the northern Tjapwurong groups, which were more closely associated with the eastern Kulin. 'The meeting places could act as nodes in the distribution network, redistributing items according to a new set of socially determined linkages' (McBryde 1984: 278).

Linguistic information also supported McBryde's interpretation (Hercus 1969; Dixon 1980). For example, central Kulin languages were closely related to those of northwestern Victoria, while the Kurnai and southern highland languages were quite distinct. The southwestern coastal languages, including those of the Mara, were also differentiated from those of the Kulin. Also, the linguistic evidence provided a degree of time depth to conclusions largely derived from geographical relationships. McBryde concluded:

> So consistency of direction derives not from trade routes determined by supply and demand, or by regional resources, but from the social affiliations of members of distinct clan territories and the political networks operating within clusters of social units. (1984: 279)

In general, these interpretations are in accord with the other western Victorian archaeological studies I have discussed earlier in this chapter. As well, not only do McBryde's results extend these socio-political patterns back in time, thus linking them closely with the archaeological trends already discussed, they also indicate that had the ethnohistorical information not existed, the archaeological patterns are still clearly visible. Complex socio-political information, therefore, *is* demonstrable archaeologically in this part of Australia, as it has been shown to be in northeastern Queensland (see Chapter Four). The evidence also indicates the close association between exchange and the main socio-political relations between groups, as discussed in Chapter One; and further, it reinforces the complex role of larger regional networks. This ranged from expansive ('open'), as in the case of the Kulin, introspective ('closed') as with the Kurnai, and mediatory, along the border between the Tjapwurong and Mara. These examples illustrate well the range of variations along the 'open'–'closed' continuum of intergroup relationships explored in Chapter One. These broad intergroup patterns, therefore, also can be expected to have influenced subsistence and settlement and to have varied through time.

Osteology and burials of the Murray River region
Osteological and burial evidence from Holocene Australia has significantly contributed to the debate on demographic and cultural changes during this period. Brown stated:

> The reduction in the size and robusticity of the cranial vault and masticatory apparatus in Australia over the last 10,000 years parallels that in other parts of the world. Elsewhere, combinations of culture change and gene flow have been argued to be the driving force behind this process. In this instance, the geographic isolation of Australia, with evidence of extremely limited gene flow from outside, and relative cultural conservatism since initial occupation would make this seem unlikely. Size reduction in Australia may in part be explained by a physiological response to increased Holocene air temperatures. (1987: 62–63)

Earlier, Thorne had also considered the biological changes as due to environmental change (1977: 195–196; see Chapter Three).

These interpretations of the evidence, however, may be challenged on a number of fronts. First, Stephen Webb (1984, 1987, 1989, 1995) has argued for significant population increases in the southeast Australian region in late Holocene times, basing his explanations on mainly late Holocene skeletal information from the area. Webb (1984) detected significant signs of health-related stress problems in prehistoric populations of the central Murray Valley, and to a lesser extent in populations from the southern coast of Victoria. In the central Murray there was a high incidence of Harris lines, suggesting disease and inadequate diet and general or annual stress upon local populations. In contrast, along the southern coast seasonal stress was indicated. Signs of anaemia, however, (and also arthritis) were more prevalent in the central Murray. Generally, this evidence suggests that the rich central Murray corridor, with its dense and relatively sedentary Aboriginal populations (as recorded ethnohistorically), was facing the effects of overcrowding and infectious diseases. In coastal western Victoria, by way of contrast, signs of stress, such as food shortages, appear to have been more regular, perhaps seasonal.

The findings of this research strongly suggest also that Aboriginal society in the central Murray was not only sedentary but must have been far higher in numbers than anything previously proposed or associated with this part of the Murray River (Webb 1984: 170). Webb (1987) has further argued that the archaeological evidence suggested considerable population increase in the central Murray region during the last 3,000–2,000 years as a result of socio-economic intensification.

While this avenue of research is still in its early stages (for example, dating remains problematical to some extent), the evidence and these interpretations do accord with results derived from other parts of southeastern Australia, such as southwestern Victoria, as well as other regions of Australia during this period (see below and Chapter Four). Given the debate on the significance of demographic and cultural (including subsistence) changes during the mid-late Holocene on the mainland, it becomes difficult to accept Brown's above assessment. I would argue that the morphological trends observed for Australian Holocene populations need to be viewed very much against the cultural, demographic, as well as environmental changes, especially those of the late Holocene. In this way, the Australian data may be seen to parallel quite closely biological, demographic and cultural trends in other parts of the world.

Evidence of burials and cemeteries from southeastern Australia, in particular the Murray River corridor, have been reviewed by Pardoe (1988, 1990; see Figure 6.20). Pardoe argues that established cemeteries may be viewed as territorial markers and thus they denote a concentration of human activity in particular locales. In this region cemeteries appear to have been established from late Pleistocene times, and include the sites at Roonka (18,000 BP to recent times) (Pretty and Kricun 1989), Kow Swamp and Coobool (13,000–9,000 BP), further burials at Coobool (6,000–2,000 BP), and Snaggy Bend (10,000 BP). The remaining burial sites are less than 6,000 years old. In general, therefore, this evidence suggests a trend towards increasing territorial behaviour beginning in

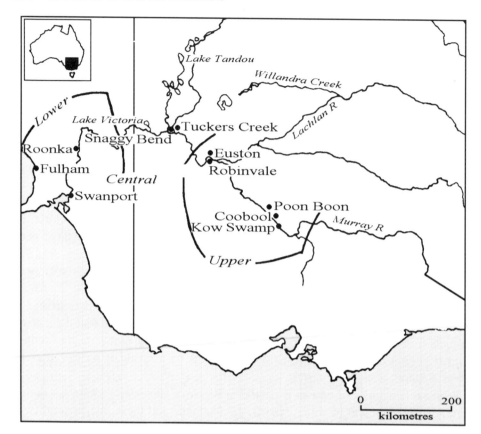

Figure 6.20 Archaeological cemetery sites of the Murray River Valley, southeastern Australia (based on Pardoe 1988: 4, Figure 1).

the late Pleistocene and becoming more pronounced in the late Holocene (when there is more evidence). Pardoe (1988) favours an interpretation of increasing regionalisation of populations from the late Pleistocene period (see also below). 'I think these graveyards arose, probably in the Upper Murray, by 10 to 13 kya [thousand years ago] and spread subsequently throughout the corridor, possibly 6 to 7 kya, to become well defined and numerous in the last 4 kya' (1988: 14).

Evidence from the more recent late Holocene burial grounds, such as Roonka (7,000 BP to the present) (Pretty 1977) and Broadbeach (Haglund 1976), indicates a wide range of burial practices which can be interpreted in a number of ways. At the very least, it suggests a widening of social differentiation at these burial places during the period. The great majority of burials at Roonka are of the last 4,000 years. Marked differences are noted in burial practices between the earlier (early Holocene) and more recent periods at the site. Elaborate burial practices are associated only with mature adults, and claims of status graves have been made by Pretty (1977). More recent investigations at Roonka, however, have failed to detect evidence of stress within the population (Pretty and Kricun 1989).

Recent analyses of skeletal evidence from the Murray River corridor, using multivariate statistical techniques (Pardoe 1990), indicate a very high incidence of morphological variation within the region. Pardoe has interpreted these results as indicating clinal patterns of 'intermarriage' along the river, with neighbouring riverine groups preferring to exchange partners in 'marriage' with each other rather than with groups bordering either side of the river. He attributes these morphological patterns with the development of more introspective, territorial socio-demographic conditions within the riverine corridor. Aspects of social 'closure', as practised by river communities, thus served to retain prime, fertile river lands within local hands, largely preventing control passing to those outside. Pardoe saw the process as beginning with the first signs of territoriality in the terminal Pleistocene and early Holocene periods.

Southern highlands

The eleven rock-shelters and one open site excavated in this region encompass the coastal ranges as well as the southeastern highlands and tablelands. All twelve sites were dated to the last 4,000 years. This late Holocene pattern was expanded with the excavation of the Pleistocene site of Birrigai (see above), which was first occupied around 20,000 BP (Flood et al. 1987). The rate and intensity of occupation of the Birrigai shelter was carefully measured by a number of parameters – artefact discard rates, charcoal quantities, sedimentation rates and sediment particle analysis (see Figure 6.3, above). The results indicate a relatively low level of occupation of the site during the Pleistocene, and this continues throughout the early to mid-Holocene periods. The changing climate of the Pleistocene–Holocene boundary does not appear to have influenced this basic pattern of long-term site use. In contrast, habitation of the site increases markedly during the last three thousand years, and continued to expand throughout this period up to the time of European contact. These trends are supported by the oriented sediment particle analysis, which indicated increased disturbance of the deposit during this period. Organic remains, which include clear, distinct lenses of charcoal, are better preserved in this more recent phase of occupation. The site, however, indicates apparently continuous, though not intensive, occupation from the time of its initial inhabitation and this chronological pattern, with its increasing occupation throughout the last three millennia, is also reflected by the other excavated sites from this region (Figure 6.21). Of the ten sites listed, only two were inhabited in the Pleistocene (Birrigai and Cloggs), the remainder less than 4,000 years ago. Half of these sites were first occupied during the last 2,000 years, and continued to be used up to the present (Flood et al. 1987: 22; see Table 6.1).

The limestone Cloggs Cave, which is located towards the base of the southern ranges in eastern Victoria and occupied during the Pleistocene (see Chapter

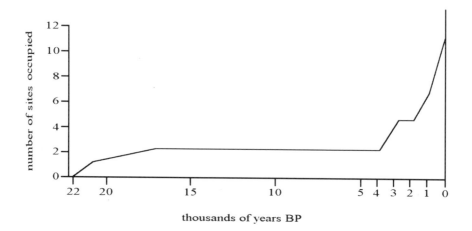

Figure 6.21 Temporal trends indicating the number of excavated rock-shelters occupied per thousand years in the southern highlands region of Australia (based on Flood et al. 1987: 22, Figure 12).

Table 6.1 Dated archaeological sites of the southeastern highlands (after Flood et al. 1987: 22, Table 4).

Site	Elevation (metres above sea level)	Earliest date occupation	Lab. no.
Birrigai	730	$21,000 \pm 220$ BP	Beta 16886
Cloggs Cave	76	$17,720 \pm 840$ BP	ANU 1044
Sassafras 1	730	$3,770 \pm 150$ BP	ANU 743
Nursery Sw 2	1140	$3,700 \pm 110$ BP	ANU 3033
Sassafras 2	730	$2,780 \pm 115$ BP	ANU 744
Caddigat	1000	$1,600 \pm 60$ BP	ANU 1049
Bogong	1433	$1,000 \pm 60$ BP	ANU 1050
Yankee Hat 2	1097	770 ± 140 BP	ANU 1051
Nardoo	762	760 ± 110 BP	ANU 1060
Hanging Rock	823	370 ± 60 BP	ANU 1047

Two), is reoccupied only during the Holocene, about a thousand years ago. During this recent phase at Cloggs Cave, occupation took place at the mouth of the cavern, where a rock-shelter is formed, rather than deeper in the main chamber of the cave system, where the Pleistocene occupation had been detected (Flood 1980: 254–275). Apart from the latter site, the preservation of organic remains at these Holocene sites is generally poor, and, therefore, questions concerning economy, land use and the like, must await new evidence and new research strategies. The stone artefact assemblages, including microliths, from this group of sites bear strong similarities to the Australian Small Tool tradition and changes are detected in raw materials, the amount of re-touch on tools, and in formal artefact types (Flood 1980: 248–253).

The general pattern of more intensive use of sites in the region during the last 3,000 years has been interpreted by the excavators to 'suggest that the type of occupation recorded for alpine and sub-alpine regions during ethnohistoric times may be no older than about 3,000 years' (Flood et al. 1987: 23). This ethnographic pattern (see Chapter Two) emphasised seasonal migrations to the highlands, and use of the Bogong moth at ceremonial and other gatherings. The excavators further suggest:

> This may indicate a starting date of around 3,000 BP for the seasonal, ceremonial-based Bogong moth exploitation events, although Bogong moth migration to the southern highlands probably began some time at the beginning of the Holocene. There is, however, no direct evidence as to when moth exploitation commenced, the earliest evidence so far coming from the moth aestivation site, Bogong Shelter, dated to 1,000 BP. (Flood et al. 1987: 23)

Stone 'pestles', perhaps used in the processing of moths, were found at this site (Flood 1980: 208–214).

The southeastern Australian highlands

Together with the southeastern highlands and the high country of Tasmania, the spine of mountains known as the Great Dividing Range continues for the length of Australia's eastern seaboard. Archaeological research has been undertaken especially in a number of areas within this upland belt, in particular in the Blue Mountains of New South Wales and the New England Tablelands (New South Wales). Syntheses and comparative evaluations of this material have been produced by Bowdler (1981; see also Lourandos 1985a; David 1987: 218–277; Flood et al. 1987). The more important information and interpretations of the material from these sub-regions will now be considered in some detail.

The Blue Mountains, New South Wales

This rugged area skirts the western margins of the Sydney basin. Archaeological investigations which span a period of over thirty years have produced sequences from a series of well-dated rock-shelters (Tindale 1961; McCarthy 1964; Stockton 1970; Stockton and Holland 1974; Johnson 1979; Kohen et al. 1984). Occupation during the Pleistocene appears to have been slight, and is represented only at King's Table (see Chapter Two) from around 22,000 BP (Stockton 1973). Four of the other shelters were first occupied during the terminal Pleistocene, that is around the time climates became more favourable for habitation. These sites are Shaws Creek KII (Kohen et al. 1984), Noola (Tindale 1961; Bermingham 1966), Lyrebird Dell and Walls Cave (both Stockton and Holland 1974), and they date to between c. 13,000 and 12,000 BP. The remaining sites, Capertee, Horseshoe Falls and Springwood Creek are first occupied during the early Holocene. A number of authors, however, have pointed out that occupation at all these sites was relatively sparse until after about 4,000 BP, when their use is considerably intensified (Johnson 1977; Bowdler 1981; Kohen et al. 1984). This interpretation has been based, to a large extent, upon the rate of deposition of stone artefacts. The more recent levels in these sites are in all cases associated with artefacts of the Australian Small Tool tradition. A further four undated rock-shelters at Capertee also conform to this chronological sequence (McCarthy 1964). This general regional sequence also has been supported by later excavations, such as Shaws Creek KII (Kohen et al. 1984) and the re-excavation of some Capertee Valley sites (Johnson 1977). The post-4,000 BP levels at Shaws Creek KII, for example, are represented by increased rates of deposition of lithic material, distinct hearths and faunal remains, which suggest hunting of the larger macropodids, birds and collection of freshwater mussel (Kohen et al. 1984). Some excavators have argued for the existence of an occupational hiatus which pre-dates the recent, more intensive levels of the last 4,000 years or so (Kohen et al. 1984: 57, 71), while Johnson (1977) has rejected this hypothesis.

Cycads, *Macrozamia*, also appear to have been used in some quantity at Capertee 3 in recent times (McCarthy 1964: 199). This also seems to have been the case at Noola (Tindale 1961:194; Bowdler 1981). Eugene Stockton's interpretations of settlement patterns for the region suggest that year-round occupation was restricted to areas of lower elevation (200-440 metres), where most of the habitation sites are located (1970: 300). Higher up in more rugged terrain (400–900 metres) sparser, perhaps seasonal, occupation is indicated and also a greater emphasis upon ceremonial activity. Stockton noted that 80 percent of art sites occur in this elevated region, and Johnson (1977: 24–38) is in agreement.

New England Tablelands, northeastern New South Wales
Isabel McBryde's research established the prehistoric model for the region (1974, 1977). The four Graman rock-shelter sites are located on the western slopes of the ranges (off the Tablelands) at elevations of less than one thousand metres above sea level. The oldest of these sites was inhabited from about 9,000 BP and there are 'backed blades' from around 5,450 ± 100 BP (McBryde 1977: 229). The mid-late Holocene deposits of the sites indicated an emphasis upon grass seeds, deduced from plant remains and seed grinders, similar to subsistence patterns of more semi-arid regions of western New South Wales. In contrast, the more elevated sites from Bendemeer were first inhabited from about 4,350 and 3,000 BP and lack evidence of seed use, a feature common to sites, including open sites, of the Tablelands (McBryde 1977). Grasses (*Panicum* and *Themeda* species), although not as abundant as those of the western slopes, grow on the Tablelands. McBryde speculated that the Bendemeer sites, with evidence of rock art, may indicate specialised, limited occupation connected with male ritual and divorced from more everyday subsistence practices, such as seed grinding, commonly associated with women (1977).

This observation was developed further by Bowdler, who argued that all Tableland sites at elevations above 1,000 metres may have served largely what she terms a ceremonial role. Sites of this region displayed patterns similar to those at Bendemeer and also there is evidence throughout the area of ceremonial sites (bora grounds and stone arrangements). 'A slight reinterpretation of the relationship between the Aneiwan people and the tablelands country might be that they had a totemic ''owner'' relationship with the higher country, but that their economic range was more generally restricted to the intermediate zone between 600 and 1000m' (Bowdler 1981: 107). Bowdler, therefore, drew connections between the late Holocene settlement and subsistence patterns of highland regions of New England and those of the Blue Mountains and southern highlands further south. Later archaeological investigation in the region by Godwin (1983) pointed to the greater ecological diversity of the Tablelands and to habitation sites above elevations of 1,000 metres. In all, Godwin's work indicated more complex patterns of land use and social interaction for recent and late Holocene times.

Southwestern Australia

Comparable information and debate concerning Holocene socio-cultural and environmental changes, apart from a few instances, is not yet generally available from this corner of the continent, with its unique environmental features and climatic history. Ferguson (1985) argued for a depopulation of forested parts of the southwest as climate became more humid and forests expanded in the early mid-Holocene (see also above, this chapter). He viewed the process as operating somewhat differentially; between 10,000 and 4,000 years ago at Kalgan Hall in the south, and between 6,000 and 2,000 years in the north, at Walyunga. More detailed environmental data, which are generally lacking for the southwest, are still needed to substantiate these models. Hallam (1975, 1987) carried out detailed archaeological surveys of the distribution of sites and stone artefacts in relation to land forms and natural resources along the coastal plain of the Swan River, near Perth. Hallam showed that Aboriginal settlement had concentrated upon the rich wetlands of the sandy coastal plain and on the riverine environment with its more fertile soils. In contrast, the habitats associated with the sea were less utilised; and the extensive jarrah forests appeared to have been only relatively sparsely inhabited. Hallam concluded that Aboriginal populations may have risen within this coastal plain during the mid-late Holocene period. But as to details concerning seasonal settlement and subsistence strategies, Hallam (1987) and Ferguson (1985) are not in total agreement.

Investigations of southwestern shell middens, by Dortch, Kendrick and Morse support Hallam's conclusions to some extent. Shell middens throughout this broad region are few and far between; they are not comparable to the dense concentrations common in other parts of the continent, like we find in Tasmania and the southeastern corner of the Australian mainland. While erosion brought about by unstable coastal land forms may be a factor accounting for this, Charles Dortch and his fellow researchers feel that it does not fully explain the pattern. Aboriginal socio-cultural practices and emphases have also to be considered. For example, the rich resource complex of the coastal plain may have been the primary focus of Aboriginal settlement and economy, with shellfish and the coastal strip itself playing a more minor role (Dortch et al. 1984).

Overview: Holocene settlement

The warm, humid post-Pleistocene climate of southern Australia was associated with rises in sea level and the drowning of the low-lying Bass Strait region, which severed the connection between Tasmania and the present-day Victorian mainland, before stabilising about 6,000–5,000 years ago. In the most humid period – the early Holocene – there was an expansion of freshwater wetlands and forest, including closed communities like rainforest, which replaced the drier, more open landscapes of the terminal Pleistocene. Drier, more stressful climate, however, followed in the late Holocene with a contraction of both wetlands and forests. The driest phase, around 3,000 years ago, was succeeded by fluctuating, slightly more humid conditions during the last 2,500 years or so.

The archaeological evidence comes from a variety of study areas and environments and, although interpretations of this material are diverse, I would argue that broad chronological trends – or general patterns – are evident in terms of Aboriginal society and demography. A summary of the main case studies follows.

The appearance of cemeteries in the Murray River corridor since the terminal Pleistocene has been viewed as a sign of increasing territoriality. In some ways this may be a reflection of amelioration in climate and of changing demographic patterns; even of some increases in Aboriginal populations. Throughout southeastern Australia a steady, general increase in the establishment and use of sites also takes place, beginning in the terminal Pleistocene and continuing throughout the Holocene. Apart from these instances, however, there appears to be not so *marked* an expansion of Aboriginal settlement during the early Holocene associated with levels of increasing bioproduction as climatic patterns would indicate; nor during the time of sea-level stabilisation in coastal areas. Instead, more complex settlement patterns still occur in the late Holocene, when climate was more stressful. This is especially so during the last 3,500 years, along with other indications of social and demographic changes.

These archaeological patterns are evident in all main southeastern Australian study areas, to varying degrees and depending on the range of information available. Included are the humid coastal plains of southwestern Victoria and southeastern South Australia, the semi-arid northwestern Victorian mallee, the southeastern Australian highlands and parts of the eastern highlands. These examples are reinforced by osteological and burial evidence and studies on exchange in wider southern and central Victoria and along the Murray River corridor.

There are changes in settlement patterns, and in land and resource use, in environments including wetlands, highlands, forests (including rainforest), coasts, estuaries, the inland Murray River region and the semi-arid Victorian mallee. Also, changes occur in technology and painted rock art, and include an increase in the number and use of sites, the appearance of new site forms (for example, earth mounds in western and central Victoria and the Murray River region), and more 'complex' sites (for example, shell middens of the Coorong estuary and Cape Otway). A case can be made for more 'logistically' organised settlement and increased 'sedentism' (or reduced mobility) from the increased use of sites and appearance of earth mounds, and from shell middens of the Coorong estuary and Cape Otway. 'Logistically' organised resource strategies include fish traps and artificial drainage systems used in fishing, both of which are linked to recent lake levels (of the last 2,000 years or so). The recent accentuation in the use of wetlands and their resources, as evidenced by earth mounds, would logically have included the latter (and is supported by ethnographic evidence; see Chapter Two). 'Complex' and extensive exchange patterns, indicating varying aspects of more 'open' and 'closed' social relations, also can be linked to recent contexts. Whether or not the latter occurred earlier in time must await further investigation.

Further support is provided by studies of osteology and burials. Osteological studies of the central Murray River suggest recent high levels of health-related stress, which have been interpreted as indicating high population densities, sedentism and general overcrowding. Seasonal food shortages were also indicated for southwestern Victoria. As well, morphological studies of Murray River valley populations indicate 'intermarriage' within the river corridor, suggesting marked patterns of regional territoriality and more 'closed' social formations. This picture is further enhanced by evidence of burial grounds and burial practices in the region which are more numerous, extensive and complex during the last 3,000 years or so. While the chronology of many of these categories of evidence remains relative and generalised, most of the evidence appears to be roughly dated to the late Holocene period.

Opinions vary on the explanations of the southeastern Australian mid-late Holocene cultural changes. Explanations of individual study areas have focused upon demographic changes (for example, population increase) and their relationship to socio-cultural change, including land and resource use strategies, settlement patterns and social relations. Others still have seen the changes as largely reactions to climatic and environmental alterations. General archaeological temporal trends, however, do not fit any general climatic or environmental chronological trend. For example, there is no evidence of a *marked* expansion of Aboriginal populations in the early Holocene along with increased precipitation, expansion of wetlands and high levels of bioproduction. Instead, evidence of more significant demographic changes, including possible population growth and changing patterns of population dispersal (for example, aggregation and 'sedentism-nomadism') occur in the more stressful, less humid late Holocene. No evidence exists for intensive use of the extensive wetlands of the early Holocene, whereas this is increasingly evident after about 2,500 BP with the introduction and spread of earth mounds linked to permanent and ephemeral wetlands.

While forests expanded in the early Holocene, signs of their use at this time are minimal. A drier climate about 3,000 years ago produced a contraction of forests, in some ways facilitating Aboriginal expansion into these areas, assisted by their firing practices. During the last 2,500 years, however, while more humid climate enabled forest to expand once more, Aboriginal habitation of these areas *continued* to expand increasingly throughout the latter period *against* the climatic trend. Changing coastal environments, and their resource structure, also do not appear to *determine* Aboriginal cultural responses. For example, changing Aboriginal use of the coast in the Coorong estuary indicates *more* intensive exploitation during a period of climatic *reversal*. In Cape Otway, however, where similar cultural changes occur, there is no evidence of contemporary changes in marine conditions and availability of resources.

I would interpret the archaeological patterns in the following way. During the terminal Pleistocene, evidence exists for increasing territoriality in the Murray River corridor, as signalled by the appearance of cemeteries, a pattern which may have been influenced, to some degree, by climatic amelioration. Although increased humidity and levels of bioproduction were highest in the early Holocene (with sea levels stabilising 6,000–5,000 years ago), apart from steady, general increases in the establishment and use of sites, further signs of significant socio-demographic changes are not apparent until the late Holocene. From about 3,500 BP, however, there are marked indications of social and demographic changes. Trends are apparent in a wide range of natural environments, indicating increased use of sites and locales. Changes to settlement patterns (for example, increasing 'sedentism' or more constant use of sites) suggest changing land and resource use. These patterns generally suggest increases in Aboriginal population and changes to population density and dispersal.

Environments where these processes are visible include wetlands, forests (including rainforest), highlands, parts of the coast and estuaries, the semi-arid Victorian mallee, the southeastern highlands and parts of the eastern highlands. New site forms – earth mounds – appear in wetlands in western Victoria and the Murray River area, and suggest expansion into these rich aquatic habitats. Wetlands were extensive during the autumn-winter seasons, and their occupation at this 'stressful' time of year may have led to increases in local population. Without mounds (which provided dry base camps), winter settlement of these extensively water-logged wetlands would have been restricted to a great degree. These patterns are reinforced by the ethnographic picture of the region which indicated permanent year-round use of wetlands, together with marked territoriality (which is covered in Chapter Two). Technological changes, such as use of mounds and fish traps, are suggestive of increasing use of what may be termed fixed (or 'logistical') facilities.

Introduction of economic use of grass seeds on the humid western slopes of the Great Dividing Range of New South Wales (outside the semi-arid zone), and possible intensive use of plants (fern root) at Cape Otway, during the late Pleistocene, are indications of more intensive plant processing techniques. New fishing technology is introduced during this phase on the southeastern and eastern Australian coast. During the late Holocene also, osteological studies and those of burial practices from the Murray River area reveal signs of health-related stress, perhaps caused by increased population densities and sedentism, and these appear to a lesser extent in western Victoria. Cemeteries were more common, extensive and complex during this period as were burial practices. Extensive patterns of exchange are documented across central and southern Victoria, indicating complex intergroup social relations, and painted rock art appears in highlands areas of New South Wales, southeastern and eastern Victoria, both roughly dated to this period by their association with stratified deposits and ochres.

In all, a general pattern emerges in southeastern Australia of a socio-demographic trend beginning in the terminal Pleistocene and generally associated with, but *not necessarily determined by*, ameliorating climate and increased bio-production. Steady, general increases in site establishment and use throughout the period suggest socio-demographic shifts. During the last 3,500 years in particular, still more complex socio-demographic patterns are evident, suggesting further changes to population size, density and dispersal – that is to say more people, more 'sedentary' practices, 'logistically' organised settlement and behavioural patterns, and more complex intergroup relations, as regards more 'open' and 'closed' aspects of social formations. These more dynamic, complex socio-demographic patterns fit no one environmental trend; indeed, they appear to be the *reverse* of the general regional climatic trend: compare Figures 6.1 and 6.17. Environmental changes similar to those of the late Holocene, for instance, had largely occurred before, but without corresponding cultural alterations. For example, the early Holocene was more humid than the late Holocene when mounds first appear, and the late Pleistocene drier. We can see, therefore, that archaeological trends more closely follow upon environmental trends in the terminal Pleistocene and early Holocene, and then diverge from these significantly in the late Holocene. Aboriginal social groups, therefore, appear to have become attuned to both natural and socio-cultural circumstances in varying ways.

CHAPTER 7

TASMANIA

Who were the Tasmanian Aborigines? Where did they come from? And what effects had long-term isolation on a large, remote island upon these people? These questions have guided investigations in Tasmania for well over a century. The mountainous island of Tasmania is a rocky extension of Australia's Great Dividing Range, and until about 12,000–10,000 years ago it was connected to the Australian mainland by a landbridge across the present-day Bass Strait (Chappell and Thom 1977; Chappell 1983). The actual time of separation of the land masses is debated, with some preferring a more recent date of about 8,000 BP (Blom 1988). As Tasmania has been geographically divorced from mainland Australia throughout the Holocene period, without cultural contact, it is discussed here separately.

PLEISTOCENE SETTLEMENT

Palaeoenvironment

A landbridge linked Tasmania with the Australian mainland at two times at least during the historical occupation of this continent, between about 37,000 and 29,000 years, and about 25,000 and 12,000–8,000 years ago (Figure 7.1). Prior to about 30,000 years BP, the climate was cool and moist, especially in the west, and much of the region was forested. But these sclerophyll and, in some cases, rainforest communities were increasingly replaced by open grassland-steppe with the onset of drier, colder conditions which culminated in the glacial maximum about 18,000 years ago (Fig. 7.2). Pollen sequences have been obtained from the northwest on Hunter Island (Hope 1978) and Pulbeena Swamp (Colhoun et al.

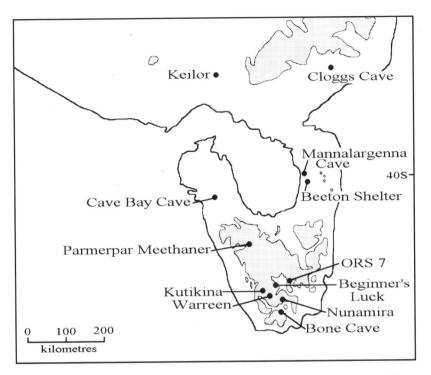

Figure 7.1 Pleistocene Tasmania, indicating the coastline about 14,000 years ago and the initial occupation of archaeological sites in Tasmania and the Australian mainland, which at that time were connected (based on Jones 1977b: 335, Figure 9).

1982), and in the west at Tullarbardine Dam (Colhoun and van de Geer 1986) and Darwin Crater (Colhoun 1988).

At this time there were glaciers in central Tasmania, on the central plateau, and in river systems such as the Upper Mersey. Low lake levels and dune building in northern Tasmania were further signs of aridity (Bowler 1982). As sea levels rose towards the end of the Pleistocene (Chappell and Thom 1977; Chappell 1983), the landbridge with mainland Australia was severed at the start of the Holocene, and forests, including rainforest, began to recolonise the island.

A group of cave sites in western Tasmania were thought to have been first inhabited between about 23,000 and 20,000 BP. Very recent finds, however, of further sites in the region indicate that the area was initially occupied by about 35,000 BP (see below).

Cave Bay Cave, which is presently located on Hunter Island off the northwestern tip of Tasmania, was the first Pleistocene site found. Its discovery ended, once and for all, speculation concerning the origins of the Tasmanian people of the ethnohistorical period (Bowdler 1974, 1984). The site is a large, dry sea cave in siltstone, and was most intensively inhabited between 22,750 ± 420 BP and 20,850 ± 290 BP (Figure 7.3). Hearths, stone artefacts and debitage,

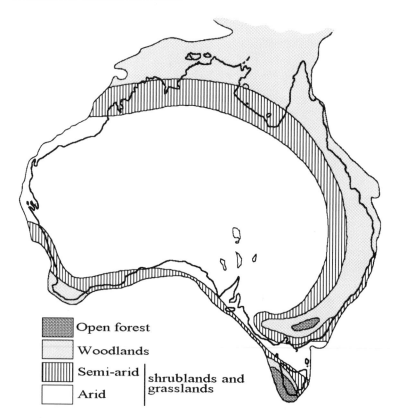

Figure 7.2 Vegetation of Greater Australia and Tasmania at the time of the glacial maximum, 18,000 years ago (based on Smith 1989: 93, Figure 2).

together with a suite of medium-to-small-sized animal and bird bones were found. The largest herbivore present was the Bennett's wallaby, *Macropus rufrogriseus*. At this stage the site served as an inland hunting bivouac. After this, the cave was used less frequently until around 18,550 ± 600 BP. Bone tools found at this stage are reminiscent of those from other Australian Pleistocene sites. Apart from one further hearth at 15,400 ± 330 BP, the cave was effectively abandoned during the time of the glacial maximum for a period of some 12,000 years. It was only reoccupied during the Holocene period. Bowdler's detailed taphonomic study of the site distinguished between the human and non-human faunal components in the bone-rich sediments, which span the full period of 23,000 years.

Beginners Luck is a limestone cave high in the Florentine Valley of southwestern Tasmania. Today the area is covered in dense rainforests, but at the time of its occupation, some time around 20,650 ± 1,790 BP, the cave was situated about three kilometres north of the outwash gravels which were the product of glacial activity in southern Tasmania. The cold, dry climate of that era, together with limestone soils, supported a grassland and herbfield vegetation

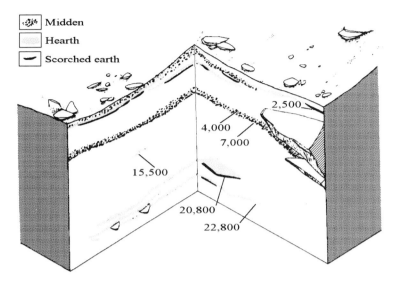

Figure 7.3 Cave Bay Cave, stratigraphic section (based on Bowdler 1977: 216, Figure 2).

with alpine shrubland. Palaeontological information from other cave sites in the Florentine Valley indicates the existence of a varied marsupial fauna (Goede and Murray 1979; Murray et al. 1980: 150).

The cultural deposits of Beginners Luck are in a limestone breccia which has been redeposited within the cave system. Some 20 stone artefacts, charcoal and faunal remains, again mainly of Bennett's wallaby, *M. rufrogriseus*, were found, together with a cuboid of the extinct megafaunal species, *Macropus titan* (Murray et al. 1980).

Southwestern Tasmania

In contrast to the above, rather sparse, information, we have plentiful Pleistocene archaeological evidence from a group of mainly limestone caves and rock shelters in southwestern Tasmania and nearby areas. Today, this is a largely uninhabited region of dense Holocene rainforests, but during the Pleistocene, after about 30,000 years ago, this area was composed largely of open stretches of periglacial vegetation, and was at this time dotted with glaciers. Together these sites comprise the possibly richest archaeological evidence from Pleistocene Greater Australia.

The dated archaeological sequences cover most of the prehistory of Pleistocene Greater Australia, from about 35,000 years until about 11,000 years ago, when warmer, wetter post-glacial climates produced the dense rainforests of today. This relatively extensive body of information is the work of a large number of researchers, the most recent including Rhys Jones, Jim Allen and Richard Cosgrove (see, for example, Kiernan et al. 1983; Jones 1984; Jones et al. 1988; Allen 1989b; Cosgrove 1989, 1991; Cosgrove et al. 1990; Anderson 1991;

Table 7:1 Time-spans of selected Pleistocene archaeological sites from southwestern and eastern Tasmania. (Some sites are located on Figure 7.4.)

Site	Oldest occupation Years BP	Last occupation Years BP	Reference
Southwest			
Warreen	34,790 ± 510 (Beta-42122 and ETH-7665)	c.16,000 (Beta-42993)	Allen et al. 1989
Nunamira	30,420 ± 690 (Beta-25881)	11,630 ± 200 (Beta-25877)	Cosgrove 1989
Acheron	c.30,000	13,000	Cosgrove et al. 1990
Bone	29,000 ± 520 (Beta-29987)	13,700 ± 860 (Beta-26509)	Allen 1989
Mackintosh 90/1	17,030 ± 430 (Beta-45808)	15,160 ± 210 (Beta-46305)	Stern and Marshall 1993
Kutikina	19,970 ± 850 (ANU-2785)	14,480 ± 930 (ANU-2781)	Kiernan et al. 1983
East			
ORS 7	30,840 ± 480 (Beta-23404 and ETH-3724)	2,450 ± 70 (Beta-27078)	Cosgrove 1991 McNiven et al. 1993

Brown et al. 1991; Stern and Marshall 1993). Seven of the sites have been reported in some detail, and are located in the following river valleys: Warreen in the Maxwell (M86/2 Maxwell River, 35,000–16,000 BP), Nunamira Cave in the Florentine (30,420–11,630 BP), Acheron Shelter in the Acheron (30,000–13,000 BP), Bone Cave in the Weld (29,000–13,700 BP), Mackintosh 90/1 at Lake Mackintosh (17,000–15,000 BP), and Kutikina in the Franklin (19,770–14,840 BP). The seventh site, ORS 7 (30,840–2,500 BP), is located just outside the southwestern geological province, on the edge of the central plateau, in eastern Tasmania. (References for these sites are given in Table 7.1; see also some locations on Figure 7.4.)

These sites have excellent preservation of abundant faunal and artefactual material, and the preliminary analyses indicate rather specialised hunting and bone processing practices. Emphasis appears to have been placed upon one species of macropod in particular, the Bennett's wallaby, *Macropus rufrogriseus*. Around 90 per cent of identifiable bone from many of these sites is of this one species of animal, although a wider range of animals is present at other sites, such as Warreen. As a great percentage of the bone from these sites is also the product of human predation, the implication here is that Bennett's wallaby was targeted as a prey animal. To what extent, however, local ecological factors limited the choice of prey is as yet unclear.

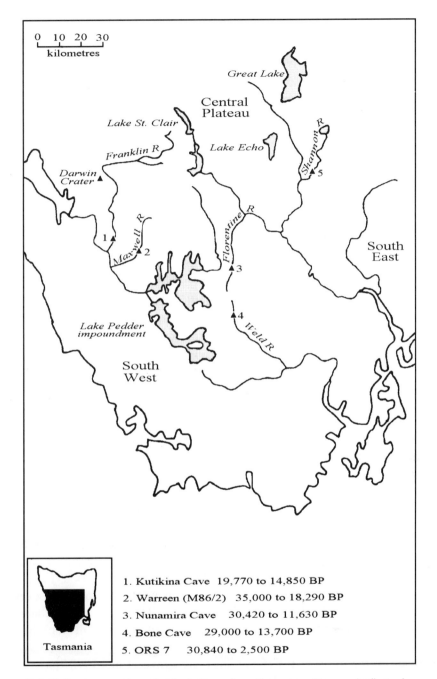

Figure 7.4 Pleistocene archaeological sites of southwestern Tasmania (based on Cosgrove et al. 1990: 65, Figure 3).

Although examination of these sites is still in the preliminary stages, some general trends are apparent. While many of the sites were first occupied from about 35,000–30,000 years ago, when the earliest landbridge with the Australian mainland existed, all the southwestern sites had been abandoned by about 11,000 years BP. And even though abandonment took place at different times at individual sites (see Table 7.1), the overwhelming impression here is that all sites were eventually engulfed by the spread of postglacial rainforests which effectively cut off these valley systems, and sites, from Aboriginal settlement. The sites appear never to have been used again by people.

Kutikina, together with other southwestern Tasmanian Pleistocene sites (below), appears to be one of the most consistently reoccupied sites from Pleistocene Greater Australia. Repeated, consistent use of the site by humans is indicated until about 15,000 years ago when it appears to have been abandoned (Kiernan et al. 1983). Even so, rather specialised, short-term and perhaps seasonal occupation is suggested with a marked emphasis upon the hunting of Bennett's wallaby. There is no evidence here, however, of a long-term base camp reflecting a broad-based set of resources and activities.

Most intensive use of these Pleistocene sites appears to have taken place in their more recent levels. During the glacial maximum, a time of severe climate in this elevated sub-antarctic zone, some of the sites – for example Nunamira and Kutikina – were used more intensively. There is, however, also evidence at Kutikina of possible abandonment at this time: for example, three sterile lenses are apparent in the stratigraphic section drawing of the site (Kiernan et al. 1983). Other sites, like Bone Cave and Warreen, however, were not more intensively used at this time; and Mackintosh 90/1 was only first occupied after the glacial maximum (McNiven et al. 1993). The suggestion, therefore, offered by this evidence is of changing Aboriginal patterns of land use, and of changing responses to alterations in climate.

While there is no reported evidence of alterations in hunting patterns through time, there is of the use and manufacture of stone artefacts. For example, following the glacial maximum, after about 17,000 years, there is an increase in use of quartz, in flaking technique (bipolar flaking) and in the increase or appearance of 'thumbnail' scrapers at both Bone Cave and Kutikina (Figure 7.5). At this time also, an increased use of exotic Darwin Glass is found in several of the sites (Jones 1990a, 1990b; McNiven et al. 1993). Once again, changes in Aboriginal patterns of land use, and possibly in patterns of mobility, are suggested.

Largely on the basis of the above sites, Cosgrove et al. (1990) have argued that the periglacial uplands of southwestern Tasmania had a distinct and long-lasting pattern of Pleistocene occupation (greater than 20,000 years), one that can be differentiated from other parts of Pleistocene Tasmania (for example the southeast) and Australia. Their model is of relatively concentrated human activity (perhaps year-round) in the region, centred upon the hunting of wallaby. Basing

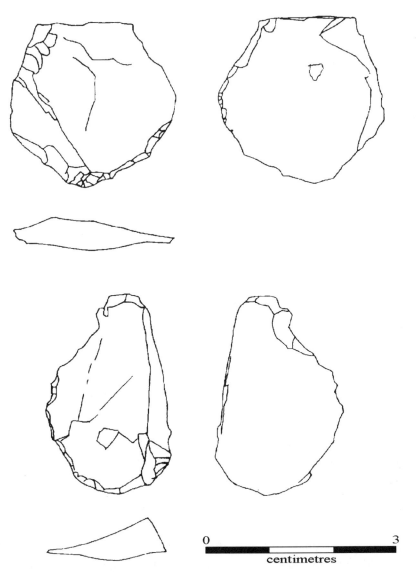

0   3
centimetres

Figure 7.5 Pleistocene chert thumbnail scrapers from Bone Cave dated to 16,000–14,500 BP (based on McNiven 1994: 79, Figure 2).

their settlement model on a reconstruction of the region's largely open grassland Pleistocene ecology, they characterise this pattern as one where 'humans move between discrete grassland patches to hunt ''ecologically tethered'' animal resources' (Cosgrove et al. 1990: 74). Bennett's wallaby, they argue, is a territorial animal and would have been distributed geographically in this fashion. Cosgrove's team considered that specialised bone marrow processing was developed to offset disadvantages imposed by an extreme 'lean meat' diet, brought about by a heavy reliance upon wallaby.

In contrast, the same researchers modelled the settlement and subsistence patterns for eastern Tasmania, where climate was even drier and vegetation more open, as more mobile, that is less sedentary, and populations as being generally more dispersed (Cosgrove et al. 1990). The archaeological evidence from the eastern site of ORS 7 seemed to be in support; sparser overall use of the site through time is indicated. As well, ORS 7 was not abandoned at the end of the last glaciation, but continued to be used well into the Holocene, perhaps because dense rainforest did not colonise this part of Tasmania.

By focusing upon this degree of cultural variation within one rather small region of Australia – Tasmania – Cosgrove et al. (1990) also argued against more generalised models that have viewed Australian Pleistocene subsistence patterns as rather specialised and settlement as largely transient (for example, Lourandos 1983a, 1985a, 1987a). In reply, I would argue that while they (and others) indeed appear to have isolated distinct regional Pleistocene patterns in southwestern Tasmania, the features of the more general model (above) also can be accommodated by their data. Is there really evidence for high Aboriginal population densities and sedentary settlement as they suggest (Cosgrove et al. 1990: 59–60)? In effect, they present a rather static model that does not take into consideration the climatic and archaeological changes which are clearly evident in their very long sequences (but see also McNiven et al. 1993; Lourandos 1993). I suggest, therefore, an alternative general model for this part of Tasmania, a model of relatively mobile populations hunting, perhaps seasonally, throughout the southwestern valley systems as well as their coastal outlets. That is, a more geographically extensive pattern, of which the upper reaches of the southwestern valley systems (and the sites described above) formed only one part. In eastern Tasmania, settlement may have been even more transient, as the evidence suggests (see above). This flexible subsistence-settlement and demographic pattern might be envisaged as having been attuned, in some ways, to climatic variations through time (see below).

In light of this more extensive and flexible pattern, the substantial cave deposits can be explained in terms of their long duration – the sequence covers some 24,000 years or more, and most cave sequences are long (see Table 7.1). Added factors to explain intensities of occupation include the prime value of the sites as places of shelter in a severe sub-antarctic upland climate, and their position as hunting stations close to the valley floors. Diets may have been mixed – a composite of terrestrial and coastal (including marine) foods – rather than the extreme lean meat diet, which Cosgrove et al. (1990: 72) themselves view, to some extent, as marginal. In other words, emphasis upon wallaby may be a feature only of inland southwestern sites, and of one aspect of a broader subsistence and settlement pattern which also incorporated coasts and estuaries as well as the upper reaches of the complex valley systems of the region. Sizes of Aboriginal territories in this sub-antarctic region can be hypothesised to have been large when compared with those of the recent ethnohistorical 'big river' people of the Derwent River basin of southeastern Tasmania, who also inhabited both upland and estuarine sectors of the valley system. This territorial group also occupied the elevated, cold central plateau area of Tasmania and had an estimated territory of approximately 7,500 square kilometres (Jones 1974: 341). Of course, territorial size is the product of both social and ecological factors, and might also be expected to change through time. As well, the recent Holocene territory of the 'big river' people is climatically quite different to that of the Pleistocene southwest but, given the sub-antarctic climate of that time, it can be argued that Pleistocene territories would have been even more extensive. Territories of this size, therefore, would have incorporated much more than the elevated inland region of the southwest where the present excavated sites are located, and arguably would have included parts of the nearby coastal strip.

In all, the archaeological evidence suggests that significant changes have taken place in climatic, as well as settlement and subsistence, patterns through time and that more dynamic models are needed to explain these processes. The implication here is of changes also in population sizes and density and in the degree of nomadism and sedentism. The evidence for this is the differential intensities in site use in both time and space (above). Given the existing archaeological information presented above, I would offer the following general scenario for Pleistocene Tasmania. Aboriginal settlement of this sub antarctic area goes back as far as 35,000 years, not very long after the earliest evidence of occupation of the continent, when the region was forested and a landbridge with the mainland existed. Settlement appears to have been relatively sparse until the time of the glacial maximum, and perhaps more intermittent with generally lower population densities. From around 20,000 years, however, settlement appears to have become increasingly more intensive and dynamic, as during the glacial maximum various patterns are represented, with some sites being more intensively used, and disuse at times is also suggested. During this harshest of periods, however, the area took on the appearance of a geographical refuge zone within which populations concentrated, but also one in which considerable rearrangement in settlement patterns occurred.

The relative ecological richness of this region stands in contrast to the drier, periglacial and semi-arid landscapes of eastern Tasmania and parts of the southeastern Australian mainland of this time. Following about 17,000 years ago, however, occupation seems to have intensified considerably, with significant changes in settlement, technology and use of raw materials. Changes also may have taken place in patterns of mobility and sedentism, with an overall implication of alterations in land use. All the sites were abandoned at various times in the terminal Pleistocene perhaps, as already noted, as closed forests, including rainforest, engulfed the area. The sequence of events, therefore, varies considerably through time, as does climate. The region, far from being an open herbfield, as has been stressed in prior models (Cosgrove et al. 1990), was forested in the first stage of settlement and experiencing trends towards climatic amelioration in the terminal Pleistocene, when the sites and region were most intensively inhabited. As an example of this, appearance of ringtail possum (*Pseudocheirus peregrinus*) in both Bone Cave and Nunamira in their most recent levels suggests increasing forestation of the region following the glacial maximum.

A certain amount of support for the arguments I have advanced here concerning the southwest is provided by McNiven (1994). McNiven presents a model of changing settlement (mobility) patterns, together with reorganisation of stone artefact technology, throughout southwestern Tasmania following the glacial maximum (post 18,000 BP). He argues that increased use of thumbnail scrapers at this time is associated with increases in mobility, 'which placed extra demands for highly portable, long-term maintainable components of the tool-kit' (1994: 80).

An extra demand was also created for use of high quality raw materials such as chert and quartz (also Darwin glass) (McNiven 1994: 80). McNiven compared information obtained from sites inhabited after the glacial maximum (including Mackintosh 90/1, Condominium Cliffs 2 Rockshelter, and Maneena Langatick Tattana Emita Cave) with caves with longer sequences which were also inhabited at this time (Bone, Kutikina and Nunamira). Strong similarities were observed in the stone assemblages from all these sites (compare with Jones 1989, 1990).

Further general support to the above interpretations is provided by a recent analysis of the temporal spread of radiocarbon dates from a number of southwestern Tasmanian sites (Holdaway and Porch 1995). The results indicate a cyclical pattern of use of sites correlated with climatic changes (based on evidence from Pulbeena Swamp). The caves appear to have been used less frequently during the periods of relatively drier and colder climate which took place every three thousand or so years. In all, '. . . the intensity with which sites were used increased throughout the late Pleistocene', peaking about 15,000 years ago (1995: 81).

Overview: Pleistocene settlement

Tasmania was a southern promontory of Greater Australia during parts of the Pleistocene and, after about 25,000 years ago, glaciated with extensive periglacial areas of open, herbfield vegetation, in place of the forests of today. Although the area was forested prior to about 30,000 years, after this time forests would have been largely confined to the southwest, and in areas later inundated by rising sea levels in the Holocene. Aboriginal settlement of Tasmania began at least 35,000 years ago and appears to have become increasingly most concentrated or intensive in the southwest where the series of excavated caves and shelters contain some of the richest evidence from Pleistocene 'Greater Australia.

Aboriginal settlement of this southwestern area appears to have undergone changes during the glacial maximum, when the region may have served as a refuge zone within which populations concentrated. Rearrangements in site use is evident at this time. Settlement of the area, however, appears to have been most intensive following this period (c. 15,000 BP). In some ways, this tendency may have been influenced by the amelioration in climate at this time and the expansion of forests in this southwestern region. Prior to the full spread of rainforests at the end of the Pleistocene, forests would have been more open and mixed, attracting a wide range of animal species. The concentration of Aboriginal populations in this area at this time, therefore, may be linked to an increase in bioproduction during this period, resulting in a corresponding rise in population densities.

In the southwest, emphasis was placed upon the specialised hunting of one species of wallaby and use of the sites appears to have been consistent, implying fairly regular use of the region, especially in the more recent period. Overall, however, changes occurred in the use of sites and in technology which suggest both long- and short-term alterations in land use and demographic patterns, including degrees of nomadism and sedentism in this region. In other parts of Tasmania, for example the east and northeast (see below), settlement appears to have been more transient.

All southwestern sites were abandoned during the terminal Pleistocene, and not reoccupied, as the spread of rainforests engulfed the valleys of the region. To what extent encroaching forests curtailed Aboriginal use of these humid, elevated regions has recently been questioned by Thomas (1993), who largely argues against these environmentally deterministic, and to some extent 'doomsday', scenarios. In general, the archaeological evidence from southwestern Tasmania presents a pattern somewhat different to that of other parts of Pleistocene Greater Australia. There is evidence of greater use of sites here than elsewhere during the Pleistocene, and even when factors such as climate and the very long period of use of the sites is considered, the suggestion is of relatively concentrated activity at certain times in the southwest. In all, the implication is of concentrations of population and settlement in the region, especially after about 17,000 years ago, and also of significant changes in settlement and land use through time. These socio-demographic patterns, I have suggested, may be linked also, in some ways, first to the influence of the glacial maximum and, following this episode, to climatic amelioration in the terminal Pleistocene.

THE HOLOCENE: ISOLATION AND TRANSFORMATION

Rising post-glacial seas isolated Tasmania from the Australian mainland some 12,000–10,000 years ago, or more recently. Today around 200 kilometres of ocean separate southeastern Australia from the island of Tasmania. Without

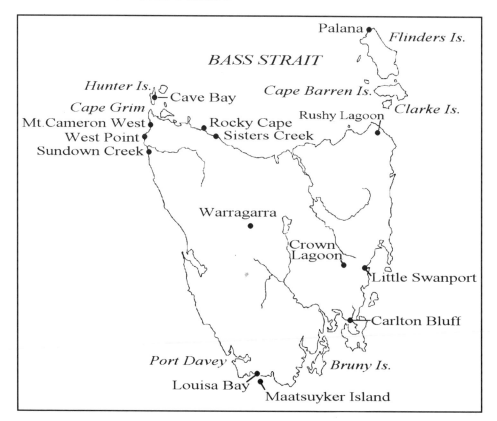

Figure 7.6 Holocene archaeological sites of Tasmania.

evidence of further contact between these two distant land masses until the historical period, Tasmania remains a case study of long-term human cultural development and isolation (Figure 7.6). Tasmania also offers us independent evidence with which to compare the Holocene prehistory of mainland Australia.

Palaeoenvironment

Pollen studies show that the glaciers had melted and that forests were expanding at the time of Tasmania's separation from southeastern Australia, sometime around 12,000–10,000 years ago. Forests recolonised the highlands, especially between about 11,500 and 9,500 years. Moist, warm conditions prevailed between about 8,000 and 4,000 years, during which period forests, including rainforests, were most widespread and dense. Following this phase, about 4,000–3,500 years ago, climate became drier and cooler with a contraction of close-canopied forests. Vegetation was most dense in western Tasmania where rainfall was highest. Eastern Tasmania, however, and especially the southeast, remained in a rain shadow and was, therefore, drier (Colhoun 1988; Macphail 1983, 1986; see also references in this chapter; Figure 7.7). By about 6,000–5,000 years ago

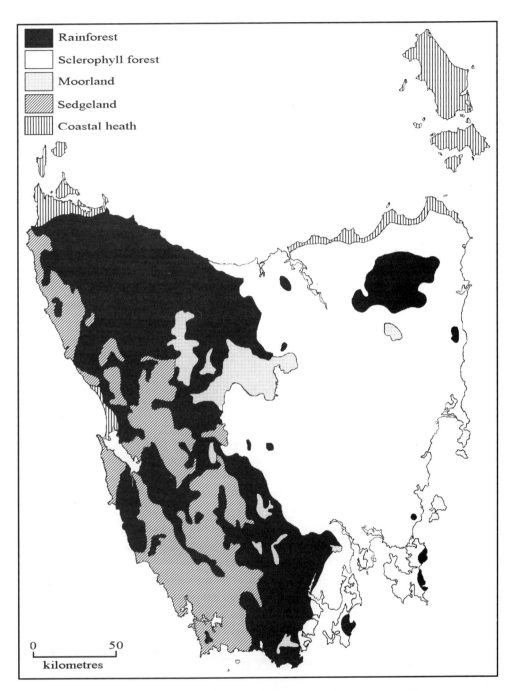

Figure 7.7 Holocene vegetation of Tasmania (based on Jackson 1965: 7).

Rainforest

Sclerophyll forest

Moorland

Sedgeland

Coastal heath

0   50
kilometres

sea levels had stabilised, forming the present coastline, and the estuaries and offshore islands of Tasmania (Chappell and Thom 1977; Chappell 1983; Blom 1988).

Northwestern Tasmania

The master archaeological sequence for this fertile coastal region comes from the Rocky Cape caves, two old stranded sea caves in quartzite (Jones 1968, 1971a,b, 1977a, 1977b, 1978). The scenic and spectacular cape extends into Bass Strait, and is today surrounded by heathland. The oldest basal dates come from the South Cave, 8120 ± 165 BP (Reber 1965; Jones 1971a: 195–198, 1977b: 343). As the uppermost levels of this cave have been destroyed since the time of European occupation, the upper half of the chronological sequence was obtained from the nearby North Cave. Both caves contain deeply stratified shell midden composed of a complex of ash and shell lenses. Shell midden rested upon sterile basal gravel, and so the date of about 8,000 BP indicates the earliest coastal foraging. Analysis of the faunal remains suggests that prior to around 3,500 BP emphasis had been placed (apart from shellfish) upon sea mammals (fur seals, *Arctocephalus* sp., and elephant seal, *Mirounga leonina*) and fish. From Jones' calculations (1977b: 342), 95 per cent of calorific intake from animal foods came from the sea and only 5 per cent from land animals (wallaby and small, wet-scrub dwellers). After about 3,500 BP however, fish is absent from the deposit, as are bone tools, which are found also in the lower levels (see below).

In the more recent levels, especially after about 2,500 BP, 'there was a somewhat greater contribution to the diet from wallabies and coastal birds especially cormorants. Stone tools were imported ready-made or as roughouts from quarries up to 100 kilometres away on the west coast, instead of being made entirely on the spot from immediately local stones as was the case previously'. (Jones 1977b: 345). An increase in efficiency of use of raw materials through time was also recorded by Jones (1971a). A broadly similar cultural sequence was obtained also from another cave, Sister's Creek, located some 11 kilometres east of Rocky Cape (Jones 1971a).

In general, Jones interpreted this sequence as indicating an early, although not exclusive, reliance upon marine foods and after about 3500 BP a greater emphasis upon terrestrial animals and birds. He associated this trend with territorial expansion by people, their use of fire allowing them into areas of previously closed forest, such as rainforest (Jones 1968; Colley and Jones 1987).

Some 80 kilometres west of Rocky Cape is the large open shell midden of West Point (Jones 1968) which is located on the exposed, high energy coastline of the west coast. The site is situated upon a sand dune and covers around half a square kilometre. Seven circular depressions (around 3–5 metres in diameter) were detected on the crest of the site. These structures seem to fit ethnographic descriptions of hut-pits, in which durable conical huts were constructed, as recorded by G. A. Robinson for the west coast (the diaries are referred to in Chapter Two). Similar structures are found on middens along the length of the west coast (Lourandos 1968; Jones 1971a; Ranson 1978). Two basal dates were obtained from the deposit which is over 2.5 metres in depth, 1850 ± 80 BP (V 69) (Jones 1971a: 609) and 2350 ± 266 BP (I 322) (Reber 1965). The site appears to have been abandoned about 1,000 years ago. A rich faunal assemblage indicated that, apart from shellfish, an emphasis had been placed upon seals, especially the elephant seal, as well as the fur seal, together with a wide range of mammals (including wallabies) and birds. Included also were large quantities of stone artefacts of fine-grained material resembling those from the upper layers of Rocky Cape. There were no bone tools, however, nor were fish represented in large enough numbers to be considered of economic importance. These last details also tally well with the post-2,500 BP levels of Rocky Cape.

Archaeological evidence from Hunter Island (Bowdler 1974, 1979, 1982, 1984), situated some 5 kilometres off the northwestern tip of Tasmania, reinforced the sequence obtained by Jones and also added a new dimension. The Holocene component of Cave Bay Cave (see also Chapter Two) begins around 6,600 ± 90 BP (ANU 1773). This thin, dense layer of shell midden (indicating the stabilisation of mid-Holocene sea levels) continues until around 4,000 BP. Apart from stone artefacts and animal bones, this layer also contains bone tools and some fish bones. It resembles, therefore, in some ways, the synchronous deposits of Rocky Cape. Following this event, the cave appears to have been abandoned until around 2,500 BP. Occupation at this time includes shellfish, animal bone, stone artefacts and charcoal, but noticeably missing are bone tools and fishbone. Whatever the reason for the abandonment of the cave, Sandra Bowdler argues 'that 2,500 years ago, Hunter Island was incorporated into the northwest Tasmanian economic system by maritime Tasmanians' (1982: 32).

Support for this interpretation is provided from a further four sites excavated on the island (Bowdler 1979, 1982). A small rockshelter, the Rookery Rockshelter, has a basal date of about 4,600 BP, and a layer of shell midden from about 1,300 BP. The three other sites, all open shell middens, are less than 1,600 years old. The Muttonbird midden is dated to around 1,600 BP. Little Duck Bay (about 1,000 BP) is a rich shell midden not unlike West Point in miniature, with two 'hut-pit' depressions on the surface and plentiful bone (including seal bone), mollusc and stone artefacts. The final site, the Stockyard site, is located in the centre of the island and includes plentiful land mammals (especially small wallabies) and seals, together with mollusc and stone artefacts (Bowdler 1981; Geering 1980; O'Connor 1980). When all this evidence is drawn together a subsistence-settlement pattern emerges which indicates a broad-range use of the island and its coastal and terrestrial resources. In all, this archaeological information reinforces the ethnohistorical picture of Hunter Island, which is of seasonal summertime visits rather than of permanent habitation (Bowdler 1982).

Figure 7.8 The Mount Cameron West rock art, northwestern Tasmania. Excavations around the carvings revealed the site to be at least 2,000 years old (Photo: H. Lourandos. Courtesy of the Tasmanian Land Council).

Extensive reconnaissance of archaeological sites by Jim Stockton (1983) in the northwestern corner of Tasmania demonstrated significant increases in site numbers during the last 3,000–2,000 years or so. The sites were located mainly along the strip of coastal heathland. This information seemed to equate with the establishment of the substantial middens in the area (for example, West Point), and overall to suggest an increase in regional population during this period.

Interpretation of the prehistory of northwestern Tasmania has been viewed very much from an environmental point of view: that is, of human adaptation to changing Holocene environments. As we saw in Chapter Two, the Pleistocene climates of this region were both cooler and drier, and vegetation was predominantly grassland; seas were lower and northern Tasmania was connected to the Australian mainland. At the start of the Holocene, or from around 12,000 years ago, open vegetation was replaced by a complex of closed forest communities, including rainforest (Colhoun 1978). Temperate rainforest are largely depauperate (have a reduced number) in faunal and floral species useful to humans, and thus are not considered to have been economically viable. Both Jones (1977a, 1977b) and Bowdler (1979, 1984) have viewed the prehistory of the region, in particular the terminal Pleistocene-early Holocene periods, in relation to the environmental events of rising sea levels and increasingly dense forests. In both cases, they argue that adaptations had to be made to geographically constraining circumstances.

Figure 7.9 The North Cave at Rocky Cape, northwestern Tasmania. Together, the North and South Caves have an archaeological sequence spanning the last 8,000 years (Photo: H. Lourandos).

Both Jones and Bowdler argued that during the late Holocene changes occurred in the regional northwestern subsistence-settlement pattern. Jones (1977a: 345) attributed these changes to the last 2,500 years and Bowdler (1979: 425) to the last 3,000 years. This process is seen by both authors as indicating a somewhat *expansive* period, which Jones describes as involving 'an enlargement of the ecological space of the Aborigines' (1977b: 345).

Jones interpreted the Rocky Cape sequence as indicating a widening of the coastal economy, with the increasing introduction of terrestrial elements in the last 2,500 years. Raw materials, he wrote, were now imported to the site from the west coast. On the west coast itself, coastal base camps were established (perhaps for the first time), for example at West Point. At nearby Mount Cameron West, a large rock art gallery was produced at this time, and offshore islands, such as Hunter Island, were now utilised. Jones considered that a major part of this expansive cultural process was linked to the burning, and reduction of the rainforest (see Chapter Two), producing in this way greater expanses of useable, open terrain (1977b: 347).

Bowdler has argued independently along similar lines, but took this discussion further and considered all of western Tasmania which has been dominated by rainforest and closed forest communities throughout most of the Holocene. In southwestern Tasmania (for example, Louisa Bay), she pointed out, settlement appears also to have been recent, that is, of the last 3,000 years (see below).

Figure 7.10 The West Point shell midden, on the Tasmanian northwestern coast, showing the completed excavation (Photo: H. Lourandos).

Bowdler suggested that 'the West coast as we know it was not successfully exploited until man had established a successful burning regime' (1979: 425). These practices, she argued, allowed for more intensive and widespread settlement and exploitation of this sector of Tasmania. As this territorial expansion progressed, economy also was reorganised.

What of the *timing* of this period of cultural expansion? Both Jones (1977b: 347) and Bowdler (1979) considered that a lapse of a substantial period of time was necessary before these new climatic and environmental conditions could be brought under control by people. Bowdler assumed that rainforest reached its climax towards the mid-Holocene, around 6,000 years ago, and asked 'Can we conjecture that it took 3,000 years or so to learn to control rainforests by burning?' (1979: 425). If an earlier settlement of western Tasmania had taken place, she speculated, it would have assumed a less intensive form (Bowdler 1982: 40).

Central highland Tasmania

This elevated inland region of mixed sclerophyll-rainforest provides a new perspective from which to view the above northwestern Tasmanian prehistoric sequence and its interpretation. It will be discussed, therefore, in some detail.

The site of Warragarra (Johnston 1982; Lourandos 1983b, 1985a, 1987a; Solomon 1985; Sutton 1985) is a sandstone rockshelter in the Upper Mersey Valley. At an elevation of roughly 700 metres, the shelter lies below some of

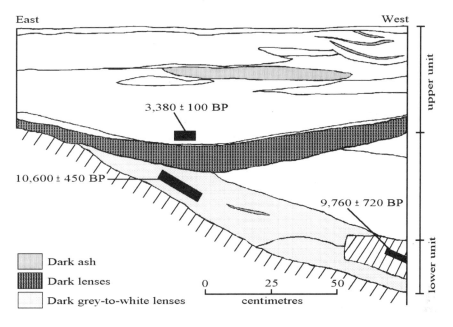

East   West

3,380 ± 100 BP

10,600 ± 450 BP

9,760 ± 720 BP

upper unit

lower unit

■ Dark ash
▓ Dark lenses
□ Dark grey-to-white lenses

0   25   50
centimetres

Figure 7.11 Warragarra Shelter, central western Tasmania: stratigraphic section of pits C and D.

Tasmania's highest terrain which includes both Cradle Mountain and Mount Ossa in the west and, to the east, the Central Plateau. Warragarra is situated some 20 kilometres within the estimated zone of Pleistocene glaciation. During the Pleistocene the Central Plateau and extensive areas of the western highlands, including the Cradle Mountain region, were glaciated. Palynological studies indicate that upslope migration of forests began around 11,500 BP (Macphail and Peterson 1975: 129), with the most rapid phase continuing until around 9,500 BP (Colhoun 1978: 7).

In light of this evidence, Warragarra would appear to have been first occupied swiftly following deglaciation of the valley. More recent radiocarbon dating of the site indicates a basal date in excess of 10,600 ± 450 BP (Beta 8466), suggesting that initial occupation took place around the time reforestation began (Figure 7.11). This archaeological evidence therefore helps to define more closely the Pleistocene-Holocene boundary, which has until now depended upon environmental analysis.

Two phases of occupation appear to have taken place at the site. The initial period of occupation may have been short, for a second radiocarbon date of 9,760 ± 720 BP (Beta 4757) was obtained from the basal unit. A stratigraphic interpretation, together with the two dates, suggests that the lower unit is between 11,000 and 9,000 years old. Use of the site at this time was not intensive according to the frequency of artefacts, faunal remains, charcoal concentrations and features such as hearths. Following this early period of occupation, the site appears to have been abandoned and only reoccupied from around 3,380 ± 100 BP (Beta 4758). This recent stratigraphic unit is composed of a complex of distinct ashy hearth floors, and overall it indicates a more intensive use of the site. In comparison with the lower occupation levels, there are increases in this upper unit of all the above-mentioned archaeological remains.

In both early and late Holocene phases the site appears to have served broadly similar functions, that is, essentially as an ephemeral hunting camp. The upper unit may represent more regular and repeated visits. A taphonomic analysis of the faunal remains was carried out by Harvey Johnston (Johnston 1982; also Solomon 1985), and of these remains the following were attributed to human predation: medium sized macropodids, such as the Bennett's wallaby, *Macropus rufrogriseus*, and the pademelon, *Thylogale billardierii*, together with a suite of smaller animals, which include bettong, brush- and ring-tail possum and rat. The grey kangaroo, *Macropus giganteus*, occurs only in the upper unit and wombat is also represented in the deposit. Exotic stone material resembling that of the west coast of Tasmania makes its appearance in the uppermost levels, which perhaps indicates the development of wider social contacts.

This sequence, although preliminary to some extent, has been viewed in relation to the Holocene climatic and floristic changes of western Tasmania. I would suggest the following model (also Lourandos 1983b): occupation of the site immediately followed upon deglaciation of the valley during a stage of mixed forests (sclerophyll-rainforest) (Macphail and Peterson 1975: 129). The site appears to have been abandoned during the mid-Holocene which was the optimum period of moister, warmer conditions (c. 8,000–3,600 BP in the southern midlands) (Colhoun 1978: 7). We may presume that rainforest and wet sclerophyll forest achieve their maximum extent at this time. Reoccupation on a more intensive level followed after about 3,400 BP, coinciding broadly with slightly drier, cooler conditions (Colhoun 1978: 7). Mixed sclerophyll-rainforest, much like those of today, may have predominated at this stage, as is suggested by the faunal remains (for example, the appearance of grey kangaroo). The firing of vegetation by people also would have been more effective during this drier phase.

More recent excavations at Warragarra have confirmed the site's basic chronology and stratigraphy (Jim Allen, personal communication 1994). I also took part in the 1992 excavation season at the site, which formed part of the Southern Forest Project, the team responsible for much of the recent fieldwork in southwestern Tasmania mentioned earlier in this chapter.

The sequence at Warragarra is to some extent reflected in the adjoining elevated Forth River Valley. This valley is drier than that of the Mersey, where Warragarra is situated, and was not subjected to glaciation as was the latter region. Here the rock-shelter of Parmerpar Meethaner has produced a very long and potentially continuous sequence of occupation, spanning both Pleistocene and Holocene periods, from about 34,000 until 780 years ago. The site appears to have been most intensively inhabited in the terminal Pleistocene, after 18,000 BP. In the late Pleistocene levels, thumbnail scrapers appear reminiscent of southwestern sites, although faunal associations (including an emphasis on wallaby) differ from the latter.

Between about 10,000 and 3,000 years ago, however, intensity of occupation is lessened, increasing once again after that, a pattern linked to expanding forests and more humid conditions (Cosgrove 1995; Cosgrove personal communication 1992; personal observation 1992). The general similarity here with the sequence at Warragarra strengthens the interpretation offered above, which is based largely around changing climate, its effect upon vegetation and resources, and upon people and the ways in which they have perceived and reacted to these events.

There is also strong accord between some of the basic features of the central highlands and the northwestern Tasmanian archaeological sequence (see also Johnston 1982). First, the less intensive early Holocene unit at Warragarra can be seen to reflect aspects of the more restricted (localised) pre-2,500 BP sequence at Rocky Cape and also to support Bowdler's hypothesis of a low-level pre-3,000 BP occupation of western Tasmania. Second, the more intensive upper unit at Warragarra, dated to about 3,400 BP, correlates in general with the 'expansive' phase in the northwest, which has been dated to around 3,000–2,500 BP.

In all, therefore, this information suggests that the 'period of cultural expansion', dated to the last 3,000 years or so in northwestern Tasmania, and to around 3,400 years ago in the upper Mersey, coincided with the onset of a cooler, drier climate and to a time when closed forests would have been more easily reduced by fire. I would suggest that this is the explanation for the *timing* of the more intensive occupation of marginal rainforest-wet sclerophyll areas (both coastal and inland) of northwestern Tasmania (and perhaps southwestern Tasmania also), rather than the indefinable 'period of cultural adaptation' to new Holocene environmental conditions as has been previously suggested. Firing practices, it could be argued, at this time would have been more effective (if only seasonally), producing corridors of more open vegetation and thus facilitating both increased travel and settlement. The indication from Warragarra, together with the palynological information presented, would suggest that the stimulus for change had begun at least by about 3,500 BP and not later as previously supposed (Lourandos 1983b: 43; see also Macphail 1983).

Environmental factors, however, should not be viewed as *determining* the nature of the cultural changes. I would argue that climatic change provided the incentive for change, the human response being largely culturally determined. Rather than seeing this adaptation to a new Holocene environment, I tend to view this process as a positive response to expanding opportunities (social as well as economic), brought about in part by climatic change (Lourandos 1983b: 43).

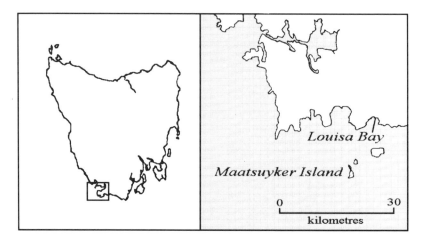

Figure 7.12 Louisa Bay and Maatsuyker Island, southwestern Tasmania.

Southwestern Tasmania

Vanderwal's research in this extremely rugged area centred upon Louisa Bay and offshore Maatsuyker Island (1978; Vanderwal and Horton 1984; Figure 7.12). Louisa Bay is flanked in the east by the towering Ironbound Range and the excavated evidence indicates that occupation of the region extends back only 3,000 years or so. The region appears, however, to have been most intensively utilised around 1,000 years ago (Vanderwal 1978: 120). This evidence has been obtained from three sites or locations within the bay. A series of cultural lenses were detected in dunes at the eastern end of the bay, the oldest of which were dated to 2,970 ± 200 BP (ANU 1771). The lowermost lenses indicated intermittent use and were overlain by evidence of more intensive occupation.

At the western end of the bay a similar site, which is also stratified within dunes, was dated to 1,250 ± 100 BP (Gak 5989), and also a small rock-shelter, Louisa River Cave site 2, with a shallow deposit, to 870 ± 90 BP (Gak 5990). The cultural remains from these sites was generally similar and indicated use of mammals and sea birds as well as shellfish. One possible hint of earlier, that is pre-3,500 BP, occupation of Louisa Bay is the discovery of a bone tool which is in some ways reminiscent of those from Rocky Cape South. The tool came from the eastern dune site, but there are stratigraphic and chronological problems with this example.

Excavations on Maatsuyker Island, which is located some 13 kilometres from the mainland, complement the evidence from Louisa Bay. Treacherous seas divide this island from the mainland. An open site on the island was dated to 570 ± 100 BP (Gak 5987), and the faunal remains were mainly of seals and muttonbirds. Both faunal groups are still plentiful on the island today and, from this evidence, sea travel to Maatsuyker Island and its rich resources appears to have been of fairly recent origin.

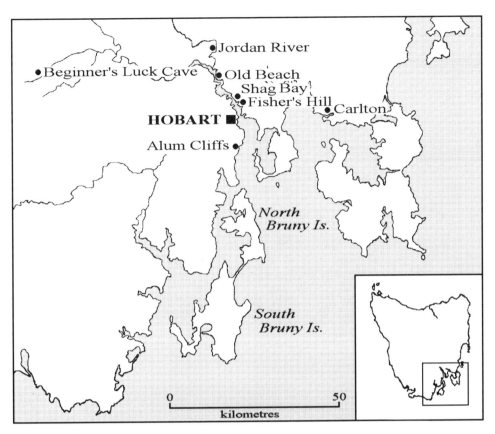

Figure 7.13 Archaeological sites of southeastern Tasmania.

Vanderwal and Horton (1984: 93–117) have proposed a speculative seasonal subsistence model for the Louisa Bay area. They suggest that the mainland, including the bay area, was occupied year-round. Maatsuyker Island, on the other hand, was visited during the summer season. They distinguished between short-term summer camps and longer-term winter sites on the mainland, and drew a close parallel between this seasonal pattern from Louisa Bay and that of northwestern Tasmania. They also pointed out the marked dissimilarities between the seasonal pattern at Louisa Bay and that of southeastern Tasmania (1984: 117).

Southeastern Tasmania

The archaeological sequence and model for southeastern Tasmania (Lourandos 1968, 1970, 1977b) has generally has been supported by more recent research (Figure 7.13). The original model was based upon extensive archaeological reconnaissance of the region. The survey stretched from Piccaninny Point in the northeast to the Huon River in the southwest. Large tracts of the interior were also surveyed, and a predictive model was established followed by the excavation

Figure 7.14 The placid Carlton estuary in southeastern Tasmania. Extensive oyster shell middens line the estuary and excavations took place below this point, closer to the water-line (Photo: H. Lourandos).

of two sites, Little Swanport and Crown Lagoon, and more recently a third site, Carlton (Lourandos and Murray, in prep.).

Shell middens located in sheltered estuaries or bays are extensive, often deeply stratified structures in this area of Tasmania, and generally are composed of mud oyster, *Ostrea angasi*, and some mussel. Some of the largest shell middens are found in the estuaries of Little Swanport and Carlton, and the site excavated at Little Swanport is an extensive shell midden, approximately 2,800 metres square in area and some 2 metres in depth. A large area was sampled to examine both spatial and chronological trends, while in contrast at Carlton a more limited excavation was carried out.

The excavations revealed that dense oyster middens had been established around 5760 ± 130 BP (Beta 2854) at Carlton and 4490 ± 120 BP (ANU 356) at Little Swanport, that is, following the establishment of mid-Holocene sea levels. Presumably the stabilisation of sea levels provided favourable estuarine habitats for oyster shell beds. At Carlton an underlying, very sparse shell layer of cockles with a basal date of 7,560 ± 70 BP (Beta 2855) is presumed to indicate early Holocene pre-optimal estuarine conditions. A basal date of around 9,000 BP had been previously reported for the Carlton site (Reber 1965), and has often been referred to as giving one of the earliest examples of Australian Holocene middens. In order to test the original chronology of the site, our excavation was located beside the trench Reber had dug nearly twenty years before. In general, our findings support those of Reber, and there is also the possibility that Reber's somewhat older date is the product of admixture with earlier stratigraphic material.

Once oyster beds had been established between 6,000 BP and 5,000 BP a fairly homogeneous cultural pattern of predominant shell gathering continued at Little Swanport and Carlton, more or less up to the historical period. At Little Swanport, although there were numerous ashy hearths, there were very sparse occurrences of retouched stone artefacts, land fauna (medium-to-small animals) and crustacea. No flaking floors were found nor quantities of waste flakes. Fewer still cultural items, apart from shell and numerous hearths, were found at Carlton. Apart from small hearths there were no indications of semi-sedentary behaviour as is found in middens of northwestern Tasmania. The remains of fish (leatherjacket) and bone tools (two spatulae) were found in the levels older than 3660 ± 95 BP (ANU 357) at Little Swanport, and this evidence seemed to support Jones' findings from Rocky Cape (see above), and suggested that the cessation of fishing was a pan-Tasmanian phenomenon (Lourandos 1968). These excavations, therefore, reinforce the impression gained from the surface survey: that southeastern Tasmanian shell middens were predominantly shell dumps with few other cultural features represented (Lourandos 1968).

Crown Lagoon is an open site and is located in the upper reaches of the Little Swanport drainage basin, some 25 kilometres inland. The site is stratified within the upper horizon of a fossil done (lunette) and it showed quite a different picture from that of the coastal sites. The cultural deposit was dated between 4,860 ± 95 BP (ANU 278) and 4,170 ± 80 BP (ANU 279). Distinct activity areas could be recognised. Areas of hearths and plentiful, although fragmented, animal bone could be distinguished from areas of flaking floors, composed of stone cores, artefacts and debitage. The only recognisable species present was the large grey kangaroo, *Macropus giganteus* (Lourandos 1970: 60–67, 1977b). Crown Lagoon in many ways appeared typical of the numerous open inland sites detected in the field survey.

I argued that the differences observed between the coastal sites and Crown Lagoon reflected complementary patterns of land and resource use (Lourandos 1968, 1970, 1977b). On the one hand, Little Swanport and Carlton indicated specialised, ephemeral marine exploitation (predominantly shellfish), with few other cultural markers. While on the other hand, Crown Lagoon represented a transient hunting camp with the emphasis on kangaroo hunting and the manufacture and use of stone artefacts, which are arguably related pursuits. As both site types conform to those of the extensive site survey, I suggested that together they represented a subsistence-settlement pattern peculiar to southeastern Tasmania. This pattern could be characterised as incorporating dispersed activities with specialised use of resources at task-specific sites – both marine and terrestrial. At Little Swanport and Carlton mud oyster was the predominant target species, and at Crown Lagoon it was grey kangaroo. As there was no evidence for complex, long-term base camps (such as those of northwestern Tasmania) in the area, overall this indicated a pattern of general mobility.

I contrasted this geographically dispersed, mobile and specialised subsistence-settlement pattern with the northwestern Tasmanian pattern, which I characterised as centred upon coastal base camps where a relatively wide range of resources and activities were represented. The archaeological patterns observed from both regions of Tasmania were supported by ethnohistorical information (such as that presented in Chapter Two).

This subsistence-settlement dichotomy can now be identified with more recent distinctions between the 'residential' ('mapping-on') as opposed to 'logistical' strategies among hunter-gatherers discussed in the first chapter. The former pattern can be associated with areas of more geographically dispersed resources, and the latter with areas where resources are spatially more concentrated. This ecological distinction to some extent fits both southeastern and northwestern Tasmania. This does not, however, provide the only explanation for the two patterns. The establishment of base camps, for example, might also have been a viable economic strategy in fertile southeastern Tasmania. In other words, resources were not so geographically dispersed in this area that mobility was the only option. Cultural factors as well, such as lower population density and a more open and flexible social system, might have influenced the mobile, spatially dispersed pattern. The northwestern pattern, in contrast, could be explained as due to a rich concentration of resources, restricted territorial range and climate. This region, for example, has heavy year-round rainfall together with relatively low temperatures but on the open, resource-rich coastline there are relatively few rock-shelters, thus necessitating use of durable huts and bases.

The southeastern Tasmanian subsistence-settlement pattern appears, therefore, to have been developed around the mid-Holocene period (about 5,000 BP) with the stabilising of post-glacial sea levels. At this time favourable coastal conditions were established, conducive to supporting sizeable shellfish populations, such as oyster. Apart from what appear to have been relatively minor cultural changes – the cessation of limited fishing and making of bone tools – this regional pattern appears to have continued more or less unchanged into recent times.

While these conclusions have greater applicability to coastal sites, long-term cultural sequences are now required from inland locations. Although in this region we do not find the more marked changes which are evident in the archaeological sequences of northwestern, central highland or southwestern Tasmania, more subtle changes thus far may have gone unnoticed. Of the latter we may consider the opening up of econiches such as areas of closed forest, and the use of inland resources.

Later investigations in southeastern Tasmania have in general supported the original model. An open midden on the Jordan River, a tributary of the Derwent, included estuarine shellfish in the main, a few stone artefacts, but no animal bone (Gaffney and Stockton 1980: 76). In the Derwent estuary also, a similar assemblage was obtained from a rock-shelter at Shag Bay which has a basal date of 5,300 ± 120 BP (Gak 5425) (Vanderwal 1977: 168). Marine shell came from a further open midden at Alum Cliffs, situated at the mouth of the Derwent estuary, and dated to 3,875 ± 160 BP (SUA 599) (Stockton and Wallace 1979: 83).

Two other shell middens have also been dated at Old Beach and Fishers Hill, to 5,220 ± 110 BP (I 324) and 5,520 ± 85 BP (ANU 1090A) respectively (Reber 1965). As with my own sites, these shell middens also date to the time of sea level stabilisation between 6,000 and 5,000 BP. Basal dates from around this time have also been obtained from shell middens on Bruny Island (Reber 1965), which might indicate the early use of large islands in the region.

A detailed archaeological survey has been undertaken on the northwestern corner of the Tasman Peninsula, the most southerly appendage of the region by Gaughwin (1985). Three transects were surveyed, including archaeological sites in both protected bay (low energy) and open coastline (medium energy) locations. Gaughwin's aim was partly to test the southeastern model of settlement and landuse (1985: 39). She concluded:

> The pattern of coastal site location identified above fits broadly that suggested for the east coast of Tasmania . . . but suggests that these models give only a brief sketch of what appears to be a more complicated pattern. (1985: 52)

Gaughwin argued that the model fitted well the pattern for the location of low-energy economies, but that a more complex pattern existed in the medium-energy coastal economies. In the latter, she states, 'they have greater quantities of stone which predominates in some sites' (Gaughwin 1985: 52). She also adds, however, that of the three locations where 'dense lithic scatters' occurred – Sloping Island, Roaring Beach and Low Point – 'the two former locations have cherty hornfels pebbles on the beaches. In general medium energy coasts provide greater access to stone resources' (1985: 51).

Perhaps the close proximity of these locations to raw materials (cherty hornfels being the most plentiful material in southeastern Tasmania) can explain the higher incidence of lithic material at these sites. Similar associations were detected during my surveys (1968). Sites located near to raw materials appear to have acted also as quarries (personal observation). Rather than more complex subsistence behaviour at these sites (for none was detected), we may have represented activities associated with the acquisition and reduction of raw stone material.

More recently, Dunnett, following a review of excavated southeastern sites, has argued that sublittoral species (including abalone, *Haliotis*) were largely avoided in the region, and that exclusive emphasis upon upper and mid-littoral species persisted here until perhaps the last thousand years (1993: 252).

Northeastern Tasmania

Less archaeological work has been carried out in this corner of the island, and some of the eastern islands of Bass Strait also have been sampled to some extent. One early Holocene site has been detected recently in the northeastern corner (Cosgrove 1985). Rushy Lagoon is today situated some 10 kilometres from the east coast. A lunette of either late Pleistocene or early Holocene age separates Rushy Lagoon from yet another lagoon to the south. Below the podzol soil of the lunette were stratified stone artefacts and charcoal and below these a hearth. From the hearth, which was stratified 40–75 cms below the surface of the lunette, a date of 8,300 ± 80 BP (Beta 8190) was obtained. No faunal remains were found but by all indications the site served as a temporary encampment. In this regard, Cosgrove (1985: 33) compares it favourably with Crown Lagoon in eastern Tasmania and with the approximately contemporary lower unit at Warragarra, in the Upper Mersey Valley, where occupation also appears to have been somewhat ephemeral. The stone tool assemblage from Rushy Lagoon also compares well with that of Crown Lagoon (Cosgrove 1985: 31–32). Further sites have also been recorded around the lunette. In all, there is evidence here of ephemeral occupation of productive wetlands during the early Holocene. At the time the site was located some 15–20 kilometres from the coast, and a broadly similar pattern is still found at Crown Lagoon some 3,500 years later.

Islands of Bass Strait

Evidence from the islands of Bass Strait presents a complex pattern of Aboriginal use of the region throughout its long-term history of transformation from cold, open Pleistocene plain to the island-studded passage of today, the product of post-glacial sea rises (Figure 7.15). Sim (1994) has drawn together the recently collected archaeological information of this area to produce a plausible prehistoric scenario of these events. Her account is largely followed here.

Separate historical patterns appear to characterise the eastern and western sectors of the strait. In the west, the sizeable King Island appears to have been ephemerally utilised in the late Pleistocene (17,000 BP), from evidence derived from rock-shelters with relatively deep Pleistocene sediments. At this time the island would have appeared as a low, rather barren plateau. Sporadic signs of occupation have also been obtained from shell middens of the last 2,000 years or so, suggesting a late Holocene re-use of the island up until some 8,000 to 9,000 years after it was severed from the Tasmanian mainland. Stone raw material associated with the latter sites suggest connections with northwestern Tasmania, and Sim offers an explanation of isolated castaways adrift from that region. Ocean currents and distance argue against more deliberate crossings. In all, the evidence from King Island indicates ephemeral and discontinuous use of the area.

From the eastern side of Bass Strait (the Furneaux Islands of today), quite a different picture emerges. Here the evidence suggests that people of the region

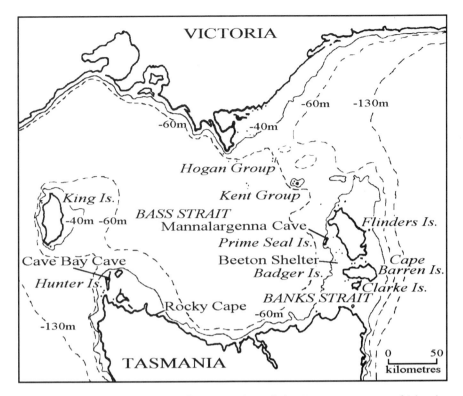

Figure 7.15 Archaeological sites of Bass Strait and the Furneaux group of islands (based on Sim 1993: 359, Figure 1).

during 'the Pleistocene landbridge phase, developed specific strategies to optimise the exploitation of locally available resources' (Sim 1994: 370). These strategies included shell artefacts and targeted food resources. These cultural patterns persisted for some 12,000 years and suggest that the Furneaux area had a distinct regional economic and possibly cultural focus. Two excavated caves have produced the Pleistocene (and early Holocene) sequence, Beeton Shelter (Badger Island) and Mannalargenna Cave (Prime Seal Island). Of the two, the latter is the best dated at present and indicates deposits of about 21,000 years in age. Ephemeral but continuous occupation is indicated, with a more intensive phase during the glacial maximum, 18,000–15,000 years ago. The grey forester kangaroo (*Macropus giganteus*), now extinct on the islands, is among the food remains (Brown 1993; Sim 1994).

Shell middens from Flinders Island, the largest island of the group, indicate that people continued to occupy the Furneaux region as seas inundated the Bassian plains. The islands are elevated, with abundant terrestrial and marine resources. A population appears to have remained on Flinders Island, isolated from the Tasmanian mainland, and the islands in closer proximity to it, until about 4,500 years ago. These middens indicate a consistent pattern of clear targeting of a small range of intertidal species. Sub-tidal marine resources, such as abalone (*Haliotis ruber*), mud oyster (*Ostrea angasi*) and crayfish, were avoided although they were available (Sim 1994: 363–364). The demise of the Flinders Island population during the late Holocene remains a mystery. Ethnohistorical accounts also clearly indicate that these resource-rich islands were uninhabited in recent times.

Overview: Holocene settlement

All available evidence points to Tasmania, including the islands of Bass Strait, remaining in cultural isolation after about 12,000–10,000 BP. That is, once the Pleistocene landbridge that had connected the Tasmanian land mass to southeastern Australia had been severed by post-glacial sea rises. No obvious clues to possible Holocene contact with the Australian mainland have been found. No microliths, which are generally typical of mid-late Holocene Australian stone assemblages, have been detected at any Tasmanian archaeological site. There is also no evidence of the dog, *Canis familiaris*, prior to its introduction by Europeans to Tasmania at the end of the eighteenth century. The survival of the Tasmanian Devil, *Sarcophilus harrisii*, and the Tasmanian Tiger, *Thylacinus cynocephalus*, is also seen as supporting the last point. These two marsupial predators, ecological competitors of the dog, became extinct on mainland Australia after the dog's purported introduction between 4,000 and 3,000 BP.

The long-standing question of the origins or homeland of the Tasmanians (also referred to on pp. 88–9) has also now been laid to rest. (It was long debated whether the people of Tasmania were a separate population – of different genetic stock – from those of mainland Australia and had possibly arrived ahead of them, maybe from a separate geographical area.) Pleistocene sites now stretch back to around 35,000 BP and a further series of archaeological sites link this distant episode to the Holocene. Pleistocene Australia, therefore, gave rise to the Tasmanian people of the Holocene and recent historical periods and osteological (see below) and linguistic evidence stand in further support. As well, the stone artefact assemblages of, for example, Rocky Cape (which begin around 8,000 BP) have also been generally associated with Australian Pleistocene lithic traditions (Jones 1971a, 1977a); similar evidence has been detected at Cave Bay Cave (Bowdler 1984; see Figure 7.16).

The question of 'devolution'

Perhaps the most controversial issue in recent Tasmanian prehistory concerns the question of devolution. This viewpoint, which was proposed by Jones, stems first from his theoretical stance, which concerns island biogeography; and second from his comparison of the Holocene prehistories and ethnohistories of Tasmania and southeastern Australia, two areas which share environmental similarities (1977a, 1977b, 1978; see also Chapter Two). Jones argued that biogeographical

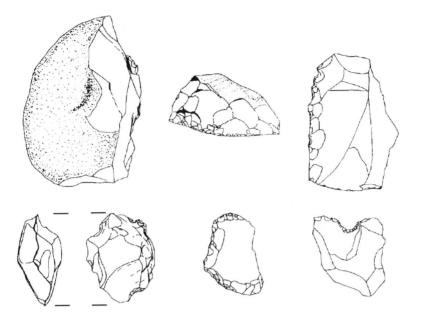

Figure 7.16 Stone artefacts from Rocky Cape (based on Jones 1977a: 191, Figure 2b). Not drawn to scale.

studies show that islands, in time, experience a reduction in their number of animal species (1977b: 317–318). Tasmania, for example, has a relatively low, or depauperate, faunal range in comparison with southeastern Australia. Jones conjectured that perhaps the same would apply to cultural traits leading in time to a cultural depauperisation (1977b: 343).

To illustrate these ideas, he pointed to archaeological evidence indicating that fishing ceased to be practised in Tasmania from around 3,500 years ago, along with the making of bone tools (see above) (Figure 7.17). Jones observed that the decision to cease fishing 'had the result of constricting their ecological universe' (1978: 44). Comparing Tasmania with mainland Australia, he suggested that many other cultural traits also may have been 'lost' in Tasmania during its 12,000 years of isolation. Included in his reckoning were items such as boomerangs, barbed spears, edge-ground axes and elementary hafting techniques (Jones 1977a: 196). While these artefacts are absent from Tasmanian contexts, the former two have been found at Wyrie Swamp in South Australia at around 10,000 BP (see Chapter Six), and the latter two from Pleistocene times – putative hafting from Devils Lair, Western Australia, and axes from Arnhem Land sites (see Chapter Two).

> This diminution I see as having been one of the consequences of the isolation of the Tasmanian segment of society from the wider continental social network. Perhaps there is here some cultural analogue of the loss of useful arts with the reduction of

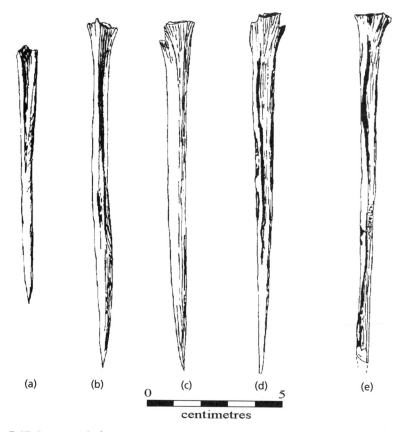

(a)   (b)   (c)   (d)   (e)

0   5

centimetres

Figure 7.17 Bone tools from Cave Bay Cave, northwestern Tasmania (a) Pleistocene; (b–e) early Holocene (based on Bowdler 1984: 124–125, Figures 38, 39).

species on continental islands. At the very least isolation may have allowed the persistence of economic maladaptations, through protection against more efficient systems replacing them from outside. (Jones 1977b: 343)

Jones justified his theoretical position, stating that, 'Demographically and culturally, Tasmania was a closed system. Indeed it would become the classic example of such a system, for no other human society which survived until modern times, has been isolated so completely and for so long' (1977a: 194). That is to say that prolonged isolation suggested to Jones a presentiment of cultural disintegration. In his words:

Like a blow above the heart, it took a long time to take effect, but slowly but surely there was a simplification of the tool kit, a diminution in the range of foods eaten, perhaps a squeezing of intellectuality ... The world's longest isolation, the world's simplest technology. Were 4,000 people enough to propel forever the cultural inheritance of Late Pleistocene Australia? Even if Abel Tasman had not sailed the winds of the Roaring Forties in 1642, were they in fact doomed – doomed to a slow strangulation of the mind? (1977a: 202–203)

Jones' explanation for the mid-late Holocene changes in mainland Australia has already been discussed in Chapter Five. His devolution scenario, as one might imagine, has drawn a good deal of attention and criticism (see, for example, Bowdler 1980). First, it should be pointed out that of the 'lost' cultural traits only fish and bone tools have been detected archaeologically. As to the loss of fish, some argue that the issue has been rather overemphasised. Horton (1979), for example, pointed out that fish may not have been as important a dietary item as Jones thought. Horton stated that fish numbers are low at Rocky Cape North, Little Swanport and Cave Bay Cave; leaving only Rocky Cape South and Sister's Creek with reasonable quantities. Horton (1979: 30) argued that on the archaeological evidence seals played a comparatively larger role in prehistoric Tasmanian diets. Allen introduced a similar point of view (1979). He argued that when comparing other hunter-gatherer societies in similarly high latitudes, dietary emphases appear to have been upon fatty foods, for example seals, mutton birds and the like. Allen pointed out that the cessation of fishing in Tasmania coincides with a drier, cooler climatic phase which may have accentuated this emphasis upon fat-rich foods and away from fish. Both Horton and Allen, therefore, have sought 'adaptive' explanations for what Jones perceived as aberrant behaviour. Further evidence suggests that exploitation of sub-tidal marine resources (such as *Haliotis*) was, as I noted above, a late Holocene development in northwestern and other parts of Tasmania (Bowdler 1988; Dunnett 1993; Sim 1994).

Other arguments have focused upon the so-called expansive trends in Tasmanian prehistory. Bowdler pointed to the recent reoccupation of Hunter Island and the possible settlement of the west coast at around the same time, aided by Aboriginal fire management strategies (1979: 426–427). Vanderwal (1978) similarly indicated the even more recent seasonal use of Maatsuyker Island and suggested that the Tasmanian water craft of the ethnohistorical period may have been a fairly recent innovation. Cessation of fishing, I suggested, in both northwestern and southeastern Tasmania was synchronous with the inferred period of territorial expansion (post-3,500 BP), which may have been triggered by a change towards drier, cooler climate. This cultural expansion, therefore, may have involved a Tasmania-wide reorganisation of subsistence strategies, as both Jones and Bowdler had suggested for the northwest. I reasoned that rescheduling of coastal practices, including fishing, needs to be viewed in terms of the large-scale island-wide terrestrial gains that this expansive cultural process implies (Lourandos 1983b: 144).

Overall, given this set of counter-arguments, it would seem unnecessary to introduce the concept of devolution in order to explain the Holocene prehistory of Tasmania.

This viewpoint has been reinforced strongly by Pardoe's osteological studies. He compared Tasmanian Aboriginal skeletal evidence with evidence from south-eastern Australia (including Victoria and the Murray River region). His conclusions indicate that 'Tasmanians have diverged no more than might be expected if Tasmania were still attached to the mainland' (Pardoe 1991: 1).

Genetic drift, for example, had little effect on so long a period of isolation. A more recent discovery from King Island in Bass Strait appears to further support this perspective. A secondary burial of a mature male from a cave, dated to 14,270 ± 640 BP (ANU 7039), has been described as morphologically gracile and reminiscent of the Victorian Keilor skull (Sim and Thorne 1990; Sim 1990; Thorne and Sim 1994).

Comparisons with Holocene mainland Australia

In view of the discussion concerning late Holocene changes in Australia (see Chapter Five), can we see any similar trends in Tasmania, and if so can similar explanations be invoked? Are there, for example, indications of resource intensification, econiche expansion and demographic change? What can be said of changing levels of production and of social relations?

With regard to econiche expansion a number of examples can be found in Tasmania. The recent seasonal use of offshore islands, both in the northwest and southwest, indicate a widening of resource opportunities. Movement into peripheral rainforest areas after about 3,500 BP suggests a similar trend. For example, movement appears to have taken place around the coastline of western Tasmania and up into the central highland region, such as the Upper Mersey Valley. Land management practices were also associated with these events. The management of rainforest and other closed forest by fire has been viewed as a key factor in this process. Use of sub-tidal marine resources in the late Holocene is a further example.

The beginnings of 'logistical' organisation (as opposed to 'mapping on' strategies; see Chapter One) can be seen in the establishment of mixed-resource base camps such as West Point on the west coast, on Hunter Island and in the post-2,500 BP levels of Rocky Cape. 'Logistical' organisation implies, to some extent, a reorganisation of economic activity; that is, activities associated with resource extraction (production) are more concentrated in both time and space. Demographic changes, including perhaps rises in population, also have been suggested for the post-3,000 BP period in northwestern Tasmania. Apart from these semi-sedentary coastal bases, other indications of territorial markers during this period are engraved rock art sites, which are found in coastal locations along the west coast and nowhere else in Tasmania. Mount Cameron West, which is situated immediately north of West Point, is the largest and most complex of these sites and has been dated to about 2,000 BP (Jones 1977a).

In relation to broader models of potential 'pathways' of hunter-gatherer resource expansion, or intensification outlined in Chapter One, none appears to have been pursued in Tasmania; as we saw, however, rearrangements in resource strategies, together with aspects of econiche expansion, were introduced. One potential avenue, that of fishing, was not only avoided but apparently abandoned in the late Holocene period, even though Tasmania is a high latitude province rich in fish. The resource-rich, offshore Furneaux Islands of the northeast were also uninhabited in recent times and apparently throughout the late Holocene. On the other hand, alternative strategies – such as use of sub-tidal marine exploitation – appear to have been introduced at roughly the same time.

Tasmanian prehistoric subsistence-settlement patterns appear to be closer to the 'immediate-return' end of the range, in contrast to those of many mainland Australian societies who practised 'delayed-return' systems. In northwestern Tasmania, after about 3,000 BP, however, there are suggestions of alterations to this basic pattern (in particular, the development of coastal base camps). In relation to production (as discussed in Chapter One), we would have to view the Tasmanian evidence as indicating somewhat less complex social relations which in time made fewer demands upon production. Ethnohistorical information appears to support this (see Chapter Two). Following this viewpoint, socio-cultural (including economic) patterns would appear to have developed, or changed, at a different pace, and in somewhat different ways, in isolated Tasmania than in Victoria and wider southeastern Australia during Holocene times. These trends cannot be explained solely as due to physical environmental factors.

An 'evolutionary' model

If we now draw together the main evidence from Holocene Tasmania and sketch an evolutionary model, one based on developmental processes and trends, the following could be proposed. Post-glacial seas rose after 12,000 BP, creating the island of Tasmania and the smaller islands of Bass Strait. A residual population remained on Flinders Island, in the east. Shortly after these events people were making intermittent forays up into the central Tasmanian highlands, in the wake of glacial retreat and as mixed forests began to recolonise once-glaciated valleys like that of the Upper Mersey. After about 9,000 BP the warmest and most humid phase of the Holocene set in, and with it the spread of closed forests such as rainforest. For people, temperate rainforest was in many ways inhospitable, being relatively poor in resources and difficult to traverse. These forests were most widespread in the more humid western half of the island, but were also distributed as a mosaic of closed-to-open forests throughout Tasmania. Around 8,000 BP ephemeral Aboriginal occupation was recorded around lagoons in northeastern Tasmania and on Flinders Island, in the Carlton estuary of the southeast and at Rocky Cape in the northwest, where there is a strong marine emphasis in the economy of the people. Closed forests achieved their maximum extent between about 8,000 and 5,000 BP.

At this time, we may surmise, Tasmanian populations would have been most constrained, territorially 'squeezed' by expanding forests, including rainforest.

For example, Warragarra, in the Upper Mersey Valley, was abandoned, perhaps due to the encroachment of rainforest (and occupation decreased at Parmerpar Meethaner perhaps for similar reasons). From around 6,000 to 5,000 BP, dense oyster middens were established in the extensive middens of Carlton and Little Swanport in eastern and southeastern Tasmania, and this settlement-subsistence pattern (found also at other sites in the region) continued with few alterations up until the present.

From this time on, and increasingly after about 4,000 BP, conditions became cooler and drier. Rainforests now began to contract and fire was most effective in containing their spread. After about 3,500 BP an epoch of Aboriginal territorial expansion is suggested in western Tasmania. Increased occupation of Warragarra took place in the Upper Mersey and in the northwest at Rocky Cape, substantial base camps were established at West Point, rock art at Mount Cameron West, and seasonal use was now made of Hunter Island. From the southwest a broadly similar pattern of increased site use (Louisa Bay) and recent island exploitation (Maatsuyker Island) is indicated, although chronological details may vary. While fishing and the making of bone tools ceased after about 3,500 BP in the northwest and southeast, they appear to have been offset by the other more extensive pursuits discussed above. At Rocky Cape, for example, there was a synchronous broadening of the diet with a wider terrestrial component, and in the southeast at Little Swanport, fishing had been only of minor importance.

When viewing the Holocene as a whole, a pattern emerges. For the first half of the period Aboriginal settlement was faced with constraining circumstances – rising sea levels and expanding rainforests and other closed forests. In the second half of the Holocene a reversal of this environmental trend took place to some extent. Aboriginal settlement was now able to expand, especially in the western half of the island, that is, in areas of marginal and peripheral rainforest, those most vulnerable to fire. Aided by climate, disclimaxes now may have been maintained by people, producing more productive (that is, faunally and florally rich) open forests and heathlands in western Tasmania. Aboriginal populations may have expanded in these areas (for example in northwestern Tasmania) at this time. While the possibility of some territorial expansion in eastern and southeastern Tasmania has been raised in this chapter, most of the archaeological evidence indicates that a more stable subsistence-settlement pattern continued there, with few significant changes throughout the period.

Territorial expansion in Tasmania, therefore, and its associated economic and demographic rearrangements, appears to have been associated with (although not necessarily determined by) climatic changes of the late Holocene. Comparable changes to Aboriginal settlement and economy may not have been possible earlier in the Holocene, especially in western Tasmania where the most dynamic environmental and cultural changes were observed to have taken place after about 3,500 BP.

We have come, therefore, quite a way from what I have called the traditional accounts of the Tasmanians. Some anthropologists argued that they suffered from some 'arrested cultural development' during their long period of isolation, only to be annihilated by British colonists in the first half of the nineteenth century, and this was long believed to have been the case. Now quite a different story has emerged from the archaeological and ethnohistorical records. For over a generation after the British settlement, the Tasmanians fought a long, bitter guerilla war against their foe. Their descendants struggled for more than a century to have their social identity recognised (Ryan 1981). Today there are as many Aboriginal Tasmanians as there ever were, perhaps more. And their social and cultural renaissance has been as strong as anywhere throughout Aboriginal Australia.

CHAPTER 8

ARTEFACTS AND ASSEMBLAGES CONTINENT-WIDE

This chapter provides a brief overview of the main Australian stone artefact classes for both Pleistocene and Holocene periods. The material culture of Australia is covered in great detail elsewhere (see, for instance, Mulvaney 1975). The classifications have been referred to throughout this book (especially in Chapters Four to Seven), but because they serve as important cultural and chronological markers I wish to discuss them here specifically in a continent-wide perspective. I also touch on the late Holocene introduction to mainland Australia of an animal which was mostly domesticated – the dingo.

The term 'tradition' in the context of stone (and other) artefacts refers to assemblages or collections of worked objects (artefacts) from specific geographical regions and periods of time. Descriptions of terms used here (such as 'scraper', 'tula adze', etc.) are covered in the glossary (p. 336).

The Early, or Pleistocene, assemblages of worked stone of Greater Australia are now generally referred to as the Australian Core Tool and Scraper tradition. This lithic (stone) tradition is most often seen to begin from the time of the earliest accepted evidence of human occupation of the continent, that is, some time before about 40,000 BP; it continues until around mid-Holocene times. During the mid-Holocene period a suite of new lithic forms was added to the Early basic tool kit, and this new complex is generally referred to as the Australian Small Tool tradition; we now turn to a discussion of these two traditions in the context of continental changes over time.

The Australian Core Tool and Scraper tradition

The Australian Core Tool and Scraper tradition was first defined in this manner in 1970 at the Mungo I site (Bowler et al. 1970), based upon a typological

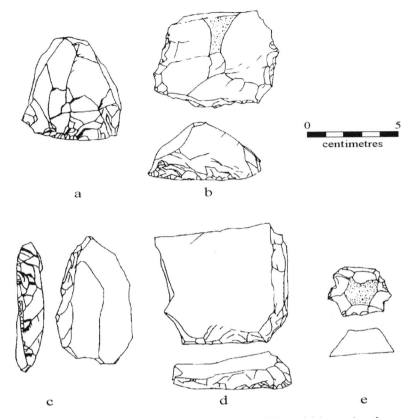

Figure 8.1 The Australian Core Tool and Scraper tradition: (a) horse-hoof core; (b–e) 'scrapers' (examples based on Lampert 1981: 154, Figure 67).

analysis of the assemblage (Figure 8.1). Descriptions of broadly similar and synchronous stone industries, however, had also been defined before by John Mulvaney, for example, at Kenniff Cave (Mulvaney and Joyce 1965). Aspects of this stone tradition have been identified at many of the excavated archaeological sites, for example Nawamoyn, Nauwalabila I, Mandu Mandu Creek, Kenniff Cave, Cloggs Cave, Burrill Lake, Bridgewater Caves, Wyrie Swamp and Kutikina. These sites spread from Arnhem Land in the central north of Australia to Mandu Mandu Creek in the central coast of Western Australia, to the southeastern Australian corner, including Tasmania. The sites date from about 30,000 BP to the terminal Pleistocene–early Holocene period. Identification of the artefacts from these sites was based on typological analyses and in some cases this has involved extensive statistical analysis. Jones (1971a), for example, carried out a detailed typological study of the stone assemblage from Rocky Cape in northwestern Tasmania, which dates from about 8,000 BP, and demonstrated the connection with the Australian Core Tool and Scraper tradition of the Pleistocene Australian mainland.

The latter tradition, however, is not thought to be represented in all Pleistocene sites from Greater Australia, although it is distributed widely across the continent. No reports of similar stone industries have come, for example, from the southwestern Australian sites of Upper Swan or Devil's Lair, nor from Miriwun in northwestern Australia, nor from the sites of southwestern Tasmania, nor from the earliest sites of New Guinea and the Bismarck Archipelago. At Cave Bay Cave in northwestern Tasmania, only a general connection with the broader Australian tradition has been reported (Bowdler 1979). Indeed, a distinctive, regional set of small 'thumbnail' scrapers are found in southwestern Tasmanian sites, mainly from about 17,000 BP until the end of the Pleistocene period (Kiernan et al. 1983; McNiven et al. 1993; McNiven 1994; see also Chapter Seven). Obviously regional as well as local factors have influenced these lithic patterns, and a broader range of variation exists within this earliest of Australian stone artefact traditions. Also, by emphasising typological factors in these systems of classification, other more behavioural factors may be masked. This is clearly borne out, for example, by McNiven's (1994) technological analysis of southwestern Tasmanian 'thumbnail' scrapers (see Chapter Seven), and Hiscock's studies from northwestern Queensland (see Chapter Five).

Other lithic forms, less common and less widespread in some cases, also have been found in Pleistocene Greater Australia. Evidence for hafting has been detected at Devil's Lair in Western Australia, from around 25,000 BP (Dortch 1979a: 269). Gum was found adhering to several stone artefacts, indicating that hafting may have been a feature of the technology. Small adzes were described by Lampert (1980) from the Seton site, beginning from around 16,000 BP, and also from southwestern Australia (see below).

One of the most surprising discoveries, at the time, was of a series of edge-ground axes from the Arnhem Land sites of Malangangerr and Nawamoyn over 20,000 years old, according to the dating (Schrire 1982) (Figure 8.2). Similar and synchronous axes were also found by other researchers in the same general area, and have now also been reported from north Queensland, in contexts perhaps older than 32,000 BP (Morwood and Trezise 1989; Morwood and Hobbs 1995). Evidence of edge-grinding was also found in the Kimberley, at Widgingarri 1, dated about 27,000 BP (O'Connor 1989, 1992), and Miriwun, around 18,000 BP (Dortch 1977). Edge-ground artefacts also have been reported from highland New Guinea in Pleistocene deposits (Kafiavana, Kiowa, Yuku and Nombe). In contrast, edge-ground axes do not appear in southern Australia until the mid-late Holocene period.

Finally, waisted 'blades' or 'axes' of broadly similar form have been found and dated in New Guinea in the Huon Terraces at around 40,000 years BP (Groube et al. 1986) and at Kosipe and Nombe from around 25,000 BP (White et al. 1970) (Figure 8.3). Typologically similar forms have been reported on the Australian mainland, from Kangaroo Island in South Australia and central east-coast Queensland (Lampert 1981). Although the Kangaroo Island artefacts have

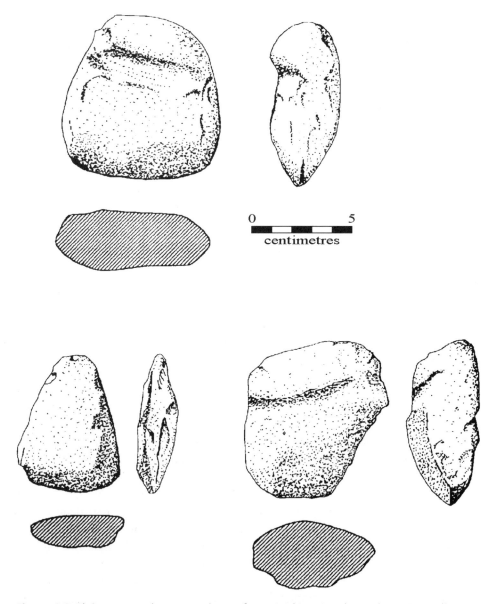

Figure 8.2 Pleistocene edge-ground axes from Arnhem Land, northern Australia (based on White 1971: 148, Figure 12.3).

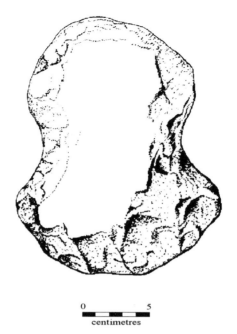

0 ___ 5
centimetres

Figure 8.3 A waisted tool from Kangaroo Island (based on Lampert 1981: 195, Figure 80).

not come from stratigraphically sound or dated context, Lampert argues for a chronological connection with the New Guinean examples on typological and contextual grounds.

Some of the earliest artefacts of bone have been found in rather old contexts, such as at Devil's Lair in southwestern Australia from around 25,000 BP (Dortch 1979a). At Cave Bay Cave, Bowdler (1984) found bone points in levels dated to about 20,000 BP, and these artefacts broadly resemble those from more recent Australian and Tasmanian contexts (see Mulvaney 1995 for further detail).

The best preserved collection of wooden items comes from the Wyrie Swamp in South Australia, dated to between 10,000 and 9,000 BP, that is from the terminal Pleistocene–early Holocene. More than 25 wooden implements were well preserved in the water-logged conditions of the site. Included in this assemblage were three complete boomerangs, which are the oldest yet discovered. A simple short spear, at least two types of digging stick and a fragment of a barbed spear carved from a single piece of wood also were excavated by Luebbers (1975, 1978).

During the Holocene period, mainland Australian stone artefact assemblages indicate marked continuities with earlier traditions and the introduction of new forms of artefacts. Significant variation occurs also in the geographical distribution of artefact types and assemblages, or traditions (as they are termed). These changes are most marked in the late Holocene, from around 5,000–4,000 years ago.

The Australian Small Tool tradition

The suite of new, smaller stone artefacts of the late Holocene were collectively termed by Gould the 'Australian Small Tool tradition' (1969: 234–235). This label has been the general usage ever since, largely serving as a convenient chronological marker. General changes in stone artefacts, together with other cultural markers of the late Holocene, had been recognised since the excavation by Hale and Tindale (1930) of the Devon Downs rock-shelter on the lower Murray River. McCarthy's (1948, 1964) pioneering excavations compounded these impressions and Mulvaney (1966, 1969, 1975: 210; Mulvaney and Joyce 1965) clearly defined this chronological phase in Australian prehistory:

> The innovations in stone tool technology chiefly depended upon the development of blade tool production (with true prismatic core production in some localities) and pressure – and delicate percussion – flaking techniques adapted to the production of the implement classes: points (in great variety), and backed microlith blades ... Burens and elouera also made their appearance. The tula adze, a woodworking chisel tip struck from the core with remarkably consistent obtuse angle, and the edge-ground axe, both types of greater antiquity, became widely adopted during this period. (Mulvaney 1975: 210)

Characteristics of the Small Tool tradition included the production of 'blades', unifacial and bifacial points, and geometric microliths, together with technological changes in core preparation, and controlled flake production (Johnson 1979; Morwood 1981; Hiscock 1994). Fine-grained raw stone materials also appear to have been used, many imported from a distance, and a reduction in the overall size of tools is also apparent. Regional diversity in stone artefact assemblages is also a characteristic of this tradition. We now turn to discuss some of the main categories of artefacts.

Backed blades

According to F. D. McCarthy, backed blades comprise 102 formal shapes. Practically, however, there are two major typological categories – geometric microliths and asymmetric points, often termed Bondi points. Some archaeologists consider the two categories to be part of a continuum but, despite their quantitative argument, differential distributions seem to undermine this. All are characterised by blunting retouch on the thickest margin (Mulvaney 1975: 211) (Figure 8.4).

These blades or flakes are generally less than 5 cm in length. Morphological variation has been observed within and between regions (Mulvaney and Joyce 1965; Glover 1967, 1969; Wieneke and White 1973), but finer definition of spatial and chronological patterns is now required. Backed blades are distributed across the southern two-thirds of the continent, and extend as far north as northwestern Queensland (Hiscock and Hughes 1980). They are found extensively in southeastern Australia, including the coastal zone, but also in

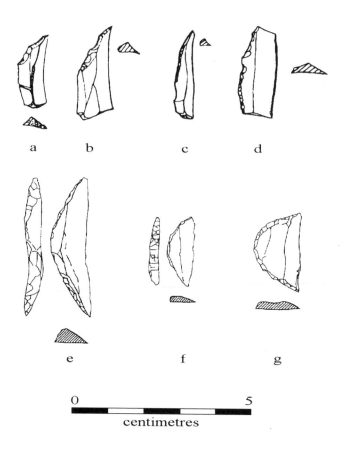

0   5

centimetres

Figure 8.4 Australian microliths. 'Backed' blades from Bridgewater South Cave, southwestern Victoria, dating from the last 500 years (a–d) (after Lourandos 1980a); and from Kenniff Cave, Queensland (e, f) and Pialago, A.C.T. (g), dating from the late Holocene (based on Mulvaney 1969: 125, Figure 29).

southwestern Australia (Dortch 1975) and central western Australia (Lorblanchet and Jones 1979). The distribution of backed blades includes, therefore, all major Australian environmental zones, including parts of the northern tropical belt. Expanded research in this region will undoubtedly clarify details for this area. Backed artefacts have been reported from the tropical Kimberley region of northwestern Australia (Dortch 1977: 117), but the closeness of their association with backed blades is disputed (White and O'Connell 1982: 113).

The timing of the introduction of these blades is also still open to question. Dates for backed blades older than 5,000 years have been reported from a number of sites, including Graman (McBryde 1974: 321), Currarong I and Burrill Lake

(Lampert 1971; Hughes and Djohadze 1980: 26), and Puntutjarpa (Gould 1977a). The reliability of all these dates, however, has been challenged (Johnson 1979). One problem, for example, is that these early backed blades have come from loose sandy deposits where disturbance is likely to have occurred. Apart from these examples, the earliest acceptable dates for the introduction of backed blades is between 4,500 and 4,000 years ago, in the central Queensland highlands (Mulvaney 1975: 290; Morwood 1981: 43).

The appearance of backed blades in New South Wales is somewhat more recent, occurring between 4,000 and 3,500 BP, and perhaps more recently. Sites where these introductions are found to have occurred include Seelands (McBryde 1974: 183) and Lapstone Creek (McCarthy 1978: 55), as well as Wilson's Promontory in southern Victoria. Evidence from the southern Australian Murray Valley sites of Devon Downs (Tindale 1957: 3) and Fromm's Landing (Mulvaney 1960: 70) also is generally consistent. At Carpetee 3, the introduction of the new artefacts appears even more recent, around 3,000 BP (McCarthy 1964; Johnson 1979).

Backed blades also appear to have been short-lived in some sites and areas, and in general to either dwindle in importance or disappear altogether in the last 1,000 years or so. Regional chronological sequences, where they have been developed, generally indicate significant variation in artefact assemblages during the last two millennia. In central Queensland, for example, backed blades are absent after 2,300 BP, and are replaced by unretouched stone chips (Morwood 1981: 44). The latter trend is also apparent in southeastern Australia (southeastern New South Wales), where the production of unretouched stone chips (often of quartz) was associated with the bipolar technique (Lampert 1975: 199). In this region, detailed sequences have been compiled of the stone artefact assemblages of the last few thousand years, where the backed blade phase is referred to as the Bondian period (Johnson 1979; Kohen et al. 1984; Attenbrow 1987).

In other areas these blades are still present in the last 500 years or so. This is the case for the New England Tablelands, the Clarence River Valley (McBryde 1974: 183, 295), the Western Desert (Gould 1977b: 103), and southwestern Victoria (Bridgewater South cave) (Lourandos 1980a, 1983a). While admixture with more recent sediments may be a problem for dating material from some sites (Morwood 1981: 44), this is not so for the southwestern Victoria information.

Many researchers have also reported that backed blades were manufactured from high quality raw materials (Gould 1977a, 1978b; Lampert 1981; Johnson 1979), the source of which was often located far from the sites in which they were found (White and O'Connell 1982: 120). Examples of the latter include coastal and coastal highland New South Wales (Hughes et al. 1973), where stone was transported over 150 kilometres (Etheridge and Whitelegge 1907); north coast New South Wales, where distances of 100 kilometres were involved (McBryde 1974: 374–379); and central Australia (Gould 1977a: 124–125, 1978a).

The function of backed blades has been widely debated and researched (Kamminga 1978). Adhering gum, or resin, on some prehistoric specimens clearly indicates that they were hafted, and probably in composite implements (McBryde 1974: 264–265; Morwood 1981: 43). It is generally assumed that many of the blades served as barbs, such as those of ethnographic ritual and hunting lances, referred to as 'death spears' (Lampert 1971; Mulvaney 1975: 108; Kamminga 1978, 1982). Lack of use-wear on many examples indicates that they did not serve as knives or gravers (Kamminga 1978, 1982; White and O'Connell 1982: 123).

Points

Items which form a second key category of late Holocene artefact are unifacial and bifacial points. Points are flakes modified by partial or total secondary working. They range in size from around 2.0 cms to 20 cms, but average sizes are at the lower end of the range. Unifacial points include the more common pirri point, and the longer lelira 'blades', which often are unretouched (McCarthy et al. 1946: 32). Smaller points, termed as 'Levallois', have also been recognised (Dortch 1977; Dortch and Bordes 1977). Bifacial points include the distinctive Kimberley points which are 2–10 cms in length and modified by percussion or pressure flaking. Kimberley points, fashioned on glass or porcelain, often have serrated edges, are up to 20 cms in length and are thought to be of post-European contact age (McCarthy et al. 1946). Serrated-edged points of prehistoric date have, however, also been found, for example at Ingaladdi in the Northern Territory (Mulvaney 1975: 217) (Figure 8.5).

Points appear to be distributed mainly in a north–south path across the middle of the continent, with bifacial points restricted to the tropical north (Mulvaney 1975: 217). Unifacial points are found throughout the region, together with bifacial points in the north, and alone in the south (South Australia, western New South Wales, and southwestern Queensland) (Morwood 1981: 44). More recent excavations, however, indicate that the distribution of points is even more widespread, with specimens coming, for example, from coastal southeastern Queensland (McNiven 1993) (see below this chapter).

A conservative reading of the chronological sequence for the introduction of stone points suggests a date some time after 5,000 BP. This evidence includes sites from the Ord River Valley (Western Australia), where around 3,000 BP a new stone industry appeared at Miriwun, which included prismatic blades, points (unifacial, bifacial, backed), edge-ground axes and grindstones (Dortch 1977: 109). Bowdler and O'Connor (1991) have recently argued, from evidence derived in the Kimberley, that the Australian Small Tool tradition in the region is no older than 4,500 BP. Sites from other north Australian regions are in western Arnhem Land, and north and central Queensland (Morwood 1981: 44; White and O'Connell 1982: 117–120). The one exception is the evidence from Nauwalabila I (Lindner), western Arnhem Land, where it has been argued by

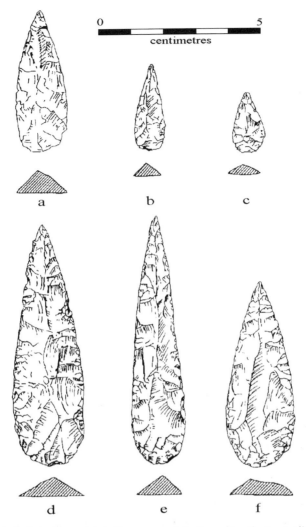

Figure 8.5 Unifacially trimmed 'pirri' stone points from South Australia (a, b, d–f) and Queensland (c) (based on Mulvaney 1969: 120, Figure 27).

the excavators that bifacial stone points were introduced prior to around 5,500 BP (also Hiscock 1993; Clarkson and David 1995) (see Chapter Four, above).

In some areas and sites, stone points have a restricted chronology. For example, in the central Queensland highlands, pirri points were used only briefly, around 4,300 BP (Morwood 1981: 44). Broken points are common in archaeological deposits and ethnographic accounts indicate that in northern Australia points were hafted as spear tips, while in South Australia they were used for engraving (see also Kamminga 1978: 328–338; 1982).

In general, stone points and backed blades overlap in both time and space across the continent. Both types conclusively appear some time after 5,000 BP,

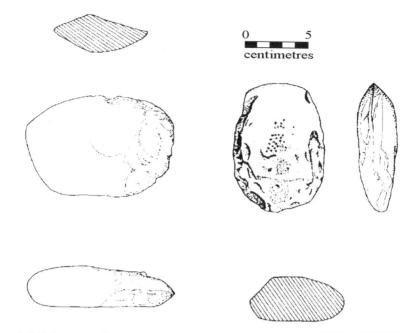

Figure 8.6 Holocene edge-ground axes from Seal Point, Cape Otway, southwestern Victoria. Both examples date to the last 1,000 years (based on Lourandos 1980a).

although not necessarily together, and are differentially distributed at a regional level.

Other stone artefact types also are included with the Australian Small Tool tradition, in particular the elouera (McCarthy et al. 1946: 28; Mulvaney 1975: 231–233; Kamminga 1978), and large juan 'knives' and other blades in northern Australia (Morwood 1981).

Adzes and axes (hatchets)

Although not strictly a part of the Australian Small Tool tradition, both adzes and ground (often edge-ground) stone axes or hatchets are associated with late Holocene assemblages (Figures 8.6, 8.7). Both forms had a longer ancestry, with ground stone hatchets occurring in Pleistocene tropical areas and adzes from late Pleistocene times in various localities (see Chapter Four). Both forms, however, were more widespread in distribution and more numerous during the late Holocene. At this time hatchets are found throughout the continent, but less so in southwestern Australia; while tula adzes are rare in the more fertile regions of southeastern and southwestern Australia. Both adzes and ground stone hatchets (or by-products of their manufacture and use) are common in assemblages associated with small backed artefacts of the last few thousand years. They also occur up to the time of European contact. Ethnographic examples of both hatchets and adzes indicate the importance of the former in exchange, and in terms of prestige and general utility (see Chapter Six). Both types were used for

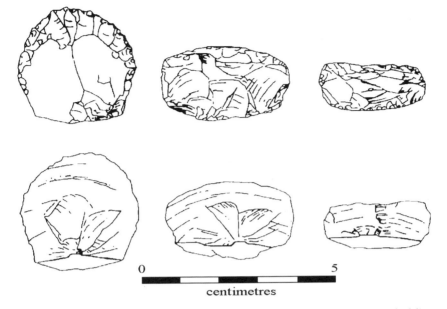

0   5
centimetres

Figure 8.7 Tula adze flakes indicating varying degrees of wear from Ingaladdi, northern Australia (based on Mulvaney 1969: 114, Figure 23).

woodworking (Mulvaney 1975; see also below). Investigation of large assemblages of ground stone hatchets suggests a rather homogeneous morphology throughout Australia (Dickson 1978).

'Burren' adzes, somewhat like small steep-edged 'scrapers', are distributed, for example, in northeastern Australia (southeastern Cape York) from the mid-Holocene and are more common in late Holocene deposits (Morwood 1993; David 1994: 143; Morwood and Hobbs 1995). In southeastern Australia, small 'adzes' appear from about 16,000 BP on Kangaroo Island, and are common in late Holocene sites, for example, along the south coast of New South Wales (Lampert 1971, 1981). Similar examples have also been detected in terminal Pleistocene–early Holocene contexts at Puntutjarpa and Devil's Lair in Western Australia.

In contrast, tula adzes are classic examples of arid region artefacts. In central Australia ethnographic examples of these small tools are used as woodworking 'chisels', often attached with spinifex gum to wooden handles or to the end of a spear thrower. They are frequently made on stone flakes, and rejuvenated by being re-used on their opposing (distal) end (Figure 8.7). Spent tula 'slugs' are commonly found in late Holocene archaeological deposits of the arid and semi-arid zones in particular, where they appear to have become a somewhat specialised tool type of this period (see Chapter Five). Tulas have also been found at this time as far east as southeast Queensland in the Caloola area, along with bifacial points; and McNiven (1993) argues for long-distance connections with inland regions via extensive social networks, such as those of southeastern Queensland established around the fruiting of the bunya nut (see Chapters Two and Four).

It is argued here that explanations of these changes in stone artefact assemblages cannot be dissociated from the wider socio-cultural changes of the late Holocene. A wide range of interpretations have been offered, however, and I now discuss some of the main ones. Taking a technological perspective, Lampert (1981) argued that the changes were the latter stages in a long-term general chronological trend of a reduction in size of stone artefacts, stemming from late Pleistocene times. On the other hand, Morwood, among others, viewed the process as a relatively sudden and rapid change (1981; but also see Morwood 1993; Morwood and Hobbs 1995). From a broader socio-cultural viewpoint, Lampert (1980) and Gould (1978a) both suggested that the increased use of raw materials and new tool types during this period indicated an expansion of exchange and ritual relations between local populations. In general, an interpretation couched in social terms was also preferred by White and O'Connell, who suggested that the new tools largely indicated stylistic and social changes:

> The extraordinarily rapid spread of new tools throughout Australia and their local variations in size, shape, raw materials and numbers are all compatible with this idea: so too is the fact that major classes occurred over almost the entire range of Australian environments, though not throughout any major environmental zones . . . (1982: 124, see also 133)

They also suggested that the spread of ground stone hatchets during this period may have been associated with a change in exchange relations (as well as food procurement) (1982: 128–129).

Mulvaney had previously considered the last thousand years or so as an expansion of socio-economic behaviour, that is, as an 'optimum adjustment to local conditions' (1969: 9). Alternatively, Jones had argued for the increased efficiency of the items of stone equipment themselves (1977a). Later studies, however, have moved away from typological approaches to the problem and have focused upon the technological aspects of stone assemblages (Hiscock 1986; Mitchell 1988; Hiscock and Hall 1988). For example, in explaining the shift to use of 'blades' in southeastern Australia during the late Holocene, Hiscock argues that this 'transition cannot be described in terms of the appearance of a blade technology; instead it represents an increase in the regularity and precision of knapping related to raw material conservation' (1993: 65). He concludes: 'the issue that remains to be investigated is the cause for this imperative to conserve material that apparently intensified during the mid-late Holocene' (1993: 75). Morwood also employs a technological approach in analysing his recent archaeological sequences in Cape York, Queensland, and in distinguishing between late Holocene occupation from that of earlier, including Pleistocene, periods (Morwood 1993; Morwood and Hobbs 1995).

The issue of whether the new tools were introduced to Australia from external sources or developed within the continent is also the subject of some debate (White 1971; McCarthy 1977: 254–256; Mulvaney 1977: 211). Backed blades and points have been reported from Southeast Asia – the Macassar area of Sulawesi – during the mid-late Holocene period (Mulvaney and Soejono 1970; Glover 1976, 1978), but are absent from regions closer to Australia, such as Timor and New Guinea.

The introduction of the dingo

Many have associated the appearance of the Australian Small Tool tradition with the roughly synchronous arrival of the dingo on the Australian continent during the late Holocene. Archaeological investigations have placed the introduction of the domesticated dog or dingo at no earlier than 4,000 years ago (Gollan 1984). Authenticated evidence positions the dingo stratigraphically between about 3,500 and 3.000 BP. These data come from sites in southern Australia, including Wombah on the north coast of New South Wales, Fromm's Landing on the Murray River and Madura Cave on the Nullarbor Plain, Western Australia (also Narcurrer in South Australia, personal observation). On the strength of this evidence, Gollan argues for a northern introduction of this animal about 4,000 years ago, and its subsequent spread throughout the continent and arrival in southern regions sometime later, as the above dates suggest.

Gollan's study linked the dingo morphologically to prehistoric dogs in India. Comparisons were made with examples from Burzahom in Kashmir, and to domesticated dogs from the city of Harappa, during the Indus Valley civilisation of between 4,000 and 3,500 years ago. Corbett's (1985) investigations are broadly in agreement, connecting the dingo to wild dogs found throughout southern mainland Asia and Southeast Asia, descendants of the Indian wolf (*Canis lupus pallipes*).

In Aboriginal society, as we know it, dingoes existed in both a domesticated and wild, or feral, state. Many Aboriginal communities cherished these dogs which performed a variety of roles, for example as domestic and hunting companions. Other groups did not keep dogs. Wild dingoes also roamed the bush, and in some parts, like the Otway forests of southwestern Victoria, they were feared by local Aboriginal people (Lourandos 1980a).

Dingoes appear to have competed with and eliminated two native carnivores on the Australian mainland. Both the Tasmanian devil (*Sarcophilus*) and Tasmanian tiger (*Thylacinus*) became extinct on mainland Australia during the last three thousand years or so, coinciding with the presence of the dingo. In Tasmania, however, where dingoes did not penetrate, both these native animals survived into historical times, that is, into the colonial period.

CHAPTER 9

INTERPRETATIONS

We now draw together all strands of arguments from the preceding chapters and consider Australian prehistory in terms of its long- and short-term dynamics. Emphasis is placed on how Australian Aboriginal society adapted to both natural and socio-cultural environments; and upon variation in all aspects, including demography, economy and society, in time and space (as discussed in Chapter One). An attempt has been made to incorporate both cultural–ecological and social theory. Also, the interpretations will consider varied spatio-temporal scales (that is, long- and short-term trends) at local, regional and continental geographical levels. The arguments included here are a development of prior studies of mine (Lourandos 1980a, 1980b: 419–424, 1983a, 1985a, 1987a, 1993) in light of new evidence.

Pleistocene patterns

First, the continent of Greater Australia must have been colonised prior to about 40,000 years ago, the time of our earliest evidence. From all indications the colonists arrived from Southeast Asia by sea, and can be counted amongst the earliest of modern human populations. The continent they traversed was colder and drier than it is today and extensively forested, with large stretches of fresh water, even in more arid regions. Even so, the evidence of these first settlers is slight, although it comes from three corners of the continent: north (New Guinea and north Queensland), southeast (including Tasmania) and southwest, suggesting that much of the continent had been traversed.

Second, between about 40,000 and 30,000 years ago, a wide range of environments, from tropical to temperate, had been occupied, if only relatively sparsely. These include New Guinea, the offshore islands of New Ireland and

New Britain, and parts of coastal northwestern and central-western Australia, where the earliest evidence exists for marine exploitation, the semi-arid zone, the southwest, as well as the southeast (including Tasmania).

Then, as climate became increasingly drier and colder, between about 30,000 and 20,000 years ago, most environmental zones of the continent were utilised, including the most extreme (the arid and highland zones). Even in resource-rich zones, however, such as inland lacustrine areas of the southeast, occupation during this period in general appears to have been rather transient as compared with more recent periods.

During the glacial maximum when seas were lowest, and climate coldest and driest, between about 20,000 and 17,000 years ago, sites generally continued to be established in most environments, along with the abandonment of some sites. In general, at this time, Aboriginal populations may have concentrated to a greater extent within the more humid belt, and its refugia, which extends around the northern, eastern and southern parts of the continent (including parts of Tasmania). Refugia, however, also were to be found in arid areas, including central Australia.

Finally, with the amelioration of climate from about 16,000 to 10,000 years ago, an increased use of many regions took place, and there is also evidence of some changes to economic and settlement patterns These areas include the more climatically marginal arid and highland zones (for example, in central Australia, New Guinea, southeastern Australia, southwestern Tasmania) and also, perhaps, New Ireland and New Britain. Further increases in forestation may have led to the final abandonment of sites in southwestern Tasmania. Territorial markers (cemeteries in this case) have been recorded in the Murray River corridor from around 13,000 years ago, perhaps indicating spatial constraints to Aboriginal settlement taking place towards the terminal Pleistocene.

The archaeological evidence, therefore, indicates a general steady occupation of new sites, and in some cases increased usage of established sites, *throughout* the Pleistocene, including the glacial maximum of around 18,000 years ago. The most significant increases, however, in site establishment and use are recorded in the late and terminal Pleistocene, that is after about 17,000 years ago (Lourandos and David in prep., b). In support of this very general observation, an examination of existing Pleistocene sites throughout Greater Australia (using thousand-year intervals) indicates a steady growth in site numbers between 30,000 and 10,000 BP (Figure 9.1) (Smith and Sharp 1993). An amendment of this general model, based upon regional differences, also has been recently suggested, principally from western Australia. This alternative general model indicates a decline in site use, and presumably population growth, during the glacial maximum (Figure 9.2). At this time also cultural rearrangements, for example in territorial size within refuges, have been suggested (O'Connor et al. 1993). Further archaeological data are now required to test these general models and at finer-grained levels.

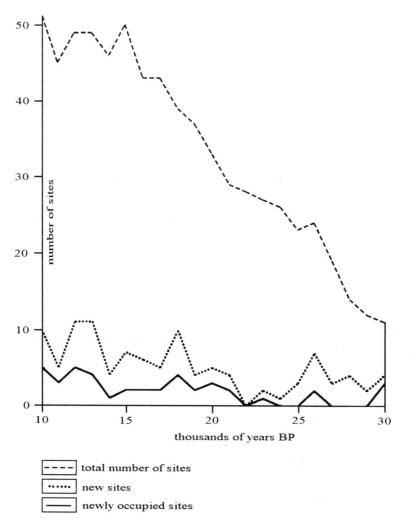

Figure 9.1 Temporal changes in the total number of occupied sites, and also in the rates of site establishment and use, between 30,000 and 10,000 BP, throughout Australia (using 1,000 year intervals) (based on Smith and Sharp 1993: 52, Figure 8).

This archaeological information, therefore, does not appear to support earlier models of rapid colonisation of the continent, followed by a stabilising of population levels which were largely controlled by environmental factors, such as the distribution of rainfall (Birdsell 1953, 1957, 1977; also Allen 1989a; see also below). Only relatively sparse signs of Aboriginal occupation (with some exceptions) existed prior to about 30,000–25,000 BP, when more humid conditions, and presumably more widespread resources, prevailed. That is, when generally higher levels of bioproductivity existed throughout the continent. Further research will undoubtedly clarify this impression. Doubt is also cast on explanations which view a stabilisation of population and economy from around

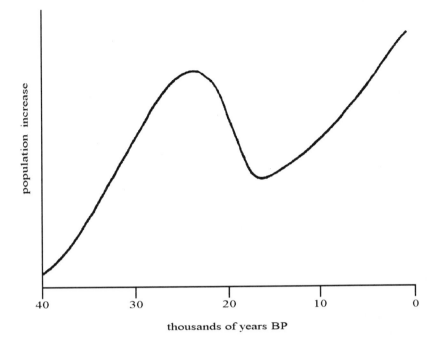

Figure 9.2 An alternative model of population growth throughout Australian prehistory indicating a decline in population towards the glacial maximum, followed by a steady increase, continuing from the terminal Pleistocene and throughout the Holocene period right up to the present (based on O'Connor et al. 1993: 95, Figure 1).

25,000 BP, the time of the Mungo I site (Jones 1979; White and O'Connell 1982: 55–56).

The introduction of the use of grass seeds is now less likely a possibility in semi-arid areas during the terminal Pleistocene. Intensification of resource use appears instead to be a late Holocene development. The Pleistocene archaeological information also fails to support hypotheses favouring major ecological destabilisation which accompany the model of rapid colonisation of Greater Australia. For example, there is no evidence for megafaunal overkill or large-scale environmental degradation, as has been speculated (for example, Jones 1968; Merrilees 1968; also Flannery 1990).

I have argued here that, in general, Pleistocene settlement patterns and economies may have been more mobile and specialised than those of more recent times in mainland Australia, with their lower population densities. While these general patterns may have varied locally and regionally (for example, in New Guinea and its offshore islands and southwestern Tasmania, especially after about 17,000 years ago), and been influenced by regional resource structure to some extent, I suggest that overall they conformed to the latter *general* pattern. Social networks *generally* may have been more 'open' and therefore less complex in form when compared to those of recent times in mainland Australia. Further support for the latter position can be obtained from Pleistocene rock art, which (although poorly dated in general) appears to be more homogeneous, suggesting more open social networks. These features may help to explain the contraction of populations around more humid areas during the most arid phase approaching the glacial maximum, a pattern or response which contrasts with those evidenced during a drier phase of the late Holocene (see below).

As the evidence stands, at the most general level of analysis, Pleistocene society appears to emphasise 'residential' ('mapping-on') economic strategies and 'immediate-return' systems, although recent data would also suggest more complex regional patterns. As far as we can tell, none of the general 'pathways' of hunter-gatherer resource intensification appear to have been expanded during the Pleistocene (as noted in Chapter One). Evidence does exist in some areas, however, to suggest alterations to economic and settlement patterns during the terminal Pleistocene, which in some ways may indicate the development of greater complexity (see also Chapter One). This takes place after about 17,000 years ago, in far-flung parts of the continent including the New Guinea Highlands, New Ireland, semi-arid New South Wales, the Murray River corridor and southwestern Tasmania. In parts of western Australia this may have taken place even somewhat earlier. Variations to the general pattern outlined above, therefore, existed and further examples may turn up in future archaeological investigations (Lourandos and David in prep., b).

Holocene patterns

Early Holocene (c. 10,000–8,000 BP)

The warmer, more humid climate and rising sea levels of this period produced significant alterations to the distribution of natural resources, including vegetation patterns and coastal landscapes. To some degree the archaeological patterns of Aboriginal settlement reflect these major environmental changes. Increases in numbers of sites and the intensity of usage of individual sites has been registered in a number of Australian regions, for example, in highland areas recolonised by forests at this time. These uplands regions include those of New Guinea, northeastern Queensland, the Central Queensland Highlands, the Blue Mountains of New South Wales, and northwestern and northeastern Tasmania. In some regions, for example the southeastern highlands of Australia, this trend has, however, not been observed. Complex swamp management practices appear in highland New Guinea before the region was severed from mainland Australia some time after about 8,000 years ago. Within the Murray River corridor also, a continuation of territoriality took place, indicated by the use of cemeteries.

The encroachment of the rising post-glacial sea upon the present coastline was announced by the occupation of sites in a number of widespread Australian locations, for example, southwestern Victoria and Kangaroo Island, the south and north coasts of New South Wales, the north coast of Queensland and Arnhem Land. Similar effects were experienced in parts of northwestern and northeastern Tasmania.

Early–mid-Holocene (c. 8,000–5,000 BP)

This was, in general, the most humid phase of the Holocene, characterised by the stabilisation of sea levels and generally more humid conditions inland, with higher lake levels in areas including southeastern Australia. Forests, including rainforest, were most extensive at this time. New sites continued to be established, and some sites were more intensively utilised at this time in coastal and inland areas. Overall, apart from these instances, however, there is no suggestion of a territorial expansion (or dispersal) of Aboriginal population commensurate with changing patterns of resource distribution and bioproduction. For example, there is no evidence of the spread of populations into arid or semi-arid areas (for example, in the northwestern Victorian Mallee) as more humid conditions became established, nor of significant use of the extensive wetlands of western Victoria and southeastern south Australia, nor of the highlands of the southeastern Australian mainland where temperatures had risen. In contrast, expansion into all these areas is more marked in the late Holocene.

Mid-late Holocene (c. 5,000 BP–the present)

The climate of this period was, in general, drier and cooler, and especially drier about 3,000 years ago with fluctuations in the last 1,000 years or so. By comparison with earlier phases of Australian prehistory, the most marked increases in numbers, establishment and use of sites took place from around 4,000 years ago, and these trends were most pronounced after about 3,000 years ago, in particular in the last 1,000 years or so. This general pattern has been detected in a wide range of Australian regions, and especially in southeastern Australia. No doubt research bias has affected the latter distribution. Aspects of these trends also have been found in a broad range of Australian environments including the temperate zone (southeast); highlands (southeastern); coastal (from temperate to tropical along the eastern seaboard of Australia, including Cape York, and northwestern Australia, and offshore islands of these areas); semi-arid (northwestern Victoria, western New South Wales); and arid zone (central Australia). Slightly different trends have been reported from southwestern Australia, where the evidence is somewhat equivocal. More information is also required now from central northern Australia, for example Arnhem Land, where, as I have argued (see above Chapter Four), aspects of these trends also are evident.

In Tasmania also, the early Holocene phase of forest expansion (including rainforest) was halted by drier conditions in the last 3,500 years or so, resulting in Aboriginal occupation of previously densely forested areas of northwestern and western Tasmania. This appears to have been associated with an expansion of Aboriginal populations in these areas, including the appearance of long-term coastal base camps and seasonal use of offshore islands. Aboriginal burning practices also must have checked the resurgence of forests, caused by more humid climate, in the last two thousand years or so.

Archaeological patterns

Broadly similar archaeological patterns to those described in the preceding section are indicated for a number of regions in southeastern Australia, which include southwestern and northwestern Victoria, southeastern South Australia, and, to some extent, the mouth of the Murray, as well as Cloggs Cave in southeastern Victoria. A similar chronological sequence and pattern has been noted in the southeastern highlands.

In general the sequences in these areas indicate that the trend towards increases in usage and rate of establishment of sites increased between about 3,500 and 3,000 years ago, with the greatest increments taking place in the last 2,000 years. Some areas and sites (for example, southwestern Victoria, southeastern South Australia, Cloggs Cave and the southeastern highlands) appear to have been most intensively inhabited in the last 1,000 years or so. In all, in this region, from around 3,500 to 3,000 years ago up to the historical period, there is a trend towards progressively more intensive habitation of sites and of the region itself.

Other factors are also related to this trend in southeastern Australia:
(i)   the most complex sites are of this recent period. These sites are larger, more complex in their range of resources, functions and activities, and more intensively inhabited;
(ii)   particular environments (including habitats peripheral to heartlands of settlement) are more intensively occupied during the last few thousand years. These environments include highlands, rainforests, arid and semi-arid areas, and parts of wetlands;
(iii) the evidence of the last 3,000 to 2,000 years, or less, also suggests more complex exchange systems and ceremonial activity as is indicated by the distribution of exotic stone, axes, art and ceremonial sites, which although they are poorly dated appear generally to be of this period.

Evidence of aspects of these trends also comes from other Australian regions including the following:
(i)   other parts of southeastern Australia including the south coast of New South Wales, the Blue Mountains, and the Upper Mangrove Creek region near Sydney;
(ii)   inland regions, including the semi-arid western New South Wales, where there is a late Holocene proliferation of sites, and where Burkes Cave is most intensively occupied in the last thousand years or so;
(iii) arid central Australia (and the Sandy desert region of the northwest), where there is an increase in site establishment and use, together with

an apparent intensification of cereal production, in the last 2,000 years or so;

(iv) southeastern Queensland during the last 2,000–1,000 years, where there is an indication of increased site establishment and use, intensification of resources (fish and perhaps plants, such as bracken fern), and greater use of certain environments (islands, highlands and rainforest);

(v) coastal Queensland where the more intensive use of islands appears to be more recent than 3,000 years ago (Keppel Islands and Whitsunday Islands). A greater emphasis upon marine resources and use of toxic plants occur on the Whitsundays during this recent period;

(vi) Princess Charlotte Bay in north Queensland, where there is an increase in site use and numbers, marine exploitation, and use of offshore islands during the last 2,000–1,000 years;

(vii) Cape York, north Queensland, where a relatively large archaeological sample indicates that there is a steady increase in site numbers and their usage throughout the early-mid Holocene, accelerating during the last 3,000 years or so, and occurring contemporaneously with significant changes in rock art styles;

(viii) rainforest regions of north Queensland, between Bowen and Cairns, which appear to have been most intensively occupied during the last 5,000 years and especially during the last 2,000 years. The processing of toxic plants, for example, appears to have been accentuated in the last 2,000 years or so;

(ix) offshore islands of the eastern seaboard of Australia generally appear to have been either first, or more intensively, utilised in the last 3,000 years and, in some cases, only the last 1,000 years;

(x) the evidence from the northwestern Kimberley area (Miriwun) and offshore islands (for example, Koolan Island) in general indicates more intensive use of these areas during the late Holocene, and more field results are now awaited to further test these propositions.

There are also some variations in the perceived archaeological trends. In the central Queensland highlands the period of greatest intensity of site establishment and use is between about 3,000 and 2,000–1,000 years ago, with some decreases indicated in the most recent phase. Aspects of this apparently decreasing trend in site use are also indicated in the New England Tablelands and Hunter Valley of New South Wales, and in the coastal region north of Sydney. Some caution also needs to be introduced, however, when evaluating supposed decreases in discard rates in the upper levels of soft, sandy deposits, as often occurred in rock-shelters.

The interpretation of archaeological sequences is less clear in some regions, for example in the Alligator Rivers region of Arnhem Land. Here rich archaeological deposits exist from the mid-Holocene, with the most complex phases (in terms of numbers of sites, site usage, economy, artefacts and rock art) taking place also in the last 3,000 years. It is not clear, however, whether these cultural changes solely reflect adaptations to changing local environmental circumstances or perhaps that they also indicate more intensive and complex occupation of the region as a whole, as is indicated in late Holocene archaeological sequences from other parts of Australia. At the very least, I would argue that both environmental and socio-cultural factors are involved, and that the second explanation is the more likely.

An evaluation of results

General support for the above results are found in the following ways. The archaeological trends of the Holocene period have been reported by a large number of independent researchers now extending over a period of some twenty-five years or so and from a wide range of natural environments. In some areas especially, a wide spectrum of archaeological site types and forms has been considered. For example, in southwestern Victoria (and southeastern South Australia) the model for the area includes caves, rock-shelters, open habitation sites (including earth mounds), drainage systems and fish traps, and these have been located in a range of environments, including the coast and estuary, the hinterland, as well as wetlands, peripheral rainforest and highlands. In recent years there has been a four-fold increase in the archaeological data base of the region.

On the debit side, however, a range of problems also exist, and many of these have attracted the attention of researchers. Sample size, for example, will always remain a problem, given the fragmentary nature of archaeological evidence. In many of the areas discussed, however, the excavated samples can be considerably expanded by the introduction of large numbers of surface sites. The distribution of surface sites generally supports the trends observed from the excavated sample. This is particularly true of areas such as southwestern Victoria (Lourandos 1980a, 1980b, 1983a), the southeastern highlands (Flood 1980), semi-arid western New South Wales (Allen 1972), the Central Desert (Smith 1985, 1986, 1988 and northwestern Australia (O'Connor 1992). Greater chronological control of this extensive surface material now needs to be developed.

A central issue concerns site formation processes. Discussion has centred upon a number of outstanding problems, which include taphonomy, sedimentology, the measurement of the intensity of site use, assessment of destruction of earlier evidence, as well as the examination of cultural and demographic patterns. These issues have been discussed by a large number of researchers in a wide range of regions, for example, south coast New South Wales by Hughes and Lampert (1982); northwestern Victoria by Ross (1981, 1985); southwestern Victoria and southeastern South Australia by Luebbers (1978, 1981, 1984), Lourandos

(1983a), Head (1983, 1986, 1989), Williams (1987), Godfrey (1989) and Bird and Frankel (1991a, 1991b); Upper Mangrove Creek, New South Wales by Attenbrow (1987); Arnhem Land by Jones (1985a); coastal Queensland by Rowland (1989); Princess Charlotte Bay, north Queensland by Beaton (1985), Cribb (1986) and David (1991, 1994); northern coastal Australia by O'Connor and Sullivan (1994); and the arid zone by Smith (1986, 1989b, also 1985) and Veth (1989a, 1989b). (See also above, Chapters Four to Six).

Broadly similar issues also have been discussed more recently in regard to earlier phases of Australian prehistory, including the Pleistocene (Lourandos in press). For example, assessment of intensity of site use (together with numbers of occupied sites) were indices employed to compare differential settlement and demographic patterns in southwestern and eastern parts of Pleistocene Tasmania (Cosgrove et al. 1989; Cosgrove 1995; Holdaway and Porch 1995), sectors of western Australia (O'Connor et al. 1993), and the sites of Pleistocene Greater Australia in general (Smith and Sharp 1993; O'Connell and Allen 1995; and compare Frankel 1993). Generally similar analyses were also used in assessing occupation of key Pleistocene sites in the southeastern Australian highlands (Flood et al. 1987) and in more northern parts of the continent – Arnhem Land (Jones 1985a), central Australia (Smith 1989b), northwestern Queensland (Hiscock 1984, 1988), northern Queensland (David 1991) and New Ireland (Allen et al. 1988).

Chronological trends and patterns

I now consider overall trends and patterns of late Holocene mainland Australia in light of the above interpretations and issues. I argue that chronological trends are recognisable especially during the mid-late Holocene period in parts of mainland Australia (also Lourandos 1985a: 398–402). The main point is that these trends and patterns do not fit any one environmental trend (regional or more general), although environmental factors may be associated. The evidence indicates that these trends are not a *direct* reflection of changes in regional resource structure during this period. Instead, often they apparently run counter to the regional environmental trend. The late Holocene evidence contrasts also with in some ways broadly comparable trends of the late Pleistocene, for example in other parts of Australia and Tasmania and sectors of western Australia (above), which can be explained as more closely linked to changing climate and the related resource structure. The Pleistocene archaeological trends in general can be seen to more closely fit environmental trends of this period (Lourandos and David in prep., b).

The argument offered here is that this late Holocene information is suggestive of more intensive use of land and resources (that is, of specialisation both extensive and intensive), more intensive use of sites and locales, or more sedentary behaviour (that is, a trend toward the establishment of longer-term base camps), and thus increasing territoriality and more intensive intergroup relations of all kinds. The suggestion here is of denser populations with perhaps long-term increases in population. It should be stressed that these characteristics appear not only along the coastal strip, but also inland, including parts of central Australia. Examples of inland long-term base camps include earth mounds and large open sites, and this trend is reinforced by the more intensive use of other sites (including rock-shelters and caves) during this same period (Lourandos 1985a: 400).

The suggestion here is of changing – that is, dynamic – patterns of land use and intergroup relations, indicating changes in territorial relationships and their impact upon people, land and resources. The latter may have been expressed in terms of increased and changing levels of territoriality, boundary maintenance, intergroup aggregations and population density; that is, of changing socio-demographic patterns and their effect upon land and resources. While increases are evident, so too are decreases in some instances, suggesting overall a dynamic series of patterns on a general continental scale, but also with distinct regional and local signatures.

These general trends can be viewed in relation to models of hunter-gatherer variation and change as outlined in Chapter One. For example, as regards the five possible 'pathways' of hunter-gatherer economic intensification, four appear to have been amplified during the mid-late Holocene in mainland Australia: (a) harvesting of grass seeds; (b) harvesting of roots and tubers; (c) gathering of tree nuts (cycads, and possibly bunya nuts); (d) fishing and hunting of aquatic mammals (dugong) (Lourandos 1980b, 1985a: 401). Management, or environmental manipulation, of some of these resource groups is also suggested. Ethnographic evidence indicates that all three plant groups (that is, a, b and c) were managed by fire, and in southwestern Victoria, fish (eels) were manipulated by extensive water controls which are still archaeologically visible.

In relation to settlement patterns, a trend is suggested towards increasing 'logistical' organisation. This is indicated by changes in settlement patterns towards an increasing use and establishment of sites and locales, and larger, more complex sites. The wider implications of these trends in settlement suggest increasingly more complex socio-economic relations which can be equated, in some ways, with 'delayed-return' systems. As we saw in Chapter One, Australian Aboriginal society has been classified in this way. No unilinear or necessarily deterministic trajectory is, however, being suggested; instead a patchwork of patterns may have appeared in time and space.

A number of significant archaeological trends have been recognised in widespread regions of mainland Australia. There trends include increases in numbers of sites, use of individual sites and use of marginal environments. Further related factors include changes in size and function of sites and the range of resources and activities represented. These trends appear to be most marked in the mid-late Holocene, from around 4,000 to 3,000 BP. In some ways the trends are most pronounced in the last one or two thousand years. In a few areas (and sites) some reversals in the trends are registered in the latter phase.

These archaeological trends are most obvious in southeastern Australia, in particular southwestern Victoria, southeastern South Australia, northwestern Victoria and the southeastern highlands. Aspects are also visible in western New South Wales, south coast New South Wales (including offshore islands), and the central highlands of New South Wales. It is argued here that the archaeological trends can be recognised in southeastern Queensland (and offshore islands), coastal northeastern Queensland (and offshore islands), and northern Queensland. More recent evidence from central Australia and the wider arid zone also indicates intensified site and resource use (that is, grass seeds) in the last 2,000 to 1,000 years. The evidence from Arnhem Land now needs to be carefully re-examined. Results from northwestern Australia indicate similar trends (for example, on offshore islands), but results from southwestern Australia are equivocal. The chronology of these archaeological trends does not fit general climatic trends for the period and so the range of possible explanations is discussed below.

Other sets of data lend support to this evaluation. Patterns of rock art (especially in northern Australia) are regionalised in the last 3,000–2,000 years with the introduction of 'new' painted styles. These have been seen as indicating the development of more 'closed' socio-demographic formations during this period. I have argued that these patterns cannot be viewed solely as products of environmental change. Increased territoriality is indicated also by the appearance of cemeteries in the Murray River corridor since about 13,000 years ago. Cemeteries are, however, also more numerous and complex (as are burial practices) during the late Holocene, which suggests further increases in territoriality (and socio-cultural complexity) at this time. Skeletal information provides further clues. Patterns of morphological variation within the Murray River region in the late Holocene suggest the formation of more 'closed', 'endogamous' social groups. Palaeopathalogical evidence from the same area, which is roughly contemporary, indicates signs of stress-related health problems caused perhaps by overcrowding and increased sedentism. Finally, 'recent' complex patterns of exchange in southeastern Australia (Victoria) show a range of 'closed' and 'open' social formations approximating to the 'super-networks' of which we have descriptions for the ethnohistorical period.

Models

We now consider the interpretation of Australian prehistory. An examination of the most influential general models allows us to understand and appreciate the current range of competing explanations, how they arose and, we hope to see, in which direction they are taking us. Explanatory models have largely taken two forms – emphasising either static or dynamic features. Also, varying emphases have been placed upon the main influential factors of environment, demography, technology and society.

'Static' models

The work of Birdsell (1953, 1957, 1968, 1971, 1977), which spans some thirty years, consolidates the static viewpoint, and has been also one of the most influential theories in the formation of the basis of Australian prehistory. Birdsell saw colonisation as a swift process, with all inhabitable Australian environments being occupied within 5,000 years. This was followed by a stabilisation of population which he saw as being closely tied to a hypothetical environmental 'carrying capacity'. He viewed Aboriginal economy, and extractive efficiency (production) especially, as being relatively homogeneous and unchanging (see Introduction).

Birdsell originally allowed for changes in population sizes in parts of southeastern Australia due to the development of more complex socio-economic practices, and for lower population levels in Tasmania, where less complex practices existed (1957: 61). But he later abandoned these ideas in preference for more environmental explanations (1977). We have already considered some of the limitations of Birdsell's model as regards its data and interpretations (Chapter One). As well, more recent computer simulation models indicate that rapid population saturation of the continent would have been most unlikely (McArthur 1976).

Further problems with Birdsell's model, as outlined above, lie in its environmentally deterministic emphasis and generally static nature. Despite these difficulties, however, the model has been the foundation of many more recent analyses of Australian prehistory (for example, Jones 1977a: 202, 1977b: 367).

Rhys Jones' (1973, 1979) interpretation of Australian prehistory and its Pleistocene beginnings followed closely the model of demographic and cultural stability and equilibrium proposed by Birdsell (see Chapter One). Jones envisaged a somewhat lengthier settling-in period than allowed by Birdsell, which he saw as drawing to a close around 25,000 BP, the time of the Mungo I site. 'The initial colonization would have been a period of imbalance and experiment, but by at least 25,000 BP, the distinctive Australian economic system was already in train in some places' (Jones 1973: 281). Jones (1968, 1973) had originally considered that the extermination of the Australian megafauna had taken place during the initial 'period of imbalance and experiment', and, like Allen (1972, 1974), argued for a shift to the use of grass seeds in arid and semi-arid zones around 15,000 BP.

> This picture of a broadly based foraging pattern extending back from ethnographic times to at least 20,000 BP, has many implications for the study of economic processes in advanced hunting societies. There were no great 'post Pleistocene adaptations'; they had been made a long time before. (Jones 1973: 281)

The cultural changes of more recent times, like the Holocene, therefore, were not considered by Jones as very significant. Later he expanded his original model by hypothesising that two waves of people were responsible for the archaeological patterns of Pleistocene Australia: a more robust archaic population before about 30,000 BP; and a more gracile modern population after that date (Jones 1979; see also 1987). The second group was characterised as technologically more advanced than the first, with higher population densities and geographical range. More recent analyses of the human osteological evidence from the Pleistocene, however, favour a homogeneous founder-population rather than two separate morphological groups (see Chapter Three). Notwithstanding this new evidence, Jones' model is still testable by archaeological information.

'Dynamic' models

More recent interpretations have placed emphasis upon more dynamic aspects of Australian prehistory, in particular those affecting society, demography and economy. Individual authors have, however, emphasised certain of these attributes over others. Static elements also have been retained, to varying degrees, in some models.

POPULATION GROWTH

Hallam (1977a, 1977b) argued strongly against Birdsell's model of Australian colonisation, and proposed an alternative model of population increase in contrast to the population equilibrium proposed by Birdsell. Hallam's model was based upon two sources of information. First she looked at the density of stone artefact distribution in a number of Australian regions (for example the Perth area of Western Australia and the Murray drainage basin). Hallam showed that Pleistocene archaeological occupation patterns were substantially different to more recent patterns, being strongly associated with now-defunct drier areas. She assumed that population continued to increase in Australia right up to the present with the most intense recent increases occurring in more humid areas. She based her conclusions upon the archaeological evidence.

Hallam viewed the earliest Australian populations as highly mobile, small groups, firstly occupying resource-rich areas such as coasts, rivers, savannas and lastly more forested regions. She speculated that for the north the collection of plant foods would have been of greater economic importance when compared to hunting in more open areas and around the arid heart of the continent, with broader-based economies in richer coastal areas. She also pointed out that large areas of Australia, for example forests, would have been opened up to herbivores through the use of fire, which both improved and degraded savanna areas. Many of the points raised by Hallam's largely intuitive model have found their way into more recent proposals.

COASTAL COLONISATION

Bowdler (1977; see also 1990c) offered a model of colonisation which in some ways is comparable to that of Hallam. She too was critical of Birdsell's bow-wave theory which presupposes an explosive colonisation across the continent, from end to end, irrespective of environmental factors. Bowdler used her own work at Cave Bay Cave, northwestern Tasmania (see above, Chapter Seven), to launch the model. After a lengthy review of existing Australian archaeological data, Bowdler pointed out that the evidence of occupation of Pleistocene cave and rock-shelter sites, including Pleistocene occupation levels within sites, is rather sparse and geographically restricted to coastal and riverine areas. In contrast, she considered that more recent occupation was both more intensive and widespread and included harsher environments, such as arid and montane zones. She thought that inland economies were centred around the hunting of smaller land mammals. Bowdler envisaged a Pleistocene coastal colonisation of the continent. The earliest populations were thought to be restricted to coastal and riverine areas, that is, the more productive environments. Occupation of arid and montane areas, she considered, took place much later in Australian prehistory when appropriate technology had been introduced.

> For Australia, I have presented a model which most economically explains the data available: that the continent was colonised by sea, by people with a coastal economy which underwent little modification for many millennia. Such modification in the initial stages merely involved a shift from marine to freshwater aquatic resource exploitation and areas away from the coasts and major river/lacustrine environments were unpopulated till rather late in the day. (Bowdler 1977: 233)

Her provocative paper stimulated much discussion and a good deal of fieldwork. More recent investigations, however, do not necessarily support all aspects of the model. Pleistocene occupation appears to have been on a much broader front, incorporating a wider range of environments than Bowdler originally allowed. Inland economies also appear to have been more complex, with the larger mammals also targeted. The association between new technology and occupation of more marginal areas (for example deserts) also does not appear to be supported by more recent evidence. Other aspects of the model, however, have to some extent stood the test of time. Bowdler's observation that Pleistocene occupation was relatively ephemeral within sites, such as caves and shelters, in general continues to be the case in many environments. Secondly, her stadial viewpoint, that of a protracted colonisation of Australia, also is still applicable although not necessarily with her chronology.

Bowdler did not distinguish, however, between the dispersal, or geographical spread, of population and population density. That is, once environments had been occupied there was no allowance made in the model for further population growth through increased extractive efficiency and other socio-economic practices.

Largely in response to Bowdler, a further biogeographical model was produced by Horton (1981), who suggested that the early colonists may have followed the forested belt, characterised by the humid zone which extends around the northern, eastern and southern parts of the continent. He considered that the arid core of Australia was largely avoided until the Holocene period, and that as the glacial maximum approached, Aboriginal settlement shifted towards the better watered coastal regions. Like many models, however, that were primarily environmentally based, this one also avoids discussing the dynamics of demography, society and economy, to name but a few aspects. It is also not generally supported by later archaeological evidence (see also Walters 1981).

Recent models
More recent interpretations of the Pleistocene have included a number of approaches; the main ones have already been considered above (also in Chapters Four to Seven). By far the greatest number of recent interpretations, however, concern the mid-late Holocene period of the Australian mainland, where abundant evidence of variation and change exists. And these will now be considered in some detail, for in these debates are discussed most key issues which relate to *all periods* of Australian prehistory, including the late Pleistocene.

Mid-late Holocene changes and interpretations
The theoretical perspectives that have been employed here are much the same as those concerning general issues of change and variation in hunter-gatherer societies (as discussed in Chapter One). The main explanations can be divided broadly into four main categories: environmental, technological, demographic and socio-demographic. Each of these interpretations will now be considered in some detail, followed by the presentation of two explanatory models of my own – demographic and socio-demographic – which are based upon the arguments developed in this book.

Environment
Late Holocene cultural changes of mainland Australia have been explained by some, as we have seen, as largely the product of changing environmental factors (for example, Jones 1977b; Rowland 1983; Beaton 1985; Bird and Frankel 1991a, 1991b; see also Birdsell 1953, 1957, 1977). While climatic changes have played a significant role in shaping some of the cultural processes outlined here, the following reasons indicate why environment cannot be viewed as the *sole* determinant of the archaeological patterns on the Australian mainland during the mid-late Holocene. Firstly, the early Holocene was generally more humid than the late Holocene which, being drier, was a more stressful period. Archaeological patterns in general, however, do not correspond with this climatic sequence, which suggests that generally bioproduction was greatest in the early Holocene, declining somewhat in more recent times. The most expansive and intensive archaeological 'phase' takes place in the mid-late Holocene, that is to say during a period of stress, rather than in the early Holocene period of greater resource availability.

Apart from coastal areas, the archaeological patterns are also found inland, for example in southwestern and northwestern Victoria, the southeastern and eastern highlands (New South Wales and central and north Queensland), as well as in semi-arid and arid zones. Climate had improved in highland areas since the late Pleistocene, and water sources were more widespread in arid belts during the early Holocene. In both these environments, however, Aboriginal occupation appears to increase only during the more recent late Holocene period. Thus the socio-cultural processes and patterns may have been, in part, responses to the more stressful conditions of the late Holocene, rather than the *direct* product of climate. Socio-cultural responses during the late Holocene, therefore, appear to have been somewhat different from those during similarly stressful periods in the past, for example during the late Pleistocene in the period leading up to the glacial maximum (c. 25,000–18,000 BP). Similarly, earth mounds appear in southwestern Victoria, and other parts of southeastern Australia, during a slightly more humid phase of the late Holocene after about 2,500 BP, rather than during the most humid phase of the early Holocene when wetlands, with which they are associated, were most extensive.

Secondly, the establishment of post-glacial sea levels around the mid-Holocene, (c. 6,000–5,000 BP), have been proposed as an explanation for the abundance of mid-late Holocene coastal archaeological sites (Beaton 1985; Jones 1977a; see also Lampert and Hughes 1974). These environmental details, however, cannot be considered an adequate explanation for the coastal archaeological patterns. The evidence of the most intensive occupation of coastal sites and locales is from the late Holocene (that is, after about 3,000 BP). This is many thousands of years after sea levels have stabilised, and longer still from the time of the first archaeological signs of coastal foraging in the Holocene (c. 8,000–7,000 BP). Mike Rowland (1983, 1989; see also Head 1986; Godfrey 1989; O'Connor 1992), for example, has argued that earlier coastal sites have been destroyed by a range of climatic and geomorphological factors (for example, higher sea levels). While this may be true of many open sites, this is less so for rock-shelters, caves and open sites on stable landforms (Hughes and Lampert 1982). Sites of the latter category largely were employed in most diachronic comparisons (above).

The notion of a time-lag between sea level stabilisation and the archaeological evidence of substantial coastal exploitation appears to depend upon the assumption of increased bioproductivity in coastal areas during the late Holocene (Beaton 1985: 18). Beaton explained the archaeological trends of this period as due to increases in Aboriginal populations following this phase of environmental enrichment; and he extended this model to all Australian coastal environments. Beaton's assumption, however, of a general continental enrichment of coastal areas during the late Holocene can be questioned. Chappell (1982) has argued strongly that during times of changes in sea level, transformations of coastal environments are very much dependent on local factors. That is, no general statement can be made about local coastal environments and their productivity, as the processes involved are dynamic. This point is reinforced when individual coastal areas are examined. For example, the dynamic nature of Holocene estuarine development is clearly indicated by recent studies in the East Alligator region of Arnhem Land (see Chapter Four). Also, two regions where a decline in coastal productivity during the late Holocene can be proposed are the Macleay River estuary of northern New South Wales (Callaghan 1980; Coleman 1982; Lourandos 1985b: 38), and southwestern Victoria (Head 1983; Lourandos 1985b: 38).

A further problem concerns the measurement of local or regional productivity. An argument based upon a limited number of factors (for example, *Anadara* shellbeds as in the case of Princess Charlotte Bay) can be misleading as many microenvironments as well as individual species are concerned. These counter-arguments are reinforced by evidence already discussed (above). First, that transgressive tropical coastal environments are not necessarily devoid of resources, and second, that a number of northern Australian archaeological sites of the early-mid Holocene indicate well developed coastal exploitation (for example Koolan Island in the West Kimberley, the East Alligator River region, and the Whitsunday Islands). The evidence from northwestern and southeastern Tasmania (Rocky Cape, Carlton Bluff, Little Swanport) does not fit a model of late Holocene exploitation, but instead indicates the foundation of shellbeds and marine economies from the early-mid Holocene. The rock-shelter at Cape du Couedic (Kangaroo Island) is another example (see above). This information does not contradict the interpretation of more intensive use of coastal sites and resources during the late Holocene, but strongly suggests that environmental factors do not fully explain the archaeological patterns; that socio-cultural practices also must be involved.

Even when socio-cultural changes appear to coincide with environmental shifts, the cultural trends do not necessarily follow those of environment. For example, drier conditions after about 4,000 BP resulted in a contraction of forests which may have facilitated firing and thus opening up of these landscapes. Archaeological trends, however, indicate that use of many such areas continued to increase even when more humid conditions, which would have promoted forestation, returned in the last 2,000 years. Examples of the latter include the north Queensland rainforests, southwestern Victoria and northwestern Tasmania.

Technology

The introduction or development of new technology, especially during the mid-late Holocene, has been viewed in a number of ways: (i) as an associated factor;

(ii) as a causal agent; (iii) as both cause and consequence of broader historical processes.

(i) The general relationship between the appearance of new technology and other cultural changes of the last 5,000–4,000 years has concerned many researchers (White 1971; Mulvaney 1975; McBryde 1977; White and O'Connell 1982; Johnson 1979; Beaton 1977, 1982; Morwood 1979; Lourandos 1980a, 1980b; Bowdler 1981; Hiscock and Veth 1991; McNiven 1993). Aside from serving as a chronological marker, new technology is viewed also as a part of the changing socio-cultural fabric of particular periods.

(ii) To some analysts, new technology is the cause of socio-cultural change. Examples which illustrate this viewpoint include the introduction of grindstone technology and the processing of grass seeds in semi-arid New South Wales (Allen 1974); processing techniques for *Macrozamia* in the south central Queensland highlands (Beaton 1977, 1982); the outrigger canoe and use of islands in northern Queensland (Beaton 1985); fish hooks on the south coast of New South Wales (Bowdler 1976); and exploitation of *Microseris* in the eastern highlands (Bowdler 1981).

Jones (1977b: 189) closely associated the introduction of new technology, in particular the Australian Small Tool tradition (in the mid-late Holocene), with widespread changes to economy, demography and social organisation (see below). Jones' assumption, however, of the increased efficiency of recent Australian stone industries (including the Australian Small Tool tradition) can be questioned. Firstly, the function and level of efficiency of many of these artefacts is, as yet, unclear. It has long been suggested that many of the microliths had more than mundane functions and also may have been used for other purposes, such as conveying social information. Many of the Australian stone artefacts also are maintenance, rather than directly extractive, equipment (White 1977). The assumption that the degree of complexity of stone tool kits reflects that of the wider economy has also been challenged. Golson (1977b) has argued convincingly, in this way, for ethnographic highland New Guinea. Here very rudimentary flaked stone industries were employed, even in recent times, in complex horticultural economies (involving intensive farming) which supported high population densities.

(iii) The introduction or development of technology also has been seen, in some more recent examples, as part of socio-demographic and environmental processes operating at various points in time. In these examples the role of technology is not always dominant, as other factors are involved, but is dependent upon the wider context. For example, the development of grindstone techniques in association with the processing of grass seeds has been viewed as an extension of existing technology, which may have given rise to still further changes (Smith 1986; see also Chapter Five). The context in which these practices were developed involved changes to environment, demography and society, as in the following example. In southwestern Victoria large-scale artificial drainage systems also appear to be a specialised local development of more widespread fishing practices (including ditches and traps), and appear to have been made within the context of environmental, social and possibly demographic changes (Lourandos 1980a, 1980b; see also above, Chapter Six). Both these cases involve the intensification of specific resources and neither is the direct product of new technology.

Demographic change

Demographic change, or more often population increase, was invoked also by many researchers to explain the mid-late Holocene Australian archaeological changes. Interpretations have focused upon two geographical levels: the regional and the continental.

Regional sequences have been interpreted in this way by a large number of researchers. The latter include Hallam (1977a, 1977b) and Ferguson (1985) for southwestern Australia; Lourandos (1980a, 1980b, 1983a) and Williams (1985, 1987) for southwestern Victoria; Ross (1981, 1985) for northwestern Victoria; Webb (1985) and Pardoe (1988, 1990) for the Murray River corridor; Luebbers (1978) for southeastern South Australia; Hughes and Lampert (1982) for the south coast of New South Wales; Morwood (1988) and Hiscock and Hall (1988) for southeastern Queensland; Beaton (1985) for Princess Charlotte Bay, north Queensland; David (1994) for Cape York, north Queensland; and Schrire (1982) for Arnhem Land.

Of all these studies of the past two decades or so, those of Ross and Williams are the most specific concerning the use of archaeological information to answer demographic questions. In spite of the difficulties of inferring past demographic information from archaeological evidence, many of the researchers argue that a general relationship can be observed between archaeological data, such as numbers of sites and the intensity of site use through time, and demographic changes. Similar interpretations regarding demographic patterns and changes during Pleistocene times have also been considered. The latter studies include those of Hiscock (1988), Ross et al. (1992), Smith (1989), Veth (1989a) for central Australia; Cosgrove et al. (1990), Lourandos (1993) for southwestern Tasmania (also see chapters Four to Seven).

The proposition that population size and density has changed throughout Australian prehistory and on a continental scale also has been entertained (Hallam 1977a, 1977b; Lourandos 1980a, 1980b, 1983a, 1983b; Beaton 1985, 1990; Gray 1985; see also Jones 1977b; Ross 1985; see also above this chapter). My own interpretation, based upon the existing archaeological evidence (and discussed in Chapters Four to Seven), indicates a general (although not necessarily uniform) population increase over time in most Australian environments. That is, demography, including population increase, may have been relatively dynamic on both long- and short-term time-scales, and at both the local or regional level (see also Davidson 1990). Perhaps the clearest example of this during the Pleistocene is in southwestern Tasmania, covering a very long time period (see Chapter Seven). Evidence of further examples occur also during the glacial maximum throughout the continent, when indications of contraction, decline and rearrangements in population are suggested (see also above this chapter). Otherwise, evidence for more widespread and dynamic changes involving demography occurs in the late Holocene on mainland Australia (also in northwestern Tasmania).

Further, I would suggest that the existing Australian archaeological evidence can be interpreted in light of three *general* continental population models: first, steady population growth throughout Australian prehistory; second, gradual early population growth with marked local increases during the late Holocene; and third, steady early growth in the Pleistocene with some reversals during the glacial maximum, followed by further increases continuing throughout the terminal Pleistocene, early Holocene and peaking during the late Holocene.

Given the fragmentary nature of the archaeological evidence, however, together with the complex and cumulative effects of population growth (Hassan 1975), it may not be so easy to clearly distinguish between these processes (Lourandos 1985a: 403; see also Beaton 1982, 1985, 1990).

Even if we accept the argument for general population increase throughout Australian prehistory, there remains the issue of causality. Pleistocene patterns are related to, but do not necessarily fit, all major climatic trends, especially prior to about 25,000 BP. Also, in what ways are the socio-cultural changes of the mid-late Holocene, related to demography? For example, it is not at all clear whether population increase *precedes* the appearance of: (a) use of grass seeds in arid Australia; (b) earth mounds, and other cultural changes, in southwestern Victoria; (c) use of toxic plants in south central Queensland, the Cape York rainforests and the Whitsunday Islands; (d) increased fishing in Moreton Bay, southeastern Queensland; or (e) changing rock art styles in Cape York. A stronger case can be made, based upon existing archaeological evidence, of population increase either *accompanying* or *following* these changes, for it is in the succeeding period that the greatest increase in site numbers and levels of site use occurred in each of these environments. Given this information, it would be very difficult to argue for population growth as *solely* an independent variable, irrespective of the considerable difficulties in measuring it archaeologically (see also Gray 1985).

I do not, however, view these late Holocene patterns and trends as necessarily, or solely, the product of rising population. Demography is a complex phenomenon, involving population density and dispersal as well as population increase, or decrease, all of which can be affected by socio-cultural as well as by natural or biological factors. Population density, for example, also can be influenced by changing settlement patterns, including those of aggregation – largely a social practice. Many of the archaeological patterns from late Holocene Australia, for example, can be interpreted in this way (as I observed earlier in this chapter), and would not necessarily require an increase in population. The lengthy intergroup gatherings in many parts of Australia in the ethnographic period (for example, southwestern Victoria) which ran for months at a time and involved hundreds, and in some cases thousands, of people would have significantly increased the population of the region in which they were held. The archaeology of these areas may indicate increased use of sites (and perhaps site size). As well, once the socio-demographic environment becomes more complex in these ways, population increase may ensue – that is, as the product rather than the cause. Given the present evidence, these patterns appear to have been stimulated by environmental factors, rather than to have been caused by them. That is, environment served largely as the stimulus, with chosen behavioural patterns (including the demographic) being largely under social control.

Socio-demographic change

Many reasearchers have considered directly or indirectly the perceived socio-cultural changes of the mid-late Holocene in Australia as indicating transformations in society and economy. A variety of these viewpoints has been discussed in relation to regional studies (Beaton 1977, 1982; Jones 1977b; Morwood 1979; Bowdler 1981; Ross 1981; Lampert and Hughes 1982; Smith 1986; O'Connor 1987; Hiscock and Hall 1988; McNiven 1990, 1991; Pardoe 1990; see also Yoffee 1985; Gamble 1986b; see also Chapters Four to Six). It has been suggested also that social networks became more complex during this period at a regional level (Lampert 1980; McBryde 1984; Lourandos 1983a, 1985a, in press; Veth 1989a; David 1990; David and Cole 1990; Lourandos and Ross 1994). The development of regional socio-cultural groups – a form of regionalisation – also has been examined in the light of the distribution of rock art styles (David 1991; Layton 1991, 1992; Morwood 1993; Morwood and Hobbs 1995; Taçon 1993) and of stone artefacts throughout this period (White and O'Connell 1982: 105–132).

One of the most important issues, however, concerns the relationship between society and demography. As I have argued throughout, the two are closely interrelated (see also Pardoe 1990). It now remains for us to explore these issues further so as to cast more light on Holocene socio-cultural changes and those of earlier periods. And in order to do this I have set out two models; the first demographic and the second socio-demographic. The models help, in my view, to explain the archaeological patterns of the Holocene period, and in particular the late Holocene, of the Australian mainland; but they are relevant also to all phases of Australian prehistory. The general issues relating to these models were discussed in Chapter One.

Two new alternative models

A demographic model

A demographic model might take into account the process as one where rising population levels lead to denser regional populations and therefore to demographic packing. The result of the latter would be increased territoriality (for example, smaller-sized, more bounded territories) and, therefore, increasingly complex methods of population management. Although neat at the outset, this model has, however, a number of problems. First, it oversimplifies the process. Second, there is no good evidence for population increase preceding the course of events, as we have already seen, nor of relatively large increases in population. Third, it does not fully account for other demographic factors such as *population dispersal* and *density* which under social control may result in a variety of patterns (for example, increased *aggregation*, see above). Fourth, it is essentially a biological model which reduces socio-cultural factors to secondary status – as agents of demographic control – thus stripping them of their independence, complexity and force (see also Chapter One). And last, I would argue against these socio-demographic patterns being reduced to a mechanical population growth model where new social groups merely 'bud off' in a more or less clockwork fashion (see for example, Birdsell 1953, 1957; Beaton 1990).

A socio-demographic model

This model is based upon discussion of the issues presented in Chapter One and is a development of earlier ideas of mine on the topic (Lourandos 1980a, 1980b, 1983a, 1985a, 1987a, 1993). It assumes that, in time, changes in demographic structure – including population density, dispersal and size – produced relatively more dynamic (competitive) and complex demographic relations. Associated with this process is the development of relatively more 'closed' social or alliance systems. The latter would have resulted in changes to intergroup relationships and to their 'open' and 'closed' aspects (that is, producing more complex patterns), and also would have made varying demands upon groups' economy. Changes in demographic structure and alliance formations are here closely interrelated, as all aspects of demography (including population density, dispersal and size) would be influenced by socio-cultural practices. As we have already seen, increases in population can be regarded as much as a product of the process as a cause. Also, relatively 'open' and 'closed' formations are not merely viewed here as *directly* related to population increase or decrease, but as part of more complex socio-demographic strategies.

This process would have produced a dynamic and complex set of socio-demographic and land use patterns. Of the latter we can include varying social and territorial constraints involving regionalisation and territorial boundary maintenance through intergroup economic activities, communal gatherings, rituals, feasting, exchange and aggression. The related expansion of alliance systems can, in some ways, be seen as a reaction to social and territorial constraints and together these may have led also to transformations in social organisation, such as the formation of hierarchies (vertical or horizontal). Changes in patterns of the use of land and resources, which are related to the above processes, might include the use of smaller-sized territories and locales, and logistical strategies (including longer-term base camps and 'sedentism'), 'delayed-return' systems (including for example, fixed facilities), and perhaps aspects of economic intensification and specialisation (involving resources) linked to both domestic and intergroup levels of economy.

All of these features can be found in the ethnography of specific Australian regions (for example, southwestern Victoria), which indicates their operation in recent times (see also Chapter Two). Aspects of the process visible directly or indirectly in the archaeological record of late Holocene Australia have already been discussed (see above, this chapter) and include regionalisation (for example, in rock art); increases in use of sites, locales and landscapes (found in a wide variety of Australian environments); use of 'marginal' or peripheral environments; more 'logistical' strategies (for example, the appearance of earth mounds and more complex sites); and changes in resource use (for example, trends towards more 'costly' foods and those from a wider range); increased territoriality (for example, cemeteries, rock art) and related boundary maintenance, competitive intergroup behaviour and expansion of alliance formation (for example, patterns of exchange). As we have already seen, more evidence exists, or may be inferred, for some of these categories than for others.

Further strengths of this model are that it allows for more detailed aspects of the socio-demographic process to be discussed. For example, I see the development through time of more complex and competitive alliance systems as central in the process. I would argue also that another key *dynamic* involved the mediating role of ceremonial and intergroup gatherings and exchange systems that helped to regulate social relations between competing populations and networks. In this way they bound together societies that otherwise lacked centralised political controls. These intergroup occasions also served as distribution centres for the dissemination of people, resources, goods, services, knowledge, and the like. These communal events, as well, allowed influential individuals (for example, clan elders) and groups to obtain power, status and prestige by attending and competing (through ceremonies, games, and arranged 'battles'). Simultaneously, the broad egalitarian or more open social structure also began to accentuate forms of gerontocracy through which, for example, clan elders extended their sphere of influence (apart from intergroup mediation) through polygyny, complex ceremonial institutions, shamanism, exchange systems and the like (Lourandos 1985a: 406; see also Chapter One).

It is also predicted in the model that when these general conditions (involving increased levels of 'closure') did not exist, alliance formations were more 'open' and flexible. More 'closed' social conditions may have existed also earlier in the prehistory of Greater Australia, in which case archaeological signs of these should be detectable.

The model also allows for a broad range of dynamic behavioural patterns in time and space, dependent on the histories of individual regions. Groups may have interrelated in a variety of ways and formed diverse patterns of alliance. The examples presented here are only a few of the manifold possibilities. Nor is there any suggestion here of a unidirectional or unilinear trend, although, as mentioned in Chapter One, a coarse-grained perspective may give such an impression.

This is a model which also accommodates *all* the data – both ethnographic and archaeological; and many aspects of it are testable. It also includes all aspects of demography – that is, population size, density and dispersal. The emphasis here has been upon the complexity of the socio-demographic process and the way human relationships can become formalised and manipulated. Demography is also about *intraspecific competition*, which is envisaged here as operating at all levels; individuals and groups were continually renegotiating their place within social and natural landscapes.

This perspective, for example, can help explain why, given similar environmental stimuli – such as increasingly stressful environments – quite different socio-cultural responses occurred. Why, for example, in arid Australia did people opt for more 'costly' grass seed practices in the mid-Holocene, when in prior dry times (including those of the Pleistocene) these practices were avoided? As we saw (Chapter Five), increasing population was not involved in this example. The answer, I suggest, lies within the socio-demographic environments of the various time periods. In the mid-Holocene, I would argue, incentives existed to intensify production, whereas in prior periods these were absent.

It is important to note that the model can also be applied to earlier stages in Australian prehistory. On present evidence, signs of social 'closure' first appear in the terminal Pleistocene, after about 13,000 years ago, with the existence of cemeteries in the Murray River corridor in southeastern Australia. More extensive and complex aspects of the process are evident in the wider region of southeastern Australia (and more widely throughout Australia), as we have seen, in the late Holocene. Thus, demographic changes might have been associated at first with the climatic amelioration of the terminal Pleistocene involving some increases in population sizes and densities. But in contrast to this example, the demographic changes of the late Holocene in mainland Australia (which indicate most clearly increases in population sizes and densities in Australian prehistory) run against the climatic trend of the period towards more stressful conditions. Indeed, if changes in population were to correspond to those of climate, then the greatest increases should have taken place in the early Holocene when conditions were more suitable. The implications here are that demography is not under *direct* environmental influence. To what extent the terminal Pleistocene climate influenced changes in demography and aspects of social 'closure' (and related socio-economic factors) in highland New Guinea (and its offshore islands) remains to be explored. Certainly, in my view the present evidence would allow such a scenario to be entertained. Increased use of sites has also been demonstrated even earlier, in southwestern Australia prior to the glacial maximum – a trend interpreted as closely linked to increased bioproduction in the region (O'Connor et al. 1993). On the other hand, in southwestern Tasmania during the late Pleistocene, the more dynamic archaeological patterns observed need to be more clearly distinguished from those of changing climate. Even so, I suggest, in this Tasmanian region also there is a strong relationship between the archaeological patterns and trends and those of climate.

Change or stability?

When all interpretations of Australian prehistory are drawn together, two main explanatory models can be isolated; the first is relatively static in form, and the alternative dynamic.

Much like Birdsell's (1953, 1957, 1977) original hypothesis, this model assumes that following the colonisation phase of the continent of Greater Australia, there have been no *significant* changes to population and economy. Population size and density were largely controlled by environmental factors (that is, by bioproduction), and were largely unaffected by any alterations to economy and society. Socio-cultural variation was essentially a response to changes in the natural environment. Aspects recognisable as, for example, 'complex', therefore, would always have been present and have appeared when 'natural' conditions arose. Birdsell viewed the colonisation era as a relatively rapid process (a few thousand years or so), whereas, as we saw earlier, more recent versions of this general argument (for example, Jones 1979) allow for a lengthier settling-in phase (but see also Allen 1989a). Recent Holocene cultural changes, for example, are not viewed as altering this steady state equilibrium in any significant way.

The alternative model assumes that population, economy and society were relatively dynamic throughout Australian prehistory. I have argued here that population, economy and society *in general* continued to expand throughout Australian prehistory. More varied patterns, however, may have formed at local or regional levels. This is so for both Pleistocene and Holocene periods. While evidence exists for changes during the Pleistocene (for example towards the glacial maximum and in the terminal Pleistocene) and early Holocene, the most significant changes appear to have taken place in the mid-late Holocene period on the Australian mainland. Environment, however, was not the only controlling factor. Opinions vary on the degree of cultural and/or demographic influences on these processes.

I have argued here also that existing archaeological evidence leans more towards the dynamic models than to the more traditional static models which it should be noted originally had been proposed *prior* to most modern archaeological investigation.

Pleistocene–Holocene trends

I suggest that four main trends can be observed throughout Australian prehistory. Once again, these should not be considered as necessarily unilinear or unidirectional. On present evidence, these trends appear most marked during the mid-late Holocene period, that is, the last 4,000 to 3,000 years.

First, the intensification of four of the five resource 'pathways', along which hunter-gatherer economies can expand: grass seeds, roots and tubers, nuts and fish.

Second, Australian settlement patterns (which include the number, form, and usage of sites) suggest a shift towards more 'logistically' organised strategies in recent times. In general, more intensive patterns of land use are indicated during the late Holocene. Examples of this were suggested also for New Ireland and the New Guinea highlands during the terminal Pleistocene; with fluctuations in patterns of site and land use in southwestern Tasmania at this time.

Third, the latter settlement trend further suggests the development of more complex socio-economic relations (for example, 'delayed-return' systems) during the mid-late Holocene period in particular.

Fourth, Aboriginal populations may have increased throughout Australian prehistory, and on present evidence this trend also appears most marked in recent times. Evidence comes from the number, form and degree of usage of archaeological sites, together with the use of more peripheral environments.

What are the dynamics fuelling these trends? While explanations of this archaeological evidence vary, these mainly centre upon four main influential factors: environment, technology, demography, and socio-cultural factors. I have argued here that environment, technology and demography cannot be viewed as causal agents in themselves, no matter how closely associated with the processes of change. I suggest that a combination of socio-cultural and demographic factors, set within the context of the natural environment, best explains the above archaeological trends. The interrelationship between these two factors and the natural environment would provide the dynamic. More dynamic patterns, it is argued here, were produced when competition between groups and social 'closure' were heightened.

By the mid-late Holocene on the Australian mainland, I argue, the socio-demographic *context* had altered. Trends towards increasing levels of 'closure' may have been influenced by rising levels of bioproduction, in regions where they occurred, in the terminal Pleistocene–early Holocene when these were most marked. This may have resulted in more complex demography, including population increase, a trend which continued by its own momentum throughout the late Holocene in the face of climatic reversals. Options, such as the intensification of resource use (including more labour-intensive foods) and land use (more intensive use or new use of sites, locales and marginal or peripheral environments, for example, by increased social aggregation), were now more viable. Some of these socio-economic strategies had been largely avoided in the past, for example during the earlier, arid period of the late Pleistocene. I suggest that the increased complexity (and competitiveness) of social networks (including aspects of both 'open' and 'closed' systems), together with their underlying demographic structure, would have provided both the context for such changes in decision-making, and the dynamic promoting their continuation, throughout the late Holocene especially. Demographic changes may have included alterations in patterns of intergroup aggregations and their duration. Changes to population densities and dispersal need not necessarily imply increased population: on the contrary, they might lead to it.

CHAPTER 10

CONCLUDING PERSPECTIVES

Ethnography and ethnohistory

I have argued that recent Australian Aboriginal ethnographic and ethnohistorical studies suggest that a broader range of socio-cultural variation existed, both geographically and through time, than previously appreciated. Aboriginal population sizes and densities were also higher than believed and had been reduced by introduced diseases and European aggression at the time of colonisation. All accounts of traditional Australian Aboriginal society must allow for this demographic decline and the associated social disruption.

Mainland Australian Aboriginal societies in more humid, fertile zones of the continent (including the tropical, sub-tropical and the temperate) appear to have been relatively sedentary, populous and with broad-based hunter-gatherer-fisher economies, including specialisation of both plant use and fishing practices, and land and resource management procedures. In harsher environments (such as arid zones), population densities were relatively lower, with reduced levels of sedentism. More complex socio-economic patterns, however, were observable even in harsh arid areas such as the Cooper Creek riverine corridor. Storage and processing of foods (that is, relatively labour-intensive practices) were widespread and intensified during, or in anticipation of, intergroup occasions (such as feasting, exchange and so on). Extensive alliance systems operated in all parts of the continent, with relatively more 'open' systems in harsher arid areas and more complex 'open' and 'closed' networks in humid, fertile regions, such as southeastern Australia. Competition existed between groups for control and access to land, resources and labour, and was closely associated with prominent leaders and their supporters. Recall that I use the word 'complex' here (as discussed at the beginning of this book) in a relative sense, referring to a cultural continuum.

Australian hunter-gatherer societies overlapped to some extent with many New Guinean hunter-horticulturalists in relation to population sizes and densities, hunting-gathering-fishing practices, levels of land and resource management (for example, plants and fish), social formation, ritual and exchange.

In contrast to the Australian mainland, Tasmanian population sizes and densities were significantly lower than in environmentally comparable regions of Australia, such as southwestern Victoria. Tasmanian economies were also broad-based, but lacked fishing practices. While populations along the Tasmanian west coast had semi-sedentary bases, generally over the rest of the island greater levels of mobility prevailed. Social networks appear to have been more 'open' and less complex than those of more humid temperate mainland regions such as southern and central Victoria.

This comparison between Australian and Tasmanian ethnographic information was interpreted largely from what may be termed an evolutionary perspective. I suggested that, along with environmental differences between the land masses, the implications were that hunter-gatherer societies of the Australian mainland had developed along somewhat different lines to those of Tasmania during their time of isolation – the entire Holocene period. In Australia, it is proposed that production of certain classes of resources had been developed (by specialisation) to varying extents. These resources include plants (among them, grass seeds, roots and tubers, and nuts to some extent) as well as fish. Specialised procurement and processing equipment, storage and management practices exist for these resource classes. It may be argued that these practices were more costly in terms of energy expenditure – and time spent in collection, preparation and the like – than other hunter-gatherer-fisher practices possible. As well, more 'logistical' subsistence and settlement patterns existed, characterised by, for instance, semi-sedentary bases, fixed procurement facilities such as weirs, fish traps, artificial drainage systems, ceremonial precincts, cemeteries and so on. In terms of socio-economic relations, the above practices were in the 'delayed-return' category, and, therefore, generally more typical of relatively more complex hunter-gatherer-fisher societies such as exist, or existed, in other parts of the world.

In contrast, only along the west coast in Tasmania were 'logistical' settlement and subsistence practices found, together with some fixed facilities (semi-sedentary bases, one type of bird snare and ritual art sites). Specialisation or expansion of particular resource classes was not evident; and fishing was entirely avoided. In all, Tasmanian socio-economic relations appear to have been generally closer to the 'immediate-return' type of system (with some exceptions) and therefore indicative overall of more mobile hunter-gatherer societies of lower population density.

In short, the Australian ethnographic and ethnohistorical evidence indicates that while natural environmental factors strongly *influenced* Aboriginal cultural patterns, as we have seen, they did not *determine* these. Cultural patterns, therefore, can be viewed as the product of the *interaction* between natural and socio-cultural forces.

Archaeology

To what extent are these trends observable in the Australian and Tasmanian, archaeological records? It has been argued here that the dominant theoretical approach to Australian prehistory has been the static model, based upon concepts of long-term equilibrium and homeostasis. Long-term adaptation to Australian environmental conditions was envisaged with few significant changes in both numbers of people or in their economy, which was defined as 'generalised'. The traditional model was essentially environmentally deterministic. In contrast to this view, however, the one main issue that I have emphasised throughout this book is that Australian prehistory should not be seen as having been *determined* by environmental change.

Although the bulk of the Australian archaeological data base has been collected only over the last thirty-five years or so, is relatively sparse, and is continually being rejuvenated by new evidence, enough material exists with which to model processes and changes through time and to evaluate past explanations. It is now known that the continent of Greater Australia has been occupied for longer than 40,000 years, and some would suggest between 50,000 and 60,000 years. It has been argued here that Birdsell's original model of rapid saturation of the continent followed by stability of both population and economy, with few significant changes, cannot be supported by recent archaeological information. Later versions of the original model which favour a stabilising of populations and economy around 25,000 BP also appear less likely.

Alternatively, I have argued that in general populations may have continued to grow, and society and economy to alter *throughout* Australian prehistory. I have viewed this as neither unilinear nor directional, although a too-general, long-term perspective may give this impression. Finer-grained spatio-temporal analyses may provide a very wide range of regional patterns and trends. On the Australian mainland, signs of change are evident in the glacial maximum, terminal Pleistocene and early Holocene periods, and more marked changes in the mid-late Holocene, in particular during the last 3,000 years or so. I am not arguing against changes – even comparable changes – having taken place during earlier periods, including those of the Pleistocene, but propose that on present evidence these appear generally more marked and widespread in recent times. I have suggested that while Pleistocene and early Holocene settlement-subsistence patterns may have varied regionally (and in time), they are *generally* indicative of relatively more mobile or nomadic economies, and of lower overall population sizes and densities. In contrast, subsistence settlement patterns of the late Holocene, and especially of the last few thousand years, demonstrate significant changes. I am not suggesting that a dichotomy existed divorcing the late

Holocene from prior periods, rather that in general they are linked clinally. Similar variations may have appeared before and trends begun earlier, for example in the terminal Pleistocene or prior glacial maximum. These are issues currently under examination. Although the archaeological data are complex and open to a range of interpretations, most writers acknowledge that the late Holocene is a period of significant cultural change in Australian prehistory. I have suggested that these changes indicate trends towards increasingly complex economies, including more sedentary settlement, and changes to demography, including increases in population size and density. Social networks also appear more complex during this recent period, with greater emphasis upon aspects of 'closure' as well as network expansion, especially in southeastern Australia. Osteological evidence suggests that no new influx of population occurred during the Holocene.

Opinions vary on the causes of these trends, with emphasis being placed alternatively upon climate or environment, demography (in particular, population increase), technology, site formation processes and socio-cultural factors. In Holocene Tasmania, geographically isolated since 12,000–8,000 BP, aspects of these trends are evident, especially in western Tasmania, but there are also variations in reactions to climatic and other changes.

Three models

Here I put forward three models to help explain the archaeological changes on the Australian mainland during the Pleistocene–Holocene period, in light of discussion developed in the first chapter of this book; the first biogeographical, the second, alliance formation and the third – which is a combination of these two – socio-demographic.

The biogeographical model

Aboriginal populations increased slowly from the time of initial colonisation, with most major environments of the continent being visibly occupied between 35,000 and 20,000 BP (that is, prior to the glacial maximum). A decline in population and contraction in its dispersal may have taken place in some regions towards and during the glacial maximum. At this time populations may have been concentrated upon the major better-watered refuges of the continent. They continued to increase and settlement continued to expand throughout the terminal Pleistocene, especially after about 17,000 BP, when regional patterns become discernible. This trend continued on into the early and mid Holocene, but with no major acceleration in trends apparent.

The period of maximum population dispersal and growth, however, was in the late Holocene, especially the last 4,000–3,000 years and more recently, when all the environments which were occupied at the time of European colonisation were utilised, and archaeological sites were generally more numerous and more intensively inhabited. The late Holocene period may be observed as a time of demographic expansion. From an ecological viewpoint, this may be seen also as a time of econiche expansion, with Aboriginal socio-economic changes largely serving to accommodate demographic rearrangements.

The strength of the model is that it has avoided the problem of viewing the process as one controlled largely by population *growth* (see Chapter One). This model can also include the idea of increasing technological efficiency. In time, the latter trend led to an overlap with, for example, Melanesian horticultural practices. This process may also be seen in ecological terms, incorporating a slow drift towards less 'complex' and more 'open' ecosystems brought about by increasing land and resource management practices. The firing of vegetation, for example, would have led to less complex stages of ecological succession, as has been argued for horticultural ecosystems (Rappaport 1967).

The are, however, also several problems with this model. First, it avoids discussing the social dynamics which underlie the demographic processes. What were the factors stimulating the increasing trend in population dispersal and growth? Second, the ecological (and economic) trend towards more open ecosystems may not be as smooth as once supposed; the dynamics of such systemic changes are often more complex (Ellen 1982: 273).

The alliance formation model

This model envisages two main, but not necessarily exclusive, stages of alliance formation, the first during the Pleistocene–early Holocene period, and the second in the late Holocene.

Stage I: During the Pleistocene–early Holocene period, alliance systems are generally more open and flexible (although regional variation may also have occurred at different times), with overall lower population densities, and greater access to allies and resource areas.

Stage II: In contrast, during the late Holocene, especially since around 4,000–3,000 BP, alliance systems are generally more complex, incorporating both more 'closed' and 'open' aspects. For example, more closed systems may contain higher population densities, less access to allies and resource areas, and higher levels of mediation (rituals, feasting, exchange) and communal aggregation. In order to overcome the constrictions of closure, however, alliance systems may also in some ways expand, or open, at other levels. For example, groups of relatively closed systems may unite in expanded networks or confederacies, as existed in parts of southeastern Australia at the time of European contact.

As I argued in Chapter One, increased closure of alliance systems would result in an increased need for regulation of social relations as access to potential allies is constrained. Intergroup behaviour associated with mediation or regulation would include rituals, gatherings, feasts, exchanges and the like. Closure would also produce a trend towards the regionalisation of social units and geographical restriction of socio-economic activities. The latter would include reduced sizes of territories, increased sedentism, economic (resource) specialisation and intensification and the like. Movement of people to intergroup gatherings would also alter the geographical dispersal of population patterns. This general process may result in greater complexity of alliance formations in both time and space, and as the interests of competing allies wax and wane.

The socio-demographic model

This composite model accommodates both the biogeographical dispersal of population and its ecological effects, together with the socio-cultural dynamics of the demographic process. It also accommodates the archaeological patterns and trends in time and space of Australian prehistory during the Pleistocene and Holocene periods. As well, this third model provides the environmental and socio-demographic dynamics behind these processes. In this way, ecological, demographic and social models are blended and linked to the archaeological data.

This model can not only explain the present archaeological data but it can also allow for the incorporation of new data with which it may be tested still further. Because of this, my preference is for the socio-demographic model, which goes somewhat further than existing models of Australian prehistory, many of which, as we have seen, are embedded in environmentally deterministic and static frames.

The following is an illustration of an environmentally deterministic interpretation. If, for example, we were to follow a model where open alliance formations were closely linked to harsh environments, and closed alliances to fertile environments (as suggested by some; see also Chapter One), then 'closure' should be evident in the early Holocene, when climate changed from the dry, cold, Pleistocene conditions towards more humid, warmer regimes; and it should be less obvious later, when climate was generally drier. Some indication of this is evident in southeastern Australia (the Murray River corridor, for example) during the early Holocene. This environmental connection, with degrees of open and closed systems, also is generally suggested by the late Pleistocene data from northwestern and central coastal (drier) and southwestern (wetter) Australia (see Chapter Nine). I argue here, however, that the process of alliance closure appears to have taken place more markedly in the late Holocene, when climates were relatively drier, that is against too close a relationship between social closure and richer environments.

It must be stressed that the models presented here are generalisations, they cover enormous stretches of time and do not necessarily suggest a unilinear trajectory. If, indeed, aspects of closure also occurred earlier, for example during the Pleistocene (and some examples have been provided here), then this should also be visible, in some way, in the archaeological record, and distinguishable from general environmental trends, as I have attempted to do here. Changes to resource structure, influencing many of the cultural trends and patterns discussed, should also be more clearly delineated and linked to the archaeological data in both general and more fine-grained contexts.

Research now needs to be directed at these broad questions, with theory developed at both the general as well as the middle-range levels of enquiry. A wider range of theoretical approaches also should be considered, for here lies the seeds of new questions and renewed enquiry. In the final section of this chapter, we will consider Australian prehistory and its interpretations in a broader, world context.

Greater Australia and world prehistory

According to available evidence, Greater Australia was colonised about the same time as modern people (*Homo sapiens sapiens*) appear on the world (or Old World) scene, that is about 40,000 years ago. The 'fully modern' Niah fossil from Borneo in Southeast Asia is of this general age, and is located at Australia's northwestern doorstep (see Chapter Three). Around the western perimeter of the Asian continent (in the Levant of the eastern Mediterranean), between about 40,000 and 30,000 years ago, populations were mixed; they were a combination of so-called archaic and modern morphologies (Stringer and Andrews 1988). This is so also for parts of eastern Europe (Gamble 1986b). It should not be surprising, therefore, that a similar broad range of morphologies occurs in Pleistocene Australian populations (irrespective of dating problems). Put crudely, at the time of Australian colonisation, that is what people of the Old World looked like, Pleistocene Australians being an extension of Southeast Asian peoples (but see Bowdler 1993; also Chapter Three). If it should transpire that Greater Australia was settled even earlier, present skeletal data would also be generally consistent, with perhaps greater accentuation on the more 'archaic' end of the range.

The spread or dispersal of modern people around the Old World (including western Europe) and further into 'uncharted' continents, including Australia and the Americas, is also an indication of changing socio-demographic patterns. One general explanation can be linked to climatic amelioration with rises in bioproductivity, another to an expansion of populations. Some (Thiel 1987) have linked these two possibilities, suggesting that in Southeast Asia climatic improvements and rising sea levels produced both an increase in human population and a territorial squeezing. This resulted, they argue, in the necessity to expand by emigration, and hence in the colonisation of Australasia. Alternative scenarios, however, in a sense countered this viewpoint by pointing to an increase of productive coastlines at this time in the island world of Southeast Asia (Bellwood 1986). Presumably the latter environmental changes might also have led to further population growth and dispersal. These explanations, however, do not take into consideration the social dynamics which promote territorial expansion and colonisation. The spread of population and cultural changes of this time, including the appearance of people around continental Greater Australia between 40,000 and 35,000 years ago, suggest more than a mechanical dispersal or radiation of population. This global (or at least Old World) Pleistocene demographic domino effect also suggests changing social relations.

Expanding social networks of a loose, open kind may have provided the dynamic associated also with population growth. That is, answers may lie also in the socio-demographic realm.

One alternative explanation is of biological change; that is to say that the development of modern people represents a biological breakthrough of some kind, with behavioural and cultural implications. In European archaeology this has been seen in terms of comparisons between 'archaic' and 'modern' populations, or the so-called 'Neanderthal problem'. Similar ideas have been discussed in relation to the development of language and other forms of social communication at this time (Davidson and Noble 1989, 1992; Noble and Davidson 1991). Biological explanations, however, do not adequately take into consideration the evidence of morphologically 'mixed' populations, including those of Australia, which existed about 40,000–35,000 years ago. They also avoid dealing with socio-cultural factors and their relationship to the demographics fuelling these processes.

The colonisation of Greater Australia has often been compared with that of the Americas. One of the main differences here relates to chronology. Two schools of thought have developed in North America regarding the colonisation of the New World; one favours a fairly recent terminal Pleistocene settlement (no older than about 15,000 BP), and the other an earlier occupation, with dates extending back beyond 30,000 years ago. The reasons behind this divergence are in some ways paradigmatic, relating to different models of colonisation. Dates older than about 15,000 BP are not accepted by the more traditional school. Earlier dates are found at key sites such as Meadowcroft (>19,000 BP) (Adavasio et al. 1990), and much earlier sites found throughout North and South America (for example, MacNeish et al. 1980, 1981; Guidon and Delibrias 1986; MacNeish 1986; Dillehey 1990).

As to colonisation models, the more traditional of the North American schools leans towards a more recent rapid settlement, with implications of marked environmental impact, swift dispersal of the population and subsequent relatively steady and increasing cultural changes. Australian prehistory is also confronting divided opinions, but these centre upon an earlier point in time; whether colonisation took place around 40,000 BP or even earlier. As in the American case, much more stringent criteria are applied to dates considered to be older than about 40,000 years ago. On both continents, Australia and North America, therefore, competing paradigms or perspectives largely control and direct the legitimation of knowledge.

In many ways Australian prehistory has also inherited theories from the traditional American school. Birdsell's (see Chapter Nine) model of rapid colonisation of Australia followed by long-term stability reflects the ecological-biological paradigm of North American cultural ecology (referred to in Chapter One). Related also is the supposed cause of the Australian Pleistocene faunal extinctions (see Chapter Three). One of the main differences, however, in the settlement of the Australian and American continents is that, whereas the north Australian region is largely an extension of the tropical island world of Southeast Asia, colonisation of the Americas was by way of the Arctic Circle, a region which would have provided considerable cultural and biological constraints.

We have already discussed in detail aspects of the debate concerning hunter-gatherer socio-cultural variation and its temporal and spatial dimensions. Comparisons, however, can be made also between Australian prehistory and other regions and time periods where hunter-gatherers predominated. For example, aspects of so-called cultural complexity, including increased population, demographic rearrangements, territoriality and more intensive land and resource use, have been documented for the late Pleistocene in southwestern France (see Chapter One) and also on the exposed Russian plain (Soffer 1985). These changes are associated with the glacial maximum and terminal Pleistocene periods in particular. Various competing explanations have been provided for these changes, including those of an ecological and social character. The Pleistocene archaeological record of Greater Australia is also beginning to reveal a complex of socio-cultural changes, also associated with the same two sub-periods.

It is during the Holocene period, however, exemplified by the Eurasian Mesolithic and North American Archaic periods, that more evidence still is to be found. As in the Holocene period of the Australian mainland, a central issue concerns disentangling natural from cultural and demographic factors. Clear similarities can, for example, be found in the Mesolithic of northwestern Europe (Price 1985). Here the complex of environmental changes is pitted against a variety of demographic and socio-cultural patterns, not easily discernible, and with no clear-cut socio-cultural signature. Similar 'grey area' patterns were seen in the Australian late Holocene data.

Less obviously comparable with Australia is the Archaic period of the North American mid-continent – the riverine Mississippi, Missouri, Illinois and Ohio areas. On closer inspection, however, similarities emerge. For example, levels of population density in rich river valleys like that of the Lower Illinois during the complex Middle Woodland period have been estimated at no more than one person per square mile (Brown 1985: 221), which is roughly comparable to ethnographic Aboriginal densities of the Murray River region in southeastern Australia (see Chapters Two and Six). Patterns of sedentism, elaborate burial practices, mortuary precincts and exchange systems vary throughout the North American riverine region and there is no direct connection with environmental factors. For example, the most complex societies of the Adena-Hopewell occurred outside the rich valley systems in less productive locales, with more dispersed settlement patterns. As Bender (1985) points out, the only common characteristic of these groups is in regard to the complexity of the socio-cultural realm. Aspects of this sketch, involving demography, settlement patterns and complex socio-cultural relations, are broadly comparable in many ways to southeastern Australia (and other areas of Australia) in the late Holocene.

As to economic patterns and trends, obvious similarities can be drawn with the Eurasian Mesolithic which demonstrate, in some ways, adaptations to changing Holocene environments, and in others, shifts towards more complex and intensive hunter-gatherer-fisher subsistence-settlement patterns. Gamble (1986b) also drew parallels between this period and late Holocene Australia. Zvelebil (1986), on the other hand, compared the temperate Eurasian Mesolithic economic shifts with contemporary changes in the Near East (Southwest Asia) where agriculture and pastoralism appear. He viewed the economic changes of temperate Eurasia within hunter-gatherer contexts as parallelling the developments in agro-pastoralism in warmer climates to the south.

Further comparisons can be drawn with late Holocene Australia. Changing hunter-gatherer relations with natural local environments and their resources in Australia compare with temperate Eurasian Mesolithic adaptations. Yen (1989, 1995) has referred to these more complex and changing relationships between people, landscapes and resources, including those of Australia, as a 'domestication of environment'. Other Australian patterns, however, for example the use of grass seeds, have parallels with classic Mesolithic Near Eastern societies (also Allen 1974). The introduction of the use of grass seeds and their later intensification in arid and semi-arid Australia during the late Holocene (see Chapter Five) is broadly comparable to the classic terminal Pleistocene Natufian sequence of events (which in a further step, sometime later, led to agriculture). It is also comparable with other archaeological examples of similar shifts to use of wild grass seeds, for example in Mesoamerica (Flannery 1968) and Peru (Cohen 1977). In all three examples, competing explanations exist in terms of the key variables: techno-environmental, demographic, and socio-cultural. Much the same set of competing explanations has been offered for the Australian examples, and largely for similar reasons.

To what extent do the cultural changes and trends observed in Australia's prehistory compare with those of neighbouring New Guinea? The two land-masses were physically connected, at least until 8,000 years ago, and peoples of the Torres Strait region, including the northeastern tip of Australia, were in close contact in recent times. The main question that has interested New Guinean prehistorians concerns the development and intensification of agriculture in the region. In Australia, by comparison, one of the leading questions posed (see above) concerns the expansion or intensification of the Australian hunter-gatherer economy, especially in late Holocene times. Both inquiries were derived from ethnographic evidence.

Some have suggested the possibility of Pleistocene agriculture in Melanesia and also northern Australia (see Chapter Four). The archaeological evidence for the New Guinea Highlands, however, indicates that while the first putative signs of horticulture, or elaborate swamp management, occur around 9,000 BP (when New Guinea was still connected to mainland Australia), it is not until around 6,000–5,000 BP that definite agricultural signs are present (Golson 1977a, 1989;

Golson and Gardner 1990; Hope and Golson 1995). Intensive horticulture and pig raising is only apparent, however, in the last two thousand years, and especially so during the last one thousand years (Golson 1977a, 1989; White and O'Connell 1982; Feil 1987). In lowland and coastal New Guinea signs of demographic changes, immigration and socio-economic rearrangements take place increasingly during the last 4,000–3,000 years, and are most pronounced in the last one thousand years or so. During these latter stages offshore islands are increasingly occupied (Allen 1977; Irwin 1978, 1992; White and O'Connell 1982; Harris 1995), and horticulture also appears to have been intensified during this recent period.

In general, therefore, until around 6,000–5,000 years ago in the New Guinea Highlands, and in the last few thousand years in both highlands and lowlands, hunter-gatherer practices predominated. Horticulture in New Guinea appears therefore to be largely a late Holocene phenomenon, and intensive horticulture (and presumably intensive hunting-fishing-gathering as well) to be of the last two millennia.

Given the structural similarities between many New Guinean hunter-horticultural and Australia hunter-gatherer economies (discussed in Chapter Two), together with the Australian archaeological data of the Holocene, it may be argued that both regions appear to have experienced an economic expansion or intensification in the late Holocene, and in particular in the last 2,000–1,000 years or so. In general, the two prehistories are also connected at least in the Torres Strait region and north Australia. The recent (late Holocene), more intensive use of offshore islands (and their marine and terrestrial foods) is common to both southern New Guinea and northern Australian regions. Trends, including common trends, towards socio-cultural complexity also have been discussed for both New Guinea and Australia in late Holocene contexts (Yoffee 1985).

I would suggest, therefore, that the cultural contexts in which the late Holocene changes occurred in northern coastal Australia are associated, in some ways, with those of coastal New Guinea. Archaeological evidence (artefacts and the like) is also in accord to some extent. This context involved socio-economic intensification and complexity, to varying degrees, in both regions. Given the chain of social and ritual connections across continental Australia during ethnographic times (see Chapter Two), it would not be difficult to suggest that these northern changes were felt across Australia. These temporal connections between late Holocene New Guinea and Australia, which have been long recognised (White 1971), would have provided a somewhat different and changing socio-cultural context to Australian Aboriginal societies.

In some ways this scenario implies a 'destabilisation' of prior Australian hunter-gatherer relations, with Australia beginning to merge with a broader Australasian system, one increasingly influenced by socio-economic and demographic changes. Such an explanation asks us to look beyond regional prehistories to those of the wider cultural area or sphere of social interaction. I am not suggesting, however, that the cultural changes of the late Holocene in Australia were due solely to external influences, but rather to an interplay of internal and external forces.

What effect could such socio-demographic changes have had upon Australian economies? One explanation would lie with economic intensification linked to inter-group occasions and relations. Similar explanations have been provided for the intensification of agriculture in the New Guinea Highlands (Watson 1965, 1977; Modjeska 1982; see Chapter One). A similar viewpoint also has been expressed here (Chapter One) for Aboriginal Australia. It has been argued that the maintenance, management and intensification of resources linked to intergroup occasions in Australia would have been affected similarly by the vagaries of intergroup social relations (Lourandos 1988b). We could hypothesise, therefore, that as socio-demographic conditions became more problematical (for example, 'closed'), the greater the impact upon the economic control of key resources (see also Chapter One).

The archaeological evidence from late Holocene Australia to some extent fits these interpretations. As socio-demographic contexts fluctuated, so too did their economic base, one that was geared to both domestic and intergroup needs. In this socio-economic climate some new directions were taken, ones largely avoided in the past. These included the incorporation of more complex and 'costly' patterns of land and resource management and use, settlement and social aggregation, and intergroup relations.

While this general overview of the prehistories of New Guinea and Australia appears to indicate directional cultural trends, this should be seen largely as a function of scale. I suggest that a more fine-grained perspective and one aimed also at the regional level would indicate a greater degree of variation in time and space. Fluctuations therefore in the key variables – social, economic and demographic – may be expected (see also Chapter One).

The prehistory, or long-term history, therefore, of both hunter-horticultural New Guinea and hunter-gatherer-fisher Australia, have more in common than at first meets the eye. The old distinction between 'resourceful' agriculturalist and 'quiescent' hunter can no longer really be seen to apply. As well, the prehistory of Greater Australia finds general parallels with the hunter-gatherer past on other continents, as we have seen. In this sense, Australia no longer has to stand as 'the continent apart', as it has so often been represented. Altogether, this new information has changed our perception and appreciation of the hunter-gatherer past. It also may help us to appreciate and understand better the present struggle of the direct inheritors of that past: in our case, Aboriginal Australians – no longer passive adaptation to changing natural environments, but active participation in complex interplays – among them, social, environmental and demographic.

GLOSSARY

adze   A chisel-edged tool used for woodworking, and often hafted onto a 'handle'.

aeolian   The product of wind action (for instance, sand dunes).

assemblage   A group of artefacts from a particular site, region or time period.

backed blade   Blades which have been blunted along one, or part, of their margins.

bifacial   Two-sided, often used of stone artefacts (*see also* unifacial, below).

biomass   The amount of energy contained in a particular environment, such as forest, island, desert etc.

biome   A geographical ecological unit or community, such as forest, island, desert etc.

bioproduction   The amount of energy produced in a particular environment, such as forest, island, desert etc.

blade   A long, thin stone flake.

breccia   A rock composed of angular fragments embedded in a matrix, which may be heterogeneous in origin.

burren adze   An adze-like stone artefact made on flakes and, for example, found in eastern Australia.

chenier (ridge)   Beach ridges formed from accumulated shell, for example along tropical coastlines.

Core Tool and Scraper tradition   An assèmblage of stone artefacts from the earlier stages of Australian prehistory (pre-c. 5,000 BP), and including artefacts such as 'horsehoof cores' and 'scrapers'.

debitage   The biproduct of stone tool manufacture and use, and generally composed of a range of 'waste' stone material.

disclimax   An arrested stage in the chronological, vegetational sequence of a region prior to the 'climax' stage, such as is produced by firing the landscape (for example, grassland as distinct from savanna; open as distinct from closed forest).

ecotone (ecotonal)   A geographical unit on the margins of two or more ecological communities (for example, forest and plain).

ethno- A prefix referring in general to ethnic groups or communities, as in ethnographic, ethnohistorical, ethnocentric etc.

forbs A non-grasslike herb.

hornfels A fine-grained rock.

industry An assemblage of artefacts from a particular time period or region (for example, backed blade industry).

Kartan The name for distinct core tools, including large horsehoof cores and steep-edge scrapers, found in the region of Kangaroo Island and wider South Australia, and often made on large water-worn pebbles.

lens A stratigraphic feature such as a 'layer' or 'level', but generally more restricted in area (for example, charcoal lens, sand lens etc).

lunette Crescent-shaped dunes formed along the eastern and southeastern margins of lake systems in southern Australia and Tasmania.

palaeo- A prefix meaning ancient, as in palaeoenvironment.

palynology The study of pollen and therefore of past and present vegetation communities.

podzol A major soil type, developed principally under forest conditions.

points Stone artefacts made on flakes, generally 'leaf shaped' in form and either unifacially of bifacially retrimmed.

progradation The process by which coastlines and other natural features are increased through deposition of new material (for example, beaches, dunes, mudflats etc).

scraper A general category of stone artefact (made either on flakes or cores) with retrimmed or utilised margins.

stratigraphy (stratigraphic) The study of strata in geological formations (for example, dunes) and archaeological sites (including layers, levels, lenses etc).

taphonomy The study of the processes by which organic materials (including animals and plants) find their way to their final place of rest (including the archaeological record).

tephra An ash-coloured volcanic rock.

tradition A general category of artefact (stone, bone, rock art etc) found over a wide geographical region and time period (for example, the Australian Small Tool tradition).

transect A cross-section of the landscape sampled, for example, during archaeological survey.

trophic Pertaining to the food chain or ecological, hierarchical sequence of organisms in particular environments.

tula adze Stone adzes made on flakes and used (in ethnographic contexts) predominantly in arid and semi-arid areas of Australia. They were often hafted with gum onto the end of wooden spearthrowers.

unifacial One-sided and often describing stone artefacts or tools worked or trimmed on one side only, as opposed, for example, to bifacial (two-sided) tools.

NOTES ON DATING METHODS

The most common method of dating in Australian archaeology is the radiocarbon (C14) method, which is based upon the half-life of the carbon 14 isotope. Organic material (for example, charcoal) can be analysed in this way; the amount of C14 remaining in the sample allows the time of death of the organism to be calculated. By this method individual strata or artefacts within archaeological sites can be dated. Generally a time range will be produced (for example, 2,500 ± 60 BP) with an inbuilt error factor (in this case ± 60 years) calculated to the present day (BP or Before Present). Such radiocarbon dates can be further calibrated to conventional time-scales.

For accuracy and to assist the serious student I have referred often to C14 dates in the above way throughout the text. As investigation of Australian prehistory is relatively recent, often only a few dates are known from individual sites. More accurate investigation requires larger numbers of dates to corroborate site and regional chronologies.

At present, however, C14 dating is limited to the last 40,000 years or so, with dates on this upper limit or older being difficult to distinguish. Because of this, more exploratory and often controversial methods of dating are also currently being investigated, such as thermoluminescence (TL). The latter does not date organic material, but the matrix, such as the sands (particles of sedimentary rock), in which archaeological material is deposited. Because TL dating can produce dates in excess of 40,000 years – and thus throw light on the earliest occupation of the continent – these methods and results come under extra-close scrutiny and, by today's standards, appear controversial in nature.

REFERENCES

Adavasio, J. M., Donahue, J. and Stuckenrath, R. 1990 The Meadowcroft rockshelter radiocarbon chronology, 1975–1990, *American Antiquity* 55 (2): 348–354.

Ainsworth, J. 1922 *Reminiscences of Ballina in the Early Days: 1847–1922*, Ballina: Beacon Printery.

Akazawa, T. 1986 Hunter-gatherer adaptations and the transition to food production in Japan, in M. Zvelebil (ed) *Hunters in Transition: Mesolithic Societies of Temperate Eurasia and Their Transition to Farming*, Cambridge: Cambridge University Press, pp. 151–165.

Alfredson, G. 1983 St. Helena Island–a changing pattern of exploitation, *Australian Archaeology* 17: 79–86.

Alfredson, G. 1984 An Archaeological Investigation Into the Aboriginal Use of St, Helena Island, Moreton Bay. Unpublished BA thesis, Brisbane: Department of Anthropology and Sociology, University of Queensland.

Allen, H. A. 1972 Where the Crow Flies Backwards: Man and Land in the Darling Basin. Unpublished PhD thesis, Canberra: Department of Prehistory, Research School of Pacific Studies, Australian National University.

Allen, H. 1974 The Bagundji of the Darling basin: cereal gatherers in an uncertain environment, *World Archaeology* 5: 309–322.

Allen, H. 1979 Left out in the cold: why the Tasmanians stopped eating fish, *The Artefact* 4: 1–10.

Allen, H. and Barton, G. 1989 Ngarradj Warde Djobkeng: White Cockatoo Dreaming and the Prehistory of Kakadu, *Oceania Monograph* 37, Sydney: University of Sydney.

Allen, J. 1977 Sea traffic, trade and expanding horizons, in J. Allen, J. Golson and R. Jones (eds) *Sunda and Sahul*, London: Academic Press, pp. 387–417.

Allen, J. 1989a When did humans first colonise Australia? *Search* 20: 149–154.

Allen, J. 1989b Excavation at Bone Cave, South Central Tasmania, January–February 1989, *Australian Archaeology* 28: 105–106.

Allen, J., Gosden, C., Jones, R. and White, J. P. 1988 Pleistocene dates for the human occupation of New Ireland, northern Melanesia, *Nature* 331: 707–709.

Allen, J., Gosden, C. and White, J. P. 1989 Human Pleistocene Adaptations in the tropical island Pacific: recent evidence from New Ireland, a greater Australian outlier, *Antiquity*, 63: 548–61.

Allen, J. and Holdaway, S. 1995 The contamination of Pleistocene radiocarbon determinations in Australia, *Antiquity* 69: 101–112.

Altman, J. C. 1987 *Hunter-Gatherers Today: an Aboriginal Economy in north Australia*, Canberra: Australian Institute of Aboriginal Studies.

Ames K. M. 1985 Hierarchies, stress, and logistical strategies among hunter-gatherers in northwestern North America, in T. D. Price and J. A. Brown (eds) *Prehistoric Hunter-gatherers: The Emergence of Cultural Complexity*, Orlando, Florida: Academic Press, pp. 155–180.

Ambrose, W. R. and Mummery, J. M. C. 1987 *Archaeometry, Further Australasian Studies*, Canberra: Department of Prehistory, Research School of Pacific Studies, Australian National University.

Anderson, I. 1991 First Australians headed south in haste, *New Scientist*, 23: 3.

Archer, M., Crawford, I. M. and Merrilees, D. 1980 Incisions, breakages and charring, some probably man-made, in fossil bones from Mammoth Cave, Western Australia, *Alcheringa* 4: 115–131.

Attenbrow, V. 1976 Aboriginal Subsistence Economy on the Far South Coast of New South Wales, Australia. Unpublished BA (Hons) thesis, Department of Anthropology, University of Sydney.

Attenbrow, V. J. 1982 The archaeology of Upper Mangrove Creek catchment: research in progress, in S. Bowdler (ed) *Coastal Archaeology in Eastern Australia*, Canberra: Australian National University Press, pp. 67–78.

Attenbrow, V. 1987 The Upper Mangrove Creek Catchment: A Study of Quantitative Changes in the Archaeological Record. Unpublished PhD thesis, Department of Anthropology, University of Sydney.

Backhouse, J. 1843 *Narrative of a Visit to the Australian Colonies*, London: Hamilton Adams.

Bailey G. N. 1983a *Hunter-gatherer Economy in Prehistory*, Cambridge: Cambridge University Press.

Bailey, G. N. 1983b Economic change in late Pleistocene Cantabria, in G. N. Bailey (ed) *Hunter-gatherer Economy in Prehistory*, Cambridge: Cambridge University Press, pp. 149–165.

Bailey, G. and Parkington, J. 1988 *The Archaeology of Prehistoric Coastlines*, Cambridge: Cambridge University Press.

Balme, J, 1980 An analysis of charred bone from Devil's Lair, Western Australia, *Archaeology and Physical Anthropology in Oceania* 15: 81–85.

Balme, J. 1995 30,000 years of fishery in New South Wales, *Archaeology in Oceania* 30: 1–21.

Balme, J. and Beck, W. 1993 Archaeology and feminism: views on the origins of the division of labour, in L. Smith and H. du Cross (eds) *Women in Archaeology: A Feminist Critique*, Canberra: Australian National University Press, pp. 61–74.

Balme, J. and Hope, J. 1990 Radiocarbon dates from midden sites in the lower Darling River area of western New South Wales, *Archaeology in Oceania*, 25: 85–101.

Balme, J., Merrilees, D. and Porter, J. K. 1978 Late Quaternary mammal remains, spanning about 30,000 years, from excavations in Devil's Lair, Western Australia, *Journal of the Royal Society of Western Australia* 61: 33–65.

Barbetti, M. and Allen, H. 1972 Prehistoric man at Lake Mungo, Australia, by 32,000 B.P., *Nature* 240: 46–48.

Barker, B. C. 1987 A Faunal Analysis From Narcurrer Shelter, South-east South Australia. Unpublished BA (Hons) thesis, Department of Anthropology and Sociology, University of Queensland.

Barker, B. C. 1989 Nara Inlet 1: A Holocene sequence from the Whitsunday Islands, central Queensland coast, *Queensland Archaeological Research* 6: 53–76.

Barker, B. C. 1991 Nara Inlet 1: coastal resource use and the Holocene marine transgression in the Whitsunday Islands, Central Queensland, *Archaeology in Oceania* 26: 102–109.

Barker, B. 1995 'The Sea People': maritime hunter-gatherers on the tropical coast. A late Holocene maritime specialisation in the Whitsunday Islands, central Queensland. Unpublished PhD thesis, Department of Anthropology and Sociology, University of Queensland.

Bar-Yosef, O. 1987 Late Pleistocene adaptations in the Levant, in O. Soffer (ed) *The Pleistocene Old World: Regional Perspectives*, New York: Plenum, pp. 219–236.

Beaton, J. M. 1977 Dangerous Harvest: Investigations in the Late Prehistoric Occupation of Upland South-east Central Queensland. Unpublished PhD thesis, Canberra: Australian National University.

Beaton, J. M. 1982 Fire and water: aspects of Australian Aboriginal management of cycads, *Archaeology in Oceania* 17: 59–67.

Beaton, J. M. 1985 Evidence for a coastal occupation time-lag at Princess Charlotte Bay (North Queensland) and implications for coastal colonization and population growth theories for Aboriginal Australia, *Archaeology in Oceania* 20: 1–20.

Beaton, J. M. 1990 The importance of past population for prehistory, in B. Meehan and N. White (eds) *Hunter-Gatherer Demography: Past and Present*, Sydney: Oceania Monograph 39, University of Sydney, pp. 23–40.

Beaton, J. M. 1995 The Transition on the coastal fringe of Greater Australia, in Allen, J. and J. F. O'Connell (eds) *Transitions: Pleistocene to Holocene in Australia and Papua New Guinea, Antiquity* 69: 798–806.

Beck, W., Clarke, A. and Head, L. 1989 Plants in Australian archaeology, *Tempus* 1, Brisbane: Anthropology Museum, University of Queensland.

Bednarik, R. 1984 Die Bedeutung der paläolithischen Fingerlinientradition, *Anthropologie* 22: 73–79.

Bell, C. 1979 Reconstruction of vegetation from spectra of pollen and spores in quaternary sediments from Moreton Bay and Maroochydore, in A. Bailey and N. C. Stevens (eds) *Northern Moreton Bay Symposium*, Brisbane: Royal Society of Queensland, pp. 29–31.

Bell, D. 1983 *Daughters of the Dreaming*, Melbourne: McPhee Gribble.

Bellwood, P. S. 1986 From late Pleistocene to Early Holocene in Sundaland, paper presented to the World Archaeological Congress, Southampton.

Belshaw, J. 1978 Population distribution and the pattern of seasonal movement in northern NSW, in I. McBryde (ed) *Records of Times Past*, Canberra: Australian Institute of Aboriginal Studies.

Bender, B. 1978 Gatherer-hunter to farmer: a social perspective, *World Archaeology* 10: 204–22.

Bender, B. 1981 Gatherer-hunter intensification, in A. Sheridan and G. Bailey (eds) *Economic Archaeology*, Oxford: British Archaeological Reports, International Series, 96, pp. 149–157.

Bender, B. 1985 Prehistoric developments in the American midcontinent and in Brittany, northwest France, in T. D. Price and J. A. Brown (eds) *Prehistoric Hunter-gatherers: The Emergence of Cultural Complexity*, Orlando, Florida: Academic Press, pp. 21–57.

Bender, B. and Morris, B. 1988 Twenty years of history, evolution and social change in hunter-gatherer studies, in T. Ingold, D. Riches and J. Woodburn (eds) *Hunters and Gatherers: History, Evolution and Social Change*, Oxford: Berg, pp. 4–14.

Bennett, G. 1834 *Wanderings in New South Wales, Batavia, Pedir Coast, Singapore and China: Being the Journal of a Naturalist in Those Countries, During 1832, 1833 and 1834*, 2 vols., London: Bentley.

Bennett, J. W. 1975 Ecosystem analogies in cultural ecology, in S. Polgar (ed) *Population, Ecology and Social Evolution*, The Hague: Mouton, pp. 272–303.

Bermingham, A. 1966 Victoria natural radiocarbon measurements I, *Radiocarbon* 8: 507–521.

Bern, J. 1979 Ideology and domination: towards a reconstruction of Australian Aboriginal social formation, *Oceania* 50: 118–132.

Berryman, A. and Frankel, D. 1984 Archaeological investigations of mounds on the Wakool River, near Barham, New South Wales, *Australian Archaeology* 19: 21–30.

Bettinger, R. L. 1991 *Hunter-Gatherers: Archaeological and Evolutionary Theory*, New York: Plenum press.

Binford L. R. 1968 Post-Pleistocene adaptations, in S. R. Binford and L. R. Binford (eds) *New Perspectives in Archaeology*, Chicago: Aldine, pp. 313–341.

Binford, L. 1980 Willow smoke and dogs' tails: hunter-gatherer settlement systems and archaeological site formation, *American Antiquity* 45: 4–20.

Binford L. 1983 *In Pursuit of the Past: Decoding the Archaeological Record*, London: Thames and Hudson.

Binford S. R. and Binford L. R. 1968 *New Perspectives in Archaeology*, Chicago: Aldine.

Binns, R. A. and McBryde I. 1972 *A Petrological Analysis of Ground-edge Artefacts from Northern New South Wales*, Canberra: Australian Institute of Aboriginal Studies.

Bird, C. F. M. and Frankel, D. 1991a Chronology and explanation in western Victoria and south-east South Australia, *Archaeology in Oceania*, 26: 1–16.

Bird, C. F. M. and Frankel, D. 1991b Problems in constructing a prehistoric regional sequence: Holocene south-east Australia, *World Archaeology* 23(2): 179–192.

Bird-David, N. H. 1988 Hunter-gatherers and other people: a re-examination, in T. Ingold, D. Riches and J. Woodburn (eds) *Hunters and Gatherers 1: History, Evolution and Social Change*, New York: St. Martin's Press, pp. 17–30.

Birdsell, J. B. 1949 The racial origins of the extinct Tasmanians, *Records of the Queen Victoria Museum* 2: 105–122.

Birdsell, J. B. 1953 Some environmental and cultural factors influencing the structuring of Australian Aboriginal populations, *American Naturalist* 87: 171–207.

Birdsell, J. B. 1957 Some population problems involving Pleistocene Man, *Cold Spring Harbor Symposia on Quantitative Biology* 22: 47–69.

Birdsell, J. B. 1958 On population structure in generalised hunting and collecting populations, *Evolution* 12: 189–205.

Birdsell, J. B. 1967 Preliminary data on the trihybrid origin of the Australian Aborigines, *Archaeology and Physical Anthropology in Oceania* 2: 100–155.

Birdsell, J. B. 1968 Some predictions for the Pleistocene based on equilibrium systems among recent hunter-gatherers, in R. B. Lee and I. DeVore (eds) *Man the Hunter*, Chicago: Aldine, pp. 229–40.

Birdsell, J. B. 1971 Ecology, spacing mechanisms and adaptive behavior in Aboriginal land tenure, in R. Crocombe (ed) *Land Tenure in the Pacific*, Melbourne: Oxford University Press, pp. 334–61.

Birdsell, J. B. 1977 The recalibration of a paradigm for the first peopling of Australia, in J. Allen, J. Golson and R. Jones (eds) *Sunda and Sahul*, London: Academic Press, pp. 113–167.

Blackwell, A. 1982 Bowen Island: further evidence for economic change and intensification on the south coast of New South Wales, in S. Bowdler (ed) *Coastal Archaeology in Eastern Australia*, Canberra: Australian National University, pp. 46–51.

Blom, W. M. 1988 Late Quaternary sediments and sea levels in Bass Basin, southeastern Australia: a preliminary report, *Search* 19: 94–96.

Blundell, V. M. and Bleed, P. 1974 Ground stone artefacts from Late Pleistocene and Early Holocene Japan, *Archaeology and Physical Anthropology in Oceania* 9: 120–133.

Bodmer, M. and Cavalli-Sforza, L. L. 1976 *Genetics, Evolution and Man*, San Francisco: W. H. Freeman.

Boot, P. 1994 Recent research into the prehistory of the hinterland of the south coast of New South Wales, in M. Sullivan, S. Brockwell and A. Webb (eds) *Archaeology in the North* Darwin: North Australian Research Unit (ANU), pp. 319–340.

Boot, P. (in press) Aspects of prehistoric change in the south coast hinterland of NSW, in I. Lilley, A. Ross, and S. Ulm, (eds) *Proceedings of the 1995 Australian Archaeological Association Annual Conference*, Brisbane: University of Queensland.

Boserup, E. 1965 *The Conditions of Agricultural Growth*, Chicago: Aldine.

Bowdler, S. 1974 An account of an archaeological reconnaissance of Hunter's Isles, north-west Tasmania, 1973/74, *Records of the Queen Victoria Museum* 54: 1–22.

Bowdler, S. 1976 Hook, line and dillybag: an interpretation of an Australian coastal shell midden, *Mankind* 10: 248–258.

Bowdler, S. 1977 The coastal colonization of Australia, in J. Allen, J. Golson and R. Jones (eds) *Sunda and Sahul*, London: Academic Press, pp. 205–246.

Bowdler, S. 1979 Hunter Hill, Hunter Island. Unpublished PhD thesis, Canberra: Australian National University.

Bowdler, S. 1981 Hunters in the highlands: Aboriginal adaptations in the eastern Australian uplands, *Archaeology in Oceania* 16: 99–111.

Bowdler, S. 1982 Prehistoric Archaeology in Tasmania, *Advances in World Archaeology*, 1: 1–49.

Bowdler, S. 1984 Hunter Hill, Hunter Island, *Terra Australis* 8, Canberra: Australian National University.

Bowdler, S. 1988 Tasmanian Aborigines in the Hunter Islands in the Holocene: island resource use and seasonality, in G. Bailey and J. Parkington (eds) *The Archaeology of Prehistoric Coastlines*, Cambridge: Cambridge University Press, pp. 42–52.

Bowdler, S. 1990a The Silver Dollar site, Shark Bay: an interim report, *Australian Aboriginal Studies* 2, 60–63.

Bowdler, S. 1990b 50,000 year-old-site in Australia – is it really that old?, *Australian Archaeology*, 31: 93.

Bowdler, S. 1990c Peopling Australasia: the 'coastal colonisation' hypothesis considered, in P. Mellars and C. Stringer (eds) *The Human Revolution: Behavioural and Biological Perspectives on the Origins of Modern Humans*, Vol.2, Edinburgh: University of Edinburgh Press, pp. 327–343.

Bowdler, S. 1991 Some sort of dates at Malakunanja II: a reply to Roberts et al., *Australian Archaeology* 32: 50–51.

Bowdler, S. 1993 Sunda and Sahul: a 30 kyr culture area? in M. A. Smith, M. Spriggs and B. Frankhauser (eds) *Sahul in Review: Pleistocene Archaeology in Australia, New Guinea and Island Melanesia*, Canberra: Department of Prehistory, Research School of Pacific Studies, Australian National University, pp. 60–70.

Bowdler, S. and O'Connor, S. 1991 The dating of the Australian small tool tradition, with new evidence from the Kimberley, Western Australia, *Australian Aboriginal Studies*, 1: 53–62.

Bowler, J. M. 1971 Pleistocene salinities and climatic change: evidence from lakes and lunettes in south-eastern Australia, in D. J. Mulvaney and J. Golson (eds) *Aboriginal Man and Environment in Australia*, Canberra: Australian National University Press, pp. 47–65.

Bowler, J. M. 1976 Recent developments in reconstructing late Quarternary environments in Australia, in R. L. Kirk and A. G. Thorne (eds) *The Origin of the Australians*, Canberra: Australian Institute of Aboriginal Studies, pp. 55–77.

Bowler, J. M. 1980 Quaternary chronology and palaeohydrology in the evolution of Mallee landscapes, in R. R. Storrier and M. E. Stannard (eds) *Aeolian Landscapes in the Semi-arid Zone of South-eastern Australia*, Wagga Wagga: Australian Society of Soil Science, pp. 17–36.

Bowler, J. M. 1981 Australian salt lakes, a palaeohydrologic approach, *Hydrobiologia* 82: 431–444.

Bowler, J. M. 1982 Aridity in the Late Tertiary and Quaternary of Australia, in W. R. Barker and P. J. M. Greenslade (eds) *Evolution of the Flora and Fauna of Arid Australia*, Adelaide: Peacock Publications.

Bowler, J. M. 1986 Quaternary landform evolution, in D. N. Jeans (ed) *The Natural Environment*, Sydney: Sydney University Press.

Bowler, J. M., Hope, G. S., Jennings, J. N., Singh, G., and Walker, D. 1976 Late Quaternary climates of Australia, *Quaternary Research* 6: 359–394.

Bowler, J. M., Jones, R., Allen, H. and Thorne, A. G. 1970 Pleistocene human remains from Australia: a living site and human cremation from Lake Mungo, western New South Wales, *World Archaeology* 2: 39–60.

Bowler, J. M. and Magee, J. W. 1990 Lake Frome: stratigraphy, facies analysis and evolution of a major playa, *SLEADS 1988*, Canberra: Australian National University.

Bowler, J. M. and Teller, J. 1986 Quaternary evaporites and hydrological changes, Lake Tyrrel, north-west Victoria, *Australian Journal of Earth Science* 33: 43–63.

Bowler, J. M. and Thorne A. G. 1976 Human remains from Lake Mungo: discovery and excavation of Lake Mungo III, in R. L. Kirk and A. G. Thorne (eds) *The Origin of the Australians*, Canberra: Australian Insitute of Aboriginal Studies, pp. 127–138.

Bowler, J. M. and Wasson, R. J. 1984 Glacial age environments of inland Australia, in J. C. Vogel (ed) *Late Cainozoic Palaeoclimates of the Southern Hemisphere*, Rotterdam: Balkema.

Bray, W. 1976 From predation to production: the nature of agricultural evolution in Mexico and Peru, in G. ge G. Sieveking, I. H. Longworth and K. E. Wilson (eds) *Problems in Economic and Social Archaeology*, London: Duckworth, pp. 73–95.

Bride, T. F. 1898 *Letters From Victorian Pioneers*, Melbourne.

Brokensha, P. 1975 *The* Pitjanjatjara *and their Crafts*, Sydney: Aboriginal Arts Board.

Brown, J. A. 1985. Long-term trends to sedentism and the emergence of complexity in the American midwest, in T. D. Price and J. A. Brown (eds) *Prehistoric Hunter-gatherers: the Emergence of Cultural Complexity*, Orlando, Florida: Academic Press, pp. 201–231.

Brown, P. 1978 *Highland Peoples of New Guinea*, New York: Cambridge University Press.

Brown, P. 1981 Artificial cranial deformation: a component in the variation in Pleistocene Australian crania, *Archaeology in Oceania* 16: 156–167.

Brown, P. 1987 Pleistocene homogeneity and Holocene size reduction: the Australian human skeletal evidence, *Archaeology in Oceania*, 22, 41–67.

Brown, P. 1989 Coobool Creek. A morphological and metrical analysis of the crania, mandibles and dentitions of a prehistoric Australian human population, *Terra Australis*, 13, Canberra: Australian National University Press.

Brown, S. 1987 Toward a Prehistory of the Hamersley Plateau, Northwest Australia, *Occasional Papers in Prehistory No. 6*, Canberra: Department of Prehistory, Australian National University.

Brown, S. 1993 Mannalargenna Cave: a Pleistocene site in Bass Strait, in M. A. Smith, M. Spriggs and B. Frankhauser (eds) *Sahul in Review: Pleistocene Archaeology in Australia, New Guinea and Island Melanesia*, Canberra: Department of Prehistory, Research School of Pacific Studies, Australian National University, pp. 258–271.

Brown, S., Kee, S., McGowan, A., Middleton, G., Nash, M., Prince, B., Ricketts, N. and West, D. 1991 A preliminary survey for Aboriginal sites in the Denison River Valley, *Australian Archaeology* 32 (March): 26–37.

Bulmer, S. 1975 Settlement and economy in prehistoric Papua New Guinea: a review of the archaeological evidence, *Journal de la Société des Océanistes* 31 (46): 7–75.

Bulmer, S. 1977 Between the mountain and the plain: prehistoric settlement and environment in the Kaironk Valley, in J. H. Winslow (ed) *The Melanesian Environment*, Canberra: Australian National University Press, pp. 61–73.

Butlin, N. G. 1983 *Our Original Aggression*, Sydney: George, Allen and Unwin.

Butlin, N. G. 1993 *Economics and the Dreamtime: A Hypothetical History*, Cambridge: Cambridge University Press.

Calaby, J. H. 1976 Some biogeographical factors relevant to the pleistocene movement of man in Australasia, in R. L. Kirk and A. G. Thorne (eds) *The Origin of the Australians*, Canberra: Australian Insitute of Aboriginal Studies, pp. 23–28.

Callaghan, M. 1980 Some previously unconsidered environmental factors of relevance to south coast prehistory, *Australian Archaeology* 11: 43–49.

Campbell, J. B. 1982 Automatic sea-food retrieval systems: evidence from Hinchinbrook Island and its implications, in S. Bowdler (ed) *Coastal Archaeology in Eastern Australia*, Canberra: Australian National University, pp. 96–107.

Cane, S. B. 1984 Desert Camps: A Case Study of Stone Artefacts and Aboriginal Behaviour in the Western Desert. Unpublished PhD thesis, Canberra: Australian National University.

Cane, S. 1987 Australian Aboriginal subsistence in the Western Desert, *Human Ecology* 15: 391–434.

Carnegie, D. W. 1898 *Spinifex and Sand*, London: Pearson.

Carr-Saunders, A. 1922 *The Population Problem*, Oxford: Clarendon Press.

Chaloupka, G. 1984 *From Palaeoart to Casual Paintings*, Darwin: Northern Territory Museum of Arts and Sciences, Monograph Series, No. 1.

Chappell, J. M. A. 1982 Sea levels and sediments: some features of the context of coastal archaeological sites in the tropics, *Archaeology in Oceania* 17: 69–78.

Chappell, J. 1983 A revised sea-level record for the last 300,000 years from Papua New Guinea, *Search* 14 (3–4): 99–101.

Chappell, J. 1988 Geomorphologic dynamics and evolution of tidal river and floodplain systems in northern Australia, in D. Wade-Marshall and P. Loveday (eds) *Floodplains Research* 2, Canberra: North Australian Research Unit, Australian National University, pp. 34–57.

Chappell, J. 1993 Late Pleistocene coasts and human populations in the Austral region, in M. Spriggs et al. (eds) *A Community of Culture*, Canberra: Department of Prehistory, RSPS, Australian National University, Occasional Papers in Prehistory 24.

Chappell, J. and Grindrod, J. 1984 Chenier plain formation in northern Australia, in B. G. Thom (ed) *Coastal Geomorphology in Australia*, Sydney: Academic Press.

Chappell, J. and Shackleton, N. J. 1986 Oxygen isotopes and sea level, Nature 324: 137–140.

Chappell, J. and Thom, B. G. 1977 Sea levels and coasts, in J. Allen, J. Golson and R. Jones (eds) *Sunda and Sahul*, London: Academic Press, pp. 275–291.

Chappell, J. and Thom, B.G. 1986 Coastal morphodynamics in north Australia, *Australian Geographic Studies* 24: 110–127.

Chase, A. K. 1989 Domestication and domiculture in northern Australia: a social perspective, in D. R. Harris and G. C. Hillman (eds) *Foraging and Farming: the Evolution of Plant Domestication*, London: Unwin Hyman, pp. 42–54.

Chen, Y. 1988 Early Holocene population expansion of some rainforest trees at Lake Barrine basin, Queensland, *Australian Journal of Ecology* 13: 225–233.

Clark, P. and Hope, J. 1985 Aboriginal burials and shell middens at Snaggy Bend and other sites on the central Murray River, *Australian Archaeology* 20: 68–89.

Clark R. L. 1983 Pollen and charcoal evidence for the effects of Aboriginal burning on the vegetation of Australia, *Archaeology in Oceania* 16: 32–37.

Clark R. L. and Guppy, J. C. 1988 A transition from mangrove forest to freshwater wetland in the monsoon tropics of Australia, *Journal of Biogeography* 15: 665–684.

Clarkson, C. and David, B. 1995 The antiquity of blades and points revisited: investigating the emergence of systematic blade production south of Arnhem Land, Australia, *The Artefact* 18: 22–4.

Cleland, J. B. 1939 Some aspects of the ecology of the Aboriginal inhabitants of Tasmania and southern Australia, *Papers and Proceedings of the Royal Society of Tasmania* 1939 (1940): 1–18.

Cohen M. N. 1977 *The Food Crisis in Prehistory*, New Haven: Yale University Press.

Cohen M. N. 1985 Prehistoric Hunter-Gatherers: the meaning of cultural complexity, in T. D. Price and J. A. Brown (eds) *Prehistoric Hunter-gatherers: the Emergence of Cultural Complexity*, Orlando, Florida: Academic Press, pp. 99–119.

Cohen, M. N. and Armelagos G. N. (eds) 1984 *Paleopathology at the Origins of Agriculture*, New York: Academic Press.

Coleman, J. 1982 A new look at the north coast: fish traps and 'villages', in S. Bowdler (ed) *Coastal Archaeology in Eastern Australia*, Canberra: Australian National University, pp. 1–10.

Colhoun, E. A. 1978 The late Quaternary environment of Tasmania as a backdrop to man's occupance, *Records of the Queen Victoria Museum* 61.

Colhoun, E. A. (Compiler) 1988 *Cainozoic Vegetation of Tasmania*, Special Paper, Department of Geography, University of Newcastle, New South Wales.

Colhoun, E. A. and van de Geer, G. 1986 Holocene to middle last glaciation vegetation history at Tullarbardine Dam, western Tasmania, *Proceedings of the Royal Society of London* B 229: 177–207.

Colhoun, E. A., van de Geer, G. and Mook, W. G. 1982 Stratigraphy, pollen analysis and palaeoclimatic interpretation at Pulbeena Swamp, north-western Tasmania, *Quaternary Research* 18: 108–126.

Colley, S. M. and Jones, R. 1987 New fish bone data from Rocky Cape, north west Tasmania, *Archaeology in Oceania* 22: 67–71.

Conkey, M. W. 1985 Ritual communication, social elaboration, and the variable trajectories of Paleolithic material culture, in T. D. Price and J. A. Brown (eds) *Prehistoric Hunter-gatherers: the Emergence of Cultural Complexity*, Orlando, Florida: Academic Press, pp. 299–323.

Connah G. (ed) 1982 *Australian Field Archaeology: A Guide to Techniques*, Canberra: Australian Studies Press.

Coon, C. S. 1962 *The Origin of Races*, New York: Knopf.

Corbett, L. K. 1985 Morphological comparisons of Australian and Thai dingoes; a reappraisal of dingo status, distribution and ancestry, *Proceedings of the Ecological Society of Australia* 13: 277–291.

Cosgrove, R. 1985 New evidence of early Holocene Aboriginal occupation in northeast Tasmania, *Australian Archaeology* 21: 19–36.

Cosgrove, R. 1989 Thirty thousand years of human colonization in Tasmania: new Pleistocene dates, *Science* 243: 1703–1705.

Cosgrove, R. 1991 The Illusion of Riches: Issues of Scale, Resolution and Explanation of Pleistocene Human Behaviour. Unpublished PhD thesis, Melbourne: La Trobe University.

Cosgrove, R. 1995 Late Pleistocene behavioural variation and time trends: the case from Tasmania, *Archaeology in Oceania* 30: 83–104.

Cosgrove, R., Allen, J. and Marshall, B. 1990 Palaeo-ecology and Pleistocene human occupation in south central Tasmania, *Antiquity* 64: 59–78.

Coutts, P. J. F., Frank, R. K. and Hughes, P. J. 1978 Aboriginal engineers of the Western District, Victoria, *Records of the Victoria Archaeological Survey* 7.

Coutts, P. J. F. and Witter, D. C. 1977 New radiocarbon dates for Victorian archaeological sites, *Records of the Victoria Archaeological Survey* 4: 59–73.

Cowgill, G. L. 1975 On causes and consequences of ancient and modern population changes, *American Anthropologist* 77: 505–525.

Cribb, R. 1986 Sites, people and archaeological information traps: a further transgressive episode from Cape York, *Archaeology in Oceania* 21: 171–174.

Cribb, R. and Minnegal, M. 1989 Spatial analysis on a dugong consumption site at Princess Charlotte Bay, North Queensland, *Archaeology in Oceania* 24: 1–12.

Crowley, G. M. 1981 The Late Quaternary Environmental History of the Lake Bolac Region of Western Victoria and its Implications for Aboriginal Occupation. Unpublished BSc (Hons) thesis, Melbourne: Monash University.

Curr, E. M. 1886–1887 *The Australian Race*, 4 vols. Melbourne: John Ferris Government Printer.

Curtain, C. C., van Loghen, E. and Schanfield, M. S. 1976 Immunoglobulin markers as indicators of population affinities in Australasia and the Western Pacific, in R. L. Kirk and A. G. Thorne (eds) *The Origin of the Australians*, Canberra: Australian Insitute of Aboriginal Studies, pp. 347–364.

Damas, D. 1968 The diversity of Eskimo society, in R.B.Lee and I. DeVore (eds) *Man the Hunter*, Chicago: Aldine, pp. 111–117.

David, B. 1987 Chillagoe: From Archaeology to Prehistory: Contributions to a Late Holocene Prehistory of the Chillagoe Region, North Queensland. Unpublished MA thesis, Canberra: Department of Prehistory and Anthropology, Australian National University.

David, B. 1991 Fern Cave, rock art and social formations: rock art regionalisation and demographic models in southeastern Cape York Peninsula, *Archaeology in Oceania* 26: 41–57.

David, B. 1993 Nurrabullgin Cave: preliminary results from a pre-37000 year old rockshelter, North Queensland, *Archaeology in Oceania* 28: 50–54.

David, B. 1994 A Space-time Odyssey: Rock Art and Regionalisation in North Queensland Prehistory. Unpublished PhD thesis, Department of Anthropology and Sociology, University of Queensland.

David, B. and Cole, N. 1990 Rock art and inter-regional interaction in northeast Australian prehistory, *Antiquity* 64: 788–806.

David, B. and Lourandos, H. (in press) 37,000 years and more in tropical Australia: investigating long-term archaeological trends in Cape York Peninsula, *Proceedings of the Prehistoric Society* 63 (1997).

David, B., McNiven, I., Flood, J. and Frost, R. 1990 Yiwarlarlay 1: archaeological excavations at the Lighting Brothers site, Delamere station, Northern Territory, *Archaeology in Oceania* 25: 79–84.

David, B, McNiven, I., Attenbrow, V., Flood, J. and J. Collins 1994 Of Lightning Brothers and white cockatoos: dating the antiquity of signifying systems in the Northern Territory, Australia, *Antiquity* 68: 241–251.

Davidson, I. 1983 On the edge of the Simpson: recent additions to the understanding of prehistoric artefact distributions in arid Australia, *Australian Archaeology* 17: 27–37.

Davidson, I. 1990 Prehistoric Australian demography, in B. Meehan and N. White (eds) *Hunter-Gatherer Demography: Past and Present*, Sydney: Oceania Monograph, 39, University of Sydney, pp. 41–58.

Davidson, I. and Noble, W. 1989 The archaeology of perception: traces of depiction and language, *Current Anthropology* 30: 125–158.

Davidson, I. and Noble, W. 1992 Why the first colonisation of the Australian region is the earliest evidence of modern human behaviour, *Archaeology in Oceania* 27: 135–142.

Davidson I., Sutton S. A. and Gale S. J. 1993 The human occupation of Cuckadoo 1 rockshelter, northwest central Queensland, in M. A. Smith, M. Spriggs and B. Frankhauser (eds) *Sahul in Review: Pleistocene Archaeology in Australia, New Guinea and Island Melanesia*, Canberra: Department of Prehistory, Research School of Pacific Studies, Australian National University, pp. 164–172.

Dawson, J. 1881 *The Australian Aborigines*, Melbourne.

Dawson, R. L. 1935 *Australian Aboriginal Words and Names: Lower Clarence District*, Sydney: W.C.Penfold and Co.

Denbow, J. R. 1984 Prehistoric herders and foragers of the Kalahari: the evidence for 1500 years of interaction, in C. Schrire (ed) *Past and Present in Hunter Gatherer Studies*, London: Academic Press, pp. 175–193.

Dickson, F. P. 1978 Australian Ground Stone Hatchets. Unpublished PhD thesis, Sydney: Macquarie University.

Dillehay, T. 1990 *Monte Verde: a late Pleistocene settlement in Chile*, Washington, DC: Smithsonian Institute.

Dixon, R. M. W. 1976 Tribes, languages and other boundaries in northeast Queensland, in N. Peterson (ed) *Tribes and Boundaries in Australia*, Canberra: Australian Institute of Aboriginal Studies, pp. 207–238.

Dixon, R. M. W. 1980 *The Languages of Australia*, Cambridge: Cambridge University Press.

Dodson, J. R. 1974 Vegetation and climatic history near Lake Keilambete, Western Victoria, *Australian Journal of Botany* 22: 709–717.

Dodson, J. R. 1975 Vegetation history and water fluctuations at Lake Leake, south-eastern South Australia, II , 50,000 BP to 10,000 BP, *Australian Journal of Botany* 23: 815–831.

Dodson, J. R. 1977 Late Quaternary palaeoecology of Wyrie Swamp, south-eastern South Australia, *Quaternary Research* 18: 97–114.

Dodson, J. 1992 *The Naive Lands: Prehistory and Environmental Change in Australia and the South-West Pacific*, Melbourne: Longman Cheshire.

Dodson, J., Fullagar, R. and Head, L. 1992 Dynamics of environment and people in the forested crescents of temperate Australia, in J. Dodson (ed) *The Naive Lands: Prehistory and Environmental Change in Australia and the Southwest Pacific*, Melbourne: Longman Cheshire, pp. 115–159.

Dodson, J., Fullagar, R., Furby, J., Jones, R. and Prosser, I. 1993 Humans and megafauna in a late Pleistocene environment from Cuddie Springs, north western New South Wales, *Archaeology in Oceania* 28: 94–99.

Dodson, J. R. and Wright, R. V. S. 1989 Humid to arid to subhumid vegetation shift on Pilliga Sandstone, Ulungra Springs, New South Wales, *Quaternary Research* 32: 182–192.

Dortch, C. 1975 Geometric microliths from a dated archaeological deposit near Northcliffe, Western Australia, *Journal of the Royal Society of Western Australia* 58: 59–63.

Dortch, C. 1977 Early and late stone industrial phases in Western Australia, in R. V. S. Wright (ed) *Stone Tools as Cultural Markers*, Canberra: Australian Institute of Aboriginal Studies, pp. 104–132.

Dortch, C. 1979a Devil's Lair: an example of prolonged cave use in south-western Australia, *World Archaeology* 10: 258–279.

Dortch, C. 1979b 33,000 year old stone and bone artefacts from Devil's Lair, Western Australia, *Records of the Western Australian Museum* 7: 329–367.

Dortch, C. and Bordes, F. 1977 Blade and Levallois technology in Western Australian prehistory, *Quartar* 27/28: 1–19.

Dortch, C., Kendrick, G. and Morse, K. 1984 Aboriginal mollusc exploitation in southwestern Australia, *Archaeology in Oceania* 19: 81–104.

Dornstreich, M. 1973 An Ecological Study of Gadio Enga (New Guinea) Subsistence. Unpublished PhD thesis, New York: Columbia University.

Dragovich, D. 1986 Minimum age of some desert varnish near broken Hill, New South Wales, *Search* 17: 149–151.

Draper, N. 1978 A Model of Aboriginal Subsistence and Settlement in the Moreton Bay Region of Southeast Queensland. Unpublished BA thesis, Brisbane: Department of Anthropology and Sociology, University of Queensland.

Draper, N. 1987 Context for the Kartan: a preliminary report of excavations at Cape du Couedic rockshelter, Kangaroo Island, *Archaeology in Oceania* 22: 1–8.

Dunbar, G. K. 1943–4 Notes on the Ngemba Tribe of the central Darling River, western New South Wales, *Mankind* 3: 140–148, 172–180.

Dunnett, G. 1993 Diving for dinner: some implications from Holocene middens for the role of coasts in the late Pleistocene of Tasmania, in M. A. Smith, M. Spriggs and B. Frankhauser (eds) *Sahul in Review: Pleistocene Archaeology in Australia, New Guinea and Island Melanesia*, Canberra: Department of Prehistory, Research School of Pacific Studies, Australian National University, pp. 247–257.

Dwyer, P. and Minnegal, M. 1992 Cassowaries, chickens and change: animal domestication by Kubo of Papua New Guinea, *Journal of the Polynesian Society* 101 (4): 373–385.

Edwards, R. 1971 Art and Aboriginal Prehistory, in D. J. Mulvaney and J. Golson (eds) *Aboriginal Man and Environment in Australia*, Canberra: Australian National University Press, pp. 356–367.

Ellen R. 1982 *Environment, Subsistence and System*, Cambridge: Cambridge University Press.

Ellen R. 1988 Foraging, starch extraction and the sedentary lifestyle in the lowland rainforest of central Seram, in T. Ingold, D. Riches and J. Woodburn (eds) *Hunters and Gatherers: History, Evolution and Social Change*, Oxford: Berg, pp. 117–134.

Enright, N. J. and Gosden, C. 1992 Unstable archipelagos – south-west Pacific environment and prehistory since 30,000 BP, in J.R. Dodson (ed) *The Naive Lands: Prehistory and Environmental Change in Australia and the Southwest Pacific*, Melbourne: Longman Cheshire, pp. 160–98.

Etheridge, R. Jr. and Whitelegge, T. 1907 Aboriginal workshops on the coast of New South Wales, and their contents, *Records of the Australian Museum* 6: 233–250.

Eyre, E. J. 1845 *Journals of Expeditions of Discovery*, Vol. II, London: Boone.

Faris, J. C. 1975 Social evolution, population and production, in S. Polgar (ed) *Population, Ecology and Social Evolution*, The Hague: Mouton, pp. 235–271.

Feil, D. K. 1987 *The Evolution of Highland Papua New Guinea Societies*, Cambridge: Cambridge University Press.

Ferguson, W. 1981 Archaeological investigations at the Quininup Brook site complex, Western Australia, *Records of the Western Australian Museum* 9: 609–637.

Ferguson, W. 1985 A Mid-Holocene Depopulation of the Australian Southwest. Unpublished PhD thesis, Canberra: Australian National University.

Flannery K. V. 1968 Archaeological systems theory and early Mesoamerica, in B. Meggers (ed) *Anthropological Archaeology in the Americas*, Washington D.C.: Anthropological Society of Washington, pp. 67–87.

Flannery K. V. 1972 The cultural evolution of civilizations, *Annual Review of Ecology and Semantics*, 4: 399–426.

Flannery K. V. (ed) 1976 *The Early Mesoamerican Village*, New York: Academic Press.

Flannery, T. F. 1990 Pleistocene faunal loss: implications of the aftershock for Australia's past and future, *Archaeology in Oceania* 25: 45–67.

Flood, J. M. 1970 A point assemblage from the Northern Territory, *Archaeology and Physical Anthropology in Oceania* 5: 27–52.

Flood, J. 1976 Man and ecology in the highlands of southeastern Australia: a case study, in N. Peterson (ed) *Tribes and Boundaries in Australia*, Canberra: Australian Institute of Aboriginal Studies, pp. 30–49.

Flood, J. M. 1980 *The Moth Hunters: Aboriginal Prehistory of the Australian Alps*, Canberra: Australian Institute of Aboriginal Studies.

Flood, J. 1989 *Archaeology of the Dreamtime: The Story of Prehistoric Australia and Its People*, Sydney: Collins.

Flood, J. 1990 *The Riches of Ancient Australia: A Journey Into Prehistory*, Brisbane: University of Queensland Press.

Flood, J., David, B., Magee, J. and English, B. 1987 Birrigai: a Pleistocene site in the south-eastern highlands, *Archaeology in Oceania* 22: 9–26.

Frankel, D. 1986 Excavations in the lower southeast of South Australia, November 1985, *Australian Archaeology* 22: 75–87.

Frankel, D. 1988 Characterising change in prehistoric sequences, *Archaeology in Oceania* 23: 41–48.

Frankel, D. 1990 Stratigraphy and argument at Koongine cave, *Australian Archaeology* 30: 71–72.

Frankel, D. 1993 Pleistocene chronological structures and explanations: a challenge, in M. A. Smith, M. Spriggs and B. Frankhauser (eds) *Sahul in Review: Pleistocene Archaeology in Australia, New Guinea and Island Melanesia*, Canberra: Department of Prehistory, Research School of Pacific Studies, Australian National University, pp. 24–33.

Franklin, N. 1991 Explorations of the Panaramitee style, in P. Bahn and A. Rosenfeld (eds) *Rock Art and Prehistory*, Oxford: Oxbow, pp. 120–135.

Fredericksen, C., Spriggs, M. and Ambrose, W. 1993 Pamwak rockshelter: a Pleistocene site on Manus Island, Papua New Guinea, in M. A. Smith, M. Spriggs and B. Frankhauser (eds) *Sahul in Review: Pleistocene Archaeology in Australia, New Guinea and Island Melanesia*, Canberra: Department of Prehistory, Research School of Pacific Studies, Australian National University, pp. 144–152.

Freedman, L. and Lofgren, M. 1979 Human skeletal remains from Cossack, Western Australia, *Journal of Human Evolution* 8: 283–299.

Friedman, J. 1979 System, structure and contradiction in the evolution of 'Asiatic' social formations. *Social Studies in Oceania and Southeast Asia*, 2, Copenhagen: The National Museum of Denmark.

Friedman, J. and Rowlands, M. (eds) 1978 *The Evolution of Social Systems*, London: Duckworth.

Furby, J. H., Fullagar, R., Dodson, J. R. and Prosser, I. 1993 The Cuddie Springs bone bed revisited, 1991, in M. A. Smith, M. Spriggs and B. Frankhauser (eds) *Sahul in Review: Pleistocene Archaeology in Australia, New Guinea and Island Melanesia*, Canberra: Department of Prehistory, Research School of Pacific Studies, Australian National University, pp. 204–210.

Gaffney, L. and Stockton, J. 1980 Results of the Jordan River midden excavation, *Australian Archaeology* 10: 68–78.

Gale, F. (ed) 1970 *Woman's Role in Aboriginal Society*, Canberra: Australian Institute of Aboriginal Studies.

Galloway, R. W. 1986 Australian snow-fields past and present, in B. A. Barlow (ed) *Flora and Fauna of Alpine Australasia: Ages and Origins*, Melbourne: CSIRO.

Gallus, A. 1971 Excavations at Keilor, report No. 1., *The Artefact* 24: 1–12.

Gamble, C. 1986a *The Palaeolithic Settlement of Europe*, Cambridge: Cambridge University Press.

Gamble, C. 1986b The mesolithic sandwich: ecological approaches and the archaeological record of the early postglacial, in M. Zvelebil (ed) *Hunters in Transition: Mesolithic Societies of Temperate Eurasia and Their Transition to Farming*, Cambridge: Cambridge University Press, pp. 33–42.

Gaughwin, D. 1985 An archaeological reconnaissance survey of the Tasman Peninsula, February 1984, *Australian Archaeology* 20: 38–57.

Geering, K. 1980 An Attempt to Establish the Seasonality of Occupation of the Stockyard Site, Hunter Island. Unpublished BA (Hons) thesis, Armidale, New South Wales: University of New England.

Gill, A. M., Groves, R. H. and Noble, I. R. (eds) 1981 *Fire and the Australian Biota*, Canberra: Australian Academy of Science.

Gill, E. D. 1957 Current Quaternary studies in Victoria, Australia, *International Association of Quaternary Research*, 5th Congress, Madrid: 1–7.

Gill, E. D. 1972 Eruption date of Tower Hill volcano, Western Victoria, Australia, *Victorian Naturalist* 89: 188–192.

Gill, E. D. 1973 Geology and geomorphology of the River Murray region between

Mildura and Renmark, Australia, *Memoirs of the National Museum of Victoria* 34: 1–97.

Gillespie, R., Horton, D. R., Ladd, P., Macumber, P. G., Rich, T. H., Thorne, A. and Wright, R. V. S. 1978 Lancefield Swamp and the extinction of the Australian megafauna, *Science* 200: 1,043–1,044.

Gillieson, D. S. and Mountain, M. J. 1983 Environmental history of Nombe rockshelter, Papua New Guinea Highlands, *Archaeology in Oceania* 18: 53–62.

Gilman, A. 1984 Explaining the upper Palaeolithic revolution, in M.Spriggs (ed) *Marxist Perspectives in Archaeology*, Cambridge: Cambridge University Press, pp. 115–126.

Glover, I. 1967 Stone implements from Millstream Station, Western Australia: Newall's Collection reanalysed, *Mankind* 6: 415–425.

Glover, I. 1969 The use of factor analysis for the discovery of artefact types, *Mankind* 7: 36–51.

Glover, I. 1976 Ulu Leang Cave, Maros: a preliminary sequence of post-Pleistocene cultural development in south Sulawesi, *Archipel* 11: 113–154.

Glover, I. 1978 Survey and excavation in the Maros district, South Sulawesi, Indonesia: the 1975 field season, *Indo-Pacific Prehistory Association Bulletin* 1: 60–103.

Godelier, M. 1975 Modes of production, kinship and demographic structure, in M. Bloch (ed) *Marxist Analyses and Social Anthropology*, London: Malaby Press, pp. 3–27.

Godfrey, M. C. S. 1988 Oxygen isotope analysis: a means for determining the social gathering of the pipi (*Donax deltoides*) by Aborigines in prehistoric Australia, *Archaeology in Oceania* 23: 17–21.

Godfrey, M. C. S. 1989 Shell midden chronology in southwestern Victoria: reflections on change in prehistoric population and subsistence, *Archaeology in Oceania* 24: 65–9.

Godwin, L. 1980 What You Can Do With 27,000 Pieces of Bone: a Taphonomic Study of Vertebrate Fauna From the Bridgewater Caves South. Unpublished BA thesis, Armidale, New South Wales: University of New England.

Godwin, L. 1983 Archaeological site surveys on the eastern margin of the New England Tablelands, *Australian Archaeology* 17: 38–47.

Goede, A. and Murray, P. 1977 Pleistocene man in south central Tasmania: evidence from a cave site in the Florentine Valley, *Mankind* 11: 2–10.

Goede, A. and Murray, P. 1979 Late Pleistocene bone deposits from a cave in the Florentine Valley, Tasmania, *Papers and Proceedings of the Royal Society of Tasmania* 113: 39–52.

Gollan, C. 1984 The Australian dingo: in the shadow of man, in M. Archer and G. Clayton (eds) *Vertebrate Zoogeography and Evolution in Australasia*, Perth: Hesperian Press, pp. 921–927.

Golson, J. 1971 Australian Aboriginal food plants: some ecological and culture-historical implications, in D. J. Mulvaney and J. Golson (eds) *Aboriginal Man and Environment in Australia*, Canberra: Australian National University Press, pp. 196–238.

Golson, J. 1977a No room at the top: agricultural intensification in the New Guinea highlands. In J. Allen, J. Golson and R. Jones (eds) *Sunda and Sahul: Prehistoric Studies in South-east Asia, Melanesia and Australia*, London: Academic Press, pp. 601–38.

Golson, J. 1977b Simple tools and complex technology: agriculture and agricultural implements in the New Guinea highlands, in R. V. S. Wright (ed) *Stone Tools as Cultural Markers*, Canberra: Australian Institute of Aboriginal Studies, pp. 154–161.

Golson, J. 1989 The origins and development of New Guinea agriculture, in D. R. Harris and G. C. Hillman (eds) *Foraging and Farming: The Evolution of Plant Domestication*, London: Unwin Hyman, pp. 678–687.

Golson, J. 1993 The last days of Pompeii?, in M. A. Smith, M. Spriggs and B. Frankhauser (eds) *Sahul in Review: Pleistocene Archaeology in Australia, New Guinea and Island Melanesia*, Canberra: Department of Prehistory, Research School of Pacific Studies, Australian National University, pp. 275–280.

Golson, J. and Gardner, D. S. 1990 Agricultural and sociopolitical organisation in New Guinea Highlands prehistory, *Annual Review of Anthropology* 19: 395–417.

Goodale, J. 1971 *Tiwi Wives*, Seattle: University of Washington Press.

Gordon, R. J. 1984 The !Kung in the Kalahari exchange: an ethnohistorical perspective, in C. Schrire (ed) *Past and Present in Hunter Gatherer Studies*, London: Academic Press, pp. 195–224.

Gorecki, P. P., Horton, D. R., Stern, N. and Wright, R. V. S. 1984 Coexistence of humans and megafauna in Australia: improved stratigraphic evidence, *Archaeology in Oceania* 19: 117–119.

Gorecki, P., Mabin, M. and Campbell, J. 1991 Archaeology and geomorphology of the Vanimo coast, Papua New Guinea: preliminary results, *Archaeology in Oceania* 26: 119–122.

Gott, B. 1982 Ecology of root use by the Aborigines of southern Australia, *Archaeology in Oceania* 17: 59–66.

Gott, B. 1983 Murnong—*Microseris scapigera*: a study of a staple food of Victorian Aborigines, *Australian Aboriginal Studies* 2: 2–18.

Gould, R. A. 1968 Living archaeology: the Ngatatjara of Western Australia, *Southwestern Journal of Anthropology* 24: 101–122.

Gould, R. A. 1969 *Yiwara: Foragers of the Australian Desert*, New York: Scribners.

Gould, R. A. 1971a The archaeologist as ethnographer: a case from the western desert of Australia, *World Archaeology* 3: 143–177.

Gould, R. A. 1971b Uses and effects of fire among the western desert Aborigines of Australia, *Mankind* 8: 14–24.

Gould, R. A. 1977a Puntutjarpa rockshelter and the Australian Desert culture, *Anthropological Papers of the American Museum of Natural History* 54 (1).

Gould, R. A. 1977b Ethno-archaeology: or, where do models come from? in R. V. S. Wright (ed) *Stone Tools as Cultural Markers*, Canberra: Australian Institute of Aboriginal Studies, pp. 162–168.

Gould, R. A. 1978a Beyond analogy in ethnoarchaeology, in R. A. Gould (ed) *Explorations in Ethnoarchaeology*, Albuquerque: University of New Mexico Press, pp. 249–294.

Gould, R. A 1978b The anthropology of human residues, *American Anthropologist* 80: 815–835.

Gould, R. A. 1980 *Living Archaeology*, Cambridge: Cambridge University Press.

Gould R. A. 1985 'Now let's invent agriculture . . ..': a critical review of concepts of complexity among hunter-gatherers, in T. D. Price and J. A. Brown (eds) *Prehistoric Hunter-gatherers: the Emergence of Cultural Complexity*, Orlando, Florida: Academic Press, pp. 427–434.

Gray, A. 1985 Limits for demographic parameters of Aboriginal populations in the past, *Australian Aboriginal Studies* 1: 22–27.

Grey, G. 1841 *Journals of Two Expeditions of Discovery in North-West and Western Australia, During the years 1837, 38, and 39*, London: Boone.

Griffith, P. B. 1984 Forager resource and land use in the humid tropics: the Agta of northeastern Luzon, the Philippines, in C. Schrire (ed) *Past and Present in Hunter Gatherer Studies*, London: Academic Press, pp. 95–121.

Groube, L., Chappell, J., Muke, J. and Price, D. 1986 40,000 year old human occupation site at Huon Peninsula, Papua New Guinea, *Nature* 324: 453–455.

Groube, L. 1989 The taming of the rain forests: a model for Late Pleistocene forest exploitation in New Guinea, in D. R. Harris and G. C. Hillman (eds) *Foraging and Farming: the evolution of plant exploitation*, London: Unwin Hyman, pp. 292–317.

Guidon, N. and Delibrias, G. 1986 Carbon 14 dates point to man in the Americas 32,000 years ago, *Nature* 321: 769–771.

Guiler, E. R. 1965 Animals, in J.L. Davies (ed) *Atlas of Tasmania*, Hobart: Lands and Surveys Department, pp. 36–37.

Haberle, S. 1993 Pleistocene vegetation change and early human occupation of tropical mountainous environment, in M. A. Smith, M. Spriggs and B. Frankhauser (eds) *Sahul in Review: Pleistocene Archaeology in Australia, New Guinea and Island Melanesia*, Canberra: Department of Prehistory, Research School of Pacific Studies, Australian National University, pp. 109–122.

Habgood, P. J. 1986 The origin of the Australians: a multivariate approach, *Archaeology in Oceania* 21: 130–137.

Habgood, P. J. 1989 The origin of anatomically modern humans in Australia, in P. Mellars and C. Stringer (eds) *The Human Revolution: Behavioural and Biological Perspectives on the Origins of Modern Humans*, Vol. 1, Edinburgh: University of Edinburgh Press, pp. 245–273.

Haddon, A. C. (ed) 1912 *Reports of the Cambridge Anthropological Expedition to the Torres Straits, IV: arts and crafts*, Cambridge: Cambridge University Press.

Haglund, L. 1976 *The Broadbeach Aboriginal Ground*, Brisbane: University of Queensland Press.

Hale, H. M. and Tindale, N. B. 1930 Notes on some human remains in the Lower Murray Valley, South Australia, *Records of the South Australian Museum* 4: 145–218.

Hall, H. J. 1982 Sitting on the crop of the bay: an historical and archaeological sketch of Aboriginal settlement and subsistence in Moreton Bay, in S. Bowdler (ed) *Coastal Archaeology in Eastern Australia*, Canberra: Australian National University, pp. 79–85.

Hall, J. 1986 Exploratory excavation at Bushrangers Cave (Site LA:A11), a 6000-year-old campsite in Southeast Queensland: preliminary results, *Australian Archaeology* 22: 88–103.

Hall, J. and Hiscock, P. 1988 The Moreton Region Archaeological Project (MRAP)—Stage II: an outline of objectives and methods, *Queensland Archaeological Research* 5: 4–24.

Hall, J. and Robbins, R. P. 1984 A working model of Moreton Island prehistory, *Queensland Archaeological Research* 1: 84–85.

Hallam, S. 1975 *Fire and Hearth*, Canberra: Australian Institute of Aboriginal Studies.

Hallam, S. J. 1977a Topographic archaeology and artifactual evidence, in R. V. S. Wright (ed) *Stone Tools as Cultural Markers*, Canberra: Australian Institute of Aboriginal Studies, pp. 169–177.

Hallam S. J. 1977b The relevance of Old World archaeology to the first entry of man into New Worlds: colonization seen from the Antipodes, *Quaternary Research* 8: 128–148.

Hallam, S. 1987 Coastal does not equal littoral, *Australian Archaeology* 25: 10–29.

Hallam, S. J. 1989 Plant usage and management in southwest Australian Aboriginal societies, in D. R. Harris and G. C. Hillman (eds) *Foraging and Farming: the Evolution of Plant Domestication*, London: Unwin Hyman, pp. 136–150.

Hamilton, A. 1980 Dual social systems: technology, labour and women's secret rites in the eastern Western Desert of Australia, *Oceania* 51(1): 4–19.

Hamilton, A. 1982a Descended from father, belonging to country: problems in the constitution of rights to land in the Western Desert of Australia, in E. Leacock, and R. Lee (eds) *Politics and History in Band Societies*, Cambridge: Cambridge University Press, pp. 50–71.

Hamilton, A. 1982b The unity of hunting-gathering societies: reflections on economic forms and resource management, in N. Williams and E. Hunn (eds) *Resource Managers: North American and Australian Hunter-gatherers*, Boulder, CO: Westview, pp. 229–247.

Hardley, R. 1975 The social life of Stradbroke Island Aborigines, *Proceedings of the Royal Society of Queensland* 86: 141–146.

Harris, D. R. 1977a Subsistence Strategies Across Torres Straits, in J. Allen, J. Golson and R. Jones (eds) *Sunda and Sahul*, London: Academic Press, pp. 421–463.

Harris, D. R. 1977b Alternative Pathways Toward Agriculture, in C. Reed (ed) *The Origins of Agriculture*, The Hague: Mouton, pp. 179–243.

Harris D. R. 1989 An evolutionary continuum of people-plant interaction, in D. R. Harris and G. C. Hillman (eds) *Foraging and Farming: the Evolution of Plant Domestication*, London: Unwin Hyman, pp. 11–26.

Harris, D. R. 1995 Early agriculture in New Guinea and the Torres Strait divide, in Allen, J. and J. F. O'Connell (eds) *Transitions: Pleistocene to Holocene in Australia and Papua New Guinea, Antiquity* 69: 848–854.

Hart, C. and Pilling, A. 1960 *The Tiwi of·North Australia*, New York: Holt, Rinehart and Winston.

Haskovec, I. 1992 Northern running figures of Kakadu National Park: a study of regional style, in J. McDonald and I. P. Haskovec (eds) *State of the Art: Regional Rock Art Studies in Australia and Melanesia*, Melbourne: Occasional AURA Publication 6, Australian Rock Art Research Association, pp. 148–158.

Hassan F. 1975 Determination of the size, density and growth rate of hunting-gathering populations, in S. Polgar (ed) *Population, Ecology and Social Evolution*, The Hague: Mouton, pp. 27–52.

Hassan, F. 1981 *Demographic Archaeology*, New York: Academic Press.

Hawkes K., Hill, K., and O'Connell, J. F. 1982 Why hunters gather: optimal foraging and the Ache of eastern Paraguay, *American Ethnologist* 9: 379–398.

Hawkes, K., O'Connell, J. F., Hill, K. and Charnov, E. L. 1985 How much is enough? Hunters and limited needs, *Ethology and Sociobiology* 6: 3–15.

Hayden, B. 1972 Population control among hunter-gatherers, *World Archaeology* 4: 205–221.

Hayden, B. 1975 The carrying capacity dilemma, *American Antiquity* 40(2)2, Memoir 30: 11–21.

Hayden, B. 1981 Research and development in the Stone Age: technological transitions among hunter-gatherers, *Current Anthropology* 22: 519–548.

Hayden, B. 1990 Nimrods, piscators, pluckers and planters; the emergence of food production, *Journal of Anthropological Archaeology* 9: 31–69.

Hayden B., Chisholm, B. and Schwarcz, H. P. 1987 Fishing and foraging: marine resources in the Upper Palaeolithic of France, in O. Soffer (ed), *The Pleistocene Old World: Regional Perspectives*, New York: Plenum, pp. 279–291.

Head, L. 1983 Environment as artefact: a geographic perspective on the Holocene occupation of Southwestern Victoria, *Archaeology in Oceania* 18: 73–80.

Head, L. 1986 Palaeoecological contributions to Australian prehistory, *Archaeology in Oceania* 21: 121–129.

Head, L. 1987 The Holocene prehistory of a coastal wetland system: Discovery Bay, south-eastern Australia, *Human Ecology* 15: 435–462.

Head, L. 1989 Using palaeoecology to date Aboriginal fishtraps at Lake Condah, Victoria, *Archaeology in Oceania* 24: 110–115.

Hekel, H., Ward, W. T., Jones, M. and Searle, D. E. 1979 Geological development of northern Moreton Bay, in A. Bailey and N. C. Stevens (eds) *Northern Moreton Bay Symposium*, Brisbane: Royal Society of Queensland, pp. 7–18.

Henry, D. O. 1985 Preagricultural sedentism: the Natufian example, in T. D. Price and J. A. Brown (eds) *Prehistoric Hunter-gatherers: the Emergence of Cultural Complexity*, Orlando, Florida: Academic Press, pp. 365–384.

Hercus, L. A. 1969 *The Languages of Victoria: A Late Survey*, Pt. II, Canberra: Australian Institute of Aboriginal Studies, No. 17.

Hercus, L. and Clark, P. 1986 Nine Simpson Desert wells, *Archaeology in Oceania* 21: 51–62.

Hiatt, B. 1967 The food quest and the economy of the Tasmanian Aborigines, *Oceania* 38: 99–133, 190–219.

Hiatt, L. R. 1965 *Kinship and Conflict*, Canberra: Australian National University Press.

Hiatt, L. R. 1968 Discussion, Part V, in R. B. Lee and I. DeVore (eds) *Man the Hunter*, Chicago: Aldine, pp. 245–248.

Hiscock, P. 1984 Preliminary report on the stone artefacts from Colless Creek Cave, Northwest Queensland, *Queensland Archaeological Research* 1: 120–151.

Hiscock, P. 1986 Technological change in the Hunter River Valley and its implications for the interpretation of late Holocene change in Australia, *Archaeology in Oceania* 21: 40–50.

Hiscock, P. 1988 Prehistoric Settlement Patterns and Artefact Manufacture at Lawn Hill, North-West Queensland. Unpublished PhD thesis, Brisbane: Department of Anthropology and Sociology, University of Queensland.

Hiscock, P. 1990 How old are the artefacts at Malkaunanja 2? *Archaeology in Oceania*, 25: 122–124.

Hiscock, P. n.d. Pleistocene abandonment of arid central Australia, unpublished paper.

Hiscock, P. 1993 Bondian technology in the Hunter Valley, New South Wales, *Archaeology in Oceania* 28: 65–76.

Hiscock, P. 1993 Technological responses to risk in Holocene Australia, *Journal of World Archaeology* 8: 267–299.

Hiscock, P. and Hall, J. 1988 Technological change at Bushranger's Cave (LA:A11), Southeast Queensland, *Queensland Archaeological Research* 5: 90–112.

Hiscock, P. and Hughes P. J. 1980 Backed blades in northern Australia: evidence from northwest Queensland, *Australian Archaeology* 10: 86–95.

Hiscock, P. and Kershaw, A. P. 1992 Palaeoenvironments and prehistory of Australia's tropical Top End, in J. Dodson (ed) *The Naive Lands: Prehistory and Environmental Change in Australia and the Southwest Pacific*, Melbourne: Longman Cheshire, pp. 43–75.

Hiscock, P. and Veth, P. 1991 Change in the Australian desert culture: a reanalysis of tulas from Puntutjarpa rockshelter, *World Archaeology* 22: 332–345.

Hobson, K. A. and Collier, S. 1984 Marine and terrestrial protein in Australian Aboriginal diets, *Current Anthropology* 25(2): 238–240.

Hodgkinson, G. F. 1845 *Australia From Port Macquarie to Moreton Bay*, London: T. and W. Boone.

Hoffman, C. L. 1984 Punan foragers in the trading networks of Southeast Asia, in C. Schrire (ed) *Past and Present in Hunter Gatherer Studies*, London: Academic Press, pp. 123–149.

Holdaway, S. and Porch, N. 1995 Cyclical patterns in the Pleistocene human occupation of Southwest Tasmania, *Archaeology in Oceania* 30: 74–82.

Hope, G. S. 1978 The late Pleistocene and Holocene vegetational history of Hunter Island, north-western Tasmania, *Australian Journal of Botany* 26: 493–514.

Hope, G. S. and Hope, J. H. 1976 Man on Mount Jaya, in G. S. Hope, J. A. Peterson, U. Radok and I. Allison (eds) *The Equatorial Glaciers of New Guinea*, Rotterdam: Balkema, pp. 225–240.

Hope, G. and Golson, J. 1995 Late Quaternary change in the mountains of New Guinea, in Allen, J. and J. F. O'Connell (eds) *Transitions: Pleistocene to Holocene in Australia and Papua New Guinea, Antiquity* 69: 818–830.

Hope, J. H. 1978 Pleistocene mammal extinctions: the problem of Mungo and Menindee, western New South Wales, *Alcheringa* 2: 65–82.

Hope, J. (ed) 1981 *Darling Surveys* 1, Occasional Papers in Prehistory No. 3, Canberra: Department of Prehistory, Australian National University.

Hope, J. H. 1993 Pleistocene archaeological sites in the central Murray-Darling basin, in M. A. Smith, M. Spriggs and B. Frankhauser (eds) *Sahul in Review: Pleistocene Archaeology in Australia, New Guinea and Island Melanesia*, Canberra: Department of Prehistory, Research School of Pacific Studies, Australian National University, pp. 183–196.

Hope, J. H., Dare-Edwards, A. and McIntyre, M. L. 1983 Middens and megafauna: stratigraphy and dating of Lake Tandou Lunette, western New South Wales, *Archaeology in Oceania* 18: 45–53.

Hope, J. H., Lampert, R. J., Edmondson, E., Smith, M. J. and Van Tets, G. F. 1977 Late Pleistocene faunal remains from Seton rockshelter, Kangaroo Island, South Australia, *Journal of Biogeography* 4: 363–385.

Horne, G. A. and Aiston, G. 1924 *Savage Life in Central Australia*, London: MacMillan.

Horsfall, N. 1987 Living in Rainforest: the Prehistoric Occupation of North Queensland's Humid Tropics. Unpublished PhD thesis, Townsville: Department of Behavioural Science, James Cook University of North Queensland.

Horton, D. R. 1979 Tasmanian adaptation, *Mankind* 12: 28–34.

Horton, D. R. 1980 A review of the extinction question: man, climate and megafauna, *Archaeology and Physical Anthropology in Oceania* 15: 86–97.

Horton, D. R. 1981 Water and woodland: the peopling of Australia, *Australian Institute of Aboriginal Studies Newsletter* 16: 21–27.

Horton, D. 1982 The burning question: Aborigines, fire and Australian ecosystems, *Mankind* 13: 237–251.

Horton, D. R. 1991 *Recovering the Tracks: The Story of Australian Archaeology*, Canberra: Australian Studies Press.

Horton, D. R. and Wright, R. V. S. 1981 Cuts on Lancefield bones: Carnivorous Thylacoleo, not humans, the cause, *Archaeology in Oceania* 16: 73–80.

Howitt, A. W. 1904 *The Native Tribes of South-East Australia*, London: McMillan.

Howitt, A. W. and Fison, L. 1880 *Kamilaroi and Kurnai*, Melbourne: Robertson.

Huchet, B. M. J. 1991 Theories and Australian prehistory: the last three decades, *Australian Archaeology* 33: 44–51.

Hughes, P. J. 1977 A Geomorphological Interpretation of Selected Archaeological Sites in Southern Coastal New South Wales. Unpublished PhD thesis, Sydney: University of New South Wales.

Hughes, P. J. 1978 Weathering in sandstone shelters in the Sydney basin and the survival of rock art, in C. Pearson (ed) *Conservation of Rock Art*, Sydney: Institute for the Conservation of Cultural Material, pp. 36–41.

Hughes, P. and Djohadze, V. 1980 Radiocarbon dates from archaeological sites on the South Coast of New South Wales and the use of depth/age curves, *Occasional Papers in Prehistory* 1, Canberra: Department of Prehistory, Australian National University.

Hughes, P. J. and Lampert, R. J. 1980 Pleistocene occupation of the arid zone in southeast Australia: research prospects for the Cooper Creek-Strzlecki Desert region, *Australian Archaeology* 10: 52–67.

Hughes, P. J. and Lampert, R. J. 1982 Prehistoric population change in southern coastal New South Wales, in S. Bowdler (ed) *Coastal Archaeology in Eastern Australia*, Canberra: Australian National University, pp. 16–28.

Hughes, P. J. and Sullivan, M. E. 1981 Aboriginal burning and late Holocene geomorphic events in eastern New South Wales, *Search* 12: 277–278.

Hughes, P. J., Sullivan, M. E. and Lampert, R. J. 1973 The use of silcrete by Aborigines in southern coastal New South Wales, *Archaeology and Physical Anthropology in Oceania* 8: 158–161.

Hynes, R. A. and Chase, A. K. 1982 Plants, sites and domiculture: Aboriginal influence upon plant communities in Cape York Peninsula, *Archaeology in Oceania* 17: 38–50.

Ingold T. 1980 *Hunters, Pastoralists and Ranchers*, Cambridge: Cambridge University Press.

Ingold T. 1988 Notes on the foraging mode of production, in T. Ingold, D. Riches and

J. Woodburn (eds) *Hunters and Gatherers: History, Evolution and Social Change*, Oxford: Berg, pp. 269–285.

Ingold, T., Riches, D. and Woodburn, J. (eds) 1988a *Hunters and Gatherers 1: History, Evolution and Social Change*, Oxford: Berg.

Ingold, T., Riches, D. and Woodburn, J. (eds) 1988b *Hunters and Gatherers 2: Property, Power and Ideology*, Oxford: Berg.

Irwin, G. J. 1978 The development of Mailu as a specialized trading and manufacturing centre in Papuan prehistory: the causes and the implications, *Mankind* 11: 406–415.

Irwin, G. 1992 *The Prehistoric Exploration and Colonisation of the Pacific*, Cambridge: Cambridge University Press.

Jackson, W. D. 1965 Vegetation, in J. L. Davies (ed) *Atlas of Tasmania*, Hobart: Lands and Surveys Department, pp. 30–35.

Jochim, M. A. 1976 *Hunter-Gatherer Subsistence and Settlement: a Predictive Model*, New York: Academic Press.

Jochim, M. 1983 Palaeolithic cave art in ecological perspective, in G. N. Bailey (ed) *Hunter-gatherer Economy in Prehistory*, Cambridge: Cambridge University Press, pp. 212–219.

Johnson, G. A. 1982 Organizational structure and scalar stress, in C. Renfrew, M.J. Rowlands and B.A. Segraves (eds) *Theory and Explanation in Archaeology: the Southampton Conference*, New York: Academic Press.

Johnson, I. 1977 Abercrombie Arch shelter: an excavation near Bathurst, New South Wales, *Australian Archaeology* 6: 28–40.

Johnson, I. 1979 The Getting of Data. Unpublished PhD thesis, Canberra: Australian National University.

Johnston, H. 1982 Testing a Model: An Analysis of Vertebrate Faunal Remains From Warragarra Rockshelter, Central Tasmania. Unpublished BA (Hons) thesis, Department of Prehistory and Archaeology, Armidale, New South Wales: University of New England.

Johnston, H. 1993 Pleistocene shell middens of the Willandra Lakes, in M. A. Smith, M. Spriggs and B. Frankhauser (eds) *Sahul in Review: Pleistocene Archaeology in Australia, New Guinea and Island Melanesia*, Canberra: Department of Prehistory, Research School of Pacific Studies, Australian National University, pp. 197–203.

Jones, R. 1968 The geographical background to the arrival of man in Australia and Tasmania, *Archaeology and Physical Anthropology in Oceania* 3: 186–215.

Jones, R. 1969 Firestick farming, *Australian Natural History* 16: 224–228.

Jones, R. 1971a Rocky Cape and the problem of the Tasmanians. Unpublished PhD thesis, Department of Anthropology, University of Sydney.

Jones, R. 1971b The demography of hunters and farmers in Tasmania, in D. J. Mulvaney and J. Golson (eds) *Aboriginal Man and Environment in Australia*, Canberra: Australian National University Press, pp. 271–287.

Jones, R. 1973 Emerging picture of Pleistocene Australians, *Nature* (London) 246: 278–281.

Jones, R. 1974 Tasmanian tribes, in N. B. Tindale (ed) *Aboriginal Tribes of Australia*, Berkley: University of California Press.

Jones, R. 1975 The Neolithic Palaeolithic and the hunting gardeners: man and land in the Antipodes, in R.Sudgate and M. Cresswell (eds) *Quaternary Studies*, Wellington: Royal Society of New Zealand.

Jones, R. M. 1977a The Tasmanian paradox, in R. V. S. Wright (ed) *Stone Tools as Cultural Markers*, Canberra: Australian Institute of Aboriginal Studies, pp. 189–204.

Jones, R. 1977b Man as an element in a continental fauna: the case of the sundering of the Bassian Bridge, in J. Allen, J. Golson and R. Jones (eds) *Sunda and Sahul*, London: Academic Press, pp. 318–386.

Jones, R. 1978 Why did the Tasmanians stop eating fish? in R. A Gould (ed) *Explorations in Ethno-archaeology*, Albuquerque: University of New Mexico Press, pp. 11–47.

Jones, R. 1979 The fifth continent: problems concerning the human colonization of Australia, *Annual Review of Anthropology* 8: 445–466.

Jones, R. 1980 Cleaning the country: the Gidjingali and their Arnhem Land environment, *BHP Journal* 1.80: 10–15.

Jones, R. 1981 Hunters in the Australian coastal savanna, in D. Harris (ed) *Human Ecology in Savanna Environments*, London: Academic Press, pp. 107–146.

Jones, R. 1984. Hunters and history: a case study from western Tasmania, in C. Schrire (ed) *Past and Present in Hunter Gatherer Studies*, London: Academic Press, pp. 27–65.

Jones R. M. (ed) 1985a *Archaeological Research in Kakadu National Park*, Special Publication 13, Australian National Parks and Wildlife Service.

Jones, R. M. 1985b Archaeological conclusions, in R. M. Jones (ed) *Archaeological Research in Kakadu National Park*, Special Publication 13, Australian National Parks and Wildlife Service.

Jones, R. 1987 Pleistocene life in the dead heart of Australia, *Nature* 328: 666.

Jones, R. 1990a East of Wallace's line: issues and problems in the colonisation of the Australian continent, in P. Mellars and C. Stringer (eds) *The Human Revolution: Behavioural and Biological Perspectives on the Origins of Modern Humans*, Vol.2, Edinburgh: University of Edinburgh Press, pp. 743–782.

Jones, R. 1990b From Kakadu to Kutikina: the southern continent at 18,000 years ago, in C. Gamble and O. Soffer (eds) *The World at 18,000 BP, Low Latitudes*, vol. 2, London: Unwin Hyman, pp. 264–295.

Jones, R. and Bowler, J. M. 1980 Struggle for the savanna: northern Australia in ecological and prehistoric perspective, in R. Jones (ed) *Northern Australia: Options and Implications*, Canberra: Australian National University.

Jones, R., Cosgrove, R., Allen, J., Cane, S., Kiernan, K., Webb, S., Loy, T., West, D. and Stadler, E. 1988 An archaeological reconnaissance of karst caves within the southern forests region of Tasmania, September 1987, *Australian Archaeology* 26: 1–23.

Jones, R. M. and Johnson, I. R. 1985a Rockshelter excavations: Nourlangie and Mt. Brockman massifs, in R. M. Jones (ed) *Archaeological Research in Kakadu National Park*, Special Publication 13, Australian National Parks and Wildlife Service.

Jones, R. M. and Johnson, I. R. 1985b Deaf Adder Gorge: Lindner Site, Nauwalabila 1, in R. M. Jones (ed) *Archaeological Research in Kakadu National Park*, Special Publication 13: 165–227, Australian National Parks and Wildlife Service.

Jones, R. and Meehan, B. 1989 Plant foods of the Gidjingali: ethnographic and archaeological perspectives from northern Australia on tuber and seed exploitation, in D. R. Harris and G. C. Hillman (eds) *Foraging and Farming: the Evolution of Plant Domestication*, London: Unwin Hyman, pp. 121–135.

Jones, W. 1979 Up the Creek: Hunter-gatherers in the Cooper Basin. Unpublished BA thesis, Armidale, New South Wales: Department of Prehistory and Archaeology, University of New England.

Kamminga, J. and Allen, H. 1973 *Report of the Archaeological Survey*, Canberra: Alligator Rivers Environmental Fact-Finding Study.

Kamminga, J. 1978 Journey Into the Microcosms. Unpublished PhD thesis, Sydney: Department of Anthropology, University of Sydney.

Kamminga, J. 1982 Over the edge: functional analysis of Australian Stone Tools, *Occasional Papers in Anthropology* No. 12, University of Queensland.

Keen, I. 1982 How some Murngin men marry ten wives: the marital implications of matrilateral cross-cousin structures, *Man* 17: 620–642.

Keen, I. 1989 Aboriginal governance, in Altman J.C. (ed) *Emergent Inequalities in Aboriginal Australia*, Sydney: University of Sydney Press, pp. 17–42.

Keesing, R. M. 1981 *Cultural Anthropology: A Contemporary Perspective*, New York: Holt, Rinehart and Winston.

Kenyon, A. S. 1928 The Aboriginal protectorate of Port Phillip, *Victorian Historical Magazine* 12: 134–172.

Kephous, K. 1981 The chronology of the Lake Victoria lunette–some recent evidence, *Australian Archaeology* 13: 8–11.

Kershaw, A. P. 1973 Late Quaternary Vegetation of the Atherton Tableland, North-east Queensland, Australia. Unpublished PhD thesis, Canberra: Australian National University.

Kershaw, A. P. 1986 The last two glacial-interglacial cycles from north-eastern Australia: implications for climatic change and Aboriginal burning, *Nature* 322: 47–49.

Kershaw, A. P., Baird, J. G., D'Costa, D. M., Edney, P. A., Peterson, J. A. and Strickland, K. M. 1991 A comparison of long Quaternary records from the Atherton Tableland and Western Plains volcanic provinces, in M. A. J. Williams and P. De Deckker (eds) *The Cainozoic of the Australian Region: A Re-evaluation of the Evidence*, Sydney: Geological Society of Australia.

Kiernan, K., Jones, R. and Ranson, D. 1983 New evidence from Fraser Cave for glacial age man in southwest Tasmania, *Nature* 301: 28–32.

Kimber, R. 1983 Black lightning: Aborigines and fire in Central Australia and the Western Desert, *Archaeology in Oceania* 18: 38–45.

Kimber, R. G. 1984 Resource use and management in central Australia, *Australian Aboriginal Studies* 2: 12–23.

Kirk, R. L. 1976 Serum protein and enzyme markers as indicators of population affinities in Australia and the Western Pacific, in R. L. Kirk and A. G. Thorne (eds) *The Origin of the Australians*, Canberra: Australian Insitute of Aboriginal Studies, pp. 329–346.

Kirk, R. L. 1987 The human biology of the original Australians, *Search* 18: 220–222.

Kirk, R. L. and Thorne, A. G. (eds) 1976 *The Origin of the Australians*, Canberra: Australian Insitute of Aboriginal Studies.

Kohen, J. L., Stockton, E. D. and Williams, M. A. J. 1984 Shaws Creek KII rockshelter:

a prehistoric occupation site in the Blue Mountains piedmont, eastern New South Wales, *Archaeology in Oceania* 19: 57–73.

Krefft, G. 1865 On the Manners and Customs of the Aborigines of the Lower Murray and Darling, *Transactions of the Philosophical Society of New South Wales* 1862–5: 357–374.

Krinsley, D., Dorn, R. and S. Anderson 1990 Factors that interfere with the age determination of rock varnish, *Physical Geography* 11: 97–119.

Kroeber, A. L. 1939 Cultural and Natural Areas of Native North America, *American Archaeology and Ethnology* 48: 1–242, University of California Publications.

Kryzwicki, L. 1934 *Primitive Society and its Vital Statistics*, London: Macmillan.

Lamb, L. 1993 A Technological Analysis of Lithic Material from Fern Cave, Queensland. Unpublished BA (Hons) thesis, Brisbane: Department of Anthropology and Sociology, University of Queensland.

Lampert, R. J. 1971 Burrill Lake and Currarong, *Terra Australis* 1, Canberra: Australian National University.

Lampert, R. J. 1975 A preliminary report on some waisted blades found on Kangaroo Island, South Australia, *Australian Archaeology* 2: 45–47.

Lampert, R. J. 1980 Variation in Australia's Pleistocene stone industries, *Journal de la Société des Océanistes* 36: 109–206.

Lampert, R. J. 1981 The great Kartan mystery, *Terra Australis* 5, Canberra: Australian National University.

Lampert, R. J. 1983 The Kartan mystery revisited, *Australian Archaeology*, 16: 175–177.

Lampert, R. J. and Hughes, P. J. 1974 Sea level change and Aboriginal coastal adaptations in southern New South Wales, *Archaeology and Physical Anthropology in Oceania* 9: 226–235.

Lampert, R. J. and Hughes, P. J. 1980 Pleistocene archaeology in the Flinders range: research prospects, *Australian Archaeology* 10: 11–20.

Lampert, R. and Hughes, P. 1987 The Flinders Rangers: a Pleistocene outpost in the arid zone, *Records of the South Australian Museum* 20: 29–34.

Lampert, R. J. and Hughes, P. J. 1988 Early human occupation of the Flinders Ranges, *Records of the South Australian Museum* 22: 139–168.

Langford, J. 1965 Weather and Climate, in J. L. Davies (ed) *Atlas of Tasmania*, Hobart: Lands and Surveys Department, pp. 2–11.

Lathrap, D. W. 1968 The 'hunting' economies of the tropical forest zone of South America: an attempt at historical perspective, in Lee, R. B. and deVore, I. (eds) *Man The Hunter*, Chicago: Aldine, pp. 23–29.

Latz, P. K. 1982 Bushfires and Bushtucker: Aborigines and Plants in Central Australia. Unpublished MA thesis, Armidale, New South Wales: University of New England.

Layton, R. 1991 Trends in the hunter-gatherer rock art of Western Europe and Australia, *Proceedings of the Prehistoric Society* 57(1): 163–174.

Layton, R. 1992 *Australian Rock Art: A new synthesis*, Cambridge: Cambridge University Press.

Leacock, E. and Lee, R. (eds) 1982 *Politics and History in Band Societies*, Cambridge: Cambridge University Press.

Lee, R. B. 1968 What hunters do for a living, or, How to make out on scarce resources, in R. B. Lee and I. DeVore (eds) *Man the Hunter*, Chicago: Aldine, pp. 30–43

Lee, R. B. 1979 *The !Kung San: Men, Women and Work in a Foraging Society*, Cambridge: Cambridge University Press.

Lee, R. 1992 Art, science, or politics? The crisis in hunter-gatherer studies, *American Anthropologist* 94 (1): 31–54.

Lee, R. B. and DeVore, I. (eds) 1968 *Man The Hunter*, Chicago: Aldine.

Leichhardt, L. 1847 *Journal of an Overland Expedition in Australia from Moreton Bay to Port Essington, a Distance of Upwards of 3000 Miles, During the Years 1844–1845*.

Levitt, D. 1981 *Plants and People: Aboriginal Use of Plants on Groote Eylandt*, Canberra: Australian Institute of Aboriginal Studies.

Lewis, D. 1988 The Rock Paintings of Arnhem Land, Australia, *British Archaeological Reports*, International Series 415, Oxford.

Lilley, I. 1984 Late Holocene subsistence and settlement in subcoastal Southeast Queensland, *Queensland Archaeological Research* 1: 8–32.

Lorblanchet, M. 1992 The rock engravings of Gum Tree Valley and Skew Valley, Dampier, Western Australia: chronology and function of the sites, in J. McDonald and I.P. Haskovec (eds) *State of the Art: Regional Rock Art Studies in Australia and Melanesia*, Melbourne: Occasional AURA Publication 6, Australian Rock Art Research Association, pp. 39–59.

Lorblanchet, M. and Jones, R. 1979 Les premières fouilles à Dampier (Australie occidentale), et leur place dans l'ensemble Australien, *Bulletin de la Société Préhistorique Française* 76: 463–487.

Lourandos, H. 1968 Dispersal of activities–the east Tasmanian Aboriginal sites, *Papers and Proceedings of the Royal Society of Tasmania* 102: 41–46.

Lourandos, H. 1970 Coast and hinterland: the archaeological sites of eastern Tasmania. Unpublished MA thesis, Canberra: Department of Prehistory and Anthropology, Australian National University.

Lourandos, H. 1976 Aboriginal settlement and land use in south western Victoria: a report on current fieldwork, *The Artefact* 1 (4): 174–193

Lourandos, H. 1977a Aboriginal spatial organization and population: south-western Victoria re-considered, *Archaeology and Physical Anthropology in Oceania* 12: 202–225.

Lourandos, H. 1977b Stone tools, settlement, adaptation: a Tasmanian example, in R. V. S. Wright (ed) *Stone Tools as Cultural Markers*, Canberra: Australian Institute of Aboriginal Studies, pp. 219–224.

Lourandos, H. 1980a Forces of Change: Aboriginal Technology and Population in Southwestern Victoria. Unpublished PhD thesis, Sydney: Department of Anthropology, University of Sydney.

Lourandos, H. 1980b Change or stability? Hydraulics, hunter-gatherers and population in temperate Australia, *World Archaeology* 11: 245–266.

Lourandos, H. 1983a Intensification: a late Pleistocene-Holocene archaeological sequence from southwestern Victoria, *Archaeology in Oceania* 18: 81–94.

Lourandos, H. 1983b 10,000 years in the Tasmanian highlands, *Australian Archaeology* 16: 39–47.

Lourandos, H. 1984 Changing perspectives in Australian prehistory: a reply to Beaton, *Archaeology in Oceania* 19: 29–33.

Lourandos, H. 1985a Intensification and Australian prehistory, in T. D. Price and J. A. Brown (eds) *Prehistoric Hunter-gatherers: the Emergence of Cultural Complexity*, Orlando, Florida: Academic Press, pp. 385–423.

Lourandos, H. 1985b Problems with the interpretation of late Holocene changes in Australian prehistory, *Archaeology in Oceania* 20: 37–39.

Lourandos, H. 1987a Pleistocene Australia: peopling a continent, in O. Soffer (ed), *The Pleistocene Old World: Regional Perspectives*, New York: Plenum, pp. 147–165.

Lourandos, H. 1987b Swamp managers of southwestern Victoria, in D. J. Mulvaney and J. P. White (eds) *Australians To 1788*, Sydney: Fairfax, Syme and Weldon, pp. 292–307.

Lourandos, H. 1988a Seals, sedentism and change in the Bass Strait, in B. Meehan and R. Jones (eds) *Archaeology with Ethnography: an Australian Perspective*, Canberra: Australian National University, pp. 277–285.

Lourandos, H. 1988b Palaeopolitics: resource intensification in Aboriginal Australia and Papua New Guinea, in T. Ingold, D. Riches and J. Woodburn (eds) *Hunters and Gatherers: History, Evolution and Social Change*, Oxford: Berg, pp. 148–160.

Lourandos, H. 1993 Hunter-gatherer cultural dynamics: long- and short-term trends in Australian prehistory, *Journal of Archaeological Research* 1 (1): 67–88.

Lourandos, H. (in press) Change in Australian prehistory: scale, trends and frameworks of interpretation, in Lilley, I., Ross, A. and Ulm, S. (eds) *Proceedings of the 1995 Australian Archaeological Association Annual Conference*, Brisbane: University of Queensland.

Lourandos, H. and Barker, B. (in preparation), Narcurrer: a limestone rockshelter from southeastern South Australia.

Lourandos, H. and David, B. (in preparation, a) The openness of 'closed' systems: cultural dynamics and social systems.

Lourandos, H. and David, B. (in preparation, b) Comparing long-term late Pleistocene–Holocene archaeological trends in Australian prehistory.

Lourandos, H. and Mitchell, S. (in preparation) Seal Point, Cape Otway: a re-analysis.

Lourandos, H. and Ross, A. (1994). The great 'intensification debate': Its history and place in Australian archaeology, *Australian Archaeology*, 39: 54–63.

Loy, T. H., Jones, R., Nelson, D. E., Meehan, B., Vogel, J., Southon, J. and Cosgrove, R. 1990 Accelerator radiocarbon dating of human blood proteins in pigments from Late Pleistocene art sites in Australia, *Antiquity* 64: 110–116.

Luebbers, R. A. 1975 Ancient boomerangs discovered in South Australia, *Nature* (London) 253: 39.

Luebbers, R. A. 1978 Meals and Menus: A Study of Change in Prehistoric Settlements in South Australia. Unpublished PhD thesis, Canberra: Department of Prehistory, Australian National University.

Leubbers, R. A. 1982 The Coorong Report. Prepared for the S. A. Department of Environment and Planning, Adelaide.

Mabbutt, J. A. 1971 The Australian arid zone as a prehistoric environment, in D. J. Mulvaney and J. Golson (eds) *Aboriginal Man and Environment in Australia*, Canberra: Australian National University Press, pp. 66–79.

Mackay, R. and White, J. P. 1987 Musseling in on the NSW coast, *Archaeology in Oceania* 22: 107–111.

Macintosh, N. W. G. 1952 The Talgai skull and dental arch: remeasurement and reconstruction, *Oceania* 23: 106–109.

Macintosh, N. W. G. 1965 The physical aspect of man in Australia, in R. M. and C. H. Berndt (eds) *Aboriginal Man in Australia*, Sydney: Angus and Robertson, pp. 29–70.

Macintosh, N. W. G. 1971 Analysis of an Aboriginal skeleton and a pierced tooth necklace from Lake Nitchie, Australia, *Anthropologie* 9: 49–62.

Macintosh, N. W. G., Smith, K. N. and Bailey, A. B. 1970 Lake Nitchie skeleton: unique Aboriginal burial, *Archaeology and Physical Anthropology in Oceania* 5: 85–101.

MacKnight, C. C. 1986 Macassans and the Aboriginal past, *Archaeology in Oceania* 21: 69–75.

MacNeish, R. 1986 The Preceramic of Middle America, *Advances in World Archaeology* 5: 93–130.

MacNeish, R., et al. 1980, 1981. *The prehistory of the Ayacucho Basin, Peru*, (2 vols.), Ann Arbor: University of Michigan.

Macphail, M. K. 1983 Holocene pollen sequences: a personal view, *Quaternary Australasia* 1: 20–30.

Macphail, M. K. 1986 Over the top; pollen based reconstructions of past alpine floras and vegetation in Tasmania, in B. A. Barlow (ed) *Flora and Fauna of Alpine Australasia: Ages and Origins*, Melbourne: CSIRO.

Macphail, M. K. and Peterson, J. 1975 New deglaciation dates from Tasmania, *Search* 6: 295–300.

Maddock, K. 1972 *The Australian Aborigines: A Portrait Of Their Society*, London: Allen Lane.

Main, A. R. 1978 Ecophysiology: towards an understanding of Late Pleistocene marsupial extinction, in D. Walker and J. C. Guppy (eds) *Biology and Quaternary Environments*, Canberra: Australian Academy of Science, pp. 169–184.

Marquardt, W. H. 1985 Complexity and scale in the study of fisher-gatherer-hunters: an example from the eastern United States, in T. D. Price and J. A. Brown (eds) *Prehistoric Hunter-gatherers: the Emergence of Cultural Complexity*, Orlando, Florida: Academic Press, pp. 59–98.

Marquardt, W. H. 1988 Politics and production among the Calusa of south Florida, in T. Ingold, D. Riches and J. Woodburn (eds) *Hunters and Gatherers: History, Evolution and Social Change*, Oxford: Berg, pp. 161–188.

Marshall, L. G. 1974 Late Pleistocene mammals from the 'Keilor cranium site', southern Victoria, Australia, *Memoirs of the National Museum of Victoria* 35: 63–86.

Martin, H. 1973 Palynological and historical ecology of some cave excavations in the Australian Nullarbor, *Australian Journal of Botany* 21: 283–283

Martin, P. S. and Klein, R. G. (eds) 1984 *Quaternary Extinctions. A Prehistoric Revolution*, Tucson: University of Arizona Press.

Marun, L. H. 1974 The Mirning and Their Predecessors on the Coastal Nullarbor Plain. Unpublished PhD thesis, Sydney: University of Sydney.

Mathews, R. H. 1903 The Aboriginal fisheries at Brewarrina, *Journal of the Royal Society of New South Wales* 37: 150–153.

Maynard, L. 1977 Classification and terminology in Australian rock art, in P. J. Ucko (ed) *Form in Indigenous Art*, Canberra: Australian Institute of Aboriginal Studies, pp. 387–402.

Maynard, L. 1979 The archaeology of Australian Aboriginal art, in S. M. Mead (ed) *Exploring the Visual Art of Oceania*, Honolulu: University Press of Hawaii, pp. 83–110.

Maynard, L. 1980 A Pleistocene date from an occupation deposit in the Pilbara region, Western Australia, *Australian Archaeology* 10: 3–8.

McArthur, M. 1976 Computer simulations of small populations, *Australian Archaeology* 4: 53–57.

McBryde, I. 1974 *Aboriginal Prehistory in New England*, London: Green and Longmans.

McBryde, I. 1977 Determinants of assemblage variation in New England prehistory, in R. V. S. Wright (ed) *Stone Tools as Cultural Markers*, Canberra: Australian Institute of Aboriginal Studies, pp. 225–250.

McBryde, I. 1978a Wil-im-ee Moor-ing: or where do axes come from? *Mankind* 3: 354–382.

McBryde, I. (ed) 1978b *Records of Times Past*, Canberra: Australian Institute of Aboriginal Studies.

McBryde, I. 1979 Petrology and prehistory: lithic evidence for exploitation of stone resources and exchange systems in Australia, *Council for British Archaeology, Research Report* 23: 113–126.

McBryde, I. 1984 Kulin greenstone quarries: the social contexts of production and distribution for the Mt William site, *World Archaeology*, 16: 267–285.

McCarthy, F. D. 1939 'Trade' in Aboriginal Australia and 'trade' relationships with Torres Strait, New Guinea and Malaya, *Oceania* 9: 405–438; 10: 80–104, 171–195.

McCarthy, F. D. 1940 Aboriginal Australian material culture: causative factors in its composition, *Mankind* 2: 241–269, 294–320.

McCarthy, F. D. 1948 The Lapstone Creek excavation: two culture periods revealed in eastern New South Wales, *Records of the Australian Museum* 22: 1–34.

McCarthy, F. D. 1964 The archaeology of the Capertee Valley, New South Wales, *Records of the Australian Museum* 26: 197–246.

McCarthy, F. D. 1977 The use of stone tools to map patterns of diffusion, in R. V. S. Wright (ed) *Stone Tools as Cultural Markers*, Canberra: Australian Institute of Aboriginal Studies, pp. 251–262.

McCarthy, F. D. 1978 New light on the Lapstone Creek excavation, *Australian Archaeology* 8: 49–60.

McCarthy, F. D., Bramell, E. and Noone, H. V. V. 1946 The stone implements of Australia, *Memoirs of the Australian Museum* 9.

McCulloch, M. T., De Deckker, P. and Chivas, A. R. 1989 Strontium isotope variations in single ostracod valves from the Gulf of Carpentaria Australia: a palaeoenvironmental indicator, *Geochimica et Cosmochimica Acta* 53: 1703–1710.

McDonald, J. J. 1994 Sydney Basin rock art: the analysis of a regional art style in the context of its prehistory, Unpublished PhD thesis, Department of Prehistory and Anthropology, Canberra: Australian National University.

McInnes, P. 1988 Sea-level Stabilisation Arguments: Assessing Their Explanatory Potential. Unpublished BA thesis, Brisbane: Department of Anthropology and Sociology, University of Queensland.

McNiven, I. 1990 Prehistoric Aboriginal Settlement and Subsistence in the Cooloola

Region, Coastal Southeast Queensland. Unpublished PhD thesis, Brisbane: Department of Anthropology and Sociology, University of Queensland.

McNiven, I. 1991 Teewah Beach: new evidence for Holocene coastal occupation in southeast Queensland, *Australian Archaeology* 33: 14–27.

McNiven, I. 1993 Tula adzes and bifacial points on the east coast of Australia, *Australian Archaeology* 36: 22–33.

McNiven, I. J. 1994 Technological organization and settlement in southwestern Tasmania after the glacial maximum, *Antiquity* 68: 75–82.

McNiven, I. J., Marshall, B., Allen, J., Stern, N., and Cosgrove, R. 1993 The southern forests archaeological project: an overview, in M. A. Smith, M. Spriggs and B. Frankhauser (eds) *Sahul in Review: Pleistocene Archaeology in Australia, New Guinea and Island Melanesia*, Canberra: Department of Prehistory, Research School of Pacific Studies, Australian National University, pp. 213–214.

Meehan, B. 1971 The Form, Distribution and Antiquity of Australian Aboriginal Mortuary Practices. Unpublished MA thesis, Sydney: Department of Anthropology, University of Sydney.

Meehan, B. 1982 *Shell Bed to Shell Midden*, Canberra: Australian Institute of Aboriginal Studies.

Meehan, B. and Jones, R. 1988 *Archaeology With Ethnography: an Australian Perspective*, Canberra: Australian National University.

Meehan, B. and White, N. 1990 *Hunter-Gatherer Demography: Past and Present*, Oceania Monograph 39, Sydney: University of Sydney.

Meggitt, M. J. 1962 *Desert People*, Sydney: Angus and Robertson.

Meggitt, M. J. 1964 Aboriginal food-gatherers of tropical Australia, *The Ecology of Man in the Tropical Environment*, International Union for the Conservation of Nature and Natural Resources, Morges, pp. 30–37.

Meggitt, M. 1966 Indigenous forms of government among Australian Aborigines, in H. Hogbin and L. Hiatt (eds) *Readings in Australian and Pacific Anthropology*, Melbourne: Melbourne University Press.

Mellars, P. 1976 Fire ecology, animal populations and man: a study of some ecological relationships in prehistory, *Proceedings of the Prehistoric Society* 42: 15–45.

Mellars, P. A. 1985 The ecological basis of social complexity in the Upper Palaeolithic of Southwestern France, in T. D. Price and J. A. Brown (eds) *Prehistoric Hunter-gatherers: the Emergence of Cultural Complexity*, Orlando, Florida: Academic Press, pp. 271–297.

Mellars, P. and Stringer, C. (eds) 1989 *The Human Revolution: Behavioural and Biological Perspectives on the Origins of Modern Humans*, Vol. 1, Edinburgh: University of Edinburgh Press.

Merrilees, D. 1968 Man the destroyer: late Quaternary changes in the Australian marsupial fauna, *Journal of the Royal Society of Western Australia* 51: 1–24.

Milham, P. and Thompson, P. 1976 Relative antiquity of human occupation and extinct fauna at Madura Cave, southeastern Western Australia, *Mankind* 10: 175–180.

Mitchell, S. 1988 Chronological Change in Intensity of Site Use at Seal Point: A Technological Analysis. Unpublished BA (Hons) thesis, Brisbane: Department of Anthropology and Sociology, University of Queensland.

Mitchell, T. L. 1839 *Three Expeditions into the Interior of Eastern Australia*, Vols. I and II, London: Boone.

Mitchell, T. L. 1848 *Journal of an Expedition into the Interior of Tropical Australia*, London: Longman.

Modjeska, C. J. N. 1977 Production Among the Duna. Unpublished PhD thesis, Canberra: Australian National University.

Modjeska, C. N. 1982 Production and inequality: perspectives from central New Guinea, in A. Strathern (ed) *Inequality in New Guinea Highlands Societies*, Cambridge: Cambridge University Press, pp. 50–108.

Morren, G. 1974 Settlement Strategies and Hunting in a New Guinea Society. Unpublished PhD thesis, New York: Columbia University.

Morren, G. E. B. 1977 From hunting to herding: pigs and the control of energy in montane New Guinea, in T. P. Bayliss-Smith and R. G. Feachem (eds) *Subsistence and Survival: Rural Ecology*, London: Academic Press, pp. 273–316.

Morse, K. M. 1988 Mandu Mandu Creek rockshelter: Pleistocene human coastal occupation of North West Cape, Western Australia, *Archaeology in Oceania* 23: 81–88.

Morse, K. M. 1993 New Radiocarbon dates from North West Cape, Western Australia: a preliminary report, in M. A. Smith, M. Spriggs and B. Frankhauser (eds) *Sahul in Review: Pleistocene Archaeology in Australia, New Guinea and Island Melanesia*, Canberra: Department of Prehistory, Research School of Pacific Studies, Australian National University, pp. 155–163.

Morwood, M. J. 1979 Art and Stone: Towards a Prehistory of Central Western Queensland. Unpublished PhD thesis, Canberra: Australian National University.

Morwood, M. J. 1980 Time, space and prehistoric art: a principal components analysis, *Archaeology and Physical Anthropology in Oceania* 15: 98–109.

Morwood, M. J. 1981 Archaeology of the central Queensland highlands: the stone component, *Archaeology in Oceania* 16: 1–52.

Morwood, M. J. 1984 The prehistory of the central Queensland highlands, in F. Wendorf and C. Close (eds) *Advances in World Archaeology* 3: 325–380.

Morwood, M. J. 1987 The archaeology of social complexity in South-east Queensland, *Proceedings of the Prehistoric Society* 53: 337–350.

Morwood, M. 1989 The archaeology of Aboriginal art in S. E. Cape York: preliminary report on the 1989 fieldwork, *Rock Art Research* 6: 155–156.

Morwood, M. J. 1990 The prehistory of Aboriginal landuse on the Upper Flinders River, North Queensland Highlands, *Queensland Archaeological Research* 7: 3–40.

Morwood, M. J. 1992 Changing art in a changing landscape: a case study from the upper Flinders River Region of the North Queensland Highlands, in J. McDonald and I. P. Haskovec (eds) *State of the Art: Regional Rock Art Studies in Australia and Melanesia*, Melbourne; Occasional AURA Publication 6, Australian Rock Art Research Association, pp. 60–70.

Morwood, M. 1993 Cause and effect: Pleistocene Aboriginal occupation in the Quinkan region, southeast Cape York Peninsula, in M. A. Smith, M. Spriggs and B. Frankhauser (eds) *Sahul in Review: Pleistocene Archaeology in Australia, New Guinea and Island Melanesia*, Canberra: Department of Prehistory, Research School of Pacific Studies, Australian National University, pp. 173–179.

Morwood, M. J. and Godwin, L. M. 1982 Aboriginal sites in the Hughenden region, north Queensland highlands: research prospects, *Australian Archaeology* 15: 49–53.

Morwood, M. J. and Hobbs, D. R. (eds) 1995 Quinkan Prehistory: the archaeology of Aboriginal art in S.E. Cape York Peninsula, *Tempus* 3, Brisbane: University of Queensland.

Morwood, M. J. and Trezise, P. J. 1989 Edge-ground axes in Pleistocene greater Australia: new evidence from S.E. Cape York Peninsula, *Queensland Archaeological Research* 6: 77–90.

Mountain, M. J. 1993 Bone, hunting and predation in the Pleistocene of northern Sahul, in M. A. Smith, M. Spriggs and B. Frankhauser (eds) *Sahul in Review: Pleistocene Archaeology in Australia, New Guinea and Island Melanesia*, Canberra: Department of Prehistory, Research School of Pacific Studies, Australian National University, pp. 123–130.

Mulvaney, D. J. 1960 Archaeological excavations at Fromm's Landing on the Lower Murray River, South Australia, *Proceedings of the Royal Society of Victoria* 72: 53–85.

Mulvaney, D. J. 1962 Archaeological excavations on the Aire river, Otway Peninsula, Victoria, *Proceedings of the Royal Society of Victoria* 75: 1–15.

Mulvaney, D. J. 1964 The Pleistocene colonization of Australia, *Antiquity* 38: 263–267.

Mulvaney, D. J. 1966 The prehistory of the Australian Aborigine, *Scientific American* 214 (3): 84–93.

Mulvaney, D. J. 1969 *The Prehistory of Australia*, London: Thames and Hudson.

Mulvaney, D. J. 1975 *The Prehistory of Australia*, Melbourne: Pelican.

Mulvaney, D. J. 1976 'The chain of connection': the material evidence, in N. Peterson (ed) *Tribes and Boundaries in Australia*, Canberra: Australian Institute of Aboriginal Studies, pp. 72–94.

Mulvaney, D. J. 1977 Classification and typology in Australia: the first 340 years, in R. V. S. Wright (ed) *Stone Tools as Cultural Markers*, Canberra: Australian Institute of Aboriginal Studies, pp. 263–268.

Mulvaney, D. J. 1979 Blood from stones and bones, *Search* 10: 214–218.

Mulvaney, D. J. and Joyce, E. B. 1965 Archaeological and geomorphological investigations on Mt. Moffit station, Queensland, Australia, *Proceedings of the Prehistoric Society* 31: 147–212.

Mulvaney, D. J. and Soejono, R. P. 1970 The Australian–Indonesian archaeological expedition to Sulawesi, *Asian Perspectives* 13: 163–178.

Mulvaney, D. J. and White, J. P. 1987 *Australians to 1788*, Sydney: Fairfax, Syme and Weldon.

Murray, P. F., Goede, A. and Bada, J. L. 1980 Pleistocene human occupation at Beginners Luck Cave, Florentine Valley, Tasmania, *Archaeology and Physical Anthropology in Oceania* 15: 142–152.

Murray, P. F. and Chaloupka, G. 1984 The dreamtime animals: extinct megafauna in Arnhem Land rock art. *Archaeology in Oceania* 19(3): 105–116.

Myers, F. 1986 *Pintupi Country, Pintupi Self: sentiment, place and politics among Western Desert Aborigines*, Canberra: Australian Institute of Aboriginal Studies.

Myers, F. R. 1988 Critical trends in the study of hunter-gatherers, *Annual Revue of Anthropology* 17: 261–282.

Nanson, G. C., Young, R. W. and Stockton, E. D. 1987 Chronology and Palaeoenvironment of the Cranebrook Terrace (near Sydney) containing artefacts more than 40,000 years old, *Archaeology in Oceania* 22: 72–78.

Neal, R. and Stock, E. 1986 Pleistocene occupation in the south-east Queensland coastal region, *Nature* 323: 618–621.

Negerevich, T. 1992 Settlement Sizes, Growth and Stability: Patterns Produced by Internal Processes. Unpublished PhD thesis, Brisbane: Department of Anthropology and Sociology, University of Queensland.

Newland, S. 1920–1 Annual address of the President, *Journal of the Royal Geographical Society of Australasia (South Australian Branch)* 22.

Noble, W. and Davidson, I. 1991 The evolutionary emergence of modern human behaviour: language and its archaeology, *Man* 26: 223–253.

Nolan, A. 1986 Sandstone Point: Temoporal and Spatial Patterns of Aboriginal Site Use at a Midden Complex, South-east Queensland. Unpublished BA thesis, Brisbane: Department of Anthropology and Sociology, University of Queensland.

O'Connell, J. F. 1977 Aspects of variation in central Australian lithic assemblages, in R. V. S. Wright (ed) *Stone Tools as Cultural Markers*, Canberra: Australian Institute of Aboriginal Studies, pp. 269–281.

O'Connell, J. F. and Allen, J. 1995 Human reactions to the Pleistocene–Holocene transition in Greater Australia: a summary, in Allen, J. and J. F. O'Connell (eds) *Transitions: Pleistocene to Holocene in Australia and Papua New Guinea, Antiquity* 69: 855–862.

O'Connell J. F. and Hawkes, K. 1981 Alywara plant use and optimal foraging theory, in B. Winterhalder and E. A. Smith (eds) *Hunter-Gatherer Foraging Strategies: Ethnographic and Archaeological Analyses*, Chicago: University of Chicago Press, pp. 99–125.

O'Connell, J. F., Latz, P. K. and Barnett, P. 1983 Traditional and modern plant use among the Alyawara of central Australia, *Economic Botany* 37: 80–109.

O'Connor, S. 1980 Bringing it All Back Home: Analysis of the Vertebrate Faunal Remains From the Stockyard Site, Hunter Island, Northwest Tasmania. Unpublished BA (Hons) thesis, Armidale, New South Wales: University of New England.

O'Connor, S. 1987 The stone house structures of High Cliffy Island, north-west Kimberley, W.A., *Australian Archaeology* 25: 30–39.

O'Connor, S. 1989 New radiocarbon dates from Koolan Island, West Kimberley, W.A., *Australian Archaeology* 28: 92–104.

O'Connor, S. 1990 Thirty Thousand Years in the Kimberley. Unpublished PhD thesis, Perth: Department of Archaeology, University of Western Australia.

O'Connor, S. 1992 The timing and nature of prehistoric island use in northern Australia, *Archaeology in Oceania* 27: 49–60.

O'Connor, S. and Sullivan, M. 1994 Distinguishing middens and cheniers: a case study from the southern Kimberley, W. A., *Archaeology in Oceania* 29: 16–28.

O'Connor, S., Veth, P. and Hubbard, N. 1993 Changing interpretations of postglacial human subsistence and demography in Sahul, in M. A. Smith, M. Spriggs and B. Frankhauser (eds) *Sahul in Review: Pleistocene Archaeology in Australia, New Guinea and Island Melanesia*, Canberra: Department of Prehistory, Research School of Pacific Studies, Australian National University, pp. 95–105.

Ohtsuka, R. 1977 The sago eaters: an ecological discussion with special reference to the Oriomo Papuans, in J. Allen, J. Golson and R. Jones (eds) *Sunda and Sahul*, London: Academic Press, pp. 465–492.

Orchiston, D. W. and Glenie, R. C. 1978 Residual Holocene populations in Bassania: Aboriginal man at Palana, northern Flinders Island, *Australian Archaeology* 8: 127–137.

Pardoe, C. 1988 The cemetery as symbol. The distribution of prehistoric Aboriginal burial grounds in southeastern Australia, *Archaeology in Oceania* 23: 1–16.

Pardoe, C. 1990 The demographic basis of human evolution in southeastern Australia, in B. Meehan and N. White (eds) *Hunter-Gatherer Demography: Past and Present*, Sydney: Oceania Monograph 39, University of Sydney, pp. 59–70.

Pardoe, C. 1991 Isolation and evolution in Tasmania, *Current Anthropology* 31: 1–21.

Pardoe, C. 1992 Arches of radii, corridors of power: Reflections on current archaeological practice, in B. Attwood and J. Arnolds (eds) *Power, Knowledge and Aborigines* Melbourne: Latrobe University Press, pp. 132–141.

Pearce, R. H. and Barbetti, M. 1981 A 38,000-year-old archaeological site at Upper Swan, Western Australia, *Archaeology in Oceania* 16: 173–178.

Peterson, N. 1976 The natural and cultural areas of Aboriginal Australia; a preliminary analysis of population groupings with adaptive significance, in N. Peterson (ed) 1986 *Tribes and Boundaries in Australia*, Canberra: Australian Institute of Aboriginal Studies, pp. 50–71.

Petrie, C. C. 1904 *Tom Petrie's Reminiscences of Early Queensland*, Brisbane: Watson.

Pianka, E. R. 1978 *Evolutionary Ecology*, New York: Harper and Row.

Pierce, R. 1971 The Effects of Aquatic Foods on the Diet and Economy of Aborigines on the North Coast of NSW at the Time of First Contact. Unpublished BA thesis, Armidale: University of New England.

Pietrusewsky, M. 1984 Metric and non-metric cranial variation in Australian Aboriginal populations compared with the Pacific and Asia, *Occasional Papers in Human Biology* 3: 1–113.

Plomley, N. J. B. 1966 *Friendly Mission: the Tasmanian journals and papers of George Augustus Robinson, 1829–1834*, Hobart: Tasmanian Historical Research Association.

Poiner, G. 1976 The process of the year among Aborigines of the central and south coast of New South Wales, *Archaeology and Physical Anthropology in Oceania* 11: 186–296.

Polgar, S. 1975 Population, evolution, and theoretical paradigms, in S. Polgar (ed) *Population, Ecology and Social Evolution*, The Hague: Mouton, pp. 1–25.

Pretty, G. L. 1977 The cultural chronology of the Roonka Flat, in R. V. S. Wright (ed) *Stone Tools as Cultural Markers*, Canberra: Australian Institute of Aboriginal Studies, pp. 288–331.

Pretty, G. L. and Kricun, M. E. 1989 Prehistoric health status of the Roonka population, *World Archaeology* 21: 218–224.

Price, T. D. 1985 Affluent foragers of Mesolithic southern Scandinavia, in T. D. Price and J. A. Brown (eds) *Prehistoric Hunter-Gatherers: The Emergence of Cultural Complexity*, Orlando, Florida: Academic Press, pp. 341–363.

Price, T. D. 1987 The Mesolithic of Western Europe, *Journal of World Prehistory* 1 (3): 225–305.

Price, T. D. and Brown, J. A. 1985a *Prehistoric Hunter-gatherers: The Emergence of Cultural Complexity*, Orlando, Florida: Academic Press.

Price T. D. and Brown J. A. 1985b Aspects of hunter-gatherer complexity, in T. D. Price and J. A. Brown (eds) *Prehistoric Hunter-gatherers: The Emergence of Cultural Complexity*, Orlando, Florida: Academic Press, pp. 3–20.

Quinn, R. H. and Beumer, J. P. 1984 Wallum Creek–a study in the regeneration of mangroves, in R. G. Coleman, J. Covavevich and P. Davie (eds) *Focus on Stradbroke*, Brisbane: Boolarong Publications, pp. 238–259.

Radcliffe-Brown, A. R. 1930 Former numbers and distribution of the Australian Aborigines, *Official Year Book*, 23: 688–696.

Ranson, D. 1978 A preliminary examination of prehistoric coastal settlement at Nelson Bay, west coast of Tasmania, *Australian Archaeology* 8: 149–158.

Rappaport, R. 1967 *Pigs for the Ancestors*, New Haven, CT: Yale University Press.

Reber, G. 1965 Aboriginal carbon dates from Tasmania, *Mankind* 6: 264–268.

Reynolds, B. 1987 Challenge and response of the rainforest, in D. J. Mulvaney and J. P. White (eds) *Australians to 1788*, Sydney: Fairfax, Syme and Weldon, pp. 166–176.

Roberts, R. G., Jones, R. and Smith, M. 1990a Thermoluminescence dating of a 50,000-year-old human occupation site in northern Australia, *Nature* 345: 153–156.

Roberts, R. G., Jones, R. and Smith, M. 1990b Early dates at Malakunanja II: a reply to Bowdler, *Australian Archaeology* 31: 94–97.

Roberts, R. G., Jones, R. and Smith, M. 1990c Stratigraphy and statistics at Malakunanja II: a reply to Hiscock, *Archaeology in Oceania* 25: 125–129.

Robinson, G. A. 1839–1849 *Manuscripts and Papers, Port Phillip Protectorate*, Sydney: Mitchell Library.

Rose, F. G. G. 1960 *Classification of Kin, Age, Structure and Marriage Amongst the Groote Eylandt Aborigines*, Berlin: Academie-Verlag.

Rosenfeld, A. 1993 A review of the evidence for the emergence of rock art in Australia, in M. A. Smith, M. Spriggs and B. Frankhauser (eds) *Sahul in Review: Pleistocene Archaeology in Australia, New Guinea and Island Melanesia*, Canberra: Department of Prehistory, Research School of Pacific Studies, Australian National University, pp. 71–80.

Rosenfeld, A., D. Horton, and J. Winter 1981 Early Man in North Queensland. *Terra Australis*, 6, Department of Prehistory, Research School of Pacific Studies, Australian National University, Canberra.

Ross, A. C. 1981 Holocene environments and prehistoric site patterning in the Victorian Mallee, *Archaeology in Oceania* 16: 145–155.

Ross, A. 1985 Archaeological evidence for population change in the middle to late Holocene in southeastern Australia, *Archaeology in Oceania* 20: 81–89.

Ross, A. 1989 Question of numbers: the interaction of people and environment in the Holocene, in T. H. Donnelly and R. J. Wasson (eds) *CLIMANZ* 3, Canberra: CSIRO.

Ross, A., Donnelly, T. and Wasson, R. 1992 The peopling of the arid zone: human-environment interactions, in J. Dodson (ed) *The Naive Lands: Prehistory and Environmental Change in Australia and the Southwest Pacific*, Melbourne: Longman Cheshire.

Roth, W. E. 1897 *Ethnological Studies among the North-West-Central Queensland Aborigines*, Brisbane: Government Printer.

Roth, W. E. 1898 *The Aborigines of the Rockhampton and surrounding coast districts, Report to the Commissioner of Police, Queensland*, Sydney: Mitchell Library, Uncat. ML MSS 216, CY Reel 208.

Rowland, M. J. 1980 The Keppel Islands—preliminary investigations, *Australian Archaeology* 11: 1–17.

Rowland, M. J. 1981 Radiocarbon dates for a shell fishook and disc from Mazie Bay, North Keppel Island, *Australian Archaeology* 12: 63–69.

Rowland, M. J. 1982a Further radiocarbon dates from the Keppel Islands, *Australian Archaeology* 15: 43–48.

Rowland, M. J. 1982b Keppel Island marine specialists: an adaptation to the Southern Barrier Reef province, in S. Bowdler (ed) *Coastal Archaeology in Eastern Australia*, Canberra: Australian National University, pp. 114–120.

Rowland, M. J. 1983 Aborigines and environment in Holocene Australia: changing paradigms, *Australian Aboriginal Studies* 2: 62–77.

Rowland, M. J. 1986 The Whitsunday Islands: initial historical and archaeological observations and implications for future research, *Queensland Archaeological Research* 3: 72–87.

Rowland, M. J. 1989 Population increase, intensification or a result of preservation? Explaining site distribution patterns on the coast of Queensland, *Australian Aboriginal Studies* 2: 32–42.

Rowley-Conwy, P. 1986 Between cave painters and crop planters: aspects of the temperate European Mesolithic, in M. Zvelebil (ed) *Hunters in Transition: Mesolithic Societies of Temperate Eurasia and Their Transition to Farming*, Cambridge: Cambridge University Press, pp. 17–32.

Ryan, L. 1981 *The Aboriginal Tasmanians*, Brisbane: University of Queensland Press.

Sahlins, M. 1974 *Stone Age Economics*, London: Tavistock.

Satterthwait, L. D. 1980 Aboriginal Australia: the simplest technologies? *Archaeology and Physical Anthropology in Oceania* 15: 153–156.

Satterthwait, L. D. 1986 Aboriginal Australian net hunting, *Mankind* 16: 31–38.

Satterthwait, L. D. 1987 Socioeconomic implications of Australian Aboriginal net hunting, *Man* (N.S.) 22: 613–636.

Schalk, R. F. 1982 Land use and organizational complexity among foragers of northwestern North America, in Koyama S. and Thomas D. H. (eds) *Affluent Foragers*, Senri Ethnological Studies No. 9, Osaka, pp. 53–76.

Schrire, C. 1980 An analysis of human behaviour and animal extinctions in South Africa and Australia in late Pleistocene times, *South African Archaeological Bulletin* 35: 3–12.

Schrire, C. 1982 The Alligator rivers: prehistory and ecology in western Arnhem Land, *Terra Australis* 7, Canberra: Australian National University.

Schrire, C. (ed) 1984 *Past and Present in Hunter-gatherer Studies*, Orlando, Florida: Academic Press.

Schwede, M. 1983 Supertrench—Phase 2, a report on excavation results, in Moya Smith (ed) *Archaeology at ANZAAS 1983*, Perth: Western Australian museum, pp. 53–62.

Shanks, M. and Tilley, C. 1987 *Social Theory and Archaeology*, Cambridge: Polity Press.

Shawcross, F. W. 1975 Thirty thousand years and more, *Hemisphere* 19: 26–31.

Sheehan, G. W. 1985 Whaling as an organising focus in northwestern Alaskan Eskimo societies, in T. D. Price and J. A. Brown (eds) *Prehistoric Hunter-gatherers: the Emergence of Cultural Complexity*, Orlando, Florida: Academic Press, pp. 123–154.

Sim, R. 1990 Prehistoric sites on King Island in the Bass Strait: results of an archaeological survey, *Australian Archaeology* 31: 34–43.

Sim, R. 1994 Prehistoric human occupation in the King and Furneaux Island regions, Bass Strait, in M. Sullivan, S. Brockwell and A. Webb (eds) *Archaeology in the North*, Darwin: North Australia Research Unit (ANU), pp. 358–374.

Sim, R. and Thorne, A. G. 1990 Pleistocene human remains from King Island, Bass Strait, *Australian Archaeology* 31: 44–51.

Simmons, R. T. 1976 The biological origin of Australian Aboriginals: an examination of blood group genes and gene frequencies for possible evidence in populations from Australia to Eurasia, in R. L. Kirk and A. G. Thorne (eds) *The Origin of the Australians*, Canberra: Australian Institute of Aboriginal Studies, pp. 307–328.

Singh, G. and Geissler, E. A. 1985 Late Cainozoic history of vegetation, fire, lake levels and climate at Lake George, New South Wales, Australia, *Philosophical Transactions of the Royal Society of London*, Series B 311: 379–447.

Singh, G., Kershaw, A. P. and Clark, R. 1981 Quaternary vegetation and fire history in Australia, in A. M. Gill, R. H. Groves and I. R. Noble (eds) *Fire and the Australian Biota*, Canberra: Australian Academy of Science, pp. 23–54.

Smith, M. A. 1982 Devon Downs reconsidered: changes in site use at a Lower Murray River rockshelter, *Archaeology in Oceania* 17: 109–116.

Smith, M. A. 1985 A morphological comparison of Central Australian seedgrinding implements and Australian Pleistocene grindstones, *The Beagle: Occasional Papers of the Northern Territory Museum of Arts and Sciences*, 2 (1).

Smith, M. A. 1986 The antiquity of seedgrinding in central Australia, *Archaeology in Oceania* 21: 29–39.

Smith, M. A. 1988 The Pattern and Timing of Prehistoric Settlement in Central Australia. Unpublished PhD thesis, Armidale, New South Wales: Department of Archaeology and Palaeoanthropology, University of New England.

Smith, M. A. 1989a Seed gathering in inland Australia: current evidence from seed-grinders on the antiquity of the ethnohistorical pattern of exploitation, in D. R. Harris and G. C. Hillman (eds) *Foraging and Farming: the Evolution of Plant Domestication*, London: Unwin Hyman, pp. 305–317.

Smith, M. A. 1989b The case for a resident human population in the Central Australian Ranges during full glacial aridity, *Archaeology in Oceania* 24: 93–105.

Smith, M. A. and Sharp, N. D. 1993 Pleistocene sites in Australia, New Guinea and Island Melanesia: geographic and temporal structure of the archaeological record, in M. A. Smith, M. Spriggs and B. Frankhauser (eds) *Sahul in Review: Pleistocene Archaeology in Australia, New Guinea and Island Melanesia*, Canberra: Department of Prehistory, Research School of Pacific Studies, Australian National University, pp. 37–59.

Smith, Moya 1982 Late Pleistocene Zamia exploitation in southwestern Western Australia, *Archaeology in Oceania* 17: 117–121.

Smith, P., Prokopec, M. and Pretty, G. 1988 Dentition of a prehistoric population from Roonka Flat, South Australia, *Archaeology in Oceania* 23: 31–36.

Smyth, R. B. 1876 *The Aborigines of Victoria*, Melbourne, two volumes.

Soffer, O. 1985 Patterns of intensification as seen from the Upper Paleolithic of the Central Russian Plain, in T. D. Price and J. A. Brown (eds) *Prehistoric Hunter-gatherers: the Emergence of Cultural Complexity*, Orlando, Florida: Academic Press, pp. 235–270.

Soffer, O. (ed) 1987a *The Pleistocene Old World: Regional Perspectives*. New York: Plenum.

Soffer, O. 1987b Upper Palaeolithic connubia, refugia, and the archaeological record from Eastern Europe, in O. Soffer (ed), *The Pleistocene Old World: Regional Perspectives*, New York: Plenum, pp. 333–348.

Soffer, O. 1989 Storage, sedentism and the Eurasian Palaeolithic record, *Antiquity* 63: 719–732.

Solomon, S. 1985 People and Other Aggravations: taphonomic research in Australia. Unpublished BA (Hons) thesis, Armidale, New South Wales: Department of Prehistory and Archaeology, University of New England.

Solomon, S., Davidson, I. and Watson, D. 1990 Problem solving in Taphonomy: Archaeological and Palaeontological Studies From Europe, Africa and Oceania, *Tempus* 2, Brisbane: Anthropology Museum, University of Queensland.

Specht, R. L. 1958 An introduction to the ethnobotany of Arnhem Land, in C. P. Mountford (ed) *Records of the American-Australian Expedition to Arnhem Land, 111, Botany and plant ecology*, Melbourne: Melbourne University Press.

Specht, J., Lilley, I. and Normu, J. 1983 More on radiocarbon dates from West New Britain, Papua New Guinea, *Australian Archaeology* 16: 92–95.

Spencer, W. B. and Gillen, F. J. 1899 *Native Tribes of Central Australia*, London: Macmillan.

Spencer, W. B. and Gillen, F. J. 1912 *Across Australia*, London: MacMillan.

Spriggs, M. 1993 Pleistocene agriculture in the Pacific: why not? in M. A. Smith, M. Spriggs and B. Frankhauser (eds) *Sahul in Review: Pleistocene Archaeology in Australia, New Guinea and Island Melanesia*, Canberra: Department of Prehistory, Research School of Pacific Studies, Australian National University, pp. 137–143.

Stanner, W. E. H. 1965 Aboriginal territorial organisation: estate, range, domain and regime, *Oceania* 36: 1–26.

Stern, N. and Marshall, B. 1993 Excavations at Mackintosh 90/1 in western Tasmania: a discussion of stratigraphy, chronology and site formation, *Archaeology in Oceania* 28: 8–17.

Steward, J. H. 1936 The economic and social basis of primitive bands, in R. H. Lowie (ed) *Essays in Anthropology* Presented to A. L. Kroeber, Berkeley: University of California Press.

Steward, J. H. 1955 *Theory of Cultural Change*, Chicago: University of Illinois Press.

Stirling, E. C. 1911 Preliminary report on the discovery of native remains at Swanport, River Murray: with an enquiry into the alleged occurrence of a pandemic among Australian Aboriginals, *Transactions of the Royal Society of South Australia* 35: 40–46.

Stockton, E. D. 1970 An archaeological survey of the Blue Mountains, *Mankind* 7: 295–301.

Stockton, E. D. 1973 *King's Table Shelter*, report to National Parks and Wildlife Service, Sydney, March, 1973.

Stockton, J. 1983 The prehistoric population of northwest Tasmania, *Australian Archaeology* 17: 67–78.

Stockton, E. D. and Holland, W. 1974 Cultural sites and their environment in the Blue Mountains, *Archaeology and Physical Anthropology in Oceania* 9: 36–65.

Stockton, J. and Wallace, A. 1979 Towards a human prehistory in the Lower Derwent area, south-eastern Tasmania, Australia, *Papers and Proceedings of the Royal Society of Tasmania* 113: 81–84.

Stringer, C. B. and Andrews, P. 1988 Genetic and fossil evidence for the origin of modern humans, *Science* 239: 1263–1268.

Struever, S. 1968 Woodland Subsistence-Settlement Systems in the Lower Illinois Valley, in S.R. Binford and L.R. Binford (eds) *New Perspectives in Archaeology*, Chicago: Aldine, pp. 285–312.

Storm, P. and Nelson, A. J. 1992 The many faces of Wadjak man, *Archaeology in Oceania* 27: 37–46.

Sullivan, H. 1977 Aboriginal Gatherings in South-east Queensland. Unpublished BA thesis, Canberra: Australian National University.

Sullivan, M. 1982 Exploitation of offshore islands along the New South Wales coastline, *Australian Archaeology* 15: 8–19.

Sullivan, M. E. 1987 The recent prehistoric exploitation of edible mussel in Aboriginal shell middens in southern New South Wales, *Archaeology in Oceania* 22: 97–106.

Sullivan, M. and O'Connor, S. 1993 Middens and Cheniers: implications of Australian research, *Antiquity* 67: 776–788.

Suttles, W. 1968 Coping with Abundance: subsistence on the Northwest Coast, in R.B. Lee and I. DeVore (eds) *Man the Hunter*, Chicago: Aldine, pp. 56–68.

Sutton, P. and Rigsby, B. 1982 People with 'politicks': management of land and personnel on Australia's Cape York peninsula, in N. Williams and E. Hunn (eds) *Resource Managers: North American and Australian Hunter-gatherers*, Boulder, Co: Westview.

Sutton, S. A. 1985 Warragarra Stone: a technological analysis of a stone artefact assemblage from central Tasmania. Unpublished BA (Hons) thesis, Armidale, New South Wales: Department of Prehistory and Archaeology, University of New England.

Swadling, P. and Hope, G. 1992 Environmental change in New Guinea since human settlement, in J. Dodson (ed) *The Naive Lands*, Melbourne: Longman Cheshire, pp. 13–42.

Taçon, P. 1987 Internal-external: a re-evaluation of the 'X-ray' concept in western Arnhem Land rock art, *Rock Art Research* 4: 36–50.

Taçon, P. 1993 Regionalism in the recent rock art of western Arnhem Land, Northern Territory, *Archaeology in Oceania* 28: 112–120.

Testart, A. 1982 The significance of food storage among hunter-gatherers: residence patterns, population densities, and social inequalities, *Current Anthropology* 23: 523–537.

Thiel, B. 1987 Early settlement of the Philippines, Eastern Indonesia, and Australia-New Guinea: A New Hypothesis, *Current Anthropology* 28: 236–241.

Thomas, N. 1981 Social theory, ecology and epistemology: theoretical issues in Australian prehistory, *Mankind* 13: 165–177.

Thomson, D. F. 1939 The seasonal factor in human culture, *Proceedings of the Prehistoric Society* 5: 209–221.

Thomson, D. F. 1949 *Economic Structure and the Ceremonial Exchange Cycle in Arnhem Land*, Melbourne: McMillan.

Thorne, A. G. 1975 Kow Swamp and Lake Mungo. Unpublished PhD thesis, Sydney: University of Sydney.

Thorne, A. G. 1976 Morphological contrasts in Pleistocene Australians, in R. L. Kirk and A. G. Thorne (eds) *The Origin of the Australians*, Canberra: Australian Institute of Aboriginal Studies, pp. 95–112.

Thorne, A. G. 1977 Separation or reconciliation?: biological clues to the development of Australian society, in J. Allen, J. Golson and R. Jones (eds) *Sunda and Sahul*, London: Academic Press, pp. 187–204.

Thorne, A. G. and Macumber, P. G. 1972 Discoveries of Late Pleistocene man at Kow Swamp, Australia, *Nature* 238: 316–319.

Thorne, A. G. and Wilson, S. R. 1977 Pleistocene and recent Australians; a multivariate comparison, *Journal of Human Evolution* 6: 393–402.

Thorne, A. G. and Wolpoff, M. H. 1981 Regional continuity in Australasian Pleistocene hominid evolution, *American Journal of Physical Anthropology* 55: 337–349.

Tindale, N. B. 1940 Distribution of Australian Aboriginal Tribes: a field survey, *Transactions of the Royal Society of South Australia* 61(1): 140–231.

Tindale, N. B. 1957 Cultural succession in south-eastern Australia from Late Pleistocene to the present, *Records of the South Australian Museum* 13: 1–52.

Tindale, N. B. 1961 Archaeological excavations of Noola rockshelter, *Records of the South Australian Museum* 14: 193–196.

Tindale, N. B. 1964 Some wood and stone implements of the Bindibu tribe of central Western Australia, *Proceedings of the Prehistoric Society* 30: 400–422.

Tindale, N. B. 1972 The Pitjandjara, in M. G. Bicchieri (ed) *Hunters and Gatherers Today*, New York: Holt, Rinehart and Winston, pp. 217–268.

Tindale, N. B. 1974 *Aboriginal Tribes of Australia*, Los Angeles: University of California Press.

Tindale, N. B. 1977 Further report on the Kaiadilt people of Bentinck Island, Gulf of Carpentaria Queensland, in J. Allen, J. Golson and R. Jones (eds) *Sunda and Sahul*, London: Academic Press, pp. 247–273.

Tonkinson, R. 1978 *The Mardudjara Aborigines*, New York: Holt, Rhinehart and Winston.

Torgensen, T., Luly, J., De Deckker, P., Jones, M. R., Searle, D. E., Chivas, A. R., and Ullman, W. J. 1988 Late Quaternary environments of the Carpentaria Basin, Australia, *Palaeogeography, Palaeoclimatology, Palaeoecology* 67: 245–261.

Torrence, R. 1983 Time Budgeting and Hunter-Gatherer Technology, in G. N. Bailey (ed) *Hunter-Gatherer Economy in Prehistory*, Cambridge: Cambridge University Press, pp. 11–22.

Troilett, G. 1982 Report on Ethel Gorge Salvage Project. Unpublished report, Perth: Department of Aboriginal Sites, Perth: Western Australian Museum.

Vanderwal, R. I. 1977 The Shag Bay rockshelter, Tasmania, *The Artefact* 2: 161–170.

Vanderwal, R. I. 1978 Adaptive technology in southwest Tasmania, *Australian Archaeology* 8: 107–127.

Vanderwal, R. and Horton, D. 1984 Coastal Southwest Tasmania: the prehistory of Louisa Bay and Maatsuyker Island, *Terra Australis* 9, Canberra: Australian National University.

Veth, P. M. 1987 Martujarra prehistory: variation in arid zone adaptations, *Australian Archaeology* 25: 102–111.

Veth, P. M. 1989a The Prehistory of the Sandy Deserts: Spatial and Temporal Variation in Settlement and Subsistence Behaviour Within the Arid Zone of Australia. Unpublished PhD thesis, Perth: Department of Archaeology, University of Western Australia.

Veth, P. 1989b Islands of the interior: a model for the colonization of Australia's arid zone, *Archaeology in Oceania* 24: 81–92.

Veth, P. (forthcoming) Before The Blast: The Prehistory of the Monte Bello Islands, Northwest Australia.

Von Sturmer, J. 1978 The Wik region: Economy, Territoriality and Totemism. Unpublished PhD thesis, Brisbane: Department of Anthropology and Sociology, University of Queensland.

Walker, D. and Chen, Y. 1987 Palynological light on tropical rainforest dynamics, *Quaternary Science Review* 6: 77–92.

Walters, I. N. 1981 Colonization of a model island continent–Australian implications, *Australian Archaeology* 12: 33–44.

Walters, I. 1987 Another Kettle of Fish: the Prehistoric Moreton Bay Fishery. Unpublished PhD thesis, Brisbane: Department of Anthropology and Sociology, University of Queensland.

Walters, I. 1989 Intensified fishery production at Moreton Bay, southeast Queensland, in the late Holocene, *Antiquity* 63: 215–224.

Wasson, R. 1986 Geomorphology and Quaternary history of the Australian continental dunefields, *Geographical Review of Japan* 59 (Ser B): 55–67.

Watchman, A. 1991 Age and composition of oxalate-rich crusts in the Northern Territory, Australia, *Studies in Conservation* 36: 24–32.

Watchman, R. 1992 Composition, formation and age of some Australian silica skins, *Australian Aboriginal Studies* 1992/1: 61–66.

Watson, J. B. 1965 From hunting to horticulture in the New Guinea Highlands, *Ethnology* 4: 295–309.

Watson, J. 1977 Pigs, fodder and the Jones effect in post-ipomoean New Guinea. *Ethnology* 16: 57–70.

Watson, P. 1983 This Precious Foliage, *Oceania Monograph* 26, Sydney: University of Sydney.

Watson, V. D. and Cole, J. D. 1977 *Prehistory of the Eastern Highlands of New Guinea*, Seattle: University of Washington Press.

Webb, S. 1984 Intensification, population and social change in southeastern Australia: the skeletal evidence, *Aboriginal History* 8: 154–172.

Webb, S. G. 1987 A palaeodemographic model of late Holocene Central Murray Aboriginal society, Australia, *Human Evolution* 2: 385–406.

Webb, S. G. 1989 *The Willandra Lakes Hominids*, Canberra: Department of Prehistory, Research School of Pacific Studies.

Webb, S. 1995 *Palaeopathology of Aboriginal Australians: Health and disease across a hunter-gatherer continent*, Cambridge: Cambridge University Press.

Wells, R. T. 1978 Fossil mammals in the reconstruction of Quaternary environments with examples from the Australian fauna, in D. Walker and J. C. Guppy (eds) *Biology and Quaternary Environments*, Canberra: Australian Academy of Science, pp. 103–124.

Wenke, R. J. 1981 Explaining the evolution of cultural complexity: a review, in M. B. Schiffer (ed) *Advances in Archaeological Method and Theory*, New York: Academic Press, pp. 79–127.

White, C. (Schrire) 1967 Plateau and Plain: Prehistoric Investigations in Arnhem Land, Northern Territory. Unpublished PhD thesis, Canberra: Australian National University.

White, C. 1971 Man and environment in northwest Arnhem Land, in D. J. Mulvaney and J. Golson (eds) *Aboriginal Man and Environment in Australia*, Canberra: Australian National University Press, pp. 141–157.

White, J. P. 1971 New Guinea and Australian prehistory: the 'neolithic problem', in D. J. Mulvaney and J. Golson (eds) *Aboriginal Man and Environment in Australia*, Canberra: Australian National University Press, pp. 182–195.

White, J. P. 1972 Ol Tumbuna: archaeological investigations in the eastern central highlands, Papua New Guinea, *Terra Australis* 2, Canberra: Australian National University Press.

White, J. P. 1977 Crude, colourless and unenterprising: prehistorians and their views on the stone age of Sunda and Sahul, in R. V. S. Wright (ed) *Stone Tools as Cultural Markers*, Canberra: Australian Institute of Aboriginal Studies, pp. 13–30.

White, J. P. 1981 Archaeology in Australia and New Guinea, *World Archaeology* 13 (2): 255–263.

White, J. P., Crook, K. A. W. and Ruxton, B. P. 1970 Kosipe: a late Pleistocene site in the Papuan Highlands, *Proceedings of the Prehistoric Society* 36: 152–170.

White, J. P. and Mulvaney, D. J. 1987 How many people? in D. J. Mulvaney and J. P. White (eds) *Australians To 1788*, Sydney: Fairfax, Syme and Weldon, pp. 114–117.

White, J. P. and O'Connell, J. F. 1979 Australian prehistory: new aspects of antiquity, *Science* 203: 21–28.

White, J. P. and O'Connell, J. F. 1982 *A Prehistory of Australia, New Guinea and Sahul*, Sydney: Academic Press.

Wickler, S. and Spriggs, M. 1988 Pleistocene occupation of the Solomon Islands, Melanesia, *Antiquity* 62: 703–706.

Wiedenreich, F. 1945 The Keilor skull: a Wadjak type from south-east Australia, *American Journal of Physical Anthropology* 3: 225–236.

Wieneke, C. and White, J. P. 1973 Backed blades: another view, *Mankind* 9: 35–38.

Williams, E. 1985 Estimation of prehistoric populations of archaeological sites in south-western Victoria: some problems, *Archaeology in Oceania* 20: 73–80.

Williams, E. 1987 Complex hunter-gatherers: a view from Australia, *Antiquity* 61: 310–321.

Williams, E. 1988a Complex hunter-gatherers: a late Holocene example from temperate Australia, *BAR International Series*, 423, Oxford.

Williams, E. 1988b The archaeology of the Cooper Basin: report on fieldwork. *Records of the South Australian Museum* 22: 53–62.

Wilmsen, E. and Denbow, J. 1990 Paradigmatic studies of San-speaking peoples and current attempts at revision, *Current Anthropology*, 31 (5): 489–524.

Winterbotham, L. P. 1959 Some native customs and beliefs of the Jinibara tribe as well as those of some of their neighbours in Southeast Queensland, transcribed by G. Langevad, *Queensland Ethnohistory Transcripts* 1 (1): 20–135.

Winterhalder, B. 1981 Optimal foraging strategies and hunter-gatherer research in Anthropology: theories and models, in B. Winterhalder and E. A. Smith (eds) *Hunter-Gatherer Foraging Strategies: Ethnographic and Archaeological Analyses*, Chicago: University of Chicago Press, pp. 13–35.

Winterhalder, B. and Smith, E. A. (eds) 1981 *Hunter-Gatherer Foraging Strategies. Ethnographic and Archaeological Analyses*, Chicago: University of Chicago Press.

Wobst, H. M. 1974 Boundary conditions for palaeolithic social systems: a simulation approach, *American Antiquity*, 39: 147–178.

Wobst, H. M. 1976 Locational relationships in palaeolithic society, *Journal of Human Evolution* 5: 49–58.

Wolpoff, M. H. 1989 Multiregional evolution: the fossil alternative to Eden, in P. Mellars and C. Stringer (eds) *The Human Revolution: Behavioural and Biological Perspectives on the Origins of Modern Humans*, Vol.1, Edinburgh: University of Edinburgh Press, pp. 62–108.

Wolpoff, M. H., Wu, X. Z. and Thorne, A. G. 1984 Modern *Homo sapiens* origins: a general theory of hominid evolution involving the fossil evidence from East Asia, in F. M. Smith and F. Spencer (eds) *The Origins of Modern Humans*, New York: Alan R. Liss, pp. 411–484.

Woodburn, J. 1980 Hunters and gatherers today and reconstruction of the past, in E. Gellner (ed) *Soviet and Western Anthropology*, London: Duckworth, pp. 95–117.

Woodburn, J. 1982 Egalitarian Societies, *Man* (n.s.)17: 431–451.

Woodburn, J. 1988 African hunter-gatherer social organization: is it best understood as a product of encapsulation?, in T. Ingold, D. Riches and J. Woodburn (eds) *Hunters and Gatherers: History, Evolution and Social Change*, Oxford: Berg, pp. 31–64.

Woodroffe, C. D., Chappell, J. and Thom, B. G. 1988 Shell middens in the context of estuarine development, South Alligator River, Northern Territory, *Archaeology in Oceania* 23: 95–103.

Wright, R. (ed) 1971a *The Archaeology of the Gallus site, Koonalda Cave*, Canberra: Australian Institute of Aboriginal Studies.

Wright, R. 1971b The Cave, in R. Wright (ed) *The Archaeology of the Gallus Site, Koonalda Cave*, Canberra: Australian Institute of Aboriginal Studies, pp. 22–30.

Wright, R. 1986 How old is Zone F at Lake George? *Archaeology in Oceania* 21: 138–139.

Wynne-Edwards, V. C. 1962 *Animal Dispersion in Relation to Social Behaviour*, London: Oliver and Boyd.

Wyrwoll, K. H. and Dortch, C. 1978 Stone artefacts and an associated Diprotodontid mandible from the Greenough River, Western Australia, *Search* 9: 411–413.

Wyrwoll, K. H., McKenzie, N. L., Pederson, B. J. and Tapley, I. J. 1986 The Great Sandy Desert of north-western Australia: the last 7000 years, *Search* 7: 208–210.

Yap, L. 1992 New Tricks From a Bag of Old bones: A Faunal and Taphonomic Analysis From An Open Shell Midden Site at Seal Point, Cape Otway, Western Victoria. Unpublished BA (Hons) thesis, Brisbane: Department of Anthropology and Sociology, University of Queensland.

Yen, D. E. 1989 The domestication of environment, in D. R. Harris and G. C. Hillman (eds) *Foraging and Farming: the Evolution of Plant Domestication*, London: Unwin Hyman, pp. 55–75.

Yen, D. E. 1995 The development of Sahul agriculture with Australia as bystander, in Allen, J. and J. F. O'Connell (eds) *Transitions: Pleistocene to Holocene in Australia and Papua New Guinea, Antiquity* 69: 831–847.

Yengoyan, A. A. 1968 Demographic and ecological influences on Australian Aboriginal marriage sections, in R. B. Lee and I. DeVore (eds) *Man the Hunter*, Chicago: Aldine, pp. 185–199.

Yengoyan, A. A. 1972 Ritual and exchange in Aboriginal Australia: an adaptive interpretation of male initiation rites, in E. N. Wilmsen (ed) *Social Exchange and Interaction*, Anthropological Papers, Museum of Anthropology, University of Michigan, 46: 5–9.

Yengoyan, A. A. 1976 Structure, event and ecology in Aboriginal Australia: a comparative viewpoint, in N. Peterson (ed) *Tribes and Boundaries in Australia*, Canberra: Australian Institute of Aboriginal Studies, pp. 121–132.

Yoffee, N. 1985 Perspectives on 'trends towards social complexity in prehistoric Australia and Papua New Guinea', *Archaeology in Oceania* 20: 41–49.

Zobel, D., Vanderwal, R. and Frankel, D. 1984 The Moonlight Head Rockshelter, *Proceedings of the Royal Society of Victoria* 96: 1–24.

Zvelebil, M. 1986 *Hunters in Transition: Mesolithic Societies of Temperate Eurasia and Their Transition to Farming*, Cambridge: Cambridge University Press.

INDEX OF ARCHAEOLOGICAL SITES

GENERAL INDEX